To Arthur:

I am still at the beginning, but much of what I know has been taught by you.

Annette Leising
Rio de Janeiro
11/97

The Medical Anthropologies in Brazil

Journal for Ethnomedicine • edited by Arbeitsgemeinschaft Ethnomedicine

Special Volume 12/1997

The Medical Anthropologies
in Brazil

edited by

Annette Leibing

on behalf of
Arbeitsgemeinschaft Ethnomedizin

VWB – Verlag für Wissenschaft und Bildung

Coverphoto:
Physician with a newborn baby on his arm; cover picture of a popular 'cordel' publication. These are stories published on cheap paper and sold on the markets. Usually they are hanging on a clothline ('cordel') were they are viewed and discussed by the public.

English Revision:
Dr. David G. Howe
Cecilía Moura Lonergan
Lorenz und Claudia von Usslar

Die Deutsche Bibliothek – CIP-Einheitsaufnahme

[Curare / Special Volume]
Curare. Sonderband - Berlin : VWB, Verl. für Wiss. und Bildung
Früher Schriftenreihe. - Früher im Verl. Vieweg, Braunschweig,
Wiesbaden
Reihe Sonderband zu: Curare

12. The medical anthropologies in Brazil. - 1997

The **medical anthropologies in Brazil** / ed. by Annette Leibing on behalf of the Arbeitsgemeinschaft Ethnomedizin. - Berlin : VWB, Verl. für Wiss. und Bildung, 1997
(Curare: Special Volume ; 12)
ISBN 3-86135-568-X

Publisher:
VWB – Verlag für Wissenschaft und Bildung, Amand Aglaster
Markgrafenstr. 67 • D-10969 Berlin • P.O.Box 11 03 68 • D-10833 Berlin
Phone: +49 [0]30 251 04 15 • Fax +49 [0]30 251 04 12

Typsetting:
Dr. Judith Schuler, Wasserburg

Printing:
GAM-Media GmbH, Berlin

Copyright:
© VWB – Verlag für Wissenschaft und Bildung, 1997

The Medical Anthropologies in Brazil

Edited by
ANNETTE LEIBING

Contents

ANNETTE LEIBING
Preface 7

PAULO CÉSAR ALVES & MIRIAM RABELO
Being a Nervous Person: Narratives and the Construction of a Self 9

LUIZ-FERNANDO DIAS DUARTE
Nerves and *Nervousness* in Brazilian Urban Culture 21

JANE A. RUSSO
Body Therapists in Rio de Janeiro:
Relations Between Social Career and Therapeutic Principles 39

MADEL T. LUZ & KENNETH ROCHEL DE CAMARGO JR.
A Comparative Study of Medical Rationalities..................................... 47

MARIA ANDRÉA LOYOLA
Social and Cultural Hierarchies and Different Ways of Healing in Brazil 59

TELMA CAMARGO DA SILVA
Biomedical Discourses and Health Care Experiences:
The Goiânia Radiological Disaster 67

SÉRGIO CARRARA
The Symbolic Geopolitics of Syphilis: An Essay in Historical Anthropology 81

SEAN PATRICK LARVIE
Personal Improvement, National Development:
Theories of AIDS Prevention in Rio de Janeiro, Brazil 97

MARILYN K. NATIONS & CRISTINA M.G. MONTE
"I'm Not Dog, No !": Cries of Resistance against Cholera Control Campaigns 115

ELIZABETH UCHÔA, HENRIQUE LEONARDO GUERRA,
JOSÉLIA OLIVEIRA ARAÚJO FIRMO, MARIA FERNANDA LIMA E COSTA
Signs, Meanings and Actions Associated with Schistosomiasis Mansoni
in a Small Village in Brazil 143

ONDINA FACHEL LEAL
Blood, Fertility and Contraceptive Practices 157

CERES VICTORA
Inside the Mother's Body: Pregnancy and the 'Emic' Organ 'the Body's Mother' 169

CONTARDO CALLIGARIS
Notebook on Migrations 177

CARLOS CAROSO, NÚBIA RODRIGUES, NAOMAR ALMEIDA-FILHO,
ELLEN CORIN & GILLES BIBEAU
When Healing Is Prevention: Afro-Brazilian Religious Practices
Related to Mental Disorders and Associated Stigma in Bahia, Brazil 195

PAULO DALGALARRONDO
Is Religious Membership and Intensity a Protective Factor
in the Course of Functional Psychosis? A Clinical Study from Brazil................. 215

ANNETTE LEIBING
Narrowing Worlds: On Alzheimer's Disease and Biography in Brazil 221

JOÃO FERREIRA DA SILVA FILHO
Psychiatry: Its Science and Its Ethics 243

About the authors 245

Preface

Maybe two—interdependent—moments were decisive for the idea to publish this book: One was on an icy morning in Boston, MA in 1996, when I was asked about Medical Anthropology in Brazil by ARTHUR KLEINMAN and his colleagues from the Harvard Social Medicine Department. Somehow, it was not easy to give a clear answer.

The second moment was when I started teaching at the Institute of Psychiatry (Federal University of Rio de Janeiro) and introduced myself as a medical anthropologist. Not always, but sometimes, the reaction to this 'label' was as frosty as the Boston winter morning described above. I wondered why.

Medical anthropology is quite a new field in anthropological teaching and research in Brazil. A first attempt to define the field was a publication edited by ALVES & MINAYO (1994) titled "The Anthropology of Health," with 'religious healing' as the main topic. In a historical overview the roots of this field were defined as part of the public health movement of the 80s. It still is an unmapped territory, where many voices try to contribute to the eternal question about Brazilian identity and suffering, a question which will probably never be answered due to the many guises of being Brazilian. Contrary to German anthropologists or to what we can observe in the US, anthropology in Brazil is almost exclusively concerned with its own culture—the different in the familiar.

The first reason for the title of this book—the many anthropologies in Brazil—is due to the above-mentioned differentiation in the field of culture and health: there are those who consider themselves medical anthropologists and those who do not. For me, medical anthropology has always been a neutral term in the way that everything that is related to the preoccupation with health and sickness in a given society, independent of whether western medicine would call it medicine or not, and analysed by an anthropological approach, could be called medical anthropology. The way of looking at the category to be analysed, distinguishes one anthropologist from the other. Or, as LINDENBAUM & LOCK (1993: x) write,

> "... our subject matter is neither simply medicine as an institutional body of scientific knowledge nor the human body as an unproblematic product of nature, but rather is a study of the creation, representation, legitimization, and application of knowledge about the body in both health and illness."

This notion of sickness (and health) as processual and not something static that is to be discovered is only possible if a dialectic of biology, society, history, and politics tries to capture the complexity of a lived experience of suffering in an ever more complicated world.

Voices critical of medical anthropology in Brasil consider the category 'medicine' too narrow to deal with health and sickness, especially if separated from religion or other forms of resolving sickness and suffering in society. Furthermore they consider medical anthropologists to be imprisioned in the (mostly bio-)medical worldview, even if they criticize it.

A second reason for the plural in the title is a continuity which refers to an earlier publication by *curare* entitled "Anthropologies of Medicine" (B. PFLEIDERER & G. BIBEAU [eds.] 1991) where North-American and West-European researchers, following a symposium on this topic in Hamburg, Germany, in 1988, reflect on the 'state of the art' of this discipline. We intended to do the same, only for the Brazilian universe(s): We asked the participating authors, that every contribution should reflect their latest research interest and contain their conception of the 'label' 'medical anthropology.' As we can see, there is no unity or theoretically dominant line of argumentation. The diversity presented in this book can be seen in regard to theory, research interest and the many co-existing realities in Brazil, often entangled with each other. We hope that with this publication Brazil's fascinating, colourful, cruel and multiple reality can be understood a little better and initiate a discussion with other researchers interested in this country and its culture as expressed in its medical systems.

ANNETTE LEIBING
Rio de Janeiro, 1997

References

ALVES, P.C. & M.C.S. MINAYO (eds.)
    1994   *Saúde e Doença, Um Olhar Antropológico*. Rio de Janeiro: Ed. Fiocruz.
LINDENBAUM, S. & M. LOCK (eds.)
    1993   *Knowledge, Power & Practice. The Anthropology of Medicine and Everyday Life*. Berkeley: University of California Press.
PFLEIDERER, B. & G. BIBEAU (eds.)
    1991   *Anthropologies of Medicine*. Wiesbaden: Vieweg Verlag.

Being a Nervous Person:
Narratives and the Construction of a Self

Paulo César Alves & Miriam Rabelo

Abstract

The onset of illness often disrupts the sufferer's sense of self leading him/her to question taken for granted aspects of his/her daily experience. The present paper discusses how self-identity is interpreted and constructed within a situation of ill-being. It examines the interplay between self-identity and narrative and argues that the biographic narratives which people produce to account for their state of suffering are an important means through which they may reflect on and reconstruct their self-identity. The paper examines the narrative of a working class woman from Salvador (Northeast Brazil) who suffers from an illness known as *nervoso* (nerves or nervousness). Within the construction of her personal narrative — which displays basic structural dimensions of the daily lives of poor urban women in Northeast Brazil — are reflected the social contexts or frameworks of an individual experience, and signs, images and metaphors that produce a certain intersubjective domain from which individuals can give shape to and communicate their own experiences.

Zusammenfassung

Der Beginn einer Krankheit zerrüttet häufig die Wahrnehmung des Leidenden von sich selbst, was dazu führt, daß Aspekte des täglichen Lebens, für selbstverständlich gehalten, hinterfragt werden. Dieser Artikel diskutiert, wie Selbstidentität interpretiert und konstruiert wird innerhalb des Krankseins. Er untersucht das Zusammenspiel von Selbstidentität und Erzählung und führt an, daß biographische Erzählungen, die jemand produziert, um den Zustand des Leidens zu erklären, wichtige Mittel sind, durch die die Selbstidentität überdacht und rekonstruiert werden kann. Der Artikel untersucht die Erzählung einer Frau aus der Arbeiterklasse aus Salvador (Nordostbrasilien), die an einer Krankheit leidet, *nervoso* genannt (nervös oder Nervosität). Innerhalb der Konstruktion ihrer persönlichen Erzählung – welche grundlegende, strukturelle Dimensionen des täglichen Lebens armer, urbaner Frauen im Nordosten Brasiliens offenbart – spiegeln sich soziale Kontexte oder theoretische Rahmen einer individuellen Erfahrung und Zeichen, Bilder und Metaphern wider, welche einen bestimmten intersubjektiven Bereich produzieren, innerhalb dessen Individuen ihren eigenen Erfahrungen Form geben und diese kommunizieren können.

Keywords: narratives, identity, biography, nerves, Bahia/Brazil

Introduction

From the viewpoint of medical anthropology sickness is not merely a 'biological entity,' a thing exterior to consciousness. It is also an experience that is socio-culturally formed and that reflects a complex process of interactions among persons, groups and institutions. Sickness refers both to subjective feelings of ill-being, that is to individual bodily experience and to the collective, cultural meanings or interpretations that are attached to these feelings (Alves 1994). Phenomenologically oriented anthropologists are especially concerned with understanding how the subjective experience of ill-being on which sickness is grounded is constituted as a socio-cultural fact.

In the field of mental health, medical anthropologists have argued that to understand the meanings attached to the experience of mental illness within a specific social group one should explore the ideas, values and feelings which form that group's notions of self and identity (see Young 1981; Littlewood & Lipsedge 1989; Jodelet 1991; Corin et. al. 1993; Good 1994). The experience of mental illness often leads the ill person — and those close to him — to question taken for granted aspects of his identity and to reflect on the particular life course that produced illness.

In reflecting on his troublesome state the individual thus turns to his biography and it is often through the elaboration of a biographical narrative that he gives meaning to the experience of illness.

> "Narrative is a form in which experience is represented and recounted, in which events are presented as having a meaningful and coherent order, in which activities and events are described along with the experiences associated with them and the significance that lends them their sense for the persons involved" (GOOD 1994: 139).

The present paper examines the biographical narrative of a working class woman from Salvador (Northeast Brazil) who suffers from 'nerves' or *nervoso*. Found in diverse social settings the category of 'nervous illness'—*doença dos nervos* or *nervoso* in Portuguese—has been widely documented in recent anthropological literature. As many anthropologists have observed, it is an illness category that encapsulates various layers of meaning (DAVIS 1989; GUARNACCIA 1989; LOW 1994), closely related to a specific notion of the person (DUARTE 1986), cultural artifacts whose meanings are learned (LUTZ 1988) and often used and manipulated in interaction (REBHUN 1993, 1994).

In Northeast Brazil working class people often explain the meaning of *nervoso* by contrasting it to madness. As opposed to the permanent and radical loss of one's capacity to interact properly that is characteristic of madness, *nervoso* is said to express a temporary absence (often crisis) of normality, a sudden loss of control over one's attitudes and emotions. Although it is said to be a reversible state, some people are thought to be more prone to having it than others. Thus there is a difference between those who occasionally become nervous (*ficam/estão nervosos*) and those who are nervous (*são nervosos*) or who suffer from *nervoso* (RABELO, ALVES & SOUZA 1995).

Many working class women that refer to themselves as suffering from *nervoso* describe such a state through the narration of problematic life events, against a backdrop of poverty, violence and lack of self-determination. The accounts that they compose about their *nervoso* and that they offer their listeners (including the researcher) articulate bodily sensations, moral judgments, discrete acts and events in a complex whole: the course of the narrated story. They do this in such a way that each aspect seems necessary and completely justified. There is no doubt that in order to better understand these illness stories one must take into account their purpose of involving an audience in the construction of reality proposed by the narrator. Nevertheless it is important to note that even the teller is not entirely free from involvement in the story he/she constructs. In a certain sense, the women too feed on the narratives they produce in order to involve and persuade their listeners: in telling the story of their *nervoso*, trying to express to others what their body seems to be saying (and why), they forge for themselves, via a reflexive effort, a sense of self. The stories are thus not simply a cognitive exercise at matching signs to causes and treatment but emotionally charged biographical accounts of how one has ended up in a state of suffering, accounts in which the attempt to grapple with illness is also an attempt to reconstruct self-identity.

Self and Narrative

The notion of self has actually loaned itself to various uses and meanings in the field of the social sciences. The most recent approaches seem to agree that far from being a permanent, fixed attribute of the individual, the self is forged in the social world. It concerns a fluid phenomena, highly moldable (WILEY 1994), even amorphous (GIDDENS 1991).

One of the most interesting approaches to the question of the self comes from American pragmatism. According to MEAD (1972) the self aims at the capacity of the individual to become an object to himself. Such a capacity develops in interaction: the individual develops a self to the extent that he interiorizes the perspective of the other. Consequently, he can experience personally the reactions that his acts would probably provoke in the other, and in this way, monitor his actions reflexively. Not only his own performance or that of others, but thoughts and affective states can be converted (to a greater or lesser extent) into an object of scrutiny within the course of a continual interior dialogue. The self is in fact defined in terms of this intrapersonal dialogue which originates from dialogue with others and organizes itself on the basis of this dialogue. (WILEY 1994). Thus, in this perspective, there exists a process of mutual determination between the self and society: on the one hand, the interior dialogue is not a movement of pure subjectivity, as it requires the incorporation of the other's point of view; on the other hand, to the extent in which the meanings are continually interpreted in the intrapersonal conversation, interpretation is always more than the mere reproduction of what is given or presented in the interpersonal sphere.

Self-identity emerges through this interior dialogue and is thus an ever-renovating realization. In this direction, GIDDENS proposes that it "*is the self as reflexively understood by the person in terms of her or his biography.*" (1991:53, italics in original). In this aspect, the concept of self must not be confused with the notion of a social model of the person. The latter refers us to a socio-cultural model, a collective representation in the DURKHEIMian sense, while the concept of self corresponds to the subjective sense that the individual confers to his/her singular existential trajectory. Nevertheless, the identity of self presupposes and is fed by a 'theory of the person' or, what amounts to the same thing, by a social definition of the subject. In this way, DUBET (1995) observes that the self is to a large extent constructed and evaluated in terms of approximation or fidelity to an ideal model of the subject/person. It is important to emphasize that the process of construction, modeled on a culturally specific notion of the person, necessarily presupposes an interpretation on the part of the individual on how is, or how should be, this 'ideal-type.'

The biographic construction of which self-identity emerges is a form of narrative. Thus GIDDENS observes that "a person's identity is not to be found in behavior, nor—important though this is—in the reactions of others, but in the capacity *to keep a particular narrative going*" (1991: 54, italics in original). This interplay between self-identity and narrative has been amply discussed by PAUL RICOEUR (1991), for whom narrative offers for the individual a privileged instance to comprehend himself to the extent in which it totalizes what is experienced as a series of fragmentary, discrete events. In producing a narrative about his life the individual grasps a sense of identity or continuity out of the innumerous and diverse meetings, accidents and actions which characterize his life. As RICOEUR notes

"[i]t is necessary that life be reunited in order that it can be put in the perspective of real life. If my life cannot be interpreted as a singular totality, then I can never hope to have a complete or successful life." (1991: 190).

Narrative analysis can thus offer important methodological resources for a socio-anthropological approach to questions relative to the constitution of self-identity. The objective of the present work is contained within this perspective. We try to explore some analytical aspects of these resources in the study of the life story of Socorro, a 62 year-old working-class woman of Salvador (Northeast Brazil), who suffers from *nervoso*.

The Narrative Process

We consider narrative to be a type of discourse which presents an isotopic chain of personages and actors who realize, in a determined time, correlative actions to a given theme. The term isotopy refers to "the characteristic property of a semantic unit which permits the understanding of a discourse as a single whole of meaning" (DUBOIS et al. 1993:355). A semantic unit of a discourse is constructed by a chain of determined 'minimum units' of narrative, that is, happenings, actions, attitudes, conceptions and evaluations. To borrow a linguistic term, such units can be conceived of as 'narrative segments.' A segment is a minimum unit of meaning or narrative expression; minimum in relation to the field of exploration chosen by the narrator. The narrative-segments in their turn are constituted by figurative elements (expressions which reveal factual occurrences), abstract elements (categorizations, opinions, evaluations, etc.) and emotional elements. A sequence of segments forms a 'someme narrative,' which is also characterized by these three elements. It is by the totality or union of these somemes that we have the 'semantic unit' of narrative.

There is a common semic nucleus (a syntagmatic unit) underlying the sequence of segments, which guarantees, in the last instance, a homogeneity (isotopy) of discourse and which represents the structure of the narrative. Such a structure is constituted by a chain of relations that involve two interlinked dimensions: combination and selection. The combination is a simple juxtaposition of two or more narrative segments. The combination presupposes a choice—hence, a selection— of elements (figurative, abstract and emotive) that are juxtaposed. In choosing and correlating occurences, actions, expressions, attitudes and emotions, the narrator establishes an organization of the narrative sequence in which each segment (or set of segments) presupposes the next. It is this organization, the chain of combinations and selections, which gives structure to the narrative and semantical/logical unity to the discourse, guaranteeing its internal 'coherence.' In the narration of his life within a determined sequence, the individual attributes to it an order, affirming for himself an identity. By thus ordering or organizing his lived experiences in the frame of the story, he imprints a basic meaning on them. This meaning is an interpretation of what he considers his position in the world to be and how he conducts himself in it.

Every narrative therefore expresses a basic or core meaning. This does not mean, however, that narratives are free from conflicting arguments, incoherences and ambiguities. Rather than pointing to a given, single meaning underlying the narrative, the idea of a core meaning should be understood as referring to the narrator's search for a unified meaning behind a plurality of facts and ideas.

Narratives which individuals elaborate about themselves are always a mixture of experience and fabulation. In this aspect, RICOEUR (1991) observes that the use of fiction is in fact important in the construction of a more complete vision of life. Clearly, should the individual intend to sustain a certain biographic narrative in a situation of continued interaction with others, then genuine, lived experiences cannot be left totally behind. Nevertheless, the application to life stories of narrative models—intrigues—borrowed from fiction, makes them more intelligible and hence, better understood in contexts of interaction.

In the intrigue subject and actions are mutually constituted: the personage is revealed by the actions that he/she undertakes and in which he/she is involved; and these, in their turn, are seen as a necessary development of the personage. In this way, the identity of the personage unfolds accordingly with the telling of the story. Thus RICOEUR argues that the intrigue makes the identity of the personage emerge from the related action within the development of the what he calls a dialectic of concord and discord. Through this dialectic, the contingent and the accidental are transformed into the necessary, and become a requirement in the development of the story:

> "The dialectic consists in such that, according to the line of concordance, the personage extracts his/her singularity from the unit of his/her life considered as a singular, temporal totality, which distinguishes him/her from any other. Corresponding to the line of discord, the temporal totality is threatened by the effect of the rupture of

unforeseen events, which punctuate it (meetings, accidents, etc.); the synthesis of concord and discord means that the contingency of occurrences contributes to the, in some way retroactive necessity, of the life-story, which is the equivalent of the identity of the personage. Here, the incidental is transmuted into destiny." (RI-COEUR 1991: 175).

Thus, weaved in the framework of a narrative, the ideas and images that the individuals nourish about themselves and about others, just as about their bodies and its sensations, are situated in the action context of the subject/personage. In its narration, the biography is constructed (or reconstructed) according to the model of the intrigue; the present pictured as the necessary, inevitable result of former actions, events and plots which related in the story (juxtaposed and selected) define the identity of self. In this light, self-identity is always subject to reorientation to the extent that the individual elaborates new narratives to account for his/her trajectory.

We may now turn to Socorro's life story and seek to understand how her *nervoso* is constructed within the frame of a narrative, that reveals an obstinate search for a coherent sense of self behind an experience of suffering and chaos. Socorro's narrative was obtained in the course of a research which is being developed by the Health and Social Sciences Centre[1]. The objective of this research is to identify and understand the processes and experiences of vulnerability related to mental health in the life trajectory of working-class urban women and the forms in which they manage to cope with those critical situations. The research involved a collection of data regarding the life trajectory of 120 women from a poor district in Salvador—Nordeste de Amaralina. Of these, 30 women, who refer to themselves as suffering from *nervoso*, have being accompanied each week (one year) by members of the research team.

Unfortunately, owing to the limits of the present article, we are unable to present the complete narrative told by Socorro, which may have left clearer the arguments developed here. In this sense, we have had to select and explore only some sections of Socorro's story with the objective of understanding the process by which narratives establish meaning for lived experiences of ill-being.

Narrating the Experience of a Nervous Life

Socorro is a black, middle-aged woman, a *baiana de acarajé* (a street vendor of traditional Bahian snack food of African origin) who lives surrounded by her children and grandchildren in a poor working class district of Salvador (Bahia, Northeast Brazil) known as Nordeste de Amaralina or simply Nordeste. The district has approximately 90,000 residents. Only 11% of its adult population have completed elementary school and almost 60% of the dwellers are migrants, most of them coming from rural areas. As in other Brazilian working class districts there is a great variety of family arrangements in Nordeste, many of them of a temporary nature. Marriages are relatively unstable and the children of different unions tend to stay in the care of their mothers. Women are the actual managers of the household—although they do not always hold formal authority in the family. If women often have to support their household and children by themselves, ideally there are very distinct expectations associated with the roles of the woman and man within the working

---

1. The research which is being developed by the Health and Social Sciences Centre (ECSAS) is entitled "Processes of Vulnerability and Protection related to the Mental Health of Working-Class Urban Women in Salvador, Brazil." It is financed by the CNPq (process 521036/93-3) and developed by PAULO CÉSAR ALVES (principal investigator), MARIA GABRIELA HITA (co-coordinator), MÍRIAM CRISTINA RABELO, IARA SOUZA and five graduate students. The account that is being analyzed in this paper was collected by MÍRIAM RABELO and SULLY MEASURED, a student on the project, who has accompanied the case (Socorro) for one year.

class family. Thus the moral character of mothers/wives is judged both in terms of the care which they dispense upon the house and their children and the manners which they display in their relations with others. The moral character of fathers, in turn, is judged mainly in terms of their engagement in work — a man is a good husband and father if he provides for the family.

Nordeste's dwellers are linked through complex networks of neighborhood and kinship. Much of what goes on in the district's daily life happens in the streets and small alleys. Information circulates in them and people usually complain of the exaggerated and immoral interest which local dwellers in general have in one another's lives. Conflicts between neighbors are routine affairs in the daily life of the district; they seem to express the tensions which exist in the relationships between persons who must continually negotiate the ill-defined boundaries between the private and public spheres of social life.

A resident of Nordeste for many years, Socorro now considers herself as suffering from *nervoso*, being subject to states of intense affliction. It is as such that she presents herself in interactions with her relatives, friends and neighbors. In her relations with them, Socorro usually behaves in an afflicted manner, she gesticulates tensely, her hands tremble, she expresses discomfort and sometimes anger; she easily breaks into tears. She feels herself to be impotent and lies down for long periods on the sofa, her eyes wet.

The description that Socorro makes about her situation characterizes, in various ways, the experience of women in her district, who describe themselves as suffering from *nervoso*. She tells us:

> "Sometimes a person would come, who wanted to meet me. 'What was it?' 'Ah, that's it.' Well, my heart started to ... that pounding. I felt sick, so I'd run below to the room that's down there, under the stair ... I'd huddle there, hide my face in the sofa and I wouldn't talk to no-one. No, nervous like that. Here on the bed like that, me looking on, swap sides, just looking at the street, the boys'd be fighting, me watchin', what's his name would curse my grandchildren and me looking on without sayin' nuthin', couldn't do nuthin'. My head thinking all the time, one day I got up, something like that, and said: 'You gonna die.'"

Socorro already looked at the world with different eyes, less distant. As a small child, she had lost her mother and suffered at the hands of her stepmother who brought her up. Later, already grown, she found herself a boyfriend, got pregnant and was abandoned by the father who "just got me pregnant." Her nervousness, which now confines her to bedrest, is closely linked to her relationships with the men in her life. Of her second husband, she relates:

> "Because I was plump, pretty, with a nice body and he was jealous of me. Even so I still had three kids by him. (Set up) a greengrocer's for me. The customers would come to buy and he wouldn't want me to serve them. Him drinking, didn't even serve the customers. When I went to serve 'em, 'cos the customer was leavin', I'd get it in my face for ... for everything. Even so I had three kids by him. When I couldn't stand it any longer I decided to throw him out. I say 'now you go, you go now from my house' ... go, don't go, go ... he went away. After midnight, he came back with some mates wantin' to come inside, drunk with liquor. I didn't want him to come inside, 'cos I say I'm not gonna forgive you, forgave him more than ten times. But then I say, 'it's no good anymore', it's no good 'cos my new baby, he beat the children. Newly-born ... Gave money for him to buy medicine for the baby, he'd drink it. And me there goin' half crazy in the street, Oh my God, my child sick. How is it that I'm gonna buy medicine for these children? Then I'd be filled with that agony, my nerves, my God, what am I gonna do now? My kids is gonna die. (...) Then he left, it didn't work out, got a new one, a new one? Look, I had my moments too ... was young, pretty, had a nice body, all my teeth perfect, long hair and everything. Got myself a new one ...."

She lived ten years with her second husband who was a good provider, always worried about the well-being of the children. However, the end of the relationship caused a lot of problems for Socorro:

Narratives and the Construction of a Self

"He stayed and stayed, but he was white and I'm black. My husband was your color and I'm black, so his mother didn't want that he liked me but even so he'd come on the sly and all here. But one day he went to Mato Grosso, I worked, gave money for him to get himself a job at Petrobrás (...) He works on the rigs. So he sent money but his mum was full of herself, 'cos she was ambitious. So he sent alot of money, asked his mum to give it to me. She'd go out and buy a little bit of everything and send it. I said, 'ah me no, I'm not used to that'... Me with a small baby with just that little bit of food, I say, 'gonna give it right back'. I was always like that ... headstrong. I say, 'I'm gonna go down there and I'm gonna give it back right now'. I got there and I called to his mum, said that that ain't no shopping ... 'Ah but that's just what you gonna eat' (...) 'In that case I'll leave it here for you'. Left that bit of shopping right there. She said: 'you ain't gonna eat not this, not nuthin' else'. So, there we are, when he arrived from Mato Grosso all content to see his newly-born son, they kept him there. And the shopping that I left there, well, she went to a house of black magic, prepared something there ... When he came back it all got worse, he did all the shopping again and those goods that were there he put more and put more in the middle (...) when I ate the sugar that he had sent, sent and sent to say that he wouldn't come, that I had maltreated his mother... and I put sugar in my coffee, sweetened my coffee, but what a thing, I felt so ill, my belly was this high, pain, pain pain, pain, my God. He didn't come here, [me] sending out for medicine ... The boy got sick and I sent for him. He said that he wouldn't give no medicine for the boy, he'd only do the boy's funeral when the boy was in Nina Rodrigues (mortuary). That's right, I let it go too ... I took him to court, everything, the case is still there at the tribunal. (...) And so I went to a house, of a man ... he works with **umbanda** (an Afro-Brazilian religion), he's a **pai de santo** (the priest of Afro-Brazilian religions like candomblé and umbanda) ... so his **caboclo** (Amerindian spirit) said: 'I'll treat you', and that's what he did, treated me. He said: 'at midnight you'll see who it was, go home and sleep 'cos at midnight you'll see who it was'. And so I lay down to sleep. At midnight I heard the bell go 'ding, ding, ding', and then I woke up ... woke up, turned over and slept again. When I woke up I saw that it was her, his deceased mother, with two men digging like below a bay tree that was there, a tobacco plant that was there, digging, taking the earth out of there (...) And then I got so nervous, I told one person then another ... and then said like; 'oh, to live a life like this, ill every day from witchcraft, and so I'm going to leave everything', left everything."

Socorro told us that the *pai de santo* managed to cure her of that affliction. A time later, however, illness and nervousness started to consume her once again. In a certain fashion, these ills seem to be the inevitable result of her daily drudgery.

"Whoever's got children has got worries. My daughters started to lose their way, and then I started to get nervous, filling the house with grandchildren, with just me to provide for, they didn't have a place to stay. Me here in this house. It was that same old story ... washing and ironing clothes and then delivering them on the right day, ah, got fed up with the boss, went back, took food for my grandchildren, my daughters would go out. They'd leave two or three in my house, all this starts to, a person starts to go thingy, no, starts to worry and so it was so when I came back from Rio de Janeiro, that I opened the door, I started to get sick. From there I got worse and worse, with a terrible headache, the doctor said I had tuberculosis. When he said I had T.B., well, I got more nervous ...."

Three events link together to compound this new phase of suffering. First, she was abandoned by her last companion:

"I feel ... I felt very sad because I lived together sixteen years with this guy ... and he was a good person but never gave nuthin' in here for the house. He treated me extremely well, and so he comes, he comes here always he comes ... he doesn't live here, no, got married, found a woman. Got married, yes, I fell even more in love, at least, me, with a belly of nine months, just about to have the baby, I saw all of that finished, he had a woman on the side, did wrong by her and had to get married, when I knew about it, he was already married. (...) I got really sad like, shocked, besides all that after I says: 'it's true, he came, he was coming here when I was well enough to cook'. He married, don't stay much in his own house, stayed more here. And now that I fell ill, he don't come no more, he passes sometimes down the alley. I stay like this, it's true, when a person only likes the other one when they're fit. And so I pray to Jesus: 'Help me, that he'll see me well again with my basket on my head, my money for him to come and ask to borrow and I won't lend him nuthin.'"

A few years later, her son is involved in an accident. He had bet on a running race with his friend, was confused for a criminal, and was shot in the foot by a policeman.

"From then on I got nervous 'cos I couldn't get this man to kill him, 'cos I was a brave one. I've already lived in the shantytown, Estácio, in Rio de Janeiro, not scared of criminals. My kids, here there's some guys who wanted to get my children stealin', yep, they came to the door, I said: 'get away from my door, my children may have been brought up without a father but he's not gonna be a thief, no, my sons is gonna be a man.' I get out a bottle to threaten them: 'Goodness, Mrs Socorro.' I say: 'get goin', I baptize my children, Thank God my sons is a man.' (…) And so I started getting nervous. On New Year's Day I had a crisis, 'cos I saw him all … 'cos here on New Year's Day, here in this street it's so lively … when I saw him there sitting at the door, when he saw me, he broke down and started to hug me: 'oh Mum, oh my God, what is it that I done, didn't do nuthin' to deserve this, my God,' and so I started to cry too, that's it. So, I started to get nervous …."

On a later occasion, late at night, as she was returning from Pelourinho, where she'd been selling *acarajé* (Bahian snack food) with her son, daughter-in-law and small grandchildren, she found herself in the middle of a fight. The vehicle was traveling at full speed; men were arguing vehemently; her daughter-in-law, in an advanced stage of pregnancy, hit the driver over the head with a pan for him to stop. At the end of all the confusion, not one of her cooking utensils was left, she lost pans, the cloth, the snack food: "and so from then on I started to get nervous."

Lying on the bed she sees the unfolding of the events, as if in another world, without involvement, distant. Her body, she feels has lost its vitality: "I'm getting smaller, smaller." Soon, she saw herself involved in a long line of doctors, examinations, collection of prescriptions and medicines. She never missed her participation in camdomblé, nor in her Spiritualist seánce (*sessão*). One day she was advised to go to a Spiritualist (Kardecist) temple; although reluctant to leave the house, she eventually did go. She took care to put on three pairs of shorts, one on top of the other, in order to disguise her thinness and not start the neighbors talking. There, however, an evil spirit descended in her, who forced her to face her decline: "I started to curse myself, say things, call myself skinny, bony, old."

The Meaning of Narrative

The narrative of Socorro includes multiple, complex meanings. The combination and selection of narrative segments bears witness to a dominant 'semantic unit': the sign of *nervoso*. This sign is described by images of oppression, a burning sensation in the head, agony, pains in the legs, headaches and fits of nervousness and irritability for any reason. On the other hand, there are marked experiences of sadness, distancing from the world and isolation. Articulated in a life-narration, Socorro selects happenings, actions, attitudes, and expressions, which juxtaposed between themselves, designate critical situations that continually put the central subject/personage of the story to the test. Thus, dramas are outlined which reveal the present as a necessary development of the arrangement of things, events, relations and established qualities of the past, i.e. as a negation of the accidental. Certain elements of the narrative play an important role in this construction. In Socorro's story, for example, the witchcraft of her jealous mother-in-law, confirmed by the dream predicted by the *pai do santo*, affirms the inevitable character of the pain and suffering which assail her. In this narrative segment, Socorro attributes to her mother-in law a negative role, stressing the inevitability of her *nervoso* as caused by her. The character of the mother-in-law represents the pole of discord which sets the intrigue into motion; constructed as a type that condenses and epitomizes the qualities of evil, she amplifies the tragic dimension of the oncoming events: the mother-in-law, who causes Socorro to suffer, is not simply a woman corroded by jealousies, but a witch supported by hidden and secret powers.

Narratives and the Construction of a Self

In Socorro's account, the sign of *nervoso*, the dominant semantic unit of the narrative, is directly associated with the disintegration of the person, who is, to a large extent, in physical and corporal decline. Within the diverse narrative segments, metaphors are present that express bodily sensations: sweat, trembling, stiff muscles, etc. The narrative segments, in their turn, are selected in such a way that they reveal the sensation that her body is diminishing or descending. It is difficult to comprehend the feeling of her nervousness divorced from this existential dimension. In the past, she had been plump, well-made, with good hair and teeth, desired, an object of jealousy; now, she was thin, bony, sick, avoided by her partner of long-standing. These new traits were not simply the products of the natural passing of time, but of time in the sense of consumption, of the suffered unfolding of events that are registered and leave their marks on the body. When talking about the deterioration of her body, Socorro not only refers to the natural process of aging, but to its almost imposed, forced quality, marked furthermore by the violence inflicted on her body. This decadence implies a change in the relation body/subject, this body, which as Socorro says had had its moments, was now uprooted from the world (thrown on the sofa), the object of the action of illness and therapies.

The bodily decline is also associated with a broader process of weakening, of a moral nature: it emerges from successive, failed attempts to see the role of husband/father/provider filled within the family and, consequently, for Socorro to occupy an ideal position, unambiguously, as wife/mother/carer. Her account expresses a marked difficulty in guiding her life—and construct a sense of self—according to this ideal. Without a firm reference of companion and father for her children, Socorro has to cope alone with the various burdens of the household, whether this belongs to the traditional dominion of the woman or not.

It is interesting to observe that according to work realized about the working-class of Salvador, many of the causes attributed to mental illnesses (madness and *nervoso*) point to the loss of a well-defined locus within the family, thought of as a network of personal and hierarchical relationships. Within this framework, the mentally-ill person is generally represented as an outsider, isolated from networks of obligation and support. (RABELO, ALVES & SOUZA 1995) With the idea in mind that the model of the person for the working-class is essentially relational or hierarchical, DUARTE (1986) suggests that the *nervoso* of the woman is partly due to her entrance into the masculine domain (the public world, of work, etc.), since such a situation negates her condition as a person, defined according to a relational logic. Nevertheless, facing a context of tensions and potential fragility, Socorro forges for herself, in her narrative, the image of a strong woman, headstrong, who threw her violent and drunkard husband out of the home, who refused to accept the crumbs from her wicked mother-in-law, who confronts criminals and who raised her children single-handed, but with pride. This image is not only the fruit of her individual creativity; it conforms to a cultural stock of feminine figures and personages found in the urban, working-class environments. The personage that Socorro appropriates and develops in her story, even though at a merely ideal level, allows her to transform a situation of weakness (linked to the difficulty to emulate the model of wife and mother given the absence of a husband/father/provider) into an affirmative experience of force and power in the face of crises and difficulties in life.

In the narrative framework, the nervous attacks which afflict Socorro appear exactly in moments of difficulty and crisis. This fact is evidenced by various segments: the violence of her husband who spends her money and leaves her unable to buy medicine for her sick child; the rejection of her companion, who, caught up in his mother's lies, refuses to give her assistance in a moment of sickness and affliction; the abandonment of the man that she loved and whom she had always helped; her son's accident; the fight on the bus which caused her to lose a large part of her *bahiana* equipment. However, Socorro's experience of nervousness cannot be reduced to a mere reaction to adverse circumstances; it stems from a specific interpretation of her own position in the state of affairs. In her story, she reveals herself to feel a sense of impotence in the different contexts, which ultimately put in check the possibility of her affirming herself as a strong/headstrong/proud woman: in the situations described, what disturbs her and makes her nervous is the perception that she is unable to maintain or put into action her self-identity. In this light, the context questions and, in the end, negates the possibility of affirmation of the image proposed and developed by Socorro. It is enlightening, in this sense, that when describing the nervous attack that overcame her due to her son's accident, Socorro relates the crisis to the impossibility to take action against the responsible policeman.

In a discussion about emotions, ROSALDO observes that: "emotions are about the ways in which the social world is one in which we are involved" (1984: 143). In the case of Socorro's nervous attacks, the relation between self and context seems marked by a strong sense of confusion, which oscillates between tension or a constant rush against a context of events and relations whose details protrude as if seen through a magnifying-glass (which is expressed as agony, anger and irritation for any reason) and a dismissal or acute estrangement from the context (marked by a sensation of distance or decreasing involvement with the world).

Conclusion

Socorro's narrative displays basic structural dimensions of the daily lives of urban working-class women; though fruit of an individual trajectory and creativity, it is composed of and articulates elements of a broader cultural narrative, belonging to a gender and class specific life experience. With this, we are not trying to say that the signification of *nervoso*, as a salient cultural category, is completely covered by Socorro's account, but that within the construction of her personal narrative are 1. reflected the social contexts or frameworks of an individual experience and; 2. developed signs, images and metaphors that produce a certain intersubjective domain from which individuals can give shape to and communicate their own experiences (ALVES & RABELO 1995).

The composition of various segments in the narrative framework expresses and configures a self, by unifying or totalizing what is experienced as a series of disconnected events and actions. This capturing of life occurs, to a large extent, through an imaginary interplay between the I and the other, which the act of narrating evokes. In telling his personal trajectory, the individual assumes the position of the other in respect to himself, as he places himself as the hero or as the symbolical figure who the saga is about. In the process of narration, a distancing occurs between the I-narrator and the I-personage of the story narrated. It is this distancing—taking himself as 'the other'—that allows the individual to reflect about his experiences and confer an order to them. The identification or recognition of the symbolic other—the hero—not only allows that the individual/narrator projects a determined definition of himself to an audience, but also helps him in the perception of his self-identity and in the formulation of a sense of continuity behind the ongoing flow of events, compromises and accidents. In the narrative, this continuity is captured by the order of the story, whose development—taken as destiny, the necessary unfolding of the trajectory – coincides with the unveiling of the identity of the narrator, who has become the personage.

It is also necessary to remember that the story is produced in the field of action and in itself constitutes action: the stories are told through or with the body—movements, expressions, postures –

and create, at least to some extent, the perspective or point of view from which the body/self is engaged in a context of objects, people and conditions. In other words, the narratives which the individuals elaborate about themselves not only reflect a perception of the world, but lead to a specific way of being in the world. In the case of the personal narratives of people suffering from *nervoso*, we can say that they indicate or point to a life experience of fragility and pain, as much as they contribute to defining this experience.

For an Anthropology interested in comprehending and theorizing about the construction of subjectivity, the analysis of narratives represents an important methodological resource which permits the discussion of relevant questions about this theme. It is a subject which seems increasingly central to this science.

Note

Sections of this paper were presented at the XX Meeting of the Brazilian Anthropological Association, April, 1996, Salvador, Brazil. The manuscript has been read by a number of colleagues in the Health and Social Sciences Centre (ECSAS) and we have benefited from their comments. Our thanks to IARA SOUZA and MARIA GABRIELA HITA. The paper was translated to English by SALLY INKPIN.

References

ALVES, P.C.
    1994   O discurso sobre a enfermidade mental. In: *Saúde e doença: um olhar antropológico*. Edited by P.C. ALVES & M.C.S.MINAYO. Rio de Janeiro: Fiocruz.
ALVES, P. C. & M. RABELO
    1995   Significação e metáforas: aspectos situacionais no discurso da enfermidade. In: *Saúde & comunicação: visibilidades e silêncios*. Edited by A.M.R. PITTA. São Paulo/Rio de Janeiro: Hucitec/Fiocruz.
CORIN, E.; BIBEAU, G. & E. UCHÔA
    1993   Éléments d'une sémiologie anthropologique des troubles psychiques chez les Bambara, Soninké et Bwa du Mali. *Antropologie et sociétés* 17(1-2): 125-156.
DAVIS, D.
    1989   The variable character of nerves in a newfoundland fishing village. *American Anthropologist* 11: 63-78.
DUARTE, L.F.D.
    1986   *Da vida nervosa nas classes trabalhadoras urbanas*. Rio de Janeiro: Zahar.
    1994   A outra saúde: mental, psicossocial, físico-moral? In: *Saúde e doença: um olhar antropológico*. Edited by P.C. ALVES & M.C.S. MINAYO. Rio de Janeiro: Fiocruz.
DUBET, F.
    1995   Sociologie du sujet et sociologie de l'experience. In: *Penser le sujet: autour d'Alain Touraine*. Edited by F. DUBET & M. WIEVIORKA. Colloque de Cerisy: Fayard.
DUBOIS, J., GIACOMO, M., GUESPIN, L., MARCELLESI, C., MARCELLESI, J.B. & J.P. MEVEL
    1993   *Dicionário de lingüística*. São Paulo: Cultrix.
GIDDENS, A.
    1991   *Modernity and self identity*. Cambridge: Polity Press.
GOOD, B.
    1994   The narrative representation of illness. In: *Medicine, rationality, and experience: an anthropological perspective*. Edited by B.J. GOOD. Cambridge: Cambridge University Press.
GUARNACCIA, P.
    1989   The multiple meanings of ataque de nervios in the Latin Community. *Medical Anthropology* 11: 47-62.
JODELET, D.
    1991   *Madness and social representations: living with the mad in one french community*. Berkeley: University of California Press.
LITTLEWOOD, R. & M. LIPSEDGE
    1989   *Aliens and alienists*. London: Unwin Hyman.

Low, S. M.
   1994   Embodied metaphors: nerves as lived experience. In: *Embodiment and experience*. Edited by T. Csordas. Cambridge: Cambridge University Press.

Lutz, C.A.
   1988   *Unnatural emotions*. Chicago: University of Chicago Press.

Mead, G. H.
   1972 [1934]. *Espíritu, persona y sociedad*. Buenos Aires: Ed. Paidos.

Rabelo, M., Alves, P.C. & I. Souza
   1995   The many meanings of mental illness among the urban poor in Brazil. In: *Urbanization and mental health in developing countries*. Edited by T. Harpham & I. Blue. Aldershot: Avebury.

Rebhun, L.A.
   1993   Nerves and emotional play in Northeast Brazil. *Medical Anthropology Quaterly* 7(2): 131-151.
   1994   Swallowing frogs: anger and ilness in Northeast Brazil. *Medical Anthropology Quaterly* 8(4): 360-382.

Ricoeur, P.
   1991   *O si mesmo como um outro*. Campinas: Papirus.

Rosaldo, M.Z.
   1984   Toward an anthropology of self and feeling. In: *Culture theory: essays on mind, self and emotions*. Edited by A. Shweder & R.A. Levine. Cambridge: Cambridge University Press.

Wiley, N.
   1994   *The semiotic self*. Cambridge: Polity Press.

Young, A.
   1981   The creation of medical knowledge: some problems in interpretation. *Social Science and Medicine* 15B: 379-386.

Nerves and *Nervousness* in Brazilian Urban Culture
Luiz-Fernando Dias Duarte

Abstract
This is a study about the Person and its physical-moral perturbations in Brazilian urban culture. The ethnographic focus is the language and experience of nerves among the working classes. The analysis is centered in a dual model opposing the individualized psychological representations typical of cultivated middle and upper classes and the relational, hierarchical representations that pervade popular, working class culture. Referring to the complex history of ideas about nerves in modern Western culture helps to elucidate the characteristics of its contemporary popular version in Brazilian society.

Zuammenfassung
Dieses ist eine Studie über das Konzept der Person und seine physisch-moralischen Störungen innerhalb der brasilianischen, urbanen Kultur. Der ethnographische Fokus ist die Sprache und die Erfahrung von Nervosität innerhalb der Arbeiterklasse. Die Analyse stellt ein duales Modell in den Mittelpunkt, welches die individualisierten, psychologischen Repräsentationen, typisch für die kultivierten Mittel- und oberen Klassen, den relationalen, hierarchischen Repräsentationen, die die Kultur der Arbeiterklasse durchziehen, gegenüberstellt. Der Bezug auf die komplexe Ideengeschichte der Nerven in der modernen westlichen Kultur hilft, die Charakteristika der gegenwärtigen populären Version innerhalb der brasilianischen Gesellschaft zu erhellen.

Keywords: person, nerves, psychology, urban Brazil

Introduction

One of the most important, current words for referring to some kind of personal sense of inadequacy or disturbance in Brazilian culture is to be nervous. To feel or to be nervous, to be in a state of nervousness, to fall prey to a nervous illness, to have a shattered nervous system or to undergo a nervous crisis are equally common expressions. More often than not, its meaning is taken for granted throughout Brazilian society. But what does being nervous really mean?

I had been doing fieldwork in working class communities around Rio de Janeiro for some years before I began to suspect that this ubiquitous expression (and all others related to it) might refer to a reality quite distant from the one my own common sense relied upon, in a cultural context that had constantly dismissed my initial and naive sense of continuity.

The ensuing research proved that those suspicions were sound. A complex and coherent model of the Person[1] could be distinguished through the semantic field of nervousness. Its structure and value-orientation led to the hypothesis of a sharp distinction between this model and the psychological one that seems to prevail in Brazilian urban upper-classes or elites (and thence in the whole 'high culture' establishment).

As it happens with nervousness, the term psychological belongs to the common sense language of a vast portion of Brazilian population. Both the nervousness and the psychological models are physical-moral systems, concerned with the regular functioning of the Person, the relation be-

---

1. The use of Person throughout the article is intentional, since it seems to convey a wider meaning — as an anthropological tool — than the otherwise more usual Individual or Self. Radcliffe-Brown's definition of the Person as opposed to the Individual is one of the first explicit mentions to the diacritic usage of the two terms (Radcliffe-Brown 1952).

tween body and mind, and the prediction, explanation and therapeutic treatment of its 'irregular' states.

The tradition of comparative studies concerning models of the Person has been almost entirely based upon ethnographic data from 'exotic' or 'classical' societies, in spite of the early programmatic synthesis of MAUSS in 1936 (MAUSS 1973). Philosophical and psychological speculation, on the one hand, or empiricist biomedical research, on the other, have been the preferred domains for it when our own Western concepts and models are at stake. This work aspires to connect these different trends in an integrated exercise of anthropological research.

I will first demonstrate the opposition between those concepts and models and their different styles of diffusion and distinction. As the hypothesis deals with the cultural diacritical theme of the opposition between social classes or groups within a national society, it will be necessary to expatiate on this particular problem.

I will further try to make clear how this research throws some light on the vast theoretical issue of modernity. The ideology of individualism—commonly considered as one of its basic characteristics—is above all a theory of the Person: peculiar; paradoxical; 'modern,' in a word. Its history has noticeably grown in recent decades; its ethnography is still otherwise largely wanting.[2]

The Nerves in a System of Cultural Differences

The foremost condition for sociological comparison is the point of view and the level of analysis that is privileged in each case. Whatever the model of Person in focus, its conception depends basically on the observer's own model, whose assumptions remain at the root of his model of the 'observed.' This seems an unavoidable frontier for a rationalist, universalistic anthropology. All that can be done is to concentrate on controlling the process; being as aware as possible of the specific effects of the previous structure of thought and analysis on 'new' knowledge.

That is why precedence must be given to the presentation assumptions; not very easy to unveil in this case. Although a certain perception of the sociological arbitrariness of the modern individualized model of the Person has been more or less present throughout the whole tradition of the social sciences, an integrated theory of its genesis, organization and ideological consequences had not become available until very recently.[3]

The first problem concerns the sociological grounding of the complex system of cultural models we will be dealing with. My model is based in the preeminence of the cultural representations, the self-identification processes by which social groups define themselves, rather than in any 'hard,' theoretically deduced entities. The use of descriptive categories that are traditionally associated with the substantialist tradition, such as 'working class' or 'middle-classes,' certainly leads to a certain confusion, inevitable in these controversial grounds. The category 'upper classes,' in my case, refers basically to the groups that embody the official, educated culture in a certain society – the 'elites,' in a sense. 'Working classes,' on the other hand, refers to those groups that define themselves as being composed of manual workers and as being dependent upon the value and

---

2. My own work is part of a larger investment and interest in that question in Brazilian social anthropology. ROBERTO DA MATTA (1979) and GILBERTO VELHO (1981) were the main pioneers in that field.
3. LOUIS DUMONT is the leading name for most levels of the question, as it is presented here (DUMONT 1972 and 1979). FOUCAULT's analysis of the individualizing effects of the 'disciplinary power' (FOUCAULT 1975) can be read in a similar direction. Other more conventional contributions among contemporaneous authors can be found in MACFARLANE 1978; MACPHERSON 1962; LUKES 1973 and TAYLOR 1989.

practice of work, within Western societies. Despite that category's great heterogeneity, it shares such basic cultural assumptions as to be considered a discrete social unit—at a certain level, of course.

This analytical option is further justified by the fact that 'upper class' members see those of the 'working classes' as different and vice-versa. At the same time, a critical mass of cultural assumptions pervades the multiple subdivisions within the so-called 'upper classes,' that can be sociologically discerned and described. Here, as in the other case, unity can be proposed only at certain levels of analysis.

The immediate, common sense recognition of difference between these two polar groups in Brazilian society is not conducive or propitious to the sociological perception of their cultural opposition. The two languages are not in an equivalent social position and many aspects or effects of this inequality are at the root of their mutual assessments. It is also important to note that one's view of the other is based upon those cultural principles or assumptions that lie at the bottom of their respective world-views; and that both in fact believe that each one's model is 'natural' and 'good.'

One very striking example of this problem is that of the relationship between nervous patients and medical agents whose world-view is based on the psychological model of the Person. All sorts of misunderstandings arise from this daily experience—always dramatic, often tragic. In all these cases, the more obvious victims are the urban workers, given their economic, political and cultural dependence on the 'upper classes.' They suffer the permanent effects of more traditional views of their 'ignorance,' 'laziness' or 'backwardness.' To this has been added the more recent suffering enticed by these 'rescuers' of good-will, who hope—in the most superficial and ethnocentric manner—to interfere in their culture in order to 'empower' them, to enable them to face and defy subjection.[4]

The opposition between the 'upper class' and 'working class' world-views is analytically based upon the definition of the first as more 'individualistic;' i.e., as being mostly dependent on the complex pattern of values that has been the backbone of Western thought at least since the Eighteenth Century. The motto of Liberty and Equality contains the most explicit principles of that Great Tradition. Nominalism and rationalization (disenchantment) are some of the concomitant processes, at different levels. Modern psychology itself has been shown to be one of the latest and most important offspring of the individualistic tendency to divide the old human totality in different layers of reality, each of which becomes the focus of a new 'science.' This tendency is coherent with a general 'flattening' strategy, which is the combined effect of 'egalitarianism' and 'rationalism.' The rejection of vertical, encompassing relations, together with a methodological contempt for the totality, has characterized it from the very beginning as a secular, anti-religious ideology. At the level of social relations, equality made it impossible to accept the legitimacy of complementary situations, replaced by the contractual and mutual model.

Most aspects of modern societies and all the institutions that have characterized them in the past two centuries are dependent on that ideology or configuration of values. This is the situation in modern economic life, both in the case of capitalism and of socialism. It is also the case of political life, from the concept of Nation to those of democracy or revolution. Power and sexuality, love and science were old concepts entirely reordered according to the individualistic ideology, to

---

4. My own position regarding this central issue of the 'social question' was exposed in DUARTE (1992) and DUARTE et al. (1993).

the point of actually becoming new entities, distinct from their traditional counterparts. A new Person arose as well—and it was called the Individual, seat of the Self.

The Psychological Model

One of the most conspicuous developments of individualistic ideology is the representation of an inner specific level of human reality called psychological (especially in its psycho-analytical, highly interiorized, version). This model is no easy target for anthropological analysis. It encompasses a very broad spectrum of meanings, that can be traced back to several and competing versions in Western thought since the Eighteenth Century (and even farther back, depending on the emphasis of the analysis).[5]

As an analytical strategy, I decided to consider the psycho-analytical, FREUDian version, as the nucleus of the model, since it corresponds to the most dynamic and integrated one, often hegemonic in the academic field.[6] A distinction will be made between a 'material' mode of the psychological model and a 'formal' one, where the category may include any of a certain number of alternative meanings.

The material form of the psychological version consists of the definition of a new order of reality, irreducible to any of the terms of the usual physical/moral dichotomy. It encompasses the whole field of the 'moral' world ('religion' included). Yet, at the same time, it relates the new order to a basically materialistic world-view; albeit at a higher, non-naturalistic level.[7]

Psychological reality aspires for a preeminence above the whole human entity, in a kind of monistic empire (encompassing the somatic dimension). It implies a whole new ontology for Man, anchoring the individualistic ideal in the radically inner reality of the libido and the unconscious, as the primum movens and the locus operandi of the modern Person. The strong emphasis of the model on the 'unconscious' character of the basic structure of human thought and action may seem to subvert the ideal of 'liberty'—one of the two guiding principles of individualism. In fact, both psycho-analytical practice and a certain level of its theoretical foundations permanently depend on the promise of a superior dimension of liberty to be attained through the 'analysis' of the relation of the self (or the ego) and the forces that both constitute and impinge upon it.[8] The principle of 'equality' was obeyed from the very beginning: the proposed model was universal and concerned the most abstract qualities of Humanity.

Wherever that model has reached a hegemonic position, all other categories related to the Person and its disturbances had to undergo a loss or shifting of meaning. Mind, spirit, soul, melancholy, hysteria, neurasthenia, mania, hypochondria, nervousness, anxiety, anguish, neurosis, psy-

---

5. MAUSS already mentioned in his seminal article the importance of the Christian tradition behind 'individualism,' following TOCQUEVILLE and DURKHEIM (see DUARTE & GIUMBELLI 1993, for a recent appraisal of that aspect of the question).
6. The value of psycho-analysis in Western culture is a source of considerable debate, depending on different national ethoses, academic traditions, epistemological dissension, etc. The very intensity of the discussions may be considered as a proof of the imposing presence of that system of ideas regarding Person and its disturbances. Regardless of its eventual 'scientific' quality, it can be considered as an important expression of the German *Bildung* tradition, concerned as it is with the unique development of the selves (as in SIMMELian 'qualitative individualism').
7. FREUD made use of arguments and imagery to construct this 'new reality' quite similar to those used by DURKHEIM to propose the *sui generis* reality of 'social facts.'
8. MARCEL GAUCHET & GLADYS SWAIN coined the expression 'personal' or 'subjective dispossession' to refer to this aspect of the question (GAUCHET & SWAIN 1980). See also SALEM 1992, for its discussion from the perspective of Brazilian social anthropology.

chosis, madness or frenzy are but a small sample of a vast semantic field that was entirely reorganized under the aegis of the new model. The very basic concepts that formed its inner scaffold were old categories, inherited from the medical-philosophical tradition, like the aforementioned libido and unconscious, or yet sublimation and identification, but invested with entirely new meanings.[9]

The rapidity and intensity of the diffusion of psychoanalysis among Brazilian urban elites has been the object of a growing number of studies, which have allowed a better understanding of their own culture and of its place in national culture. These studies have further stressed the necessity—even if not always at an explicit level—of investigating the alternative or competing concepts available in Brazilian culture and their distribution inside a complex nationwide social framework.[10]

The formal mode of the psychological model consists, on the other hand, in the presence of its lexical forms, dissociated from the ontological, semantic dimensions I have just eschewed—for reasons that will be examined.

Formal and Material Subsumption to the Psychological Model

The analytic model I have devised to present the available data is a fourfold one. The first position is that of the presence of the psychological model under its formal and material mode. The second one is that of its complete absence, both at the lexical and semantic levels. A third position can be distinguished by the formal presence of the psychological model (i.e., at 'lexical' level) and its absence under the material mode. The final one implies the material presence of that model and the absence or refusal of its lexical or formal mode.

Figure 1: Concepts of the Person: table of positions
from the point of view of the subsumption to the psychological model.

	1	2	3	4
formal	+	–	+	–
material	+	–	–	+

1. 'modern' and 'cultivated' middle and upper-classes (more established and official)
2. working-classes
3. lower middle-classes and 'non-cultivated' middle-classes; 'traditional' and 'cultivated' middle and upper-classes
4. 'modern' and 'cultivated' middle and upper-classes (less established or more marginal)

The first position—i.e., positive formal and material subsumption to the psychological model—finds its place in the culture of the established elites. As I mentioned before it has become ac-

---

9. The use of psychological to refer to that model is therefore very ambiguous, but inevitable, since the words coined by Freud to distinguish his novelty from old introspectionist or psycho-physicist psychologies never did become real alternatives (e.g. 'metapsychology' or 'deep psychology') and the word 'psycho-analytical' rather conveys a sense of methodology than a sense of world-view. 'Psychic' could have been used, weren't it for the 'mediumship connotation' it has come to have in the English language.
10. The need for further investigation did partially arise from within the very ranks of the psychological establishment, which was facing difficulties both in their conventional and unconventional efforts to propitiate a psychologically-oriented therapeutic to low-income, popular culture patients in the late 1970's and the 1980's (see ROPA & DUARTE 1989).

ademically predominant, it is widespread among the national intelligentsia and has a growing presence at the 'highest' levels of mass media. The medical and psychiatric establishment that strongly resisted it until the 1950's is now deeply pervaded by that model, and this is a very powerful factor in the pace and manner of its diffusion.[11]

The second position—i.e., negative formal and material subsumption to the psychological model—corresponds to the very specific case of the nervous model that is current and preeminent among urban workers. It was the focus of an ethnographic research and its description is at the core of this article. At the formal, lexical level, it can be considered to be a variation of the model of nervousness that grew in opposition to the humoral or melancholic one since the end of the Seventeenth Century. The apex of its academic hegemony had just been reached by the time psychoanalysis began to lay the basis for the new psychological model, and its association with the Hygienist movement accounted for a deep pervasiveness and widespread diffusion. It is a quite singular model, based upon concepts and values neatly opposed to those of its present 'upper-class' counterpart.

The next position—i.e., positive formal and negative material subsumption to the psychological model—comprehends two sets of variations (being as it is rather residual regarding the chosen focal point). The first group is that of the 'explicit' theories regarding the Person, which at present can be considered more or less openly opposed to the Freudian influence. In this group, the strongest position is held by the heirs to the positivistic tradition, in its learned, academic version—still much present in the medical-psychiatric establishment. Quite a similar position is held (paradoxically as it may seem) by classic liberal ideology and by the official doctrines of established Christian churches, which is mostly the case with the Roman Catholic Church in Brazil. These trends emphasize very firmly the attributes of 'will,' 'will power,' 'free will' and 'consciousness;' in the first case as the superior functions of matter (equivalent to a lay, 'civilized morality'); in the second, as the signs of the divine character of the Christian soul. Although both the positivistic and the Christian doctrines are based on theories of determination (either physical preeminence in the first case, as the ideas of 'heredity' or 'degeneracy' suggest, or spiritual preeminence, in the second, as demonstrated by the idea of 'original sin'), they conceive of psychoanalysis as an unacceptably deterministic concept of the Person, 'mystical' for the former, 'materialistic' for the latter. Liberal tradition denounces plainly its deterministic ambitions.

The second group belonging to the third position is very badly known, although it is socially perceptible. It seems to make use of the psychological model categories probably just as often as of the nervousness model ones. Its sociological basis can be described as 'lower middle-classes,' but this is a most imprecise definition. In fact, all that can be said here is that it encompasses groups that do not participate entirely either in the nervousness model, at least under the manner in which it presents itself within urban working class culture, or of the psychological model, in the strict sense defined here as the axis of 'upper-classes' concept of the Person. At the same time, being a folk conception, it does not present explicit, written, formalized versions easy to examine. It is highly probable that it has been influenced successively, through clinical, educational or pastoral experience, by the two learned doctrines just described.

Finally there is the fourth position—i.e., positive material and negative formal subsumption to the psychological model—that competes currently with that model within the same upper class

---

11. There is an important literature on the diffusion of psychoanalysis in France, in England, in the USA and in the German speaking countries. Some studies are now available for the case of Brazil (FIGUEIRA 1981, 1985; SAGAWA 1985; RUSSO 1993; VENANCIO 1993).

groups. Some of its versions would certainly accept the label of 'post-psychological' or 'post-psychoanalytical.' In fact this is a very broad category, whose common characteristics are a kind of contempt for or a refusal of the formal use of psycho-analysis and the search for alternative models of the Person. These alternatives concentrate concomitantly or alternatively on naturalistic or spiritualistic reorientation, having led to the formation of a host of sects, circles or networks, ranging from New Age to Zen-Buddhism. The most interesting aspect of it all is that the basic assumptions of the psychological model seem to lie at the bottom of all these variations, like the beliefs in an 'unconscious' and in inner 'drives,' the presence of an extreme form of ego-cult and the faith in the ultimate reality of self experience. This model has a very peripheral presence in the academic field, in spite of recent efforts to legitimize some of its versions. REICHian psychology and the 'new homeopathic' movement have been so far among the most successful. Nonetheless, it is being vigorously diffused, mainly through its influence in the avant-garde artistic world and in a certain level of mass media.

It must be stressed that all through the groups that embody the third and the fourth positions, the word 'psychological' can be used as a common sense expression to replace the now almost obsolete 'moral' category or to designate the intuitive techniques of interpersonal exchanges. In the first case, for instance, 'psychological effect' would be commonly used in the place of 'moral effect.' This kind of usage is also certainly common to the supporters of the first position, but it is strikingly rare among those of the second.

The *Nervousness* Model

The question of the diffusion and organization of the nervousness model is quite different. The formal/material strategy can not be used, since there are at least two material versions to oppose to the mere lexical usage. On the other hand, the presence of the formal/lexical mode does not have a diacritical function, being as it is nationally widespread. What is certain is that the use of the nervous category (and of its concomitants) is purely residual in the area dominated by the material mode of the psychological mode, i.e., both in its first and fourth positions (the most 'individualistic' and 'modern' ones). In clear contrast stands its value in the second position, i.e., among urban workers; where it serves to the expression of the popular nervousness model in its fullest form.[12] The situation is not clear concerning the sociological groups embracing the third position in the psychological-oriented model. In fact, it must remain an open question whether lower middle-classes can be defined as a cultural group at all. The available data is very sparse, as mentioned before. The academic version of the positivistic alternative within the third position is directly connected to the learned, Nineteenth Century configuration of nervousness, which is neatly distinguishable from its contemporary working class version.

The nervousness model, in its learned version, was one of the first systematic manifestations of individualistic ideology. Its origins can be found in the intense efforts of Eighteenth Century natural scientists to extend to the biological realm (mostly through Physiology) the mechanistic conception that sustained Galilean and Newtonian representations of the physical world and — at the same time — to endow the recently predominant concept of the economic and political Individual with a coherent image for its physical and moral structure and functioning (normal or pathologi-

---

12. I am considering here working class culture as the dynamic nucleus of contemporary 'urban' popular culture — for reasons I have developed elsewhere (DUARTE 1986).

cal).[13] The idea of a nervous system was the central weapon in the fight against the humoral configuration, which had sustained for centuries—together with the Christian antinomy between body and soul—Western ideas about the Person and its disturbances.

The Christian and the humoral models were holistic, dualistic and complementary: the two levels of Man, the four humors, the nine temperaments and the twelve positions of Zodiac formed a highly complex system of equivalence and exchanges based upon a logic of complementary differences subsumed to the ultimate unity of an encompassing God.[14] The nervous 'system' was indisputably physical and unitary; the temperament was physical-moral and composite. It was also universal, fundamentally identical for all; and it could represent the interior unity of each human being. The brain (the central organ of the system) was conceived as the seat of Man's higher functions, like thought and reason. These characteristics were the basis for a series of proposals and models that competed throughout the Eighteenth and Nineteenth Centuries for hegemony concerning the concept of the Person. It is possible to subsume all these movements under the single label of the nervousness model or configuration; at least at that highly abstract level where its opposition both to the humoral and the psychological models is clear.[15]

In Brazil there is evidence of the presence of the nervousness model since the first decades of the last century through French influence in the medical faculties. Under different versions or emphases, it remained predominant until very recently—as everywhere in the Western world.[16] Together with the influence of evolutionism and positivism it constituted the ground for the hygienist movement and crusades, responsible for the diffusion of the languages of nervousness throughout a country of such intense cultural heterogeneity. As I stressed before, it is still present under that learned form in certain sub-areas of higher culture.

Popular *Nerves*

Despite lexical continuity, the nerves of contemporary Brazilian urban workers have little in common with those of the Dutch and Scottish physiologists who first described their existence as a system in the Eighteenth Century, the Viennese doctors who opposed FREUD's views at the turn of the century, or the Brazilian psychiatrists who created the League for the Promotion of Mental Hygiene in the 1920's. Instead of the radical physicality of the original conception, one finds here a nervous system that may be host to all kinds of spiritual entities and may carry moral qualities together with sensory impressions. Instead of the original, universal support for equality, it serves here as the confirmation of difference; between men and women, for instance. Instead of being the

---

13. For different aspects of that historical cluster of ideas, see CARLSON & SIMPSON 1969, FIGLIO 1975, LAWRENCE 1979, and ROUSSEAU 1975 and 1990.
14. The most systematic depiction of that cosmological system from a modern perspective is LOVEJOY's book on the Great Chain of Being (LOVEJOY 1993)
15. There is an important difference to be noted in the opposition between the humoral and the learned nervousness model, on the one hand; and between the latter and the psychological one, on the other: in the first case, an individualistic model supersedes a holistic one; in the second case, a new and perhaps more radically individualistic model faces and defies another one which is also individualistic. For greater detail and precision, see DUARTE 1986.
16. DONA DAVIS' work on the development of neurasthenia in the USA is most inspiring (DAVIS 1989). I have analyzed elsewhere the presence of the nerves in French literature and in turn-of-the-century social science authors (DUARTE 1990), and in KRAFFT-EBING's organization of the system of the 'sexual perversions' (DUARTE 1989).

inner tissue of individuality, it is the vehicle of relationship between all persons and between persons and the world.

Nervousness became thus an overt physical-moral model, explicitly dualistic, and expressive of a holistic and hierarchical conception of the Person and the world. Even so, when one approaches the inner model, the architecture of this Person, its sauvage physiology, most of the themes of the learned version recur, in a most impressive demonstration of the combined action of continuity and change in the history of ideas. Here is the same concern with substance, communication, irritation/sensibility and obstruction that has pervaded the tradition of human physiology since the Eighteenth Century. But what does it all mean now? Substance is fundamentally a question of força (force, strength, power) and fraqueza (its opposite). These are important and quite general qualities. There is a physical força and a moral força. Their connecting point are the nerves, which serve as a bridge between the realm of the body, whose blood is the substance of physical force, and the realm of the head, where the brain is the seat of mental and moral force. As the brain is, however, the very nucleus of the nervous system, this connection implies a hierarchical relationship between the two terms: moral life, through the brain and the nerves (that are considered to be white) encompasses physical life, as represented by the body and blood (that are red). It is exactly the same scheme that stresses the sovereignty of God over Nature — as I was so often told. Hierarchy here doesn't mean mere domination. Rather, it means the kind of logical opposition in which the encompassed element is at the same time similar to and different from the encompassing one. In our example, the blood is a common element of the whole organism, but it belongs basically to the body proper and can thus be opposed to the head. A whole range of physical-moral disturbances is attributed to the illegitimate invasion of the brain (or the head) by blood.

The difference between man and woman depends heavily on the nerves/blood nexus. Man draws his hierarchical preeminence over the woman from the fact that he is the master of three concomitant forças: the physical, the mental (or intellectual) and the moral ones. The woman, on the other hand, is considered as a basically moral entity, incompatible with mastery at the level of physical and mental forces. It can be inferred from that model that, at a basic level, man — preeminent as he may be — is on the side of blood; and woman — encompassed as she may be — is on the side of the nerves. This means that inner accidents concerning blood are extremely dangerous in women, such as those that may occur in menstruation, pregnancy and childbirth. Women's moral quality corresponds thus to a basically nervous quality, which accounts for the fact that they are the most common victims (the natural victims, so to speak) of the wide range of disturbances related to nervousness. The characteristics of this model have wider consequences, at the level of the casa (house/home) for instance, that will be examined later.

The theme of communication has already been introduced in the question of blood and nerves. Both blood and nerves constitute internal networks concentrating the Person around the heart and the brain. A strict set of rules determines the appropriate flows and its foreseeable accidents. The theme is closely related to that of 'irritation/sensitivity.' In this case, emphasis is laid upon those qualities of the nerves that enable them to receive and transmit moral and physical impressions through the body, to and from the brain, under normal or pathological conditions. Irritability is the physical pole of a continuum whose moral pole is sensitivity. The irritation caused to the nerves by any accident reaches internal sensitivity, just as any peculiar state spreads through the nervous system under the form of irritation. The word atacar (literally, to attack) most commonly designates the different processes that can take place at that level. The nerves can be directly 'attacked' by moral injury, or by physical damage to the head. It can also be indirectly 'attacked' by processes regarding the body and mediated by the blood and the liver (considered of paramount importance because of its 'filter-like' functions). The following table may be useful:

Figure 2: Body processes

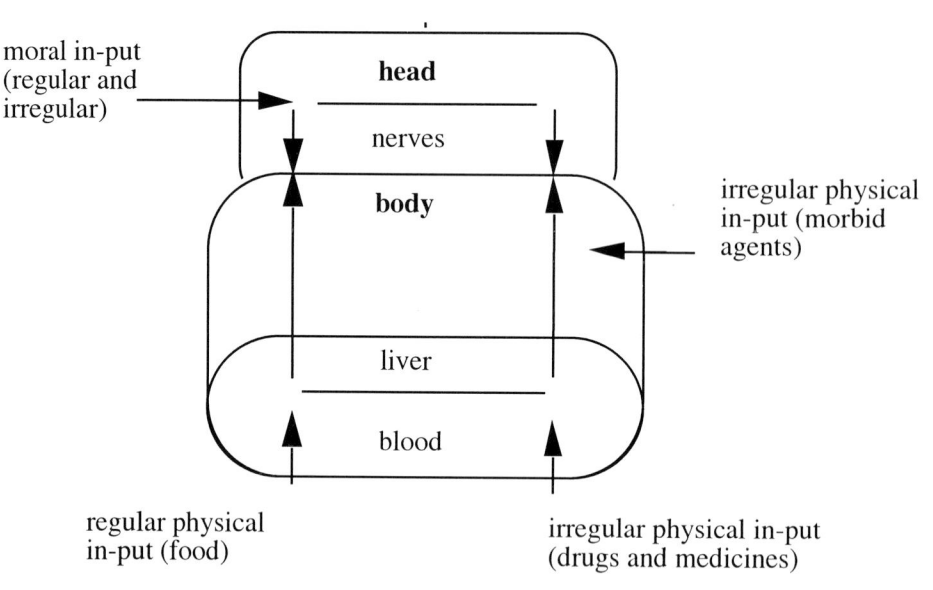

```
moral in-put
(regular and                    head
irregular)
                               nerves
                                                    irregular physical
                                body                in-put (morbid
                                                    agents)

                                liver

                                blood

    regular physical                    irregular physical in-put
    in-put (food)                       (drugs and medicines)
```

The last theme evoking the structure of the learned model of nervousness is 'obstruction.' All these flows, in-puts and out-puts, this entire 'physiology' may be interrupted by more or less dangerous accidents. They are often related to physical facts with moral consequences, but they can also operate in the opposite direction. In women, amenorrhea is probably the most common example of the first case; in men the impossibility of ejaculation. In the latter case, one of the most striking examples is 'excess of ideas in the head,' leading to the worst physical-moral disturbances.

The urban workers' version of the nervousness model is an excellent guide into their general world-view. At the same time, it is impossible to understand more fully the logic of nervousness, without taking into consideration the wider frame of their cultural premises.[17]

Family is probably the foremost level of identity in those social groups. No Person leads a full existence outside the family. The home is a very strong symbolic and concrete focus of life. A great many structural oppositions can be derived or composed around that element. It is in itself a complex, hierarchical unit, based on the reciprocal opposition between husband and wife. As we have seen, man is the encompassing element. He has the physical and mental forças that endow him with both the ability and the responsibility (the obrigação) for the maintenance and protection of the casa. He is its public face, representing the family in the outside world. Woman is the en-

---

17. It is impossible to review here or even to make most of the otherwise necessary cross-references to Brazilian literature concerning popular or working-class culture. Besides my own contribution (DUARTE 1986; 1987a, b), LOPES 1978; LOYOLA 1984; CALDEIRA 1984; ZALUAR 1985; LEAL 1995 and SARTI 1994 may offer a good overview.

VWB – Verlag für Wissenschaft und Bildung

compassed element, and represents its moral level. She must keep intact the honor of the family and be able to bring up the children according to the best moral standards. She is the inner face of the casa. Her passage through the public world must be carefully limited and controlled.

It is not difficult to see how theories concerning the structure of the Person are homologous to those concerning the structure of the casa. Man could be said to be the blood of the house, as the woman is its nerves. In another sense, however, he is the head of the house, just as she is the body. Figure 3 shows how the scheme undergoes a 'hierarchical inversion' as we pass from the outer to the inner levels of the Person: man is the external head, woman the internal one.

Figure 3:

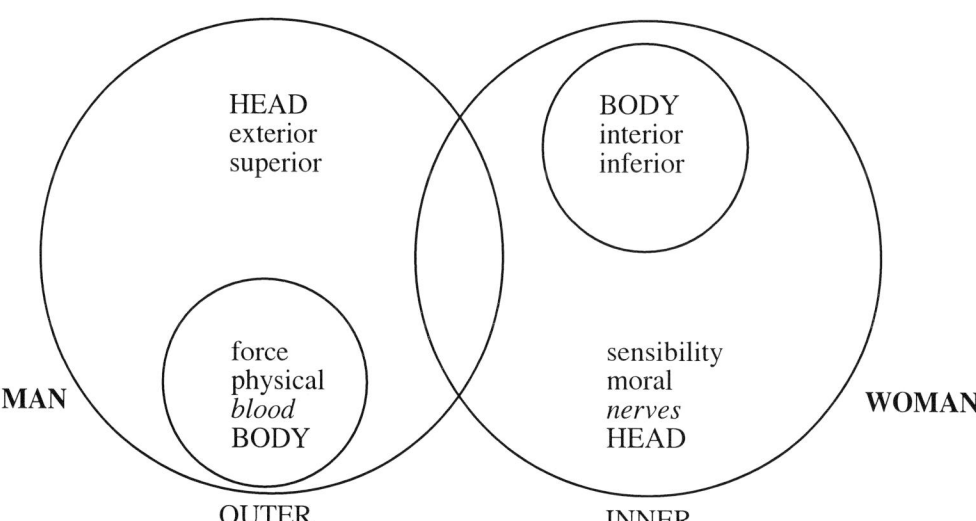

Family depends on hierarchy at yet another level: that of 'age' (or rather 'age status sets'). Seniority is the basis for a strict code of respect; respect towards other people, but above all respect towards oneself (dar-se o respeito), towards one's own status (reminiscent of the 'honour' values). The complex system of 'presentation of the self' in these groups includes the nervousness question, under the frequent category of nervous crisis. It may be a matter of considerable discussion whether this or that behavior can be legitimately attributed to a nervous crisis or breakdown, or considered as a blemish of one's moral façade, a falta de respeito (lack of respect).

In this case—as in all others—nervousness is one of the main instruments available for social evaluations. The sequence of categories related to nervousness is long, from lighter to more serious situations. It is possible to say that someone is simply nervous, that he is maluco (a lighter kind of madness) or that he is doido or maluco de verdade (really mad). Although everyone would agree that this scale has descriptive value, it is almost always impossible to discern in those thus evaluated any actual diacritical signs. The logic that presides over these classifications is fully 'situational'.[18] The choice between a positive or a negative classification, and the intensity of the label chosen depends on the 'structural distance' between subject and object, on the quality of the intermediate relationship, and on the situation. The wide range of categories offered by the ner-

---

18. In the sense EVANS-PRITCHARD (1968) employed that category in the analysis of Nuer social logic.

vousness model and its physical-moral quality account for its outstanding role in inter-personal appraisals.

Responsibility or madness are two of the dimensions that can be involved in these cases, which also include religious experiences and encosto. This last category represents a very frequent situation in urban working-class life: a temporary leave from regular work while receiving an allowance from the national welfare institution as a result of an accident or disease. The highest incidence of encosto is in the category of 'mental diseases' and 'psychiatric disturbances' (according to medical classification) or 'nervous diseases' (according to the patients). It is a very ambiguous institution, from the point of view of the urban workers, since it may include the very negative stigma of madness and the highly positive value of the esperteza (cleverness). Most people stress that their own madness was simulated (although they actually felt nervous), and that they malingered just in order to get the highly prized encosto. In this situation they can earn a salary from the 'informal' labor market, together with the encosto monthly allowance. For anyone who knows the extreme difficulties faced by Brazilian workers even to obtain physical subsistence, it is no wonder that such a resource has a very strong appeal. The encosto strategy will not be used however, unless the family situation is at its worst, because the bureaucratic procedures involved are very complicated and, above all, there is a fear of stigmatization, commonly associated with nervous disorders. It is impossible, furthermore, to assess whether the people who resort to the encosto really feel the need for medical-psychiatric help (or if they do need it somehow). All one can say is that they must be under the strain of a severe family crisis.

The ambiguous quality of encosto is therefore another important element in the interpersonal evaluations mentioned above. It may be of some help to observe how these processes take place in the case of the most obviously abnormal behaviors, such as the public display of personal disorder or disturbance. The following table presents five typical classifications in such cases. The final 'verdict' is 'situational,' and concerns the alternative or simultaneous presence of 'consciousness' and 'responsibility' for possible anomalous behaviour:

Figure 4:

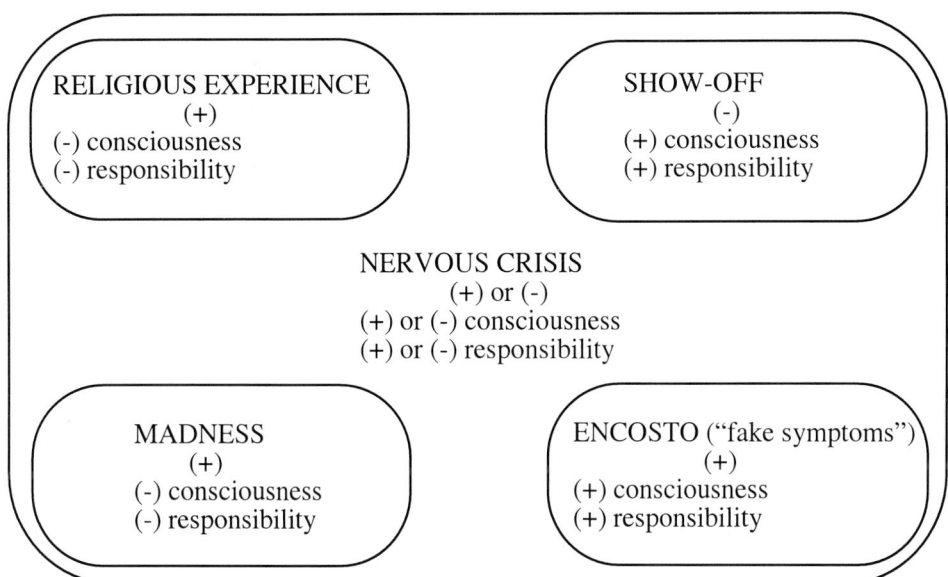

Once again it is possible to observe the encompassing role of nervousness. It represents the intermediate category among four extreme possibilities of classification, since, in any case, it is through the nerves that they take place. Two of the positions—religious experience and encosto—correspond to positive labels, and the two others—madness and show-off—to negative ones. Show-off is certainly the most negative, although the consequences of madness are more radical. What is called 'religious experience' in the table may be evoked by many names in that culture, depending on the religious definitions of what is known academically as 'possession' or 'trance.' The actual usage of the 'nervous crisis' label can be more neutral, although it may encompass an entire range of physical-moral nuances.

The 'victim' of these disturbances may not feel himself able to classify them and to deal accordingly with their symptoms and causes. One of the most interesting aspects of nervousness is the way it may encompass all kinds of abnormal states and behavior, while still allowing the 'victim' to 'choose' a more specific meaning for them ('religious' or 'psychiatric,' for instance) without really moving out of the symbolic field of nervousness.

Another characteristic that certainly accounts for its importance is the physical-moral nexus. In this sense, the nerves play a mana like role (in the LÉVI-STRAUSSian sense): a category whose actual meaning is less important than its role as a condition for thought, as a switching device for assigning significance.

Relational Causes of Popular Nervousness

Urban working-classes' nervousness—at all its multiple levels–is seen by its victims as resulting from the disruption of the basic rules of their cosmology. This may happen in the most specific and concrete situations, as in the 'physiological' accidents mentioned here—that subverted or attacked 'natural' rules. It may occur nonetheless at many other, more complex levels.

It may occur at the 'inter-personal' level. In this case, any damage or danger to family values can be the immediate cause of nervous disturbances. Women are especially prone to this kind of nervousness, given their domestic, internal quality. Among the causes of 'nervous diseases' among women, the most important are the loss of a member of the family or the failure of husbands to provide for household sustenance. All the situations that subvert the hierarchical scheme of the casa are also eminent causes of nervous disturbances: the growing number of women who must trabalhar fora (literally, to work outside the home) invariably complain of their nervous suffering.

For men, problems related to work are foremost among the causes of nervousness. They can range from unemployment to inconvenient or dangerous conditions of industrial labor. It must be stressed that any physical accident or disease contracted as a result of labor conditions may restrict men to a life at home. Though temporary, confinement in the domestic sphere makes them nervous, as it threatens man's legitimate social role.

The disruption of order at the level of local life (the bairro, favela, pedaço, etc.) also conduces to nervousness. Local identity is almost as important as family identity. A strong sense of belonging to one's own place and being a part of a wider social entity that can be positively contrasted with many others at different levels of urban structure plays a fundamental role in their worldview. That identity depends however on the maintenance of adequate levels of moral behavior and of appropriate patterns of interpersonal relationships. Many accidents could subvert this model in daily life. Most could be considered as falta de respeito (lack of respect), that is, a breach of hierarchical rules of etiquette, or falta de consideração (lack of consideration), a break of reciprocity links.

The same kind of paradox lies at the root of urban workers' denunciation of evil at the level of industrial, urban and political life—and its effects upon their own life, their nervous life. In all cases, it is the disruption of reciprocity, the subversion of the appropriate rules that must preside over the relationship between different persons or groups, that is disturbing. There are many concrete causes of unrest and dissatisfaction at work, but they become unbearable only when they can be attributed to the owner's or the manager's unwillingness to be fair, i.e., to reciprocate at a certain level of an unwritten code. The same process seems to preside over their complex attitudes towards politicians and political life at all the levels of the Brazilian system. The few revered politicians of the past are seen either as benign patrons who didn't 'forget the poor' when in power or as cultural heroes who passed laws that gave guarantees to the weak against the greed and injustice of the evil rich.

Urban life is another source of disturbance. It is of course enmeshed with most other levels of their lives, but one can easily discern the denunciation of conditions in the cities as compared with rural life (the background of many Brazilian urban workers) as a specific kind of problem. That denunciation can be attributed to a certain version of the reciprocity theme. Cities are seen as the realm of abundance, intensity and consciousness against the image of the backward, hard-living, isolated rural conditions of life. Yet, their continuous efforts, their lifelong pursuit of urban opportunities has never allowed them to participate of its riches. Quite the contrary, they must dwell in the worst possible conditions, confronted by violence and lack of water, energy, sewage systems, transportation, education, medical and commercial facilities; a composite of the most disturbing and unsettling circumstances.

The intimate relationship between nervousness and religion can be approached from the same point of view. Religion is the ultimate level of reciprocity, the highest instance of the hierarchical world-view. Just as nervousness can be considered a result of the disruption of reciprocity and hierarchy, religious experience also seems to be the place to reassert those values, to confirm their ultimate preeminence, to get solace against their subversion and—eventually—the correction of illegitimate situations.

The Brazilian urban religious market is very broad and complex. Most of its agencies and models offer urban workers a symbolic instrument to deal with nervousness. Some, like the Pentecost and Afro-Brazilian sects, try to encompass its characteristics and symptoms in the context of possession and trance (one of the ways nervous crises can be classified, as shown above). There are many levels of intensity and forms of adhesion and belief. Overlapping membership is frequent and it is impossible to separate the search for therapeutic effects in religious experience from the search for medical or paramedical services. This is true for 'common' diseases just as for nervousness in its different forms; but it is much more evident in the latter, because of their immediate 'physical-moral' quality.

Final Remarks

This is not all one can say about what it means to be nervous. I have indicated that it almost amounts to saying what it means to be as a Person for a huge part of the Brazilian population. My field research took place in several working-class communities around Rio de Janeiro, between 1974 and 1984; but I relied on a vast literature concerning the situation and the culture of working class groups throughout Brazil in the last three decades to build my hypothesis and analysis. There is still much to be learned about competing concepts of the Person in Brazilian society. There is also an urgent need to compare these data with those concerning other societies in general, but especially other 'modern,' 'western' societies—metropolitan or peripheral.[19]

This kind of research may have many levels of relevance. It may help in recognizing the legitimacy of differences within modern societies: the legitimacy of different concepts of disease and disturbance, the legitimacy of different concepts of the Person, the legitimacy of different concepts of the world and its future. It may also help in understanding the complex interplay within contemporary societies of modern Western cultural ideals (like equality or rationality) and the deeper sociological forces they have to face, obey or defy.

References

CALDEIRA, T.P.R.
    1984   *A Política dos Outros. O Cotidiano dos Moradores da Periferia e o que Pensam do Poder e dos Poderosos.* São Paulo: Brasiliense.
CARLSON, E., & M. SIMPSON
    1969   Models of the nervous system in Eighteenth Century Psychiatry. *Bulletin of the History of Medicine* 63(2): 101-115.
DA MATTA, R.A.
    1979   *Carnavais, Malandros e Heróis.* Rio de Janeiro: Zahar Editores.

---

19. A critical review of the abundant North American medical anthropology literature on the nerves since 1981 can be found in DUARTE (1993).

DAVIS, D.L.
  1989   George Beard and Lydia Pinkham: gender, class, and nerves in late 19th. Century America. In: *Gender, Health and Illness. The case of nerves*. Edited by D.L. DAVIS, & S.M. LOW, pp. 93-114. New York: Hemisphere Publishing Corporation.
DUARTE, L.F.D.
  1986   *Da Vida Nervosa (nas Classes Trabalhadoras Urbanas)*. Rio de Janeiro: Jorge Zahar Editor / CNPq.
DUARTE, L.F.D.
  1987a Identidade social e padrões de agressividade verbal em um grupo de trabalhadores urbanos. In: *Cultura e Identidade Operária*. Edited by J.S.L. LOPES, pp. 171-201. Rio de Janeiro/São Paulo: Universidade Federal do Rio de Janeiro/ Marco Zero / PROED.
  1987b Pouca Vergonha, Muita Vergonha: Sexo e moralidade entre as classes trabalhadoras urbanas. In: *Cultura e Identidade Operária*. Edited by J.S.L. LOPES, pp. 203-226. Rio de Janeiro/São Paulo: Universidade Federal do Rio de Janeiro / Marco Zero / PROED.
  1989   A 'Psychopathia Sexualis' de Krafft-Ebing, ou o progresso moral pela ciência das perversões. *Jornal Brasileiro de Psiquiatria* 38(2): 83-86, and (3): 119-123.
  1990   A representação do nervoso na cultura literária e sociológica do século XIX e começo do século XX. *Anuário Antropológico* 87: 93-116.
  1992   Légalité et citoyenneté dans le Brésil urbain contemporain: La question du particularisme des quartiers populaires. *Cahiers du Brésil Contemporain* 17: 53-64, MSH/Paris.
  1993   Os nervos e a Antropologia Médica norte-americana: Uma revisão crítica. Physis. *Revista de Saúde Coletiva* 3(2): 43-74.
DUARTE, L.F.D. ET AL.
  1993   Vicissitudes e limites da conversão à cidadania nas classes populares brasileiras. *Revista Brasileira de Ciências Sociais* 22 (ano 8) junho: 5-19.
DUARTE, L.F.D. & GIUMBELLI, E. A.
  1994   As concepções de pessoa cristã e moderna: paradoxos de uma continuidade. *Anuário Antropológico* 93: 77-111.
DUMONT, L.
  1972   *Homo Hierarchicus*. London: Palladin.
  1979   *Essais sur l'Individualisme*. Paris: Seuil.
EVANS-PRITCHARD, E.E.
  1968   *The Nuer*. Oxford: Oxford: Clarendon Press.
FIGLIO, K.M.
  1975   Theories of perception and the physiology of mind in the late Eighteenth Century. *History of Science* 13: 177-212.
FIGUEIRA, S.A.
  1981   *O Contexto Social da Psicanálise*. Rio de Janeiro: Francisco Alves Editora.
  1985   *Cultura da Psicanálise* (Ed.). São Paulo: Brasiliense.
FOUCAULT, M.
  1975   *Surveiller et Punir*. Paris: Gallimard.
GAUCHET, M. & SWAIN, G.
  1980   *La pratique de l'esprit humain (l'institution asilaire et la révolution démocratique)*. Paris: Gallimard.
LAWRENCE, C.J.
  1979   The nervous system and society in the Scottish Enlightenment. In: *Natural Order*. Edited by B. BARNES & S. SHAPIN, pp. 19-40. Sage Publications.
LEAL, O.F.
  1995   *Corpo e Significado. Ensaios de Antropologia Social*. (Ed.) Porto Alegre: Editora da Universidade Federal do Rio Grande do Sul.
LOPES, J.S.L.
  1978   *O Vapor do Diabo: o Trabalho dos Operários do Açúcar*. Paz e Terra: Rio de Janeiro.
LOVEJOY, A.
  1993   *The Great Chain of Being*. Cambridge: Harvard University Press.
LOYOLA, M.A.
  1984   *Médicos e Curandeiros, Conflito social e saúde*. DIFEL: São Paulo.
LUKES, S.
  1973   *Individualism*. New York: Harper & Row.
MACFARLANE, A.
  1978   *The Origins of English Individualism*. Oxford: Basil Blackwell.

MACPHERSON, C.B.
　1962　*The Political Theory of Possessive Individualism.* Oxford University Press.
MAUSS, M.
　1973　Une catégorie de l'esprit humain: La notion de personne, celle de 'moi'. In: *Sociologie et anthropologie.* Edited by G. GURVITCH, pp. 333-362. Paris: PUF.
RADCLIFFE-BROWN, A.R.
　1952　*Structure and Function in Primitive Society.* London: Cohen & West.
ROPA, D. & DUARTE, L.F.D.
　1985　Considerações Teóricas sobre a Questão do Atendimento Psicológico às Classes Trabalhadoras. In: *Cultura da Psicanálise.* Edited by S. FIGUEIRA, pp. 178-201. São Paulo: Brasiliense.
ROUSSEAU, G.S.
　1975　Nerves, Spirits and Fibres: Toward the Origins of Sensibility. In: *Studies in the Eighteenth Century.* Edited by R.F. BRISSENDEN, pp. 137-157. Canberra: The Australian National University Press.
　1990　*The Languages of Psyche: Mind and Body in Enlightenment Thought.* Berkeley: The University of California Press.
RUSSO, J.A.
　1993　*O corpo contra a palavra: as terapias corporais no campo psicológico dos anos 80.* Rio de Janeiro: Editora da Universidade Federal do Rio de Janeiro.
SAGAWA, R.Y.
　1985　A Psicanálise Pioneira e os Pioneiros da Psicanálise em São Paulo. In: *Cultura da Psicanálise.* Edited by S. FIGUEIRA, pp. 15-34. São Paulo: Brasiliense.
SALEM, T.
　1992　A 'Despossessão Subjetiva': Dos paradoxos do individualismo. *Revista Brasileira de Ciências Sociais* 18(7): 62-77.
SARTI, C.A.
　1994　*A família como espelho, Um estudo sobre a moral dos pobres na periferia de São Paulo.* São Paulo: FAPESP/Editora Autores Associados.
TAYLOR, C.
　1989　*Sources of the Self. The Making of the Modern Identity.* Cambridge, Massachusetts: Harvard University Press.
VELHO, G.
　1981　*Individualismo e Cultura.* Rio de Janeiro: Jorge Zahar Editores.
VENANCIO, A.T.A.
　1993　A Construção Social da Pessoa e a Psiquiatria: Do Alienismo à "Nova Psiquiatria." *Physis. Revista de Saúde Coletiva* 3(2): 117-136.
ZALUAR, A.
　1985　*A Máquina e a Revolta. As Organizações Populares e o Significado da Pobreza.* São Paulo: Brasiliense.

Body Therapists in Rio de Janeiro:
Relations Between Social Career and Therapeutic Principles

JANE A. RUSSO

Abstract
The article examines the appearance and growth of body therapies as an occupational alternative in the field of psychological practice in the city of Rio de Janeiro. It intends to show the relationship between the life histories of those who pioneered the technique of body therapy within Rio's psychology community and the theoretical and ideological principles of this kind of therapy.

Zusammenfassung
Der Artikel untersucht die Anfänge und das Wachsen von Körpertherapien als eine Beschäftigungsalternative im Feld der psychologischen Praktiken in Rio de Janeiro. Er versucht, die Beziehung herzustellen zwischen den Lebensgeschichten der Pioniere, die die Technik von Körpertherapie in Rios psychologischer Gemeinschaft eingeführt haben und den theoretischen und ideologischen Prinzipien dieser Art von Therapie.

Keywords: body therapies, life histories, urban Brazil

Body Therapies and the Psychological Culture

This paper is part of a wider research project on the origins and development of body therapies in Rio de Janeiro, a tendency that started in the late 1970's and early 1980's, and was part of a widespread 'psychological culture' among the urban middle-classes. The starting-point of this 'psychological culture' was the psychoanalytic boom that occurred in the 1970's.

It should be emphasised that 'body therapies' belong in the field of 'psychological' therapies. Its basic characteristic is the belief that ailments and indispositions usually classified as 'psychological' are located in the body and must be treated with exercises and physical activities. In other words, they are grounded on the principle that psychological complaints have their origins in the body.

Body therapies originate, in a large extent, from the theory by Wilhelm Reich, a psychoanalyst banned from the Psychoanalytic Association of Berlin in 1934, because of his disagreements with the official doctrine. They include the therapies actually created by REICH ('characteranalytical vegetotherapy' and 'orgonotherapy') and also the so-called neo-REICHian therapies or practices, such as bioenergetics, biosynthesis, biodynamic massage, etc.[1]

They were linked, especially at their beginning, to a wider movement of criticism and challenge of custom and traditional behaviour—the counter-culture movement of the 1960's. There sprang themes, at that time, which became fundamental to the late development of the body-therapy universe: the body and sexual liberation, the criticism of the 'repressive' society, the search for authenticity and spontaneity, etc. In the field of psychological practices, body therapies

---

1. It should be emphasised that although all the therapies created by REICH are chronologically previous, the movement of body therapies that sprang in the 1970's is actually *neo-REICHian* (or post-REICHian). From the new therapies, there happened a rediscovery of REICH and his techniques.

appear as an alternative to those practices already approved and accepted as 'official' (especially psychoanalysis) which were criticised for their 'intellectualism,' 'elitism' and 'conservatism.'[2]

In this paper I deal with the emergence of a new occupation or *occupational group (*the body therapists (in the field of psychological professions. My aim is to establish relations between the emergence or creation of this new psychological activity and the life-history (and thus the social career) of the individuals responsible for this emergence. In order to do that, I will try to demonstrate the actual affinity between the ideology of body therapies and the career of these individuals.[3]

Before starting this discussion, I would like to dwell upon the relation between *ascendant* social career in the middle-classes and the issue of the prosperity of a 'psychological culture.'[4]

'To get on in life' is far from meaning only material or financial success. The physical and geographical distance from one's original milieu is accompanied inevitably by a symbolic distance, that is to say, the abandonment of certain paradigms and orientation for new ones. Ascendant mobility is a situation when one breaks with a traditional universe, in which repetition, permanence, the place of the individual in a group, the maintenance of this group's hierarchical codes, etc. are highly emphasised. To ascend socially, therefore, involves, far beyond its financial aspects, a *change of worlds*. What is more, this 'change of worlds' is often so crucial that it is experienced as the very *aim* of the move. The ascendant course ('getting on in life') in this picture becomes, for the individual, a *consequence of his/her wish to change*. A change that passes from external to internal, resulting in a radical transformation of the very individual. Psychological theories and practices provide the meaning and direction to such an 'internal mobility' for these people who are obliged to 'change their worlds.'[5]

The Body Therapists

The most striking characteristic in the life-history of the individuals interviewed is their geographic and social mobility in relation to their families. The ascendant mobility usually takes place by means of an academic degree. With two exceptions only, none of the individuals surveyed had parents with a degree. Thus they endeavoured to find something missing in their families as they changed their own destiny. On the other hand, studying meant, in most cases, to live physically distant from their original universes. Out of the twenty therapists surveyed, only six were from Rio. Some of them came from small towns inland; there were others from localities on the outskirts of Rio de Janeiro. Even for those who were from other big cities, there was always the notion of 'decentring': two of the pioneers from São Paulo were born to foreign parents who left their countries to escape armed conflicts.

---

2. According to ROBERT CASTEL, body therapies and all the further alternative therapies spring, in fact, *from* the success and dissemination of psychoanalysis, that is to say, *they are a part of this dissemination*, actually maintaining part of the psychoanalytical message (CASTEL 1987).
3. I tried to interview all those responsible for the introduction of body therapies in Rio. Out of the probable 16 pioneers, I interviewed 12. I still interviewed eight therapists who, although they were not among the pioneers, were responsible for the creation of institutions that offer training in body therapies.
4. It is interesting to note the frequent association between the psychoanalytical boom in the 1970's and the Brazilian 'economic miracle.' The following discussion is largely inspired by the works of GILBERTO VELHO (1975, 1981 and 1986) and other authors who worked with middle-class groups, especially TANIA SALEM (see SALEM 1987).
5. For a detailed discussion of this argument, see RUSSO 1992: 52-60.

More than a move from bottom to top, the mobility of the individuals seemed to consist in a displacement from the margin (periphery) to the centre. Geographic and social margin. All the individuals belonging in the pioneer nucleus came from families of scarce financial resources. Their parents were usually shop owners, public officials, and there were even the cases of a field labourer and a taxi driver; some had been to primary school only and others to secondary school. The belief in formal education as a means of social ascendancy is very much cherished and encouraged in this universe of lower middle-class families. In this sense, the individuals, as they stand distant and break with their original milieu, are keeping to a sort of *family inclination*. The intention of 'succeeding' is in consonance with their parent's project. At the same time, this drive to change, to go away, to leave the periphery and go to the centre, to find a position in the social scale, comes together with a reasonable amount of indeterminacy.

If these individuals saw themselves somewhat pushed away from their original milieu, the very inclination that pushed them was nothing more that that: an inclination. The indications as to what to do to 'get there' (and even those as to where was 'there') were vague and not very precise. Expectations concerning the advisability of pursuing an academic career, for example, were generic and not clear as to what profession the children should have. It may be said that their family's basic advice was only: 'be different from us,' as if to be different was something to be decided (or constructed) by the individuals themselves.

It is evident, however, that the indeterminacy was not complete. Many career alternatives were excluded since the beginning from the possibilities of this group. We know that college education does not work automatically as a mechanism that promotes social ascendancy. It should be combined with a certain amount of cultural and/or social capital.[6] In other words, success through formal education does not always depend on what is learnt at school, but exactly on that which it does not provide.[7] It is this 'something else' that is not to be found at school, which the group in question had to compensate for.

A way of eschewing a possible exclusion was to adhere to professions whose indeterminacy did not imply any *a priori* exclusion, such as Psychology. In the case of Medicine, their point was to explore exactly its shaded areas, turning to the so-called 'alternative medicine' or, in the area of Psychiatry, to new and little established psychotherapeutic practices (fields in which, because they are still being expanded and considered as a relatively marginal activity, new-arrivals are usually included rather than excluded).

Psychology and the 'psychological' specialities seem generally to possess a great affinity with the structural indeterminacy present in the life-histories of these people.[8]

---

6. PIERRE BOURDIEU proposes a distinction between 'economic capital' and 'cultural capital.' The latter is defined as the ability to correctly perceive and appreciate symbolic goods (or the symbolic aspects of material goods), see BOURDIEU 1979.
7. It is worth quoting BOURDIEU here: 'Abstaining from offering explicitly to every one what it demands implicitly from every one, it wants to demand from everyone uniformly that they have what they were not given, namely, linguistic and cultural competence and an intimate relation with culture and language, which are instruments only familial education can provide when transmitting the dominant culture.' (BOURDIEU 1974: 306-07, translated from Portuguese).
8. Psychology is a recent profession, with wide and generic attributions. Psychologists do not have a defined area of activity or precise attributions. They can work in many different sectors of social life (schools, companies, hospitals, prisons, orphanages, mental hospitals, community homes, football teams, in the judicial system and even in the 'community'). Their attributions in each of these activities may vary indefinitely. In private clinics, there is a large number of orientations and practices to be adopted. Hence it is an occupation with a high degree of indeterminacy.

From the choice of an area of reasonable indeterminacy and low rate of exclusion, the group *invents* an occupation. One whose relation with a college degree is faint and not very defined, and whose exigencies parallel to a school education are also not clear or even non-existent. They invent an occupation in the sense of inventing rules of access to it, as well as a criterion for assessment of those who practise it.

The individuals surveyed, however, did not invent only a profession. All of them 'succeeded' after a lot of struggle, practically without any help from their families. More than a profession, these people have invented themselves: the process of constructing a new profession (body therapist) is intertwined with a sort of self-constructing process. It should be remembered here that we are dealing with individuals who were destined to leave their original milieu, including its directions and meaning (that is to say, their destiny was to become different from what they should have been). This distance from their original background is accomplished through their professional choice. It is going to college that makes this distance necessary and inevitable. Their professional choice had a double character, since it was both indeterminate and crucial. It is through it that these individuals will 'succeed' and, at the same time, acquire an identity (since the identity that might have been provided by their original environment is necessarily left behind along the way). So it is possible to say that their professional definition contaminates their whole lives. The 'invention' of an occupation coincides with the 'invention' of their own selves. This is still more noticeable when the invention involves a psychological profession. It provides both the possibility of earning a considerable amount of money (in an occupation that keeps them away from their original milieu) and *finding oneself* by means of this occupation.

At the same time, what these individuals chose, within the possibilities offered by the psychological professional field, was a fairly marginal way: an occupation that did not have a name, whose implementation and dissemination occurred on the margin of other practices more 'official' or institutionalised, and whose ideology goes strongly against stock styles of life and behaviour. It should be emphasised, however, that the degree of success involving these practices derives from their very marginal and revolutionary character. In other words, they are practices that derive their value from the opposition to the official psychological world. Likewise, it is through them and their principles that the individuals surveyed were able to transform their own marginality into a virtue.

Body Therapy Principles

It is possible to say that the principles of body therapy centre round three basic oppositions that overlap and interpenetrate.

The first of them opposes *individual* and *society*. The latter hinders the natural development of the former, that is to say, as it prevents the individual from following his natural impulses, it makes him eventually ill. Altering ROUSSEAU's phrase a little, we could say that the individual is born sound and society corrupts him. In a lecture against the Freudian concept of 'death instinct,' REICH stated that

> "anti-social tendencies in the unconscious are a product of our civilisation, which represses the bioenergetic emotions given by nature ... since their birth children are conditioned and adapted to a civilisation based on the repression of secondary impulses." (REICH quoted in HIGGINS & RAPHAEL 1972: 78-79).

There we have a second opposition (between *natural* and *social*) that doubles and covers the first. That which society represses in individuals is their 'biological core,' where their natural development is located. Health means a return to that which 'man is naturally.'

In fact, 'individual' and 'natural' seem to be almost synonymous. Both nature and the individual are *previous* to society. Social repression on the individual falls upon his natural biological impulses. Society, apparently, does not have any positive role in the production of this individual who is conceived basically as a pre-social being, that is to say, a natural being. The conception of the individual and the conception of nature overlap and both are supported by a negative conception of society.

Another duality that serves as a basis for body therapy ideology is that which opposes body and mind.

We saw that man is born in nature. Nature, as an encompassing concept, comprises human beings as a part of the animal realm and the cosmos as a whole. This means that the different levels of life or existence that make up the universe are flattened into one unique level. From this viewpoint, what distinguishes human beings is of no importance, and one sets value on that which makes man closer to any other animal. Speech, for instance, is considered to be an irrelevant characteristic of mankind. Mind (or reason) is not necessarily contrary to nature, but it is encompassed by the natural/biological principle. Thus, the body is the centre of natural processes (housing passions, appetites, sensations, affections, and the main appetite: sex). The body is, in this sense, inherently biological/natural. The above-mentioned pairs of opposites could be organised in two columns, summarising the duality present in the principles of body therapies:

Individual	Society
health	illness
natural	artificial
body	mind
positive	negative

There is an aspect in the principles of body therapies that does not appear under the guise of a dualism, but as a sort of combination of contraries, manifesting itself on the one hand, as a 'physicalist mysticism' and on the other, as a 'sexualist morality.'

The REICHian theory has a wholly functionalist and mechanicist conception of the human being. The perfect working of one's organism depends on a charging and discharging energy mechanism whose origin is sexual. The mechanicist functionalism of the tension/charging/discharging model is allied to the central role of (genital) sexuality. In both cases, the materiality of REICHian ideas is clear. FREUD's concept of libido, for example, was transformed into something measurable and visible—the orgonic energy.[9]

It is possible, however, to observe that this physical materiality goes side by side with a large amount of esoteric belief. The concept of a cosmic energy that unites all beings and things in the universe (no matter how palpable it can be) has an almost mystical foundation, not to say reli-

---

9. 'Energy' is a central notion that pervades not only body therapies, but also alternative therapies and practices as a whole. LUIZ EDUARDO SOARES calls it as the 'cultural currency of the alternative world' (SOARES 1989:129). It is a cosmic energy that, complementing the encompassing conception of 'nature,' actually unites the different levels and phenomena that make up the universe.

gious. In his last works, REICH spoke about a Vital Cosmic Energy (which corresponds to what men usually call 'God') and claimed that he had discovered the origins of life through experiments carried out in his laboratory.

On the other hand, REICH also 'materialised' the fluid and subtle concept of sexuality conceived by Freud. If to the latter, sex was not restricted to physical sexuality, to REICH's followers sex is just sex.

The concrete and physicalist way of conceiving sexuality led REICH and his followers to think that neurosis (and other disorders) can only be cured by means of sexual liberation. What is more, the concept that society blocks and warps natural impulses led to the assertion that the prevention of neurosis and unhappiness in general is an actual possibility.

Just as sexual energy replaces God,[10] traditional morals should be abandoned in favour of a rational and scientifically determined morality. A morality determined by the orgonic science or, as Reich wished, by the 'purely medical representation of biological exigencies.' A sort of natural morality, governed by charging and discharging necessities of live organisms, that, having been neglected for so long, should be rediscovered by human beings.

In this sense, REICH's followers, with their curious combination of mysticism and mechanicist scientificism, point towards an utopia: a society in which natural (genital) sexuality would not be repressed; children would be educated according to self-regulating natural principles, and the democracy of work would be paramount.

Career and Principles

It is possible to see a common ground between the principles of body therapies and the personal and professional career of the group surveyed.

Firstly, we are dealing with people that 'invented themselves,' that is to say, people that 'succeeded' against all the scarce possibilities of their social origins and also against all drawbacks and obstacles that stood on their ways: difficulties at school and in finding a respectable professional career, inherited cultural and social handicap. The principles that support their professional practice provide meaning to their careers.

It should be remembered what was said in the previous chapter: individuals exist in opposition to a 'repressive' and 'circumscribing' society. The possibility of 'liberation' from these social constraints, on the other hand, takes place through the body. By means of exercises, expressive practices, individuals build up another body for themselves. A body that will lose not only the marks of social distinctions but also those that result from belonging in any social group, as it becomes the *natural body* rediscovered. As they succeed professionally, therefore, these individuals 'remake' themselves as people and negate likewise a society that wishes to leave them prey to a marginal existence.

The adoption of the body as the basic instrument for change and 'self-construction' also means an opposition to words (the instrument, par excellence, of rationality and school logic). The individuals surveyed chose to 'make themselves' on the margins of the legitimate or 'official' academic institutions, in which success is obtained by means of words (or by the skill in a specific linguistic code). The legitimacy of their choice was sustained by the belief that the 'language' of the body is superior to words as a means of communication.

---

10. According to REICH, that which men call 'God' is in fact their perception of the Cosmic Vital Energy.

The combination between utopia and pragmatism, in turn, provides meaning for the inclination inscribed in these individuals' careers.

It provides meaning, initially, for the very 'change of worlds' operated by them in the inevitable departure from their original milieu, inspired by the concept that 'changing worlds' is not only something possible but also necessary, positive and good.

Secondly, it provides some parameters for individuals who have as their only direction the idea of 'being different.' The significant degree of indeterminacy implied in this kind of career finds its counterpart in the absolute determinism of a 'natural' moral that is not based upon any social contingency, which can always be relative.

Thus their career loses its character of pure possibility, its randomness, to become the right way that leads human beings towards their own essence. The lack of parameters is supplied not by the adoption of any parameter whatsoever, but the right and unchangeable ones, grounded on a nature that does not wish to know anything about origins or social destiny.

References

BOURDIEU, P.
　1974　O mercado dos bens simbólicos. In *A economia das trocas simbólicas*. São Paulo: Perspectiva.
　1979　*La Distiction*. Paris: Minuit
CASTEL, R.
　1987　*A gestão dos riscos*. Rio de Janeiro: Francisco Alves.
HIGGINS, M. & RAPHAEL, C. (eds.)
　1972　*Reich parle de Freud*. Paris: Payot.
RUSSO, J.A.
　1992　*O corpo contra a palavra*. Rio de Janeiro, Editora UFRJ.
SALEM, T.
　1987　*Sobre o casal grávido: Incursão em um universo ético*. PhD thesis, Museu Nacional/UFRJ, Rio de Janeiro.
SOARES, L.E.
　1989　Religioso por natureza: Cultura alternativa e misticismo ecológico no Brasil. In: *Tradições religiosas no Brasil*. Edited by L. LANDIN. Rio de Janeiro: ISER.
VELHO, G.
　1975　*Nobres e anjos: Um estudo de tóxicos e hierarquia*. PhD thesis, Faculdade de Filosofia Letras e Ciências Humanas, USP.
　1981　*Individualismo e cultura*. Rio de Janeiro: Zahar
　1986　*Subjetividade e sociedade: uma experiência de geração*. Rio de Janeiro: Jorge Zahar Editor.

A Comparative Study of Medical Rationalities

MADEL T. LUZ & KENNETH ROCHEL DE CAMARGO JR.

Abstract
This paper reports the main hypothesis and the initial findings of an ongoing project for comparing different medical systems, studied as medical rationalities and defined in terms of six dimensions: cosmology, medical doctrine, diagnosis, morphology, vital dynamics and therapeutics. The comparative study of four rationalities (Contemporary Western, Homeopathic, Traditional Chinese and Ayurveda Medicines) yielded two different paradigms, one denominated vitalist or bioenergetic (shared by the last three) and the other termed biomechanical, specific to the first. Nevertheless, several similarities were noticed, especially when approaching actual therapeutic practice. The initial findings related to one of the rationalities (Contemporary Western Medicine) are presented in the closing sections of the paper.

Zusammenfassung
Dieser Text bespricht die hauptsächlichen Hypothesen sowie anfängliche Ergebnisse eines bestehenden Forschungsprojekts über den Vergleich unterschiedlicher Medizinsysteme, welche als medizinische Denkweisen untersucht, und in sechs Dimensionen definiert werden: Kosmologie, medizinische Doktrin, Diagnose, Morphologie, vitale Dynamik und Therapie. Die vergleichende Untersuchung von vier Denkweisen (zeitgenössisch-westliche Medizin, Homöopathie, traditionell chinesische Medizin sowie Ayurveda Medizin) ergaben zwei verschiedene Paradigmen; das eine wird vitalistisch oder bioenergetisch genannt (und gehört zu den letzten drei Medizinmodellen), das andere, das biomechanische Modell ist spezifisch für das zuerst genannte Modell. Nichtsdestotrotz wurden Übereinstimmungen gefunden, speziell, in Bezug auf die aktuellen therapeutischen Praktiken. Erste Ergebnisse zur Denkweise des einen Modells (zeitgenössische westliche Medizin) werden in den letzten Teilen des Textes aufgeführt.

Keywords: biomedicines, alternative medicines, Brazil

Introduction

This paper describes the initial findings of a research project that started in 1991 with the purpose of performing a comparative study of four different medical systems (Contemporary Western, Homeopathic, Traditional Chinese and Ayurveda Medicines), both in theoretical and practical terms. The closing sections of this paper also bring some detail, as an illustration, of the findings related to the first of them. The mainstay of this effort is an operational definition of *medical rationality* as a structured system of five components, or dimensions, as follows: a) medical doctrine; b) morphology; c) vital dynamics; d) diagnostic system; e) therapeutic system.[1] The core hypotheses of the study was that there is more than one medical rationality, and that the different rationalities that coexist within our culture may be compared to each other without assuming, in an ethnocentric fashion, that one of them (usually the Western 'official' Medicine) is 'real' or 'correct' and then just contrasting the others to it, enhancing the most unusual or 'exotic' aspects of their theory and/or practice. This paper presents basically the findings related to the first phase of our study, that lasted until 1994.[2]

---

1. Each of these dimensions will be described in detail further ahead; the definition of medical rationalities was structured as an *ideal type*, inspired by WEBER's concept.
2. The practical aspects are still being researched through several field studies, taking place in nine different outpatient units of the local (Rio de Janeiro) Public Health System.

We were well aware, from the beginning of our research, of the complexity of these systems, developed over long time spans (literally centuries in the cases of Chinese and Ayurveda Medicines), which are riddled with internal contradictions, even in the case of Western Medicine. Dealing with them as if they were a solid block, without historical background or the subtle variations and changes that permeate each of them would be a crude oversimplification; however, our intention was not to historically retrace the steps that led to the construction of each rationality, a task that belongs to Historians and Anthropologists but might consume their lifetimes.

Our objective was far simpler: we intended to *describe* the main attributes of the already mentioned dimensions of each of the rationalities *as they present themselves today, in our society*. This allowed us to avoid a recurrent pitfall in such endeavours, that of being lost in the mazes of trends and schools of thought in different time frames or institutional settings. Put in other words, since we focused on the present, we were able to dismiss the lengthy—and tedious—argument of "which medical rationality (of any of the four) is being discussed?"

We were not overlooking the fact that the present configurations of these systems were slowly built within the sociocultural framework that supports them, and in many ways they are the result of *collages* and patchworks originated from different cultural instances, throughout successive historical periods, cast into a theoretical-practical kaleidoscope that joins medical art and knowledge in an ingenuous logical arrangement which is not, however, fully subject to formal requisites of analytic nature. This fact is easily noticed when considering Eastern medicines, but we could, surprisingly enough, detect this sort of arrangement in the Western medicines, even the so-called 'Scientific Medicine.' In the West there's a tendency to assume knowledge originated from the sciences as *natural*, that is, it is dealt with as if it had no origins, or if these origins (historical, cultural, imaginary) did not impregnate, *up to present days*, scientific knowledge (LUZ 1988).

The notion of progress and superseding the past has marked the scientific rationality through the last three centuries, implying the progressively dominant conception that the history of human knowledge is made of ruptures and turnovers, associating past with regression and future with innovation, being the present a temporary bridge between both. This is, evidently, an ideological conception, since in fact the 'past,' that is, the historical traces lived through and considered superseded, in a determinate moment of a specific knowledge-practice (medicine, in this case), never disappear completely, integrating into new procedures or theories in a subordinate fashion, in the latter case, or implicitly, in the former situation. Such traces form the kaleidoscope to which we referred to in the previous paragraph, thus establishing a theoretical-practical *continuity* between past and present within such knowledge-practice.

With these guidelines in mind, we got to the task of designing the basis for the comparative study of the already mentioned rationalities, which meant, in practice, a one-year period of preparation during which we researched thoroughly several sources of information on the theory, practice and history of each of the studied rationalities. During this period we sketched their portrait in terms of the basic description of a medical rationality, comprising the following axes or dimensions:

1. *Medical doctrine*, meaning the general conceptions about health and disease, healing, the practitioner's role, and so forth;
2. *Morphology*, that is, the general description of the human body(ies)[3] and its (their) structures;

---

3. The plural may sound odd, but to most of the rationalities there are more bodies than *the* body of Western culture.

3. *Vital dynamics*, or the conceptions about the functionality of the body(ies) in question (what would classically be termed 'Physiology' in Western Medicine, but we intentionally avoided this term due to its intimate connection with one of the rationalities under study);
4. *Diagnostic system,* comprising the diagnostic conceptions, practices and tools;
5. *Therapeutic system,* which, in analogy to the latter, included the set of conceptions, practices and tools closely connected to the therapeutic acts.

In the last two cases, the word 'conception' refers to those closely related to actual practice, and not the more general ones, closer to a sort of worldview, that are referred to in the first item.

Early in the research we realised that these dimensions were actually based, even if implicitly, in yet another, unanticipated in the initial design of the study, which we named *Cosmology*. The choice of this particular term may lead to a certain confusion in this case, since we're not referring to the branch of modern Western Physics also designated by this word, but rather, anthropologically-wise, to the general conceptions of the world around us, ethical values, shared with the whole of a given culture that shape in many ways the other five dimensions. This dimension determines what is to be accounted for as an 'objective data,' what are the adequate research tools, so to speak, that form the general framework from which the rationalities emerged. Although this might seem rather obvious in the case of non-Western medicines, which refer in very explicit ways to their original cosmologies, even in the Contemporary Western Medicine we were able to find an implicit link to the general conceptions of classical (mechanic) Physics.

This perception drove us into an epistemological issue, that of dealing with the apparent opposition of the idea of rationality and its relation to cosmologies that were in every other case except that of Western Medicine of a religious nature. We were until then working with a Weberian conception of rationality that was very close to that of *'scientificity,'* something set apart from religious or even philosophical thought systems. The finding that each of these complex medical systems is founded in some sort of cosmology, and that the latter, in turn, is the expression of metaphysical (religious or not) conceptions, forced us to deepen an aspect not foreseen in the original project.

This conceptual framework allowed us to produce a synoptic comparison table of the four rationalities (which will be presented below), and to identify common traces in all these rationalities, as was originally sought by the project. We soon noticed that any straightforward comparison would be impossible in terms of *cosmology,* and at least extremely difficult concerning *doctrines.* Due precisely to their deep roots in the cultures that originated the several rationalities, any comparison would tend only to underline differences and oppositions. On the other hand, it also became clear that as we got closer to actual practice, as reflected by the diagnostic and therapeutic dimensions, similarities became more evident and numerous.

In terms of broad categories, we noticed two different paradigms that helped the subsequent work. In one hand, there is what we called a *vitalist* or *bioenergetic* paradigm, common to Homeopathic, Chinese and Ayurveda Medicine, opposed, on the other hand, to the *biomechanical* paradigm characteristic of Western Medicine. This leads to a fundamental difference in terms of objects and goals, between the 'vitalist' or 'energetic' and Western medicine. While the latter has the diseases as an object and the fight against them as a goal, the other medicines have the unbalanced individual as their object, and their goal is the recovery, or even enhancement, of their health.

In the first case, the core categories are *disease, pathology, normality* and in the second they are *health, equilibrium* (as a synonym to harmony), and *disharmony* (of subjects/individuals). In the first case the medical system tends to display itself as *a science of diseases,* in the second, as a *healing art.*

Medicine as an Active Synthesis of Science and Art

The medical rationality, whichever paradigm it belongs to, has been historically characterised as a synthesis within a professional activity (*praxis*) of healing art (*tekné*) and knowledge of diseases (*gnosis, episteme*). The History of this activity is, perhaps, as ancient as Humanity itself, and through thousands of years there was no apparent split between knowledge and art in the *praxis* of this social mediator between men, suffering and death. The origin of medical knowledge was *sacred*, and in his personal, *lived through* experience, which included specific forms of socialisation and a training of esoteric nature, the practitioner synthesised *episteme* and *tekné*. Until two and a half millennia ago, both in the East and the West, that is, either in Greece or China or India, the knowledge-practice of the practitioners had a strong connection to sacerdotal functions; the nature of their knowledge was basically philosophical (be it religious or not).

In the History of the last two thousand five hundred years of this civilisation, typical cultural changes related to the medical rationality took place, giving Western Medicine its *sui generis* character. These changes sometimes amounted to important crises, that meant ruptures with prevailing patterns and deep consequences to the *episteme-tekné* synthesis mentioned before. There was a progressive separation between the two terms that constitute the kernel of any medical system, that is, the knowledge of diseases and the healing art, which was not followed by Eastern medicines. A clear-cut distinction emerges in modern knowledge, that seeks scientific status as a truth ideal since the XVII century. In this context, Western medicine may be seen as a specific medical rationality, inserted in a similarly specific cultural History, that of *Western Civilisation*.

The case of Homeopathic medicine in the XIX Century is a bit more complex, since it, although a Western production, kept part of the traditional Western cosmology, even implicitly, with its pre-Christian and Christian roots.

Crisis and Mutations in Western Medical Rationality

Later we will discuss Western Medicine in more detail, as an example of the findings of the first phase of the project; for now, we'll present a brief overview of the historical turning points that place this Medicine clearly apart from the others in this study.

The first of such crises took place during what we call the *Hippocratic period* (as opposed to *Hippocratic school,* as is usually designated), which comprised several medical schools, and spanned over a century. During this period medical thought assumed a strong tendency to rationalisation (opposing the magical and/or shamanic healing practices), to establish theories on diseases and therapeutic methods, and to speculate about the roles of philosophy and nature in medicine as a theory and practice (art) of healing. This was also accompanied by the strengthening of the role of the medical corporation as the carrier of philosophical knowledge on diseases and diseased people, with a strong *esprit de corps*, met with opposition from other segments of the society — as is witnessed by Aristophanes' caricatures of medicine men in his plays. This moment signals the beginning of the movement of Western medicine towards *science,* that is, becoming a systematic pursuit of ways to classify symptoms, diseases, syndromes, and seek causal explanation of such phenomena. Even then, however, the healing powers of Nature (*vis medicatrix naturae*, as this was later called in Latin), were still acknowledged.

The second turning point can be located between the end of Renaissance and the beginning of Modern Classicism, that is, between the XVI and XVII Centuries. The basic scientific disciplines in medicine, such as Anatomy, Physiology and Pathology, began their accumlation process, and the ideal of structuring medical knowledge in scientific terms became dominant over knowledge about diseases as a result of the experience of healing people, that is, *episteme* became more important than *gnosis* and *tekné* (LUZ 1988). The ascent of science as a legitimate—and ultimately *legal*—process of producing knowledge is a cultural fact with far more implications than just an internal reworking in medical knowledge/practice. From our point of view, the transformations in medicine express and illustrate a process that took place in the West beginning in Classical Greece but increasingly and more deeply with modern capitalism, as was pointed out by philosophers, historians and sociologists such as Max Weber, one of the theoretical references in this study.

As a result of this process, medical knowledge became progressively concerned with theories of disease, with a corresponding decrease in the status of the healing arts. In terms of the dimensions of the rationality, diagnosis acquired progressive hegemony over therapeutics; even the latter became increasingly oriented towards the systematic search for and fight against diseases.

The third crisis corresponded to the moment, examined by FOUCAULT in his *The Birth of the Clinic*, when the formal basis of contemporary medical clinics, centred on pathological anatomy, was firmly established. Death becomes the revealing device through which diseased bodies give away their secrets. Another important aspect is that, as this practice was more than ever concerned with disease and death as *collective* phenomena to be fought against, the new clinic that emerges by the end of the XVIIIth Century is, from its birth, *social medicine* as well, as the same FOUCAULT pointed out (FOUCAULT 1978; LUZ 1988).

Hospitals become increasingly the centres of medical experimenting and learning; correspondingly, medical teaching shifts progressively from medical schools, confined to the 'basic' disciplines (such as anatomy, physiology, biochemistry and so on), and some of the theoretical aspects of medical disciplines.

In this context, which began by the end of the XIXth Century but gained momentum in this century, soon after World War II, we notice a fourth critical step in the shaping of contemporary Medicine, corresponding to a rupture in medical *practice*; the ever increasing intervention of medical apparatuses further widened the already existing gap between doctors and patients, leading to a major disruption in millenary medical/patience relationship patterns.

Summarising, we could point out three ruptures within contemporary medical practice in the West: that between the science of disease and the healing arts; that between diagnostic and therapeutic practices; and, finally, that between doctors and patients. This triple rupture expresses, in our view, one of the socio-anthropological explanations of the great demand for other medical rationalities, leading in the last twenty or so years to the flourishing of the so-called 'alternative medicine,' or, more recently, the 'paradigm crisis of medicine' in Western society.

Medical Rationalities and 'Alternative Therapies'

Despite the radical differences in their systems, in recent years medical practice in Western countries has displayed a clear trend towards assimilating therapeutic techniques from other rationalities. Although this assimilation has been achieved in many cases at the expense of mechanical incorporation of certain aspects of a complex and integrated system, otherwise rejected, this also goes to show that when considered in terms of actual procedures the differences tend to wane.

This does not mean that they disappear; while non-Western and Homeopathic medicines rely heavily on the conception of men and women as integrated within themselves and also with nature, this integration is considered irrelevant—that is, non-existent for practical purposes—to scientific knowledge in Western medicine. The other three medicines, on the other hand, view disease as a result of some imbalance, a rupture in harmony, of a certain cosmic order in motion, which includes human beings as both expression and element; thus, it would be absurd *not* to take into account these elements in medical practice. These rationalities rely more on analogical, as opposed to analytic, reasoning, and general principles of similitude and sympathy such as FOUCAULT describes in *The Order of Things*, are dominant, while in Western culture this status belongs to the principle of difference.

In any case, the rationalities display considerable parallelism and even convergence, despite their deep differences, when the actual diagnostic and therapeutic practices are compared, especially the latter. We could presume that once the immemorial goal of medical practice—healing the sick—is put into action, therapeutics assume the main role, the differences in doctrine are set aside, and there is a clear opening to other practices, especially in Western medicine.

As to diagnosis, the similarities are more evident when considering the rationalities that share a vitalist paradigm (Homeopathic, Traditional Chinese and Ayurveda Medicines), since they share the same object—the sick person, as opposed to a disease—and the same goal, to heal the individual, re-establishing or expanding his/her health. Moreover, their respective cosmologies are similar in their views of human and natural as integrated domains, and also of a fundamental integration of natural and spiritual (supernatural) aspects in human existence.

Other diagnostic elements of symptoms, qualitative data such as duration, intensity, mode, laterality, rhythm and so forth, in several planes (organic, sensorial, emotional and spiritual), are greatly valued in the diagnostic systems of these medicines, originating a detailed and rich semiology, with a wide range of examining techniques. The similarities with Western medicine are few, but still exist; the traditional, low-tech physical exam has many resemblances to these techniques, even if with different goals.

The vital dynamics are also more closely related when considering the rationalities oriented by the bioenergetic paradigm, which regard *life* as both movement and energy, power or force. Since Western medicine left vitalism far behind in its history, the dynamics in this case is, once again, disease-oriented.

Finally, the morphologies express greater differences, having different references to the human body but also with a deep difference in the conceptions of *body*. The traditional medicines include in the latter category the notion of energetic body(ies), such as the meridian channels and points of Chinese medicine, or the range of bodies from the most subtle to the most 'coarse,' or dense, in Ayurveda medicine, or even with the implicit notion of a vital force inherent to the organic system, in Homeopathic medicine. The definition of organs and systems are much different, expressing different cultural contexts and their respective symbols; analogies and convergences, however, may be pointed out even in this aspect.

A comparative table of the dimensions of the four rationalities follows, as a synopsis of what the first phase of research produced.

A Comparative Study of Medical Rationalities

Table 1: Summary of the Comparative Analysis

Medical Rationality	Cosmology	Doctrine	Morphology	Vital Dynamics	Diagnosis	Therapy
Contemporary Western	Classical (Newtonian) Physics (causality)	Causal theory(ies) of disease and its defeat	Organic systems (macro and micro)	Pathophysiology and system physiology	Semiology; amanuensis; physical exam; support exams	Drugs; surgery; hygiene/preventive
Homeopathic	Implicit Traditional Western (Alchemy) and Classical (Newtonian) dynamics	Vital force and its imbalance in individual subjects	Material organism (systems) and vital force	Energetic physiology (implicit); System physiology; Patophysiology of drugs and illnesses	Semiology and amanuensis of individual imbalance; Diagnosis of drug and individual illness	Drugs; hygiene
Traditional Chinese	Chinese Cosmogony (Microcosm generated from Macrocosm)	Yin-Yang and the Five Phases (or Elements) and their equilibrium (or harmony) in individual subjects	Meridian channels and acupuncture points (subtle body) Solid and hollow organs	Vital 'breath' (Qi) physiology Organ physiology Yin-Yang dynamics within the organism and related to the environment	Semiology and amanuensis of Yin-Yang imbalance Diagnosis of subjects' imbalance	Hygiene; exercise (martial arts, meditation, etc.); diets; phytotherapy; massage acupuncture; mosha
Ayurveda	Indian (Microcosm generated from Macrocosm)	Five Elements and Humoral; Constitutions (Tridosha) in individual subjects	Several bodies (dense and subtle); Constitution of vital tissues, organs and senses	Energetic physiology (circulation of Prana and other energies within several bodies); Tridosha balance	Semiology and amanuensis of Tridosha imbalance; Eight Point observation system; Diagnosis of subjects' imbalance	Diets; purifying/ eliminating techniques; exercises (Yoga, meditation, etc.); massages; phytotherapy, drugs (substances of vegetal, animal and mineral origin)

In other words, those rationalities are *comparable* in their dimensions (even if not fully subject to complete translations from one system to the other), opening the possibility of establishing criteria to assess effectiveness adequate to each of them, that is, not subject to the usual reductionism to one culturally and politically dominant rationality, while retaining, on the other hand, the possibility of comparative studies. This has been the subject of the most recent steps in the research project; for now, we will present in the final pages of this paper an outline of one of the studied rationalities in terms of the defined categories.[4]

Contemporary Western Medical Rationality: An Outline

As was stated earlier in this paper, the beginning of modern medicine may be seen as a particular case of the deep cultural changes that affected Western culture in the passage Renaissance to Modern Classicism, frequently referred to as the 'Scientific Revolution.'

---

4. The same method was applied to the other three rationalities; due to reasons of space only one will be presented here. This work was published by the Instituto de Medicina Social, Universidade do Rio de Janeiro; see LUZ, H.S., 1993; LUZ, D., 1993; MARQUES, E.A., 1993.

It is not within the scope of this work to present a detailed account of this process, that in one sense has not yet finished, spanning across near four Centuries. We would just like to point out some aspects of this process that have had deep effects in bringing medical theory and practice into their present configuration. First of all, the social arrangement based on a theologically centred worldview gave way to a scientifically centred one; in our days, stating that something is 'scientific' is usually meant (and understood) as a synonym to being *true*. It thus follows that the main source of legitimacy in our society (at least in terms of discourse) is the world of Science; it is a logical consequence that medical knowledge would seek to be more and more 'scientific.' In broad terms, the model of science that emerged from the already mentioned revolution takes classical (Galilean/Newtonian) physics as a model of scientific production of knowledge; this rationality could be summarised in three main propositions:

- it seeks the production of discourses with universal validity, proposing models and laws that are generically applicable, not taking into account particular cases. It is, then, *generalising*;
- the aforementioned models tend to naturalise human construction, therefore reducing the universe to a gigantic machine, subordinated to principles of linear causation that can be translated in terms of composing mechanisms. It is, also, *mechanicist*;
- the theoretical and experimental approach derived from the previous principles are adopted to elucidate the 'general laws' of the functioning of the "universal machine" and determine proceedings that isolate certain parts of processes studied, assuming that the workings of the whole is given by the summation of parts. It is, finally, *analytical*.

Needless to say, modern science has somewhat overcome these conceptions, at least in the leading areas of research. We contend, however, that the cosmology of Western medicine is deeply impregnated with these already dated conceptions about the world around us and how one should proceed to understand it. The main problem here is that such conceptions are for the most part implicit, making it difficult, sometimes, to elicit them.

Another source of difficulty is the fact that, being hegemonic in our society, and given the tendency that our culture has to 'forget' the history of scientific creations, additional effort has to be made not to regard the constructions of Western medicine as 'natural' or 'real'; once again, anthropological reasoning, if not methodology, comes to our rescue.

The final sections of this paper will give a brief description of this rationality in terms of its other five dimensions, since its cosmology has already been presented here.

Medical Doctrine

Generic medical theories, in fact, tend also to be implicit and even contradictory. Old and new conceptions live together in the patchwork that makes up medical knowledge, and the relation of the latter to actual practice is far more contingent than the average doctor would like to admit. As was stated before, the formal aspects of medical theory are in a sense far apart from therapeutics in concrete situations.

The role of a general theory of medicine could be summarised in a restricted number of propositions, equally implicit, that might be referred to as a 'theory of diseases': diseases are natural entities, with little or no variation in different times and places, expressions of lesions which in turn are caused by some biological agent, or of an agent that exerts biological effects on the human body.

Two other important—and complementary—aspects in medical discourse are the ever recurring reference to 'multicausality' on one hand and to three domains that supposedly would encompass the whole of human experience, expressed by the adjectives biological, psychological and social, frequently collapsed into a single word: biopsychosocial. The rather naive conception that the fragmentation of objects intrinsic to modern science could be reverted by linguistic association is not enough to disguise the preponderance of the 'bio' term and the reduction of multiple causes to single really important ones, that should be subjected to concrete medical intervention—meaning either surgery or drugs, far more valued than any other type of intervention.

It is a paradox, however, that despite the general aspiration to scientific status, the individual experience is a shared value in the profession; the tension between the generalising discourse and individualised practice is just yet another example of the numberless contradictions that permeate the medical field.

Morphology

The main conception is the assimilation of the individual to his/her body, or in a more appropriate term, organism. The human body is perceived as naturally organised in discrete units, grouped in several systems. Three disciplines are related to this field: anatomy, histology, and pathological anatomy. The historical development in this dimension has been from macro to microscopic level, currently reaching atomic components of organic molecules and their arrangements.

Vital Dynamics

This comprises mainly physiology, pathophysiology, immunology and biochemistry (and, possibly, genetics as well), disciplines that are more directly related to the experimental method.

Some conceptions form a common core in this dimension: the notion of an internal environment, isolated from the exterior by epithelial barriers; system regulation within relatively narrow tolerance limits, known as homeostasis; the conception of life as a summation of biochemical and biophysical interactions.

The picture that emerges from these conceptions is strongly connected to system theory; the maintenance of homeostasis is described in terms of regulatory mechanisms connected through several feedback loops; this is a contemporary view in scientific terms, that coexists with the classical rationality described above.

Diagnosis

Diagnosis is made up of a diverse set of techniques collectively known as semiology. It is performed through certain pre-established steps that comprise amanuensis (medical history), followed by the physical exam, which in turn consists of four items—inspection, palpation, percussion and auscultation—systematically applied to every body component. This is usually followed—sometimes replaced—by an ever growing series of tests.

The core discipline here is medical clinics, that perform two basic operations: the gathering of medical data (through the semiological techniques described), and the placement of these within the conceptual grid of the known diseases. Although theoretically these two moments are separated in time and necessarily follow the order in which they were described, in actual practice there is a wide intertwining of both; diagnostic hypotheses arise pretty soon, influencing the collection of data itself. Another noteworthy aspect is that the already mentioned conceptual (nosological) grid is the result of a common enterprise that joins clinics and epidemiology in a curious alliance: each of these two disciplines overlooks the internal workings of the other; as a result, constructions from one field are viewed by the other as 'natural facts': the clinical descriptions of diseases are assumed as hard facts in epidemiological investigations, and the epidemiological findings about the same diseases are integrated into the clinical description as additional clinical evidence, as can be witnessed by browsing any modern manual of medical clinics. This peculiar vicious circle lies beneath the formal description of every diagnostic category.

Therapeutics

Western medicine does not hold general principles in therapeutics; the actual intervention is specific to each of the diseases figuring in its catalogue. Although theoretically several different techniques should be used, like physical therapy, diets, exercises, they do not share the same status that the 'real,' hard-core interventions—drugs and surgery—hold.

It might be argued that a general principle, the inverse of Homeopathy's *simillium*, does exist, since the therapeutic intervention aims to combat diseases; but when examined closely, there is a wide diversity, since while some agents are indeed devised as contrary to postulated agents of disease, such as antibiotics in the case of bacteria, there is a wide gamut of situations when the intervention aims at the enhancement and/or regulation of some body function, or even uses what might be regarded as 'identical' agents, such as with immune therapy.

The Structure of a Disease

In several places through this paper we argued that most of the general theories in Western medicine are implicit, being defined for particular cases such as the description of individual diseases; as was also stated before, this can be observed by browsing through any contemporary medical textbook; although the description of individual diseases is detailed and abundant, usually a very simple question remains unanswered: what is *a* disease? This can be observed even in the catalogue of diseases used world wide, WHO's International Classification of Diseases (ICD), currently in its tenth edition: although a thorough and exhaustive listing of every disease known to man is presented, a general definition of what a disease is is not even attempted.

This does not mean that such a definition does not exist, and the purpose of this final section is to present a conceptual framework for the construction of diagnostic categories,[5] summarised in the table below.

---

5. A detailed account of this model and its application to the study of the emergence of a specific disease in recent times, AIDS, was the object of the doctorate thesis of one of the authors (CAMARGO JR. 1994).

Table 2: The Structure of a Disease

Axes Elements	Explanatory	Morphologic	Semiologic
Discipline-type	Pathophysiology	Pathological anatomy	Medical Clinics
Core category	Cause Lesion	Lesion	Case
Definition of disease	Process	Expression of lesion(s)	Semiologic *gestalt*
Characteristic method	Experimental	Descriptive	Indiciary / observational
Historical period	Second half of XIXth Century	End of XVIIIth/ beginning of XIXth Centuries	XVIIIth Century

The first axis corresponds to the characterisation of diseases as processes, possessing one or more causes and a 'natural history.' It is in this axis that medical knowledge comes nearer the hard sciences, in the biological domain.

The second axis relates to the description of characteristic—pathognomonic—lesions, arising from the transition described by FOUCAULT in his *The Birth of the Clinic*. It must be noted, however, that the concept of *lesion* mutated through time, migrating from relatively large structures, visible to the naked eye, to ever diminishing portions of the human body; currently many lesions are described at the molecular level. Taking this into account, the laboratory instruments and tests used as part of the examining process are part of this same axis, and it might be said that an altered result may be seen, in this context, as a logical equivalent of a lesion.

Finally, the last axis describes diseases in terms of clusters of signals and symptoms, configuring semiologic *gestalts*. Characterizing this axis in the present moment is no easy task, since the semiologic definitions of disease are deeply intermixed with the preceding axes. It must be remarked, however, that the nosological grid—today best represented by the already mentioned ICD—precedes the last in centuries. Medicine is still classificatory, and the taxonomic system that existed in the past became the terrain in which the anatomoclinical descriptions developed. It is clear then that this axis comprises two different dimensions: on the one hand, the individualisation of single cases, using techniques described by Ginzburg as an indiciary paradigm to sketch a specific semiologic *gestalt*; on the other hand it also implies a generalisation, fitting the studied case into the aforementioned nosological grid. This, in turn, was developed conjointly by medical clinics and epidemiology, as was described previously.

The order in which these axes were presented is not casual; in effect, they are displayed in a decreasing order of valuation, in 'scientific' terms, since it is this value that lends social legitimacy to Western medicine. On the other hand, in terms of actual practice, this order is reversed, and the clinical method prevails, illustrating, once more, the separation between the science of the diseases and the healing art.

References

CAMARGO JR., K. R.
  1992 (Ir)racionalidade médica: Os paradoxos da clínica. *Physis* 2(1): 203-228.
  1993 Racionalidades médicas: A medicina ocidental contemporânea. Série *Estudos em Saúde Coletiva* no. 65, IMS/UERJ, Rio de Janeiro.

1994 *As ciências da AIDS e a AIDS das ciências*. Editora Relume-Dumará, Rio de Janeiro, 1994.
1995 Racionalidades médicas: A medicina ocidental contemporânea, *Cadernos de Sociologia,* Porto Alegre, V.7, pg. 129-150.

COULTER, H.
1982 *Divided legacy.* (3 volumes), North Atlantic Books, California.

FLECK, L.
1979 *Genesis and development of a scientific fact.* Chicago: University of Chicago Press.

FOUCAULT, M.
1966 *Les mots e les choses*. Paris: Gallimard.
1972 *La arqueología del saber*. Siglo Veintiuno, México. (Spanish translation from *L'archeologie du savoir*).
1978 *O nascimento da clínica*. Forense-Universitária, Rio de Janeiro. (portuguese translation from *La naissance de la clinique*)

GINZBURG, C.
1989 Sinais: raízes de um paradigma indiciário. in: *Mitos, Emblemas, Sinais*. São Paulo: Cia. das Letras.

LUZ, D.
1993 Racionalidades médicas: Medicina tradicional chinesa, Série *Estudos em Saúde Coletiva* no. 72, IMS/UERJ, Rio de Janeiro
1993 Racionalidades médicas: A medicina homeopática, Série *Estudos em Saúde Coletiva* no. 64, IMS/UERJ, Rio de Janeiro.
1988 *Natural Racional, Social: Razão médica e racionalidade científica moderna*. Rio de Janeiro: Campus.
1993 Racionalidades médicas e terapêuticas alternativas, Série *Estudos em Saúde Coletiva* no. 62, IMS/UERJ, Rio de Janeiro.
1994 *A arte de curar e a ciência das doenças: sócio-história da Homeopatia no Brasil*. Rio de Janeiro (thesis for the admission as full professor at the Instituto de Medicina Social, Universedade do Estado do Rio de Janeiro).
1995 Racionalidades médicas e terapêuticas alternativas, *Cadernos de Sociologia*, Porto Alegre, V.7, pg. 109-128.

MARQUES, E.A.
1993 Racionalidades médicas: Medicina ayurvédica—tradicional arte de curar da Índia, Série *Estudos em Saúde Coletiva* no. 75, IMS/UERJ, Rio de Janeiro.

UNSCHULD, P.
1985 *Medicine in China—An History of ideas*. Berkeley: University of California Press.

Social and Cultural Hierarchies and Different Ways of Healing in Brazil[1]

Maria Andréa Loyola

Abstract
Using data from two research studies conducted in Rio de Janeiro, Brazil—one involving clients of traditional and religious medicine and the other, homeopathic clients—the article shows how the option to use one type of medicine or another is influenced by the user's perception of health and sickness and by body use. This perception in large part reflects the user's class position, that is, his place within the social structure. This holds true both for clients as well as for doctors and specialists in different forms of healing.

Zusammenfassung
Der Artikel resultiert aus dem Material von zwei Studien, die in Rio de Janeiro durchgeführt wurden – eine zum Klientel der traditionellen und religiösen Medizin, die andere über Patienten der Homöopathie. Er zeigt, daß die Entscheidung für eine bestimmte Behandlung und gegen eine andere davon abhängig ist, wie der Betroffene seine eigene Gesundheit bzw. Krankheit wahrnimmt und welches Körperbild er hat. Diese Wahrnehmung reflektiert zu einem großen Teil die soziale Stellung des Betroffenen, das heißt, seinen Platz in der sozialen Struktur. Das trifft sowohl auf die Klienten als auch für die Ärzte und Spezialisten der verschiedenen Heilungsformen zu.

Keywords: homeopathy, traditional medicine, social structure, Brazil

When one examines the issue of traditional medicine, the initial question that arises is just what the term should embrace: all indigenous, *caboclo,* magical, and religious therapies; all therapies used by low-income populations; or all therapies used in rural areas, in isolated communities, and in the country's most backward regions?

Whatever aspects we emphasize when attempting to mark the boundaries of traditional medicine—technical ones, agents, consumers, or the socioeconomic realm—we run into the second, and main, problem: the presupposition (reflected in the very term *traditional medicine*) that we are dealing with knowledge and therapeutic techniques left over or surviving from a past era and which tend to disappear as official medicine gains ground. When this type of medical knowledge resists, it is out of ignorance, superstition, or fanaticism on the part of the populations that use it. As illiteracy is done away with and formal education expands, this resistance is expected to fade away.

Ignoring the character of this presupposition is tantamount to adopting the viewpoint of official medicine and thus opting from the outset to ignore the knowledge found in these practices. These practices not only exist and resist in urban centers and Brazil's more developed regions but also are responsible for curing countless illnesses which the official health system is unable to absorb and physicians are want to explain.

---

1. The original version of this article was presented at the Conference on Traditional Medicine and Western Medicine in the Amazon, held in Belém do Pará between November 27 and December 1, 1989.

Hierarchies of Knowledge and the Social Hierarchy

Whatever the classificatory term used—traditional, popular, magical, or religious medicine, for example—I believe it important to bear in mind that we are dealing with a set of healing techniques employed by specialists who are sometimes tolerated yet not recognized by official medicine. These techniques and this knowledge are therefore not offered to the population on the same footing with official medicine, or as true alternatives, being instead intermediated by relations of power.

Besides studying specific techniques, an investigation of this topic should include a study of representations regarding the body, health, and sickness. Since these techniques and representations constitute a dynamic system of signifiers that are continually being created and recreated on the basis of power relations among agents and between these agents and their clients, this investigation must also explore: 1. relations between those who employ these techniques (shamans, for example), on the one hand, and, on the other, official health agents and non-medical agents engaged in the same areas (*pajés* or *pais-de-santo,* for example); and 2. the relations between those who employ these techniques and the people to whom they provide services. This lets us take into account the class relations or relations of domination/subordination implicit to the issue, without falling into a mechanistic fallacy.

These ideas guided the research I conducted in the working-class neighborhood of Santa Rita, municipality of Nova Iguaçu, Rio de Janeiro, where most residents belong to the informal labor market. Results have been published in a book and a number of articles (LOYOLA 1982, 1984, 1987a) where I have endeavored to show that the relations between different healing systems (official medicine; *curandeirismo* or shamanism; Afro-Brazilian Umbanda/Candomblé; and Pentecostal Protestantism) are a product of the relations between different social agents, reflecting social class relations in a specific fashion.

I would like to underscore some aspects that interfere with or even dictate the use of these services—specifically, the role played by representations of the body, health, and sickness in the choice of a healing specialist and, above all, in safeguarding alternative healing systems from the prepotency of official medicine. In other words, I would like to show—however briefly—how these representations play not only a symbolic role (ranking signifiers) and a practical one (allowing the sick to rely on different types of specialists) but also a political one: defending knowledge that official medicine discredits as non-scientific, magical, and/or religious.

The Conception, Origin, and Classification of Sicknesses

In Santa Rita, the population looks at sickness (or health) as something that in the final analysis, within the overall scheme of life and death, escapes man's control, something that may be the product of supernatural forces or, more often, of God's will. Death occurs when the spirit leaves the body to which it has given life and goes to answer to God, or else to continue its journey of sorrow as a wandering soul or its journey of successive reincarnations, until reaching its final rest. The spirit is therefore greatly important to the state of one's health because it lends the body its vital energy. There is no such thing as a healthy body without a healthy soul, and a sick body often contributes to a sickness of the soul, and visa versa.

Based on this general conception of a complementary duality between body and soul, and adhering to a system of representations that allows most religious specialists to legitimate their prac-

Social and Cultural Hierarchies and Different Ways of Healing in Brazil

tices vis-à-vis official medicine (this applies especially to Umbanda's and Candomblé's *pais* and *mães-de-santos,* the Pentecostal Assembly of God's pastors, and *rezadores* - lay members who in rural Catholicism prayed in the place of priests and who now give blessings and pray for healing in urban areas), the population of Santa Rita distinguishes two main categories of sickness—*sicknesses of the body* and *sicknesses of the soul,* or *material sicknesses* and *spiritual sicknesses*—each of which requires a different type of healing agent.

Like religious specialists, the population generally classifies as spiritual illnesses those maladies whose origin defies practical verification and that are eventually, through a process of elimination, perceived and explained as non-material sicknesses. This means that quite similar symptoms may in point of fact be linked to any of the causes included within the classification system. Spiritual sickness can be caused by the 'evil eye' (healers or lower-class Catholicism, Umbanda, and Candomblé); spirit possession (the *espírito encostado* of Umbanda and Candomblé); or by Satanic possession or punishment from God (Pentecostal Protestantism), depending upon each individual's religious belief. The latter is what largely determines the type of treatment sought—that is, whether the individual will turn to a specialist from the official health system or to a religious specialist.

But while religious belief tends to encourage classification of a spiritual sickness according to its origin, this does not suffice to exclude definitions established by competing beliefs, other profane forms of knowledge, or simple common sense suppositions. In truth, the population often not only assigns more than one religious cause to one same spiritual sickness (for example, spirit possession and punishment from God can be present simultaneously) but also classifies certain sicknesses as spiritual not on the basis of their causes but on their accompanying symptoms and on the results of the doctor's recommended treatment. A spiritual illness can thus be defined as one that makes an individual 'lose his reason' or exhibit behavior that deviates from the norm. Likewise, and once again based on behavior, the term *spiritual illness* may designate a malady of a psychological or nervous order. In this system of representations, however, the category *madness* does not exist; madness is seen simply as the name doctors apply to spiritual sicknesses they cannot cure.

From the perspective of healing techniques, spiritual sicknesses encompass not only those a physician knows nothing about or does not understand but those he fails to cure as well. Unlike material sickness, a spiritual illness can be deduced from the rather rebellious nature of the malady - in other words, according to how long it takes to treat.

These representations are formed not from a general principle embracing the notions of cause and effect but through an analogic type of reasoning that works with simple binary oppositions and where reality is gradually clipped apart and reconstructed through the inclusion and exclusion of the elements in play. The body thus stands in contrast to the soul, matter to spirit, 'man's sicknesses' to 'God's sicknesses.' These categories also embrace other, simpler or more universal categories, such as those related to time—fast or slow healing—or to space—internal and external; superior and inferior (God, spirits, and men). As BOLTANSKI (1968:94) points out, the categories that members of the lower classes use in constructing their discourses often correspond to the more universal properties of things and are almost inseparable from the normal workings of the spirit (see also DURKHEIM 1960:13). These categories—as MAUSS warns us—are "constantly present in language, although not necessarily made explicit" and "generally exist more in the form of directive habits of the consciousness" (1967). In addition to the spatial and temporal categories already mentioned, in most cases these are categories of substance or attribute (strong and weak, etc.). But in Santa Rita, they are likewise associated with social categories, where each of the symbolic poles (body and soul, man and god, inferior and superior) is linked to sector specialists: medical and religious agents, those who use scientific technique and those who use prayer.

These categories also underlie the population's classification of material sickness. Depending upon whether the causes are internal or external, these illnesses can be subdivided into 1. *hereditary*, or something an individual is 'born with,' that 'comes from inside him,' that is specific to that individual and his biological cycle, and 2. *contagious* diseases, such that 'come from the outside,' that a person 'catches,' and that have to do with the organism's relationship with its physical and social environment. Since in a way they are specific to an individual and tend to be inseparable from him, a hereditary illness or a malady one is born with clearly presupposes the idea of predestination, making it possible to draw a bridge between hereditary and contagious illness (as well as between spiritual and material illness, since a weak spirit is more vulnerable to sickness than a strong one).

Material sicknesses are generally classified as *mild* (malaise, minor illnesses) or *serious*, depending upon how life threatening they are. This distinction has more to do with the intensity of the malady than with its origin or nature, and it is based on symptoms of which fever is the most decisive. Mild illnesses may become serious if they do not respond to the customary treatment. The qualifications *mild* and *serious* are associated, respectively, with *common* illnesses and *doctor's* illnesses, the latter requiring the intervention of a physician and not diagnosable by merely observing symptoms. Furthermore, data suggest that material sicknesses are classified as either *serious* or *less serious*, depending upon whether their treatment is associated with modern scientific medicine or traditional medicine.

Thus, sickness caused by fear, fright, chilly air, violation of the lying-in period, etc., along with other everyday illnesses whose symptoms and treatment fall within the realm of experience or tradition (inflammation of the nails, 'upset tummy,' 'dropped breastbone,' etc.), are generally included in the group of sicknesses that should be dealt with by healers or by *pais* or *mães-de-santo*. On the other hand, sicknesses about which little is known or that are considered serious, that cause persistent fever, or that require hospitalization or surgery are considered doctor's illnesses.

Since this classificatory system is based on practical experience, the lines between different categories are very finely drawn. Placed along a continuum, we can state that a reasonable number of sicknesses fall in the middle and may shift from one category to the other, depending upon whether they have been diagnosed or treated by a doctor or pharmacist, by a religious specialist, or even by a relative or neighbor.

The interference of agents in this classificatory system does not invalidate but rather reinforces this population's basic representations regarding the health/sickness process. The distinction between material and spiritual sickness, for example, does not contradict a totalizing conception of sickness in itself, as something that affects both spirit and matter. Instead, this distinction has more to do with the notion of what gave rise to the sickness (the cause often times being identified by analogy with the agent); once illness takes hold, it will affect the body as a whole. In counterpart, this system lets clients rely on one or the other healing system without any need to question the superiority or competence of non-medical specialists. For example, it allows those of the Umbanda faith and healers to allege that a given case is a material and not a spiritual illness, in this way permitting more serious cases to be referred to medical doctors while not jeopardizing the prestige or calling into question the skill of the traditional practitioners. It allows pastors to send most of the ill to a doctor, leaving the church to take care of the spiritual side—without which healing cannot take place. Above all, it allows the population on the whole to defend itself from the authoritarianism of official medicine and to complement medical treatment where the latter falls short from the perspective of popular culture: in its symbolic aspects.

Body Use and the Perception of Sickness

In examining the issue of how body use affects perception of sickness, I will use data not only from the Nova Iguaçu study but also from a more recent survey conducted among homeopathic clients in the city of Rio de Janeiro (1987b), which should help underline the importance of the problem.

Forced to use their bodies intensively—as the only tool available for providing their sustenance—clients of popular medicine in Santa Rita, who are for the most part heavy laborers, define health by reference to the categories of strength and weakness. Their representation of health is closely linked to the idea of strength—strength that can be used to work and which is sustained and stimulated by food intake. Sickness is seen as a state of weakness that keeps an individual from using his body normally, that is, to work.

The homeopathic clients surveyed all belonged to Rio de Janeiro's middle social strata. For them, the fundamental categories around which they organize their representations regarding health and sickness are *balance/imbalance*—categories that on a symbolic level reproduce their position within the social hierarchy, both as balancing and balancers between the privileged strata and the underprivileged. In their eyes, health is synonymous with organic and emotional balance, while sickness, whatever its nature (chronic, acute, viral, bacterial, degenerative, etc.), represents a breakdown of this balance prompted by an unbalanced life: poor nutrition, nervousness, stress, hurry, the jitters, worry, hatred, resentment—in short, by factors that affect or derive from these people's style of life.

What these homeopathic clients and the clients of popular medicine have in common is their negation both of dualism between body and spirit, or body and soul, and between objectivism and subjectivism, and of official medicine's organic mechanicism. But while clients of popular medicine think above all in terms of the categories *spirit* and *matter* and deny the existence of mental illness—in their symbolic universe identified as a spiritual disease—the clients of homeopathy think mainly in terms of the categories *body* and *mind*. Their representations concerning health and sickness are not untouched by the theories espoused by the religions to which they belong (mainly Kardecist spiritism), but on the whole those interviewed did not mention the category of spiritual sickness. When led to speak about the health/sickness process, they almost always stress the important role played by the 'mind' and therefore by the individual's own participation in this process - in a kind of volunteerism characteristic of these social strata, strongly driven by the notion of social mobility. 'Mind' may refer to a set of feelings and sentiments lying either closer to the religious universe ('good, lofty thoughts' and 'a forgiving spirit') or closer to the psychoanalytical universe ('relaxing,' 'psychological balance,' 'a productive mind'), but what is striking about the homeopathic clientele is the centrality of this category, almost never or rarely mentioned by the lower-class population. This representation is no doubt related to the clientele's class *habitus* (see BOURDIEU 1979) and their expectations for climbing the social ladder, a clientele who earns their living less by using their bodies and physical strength than by using their minds—that is, by using their ability to assimilate more or less specialized attitudes, techniques, and knowledge conveyed and legitimated by schools.

Once again similar to Santa Rita's low-income population, the homeopathic clientele values food as a source of good health and an important element in disease prevention. The former population, however, organizes its representations regarding health and sickness around the idea of strength sustained and replenished by food, while it is forced to eat a qualitatively and quantitatively minimal or highly limited diet (if not to go hungry); food therefore holds a central place in describing the health/sickness process. For the homeopathic clients, on the other hand, the importance of food derives from a lifestyle (eating the wrong food, an unbalanced diet, or polluted, industrialized, or non-natural foods, etc.) and never from want. On the contrary, over-eating, the 'abuse' of certain foodstuffs, and diversified eating habits fit in with the idea of a balanced diet — and this is fundamental for the homeopathic clients.

At the same time, while the clientele of popular medicine prefer foods that are classified as strong or heavy, because they 'weigh' in the stomach, like black beans, meat, pasta, etc.; that give the body strength and make it stout and resistant; and that leave you feeling full and satisfied, with the sensation you have eaten well — that is, a lot — the homeopathic clients prefer foods that the working class sees as weak or light, foods that nourish yet don't weigh heavy in the stomach: vegetables, white meats, etc.

If on the one hand the taste preferences of the homeopathic clients incorporate the recommendations of official dietetics (i.e., a balanced intake of vitamins, mineral salts, proteins and amino acids), on the other hand they tend towards alternative diets, like vegetarianism and macrobiotics, which are not always approved by official medicine but where the idea of balance (cosmic, biological, energetic, etc.) is basic and/or primordial.

Conclusion

In other papers on this topic (especially LOYOLA 1983 and 1987b), I offer further examples and endeavor to explore in greater depth the complex relations that exist between clientele and different medical and non-medical specialists who treat sickness in this region of Brazil, relations that grow out of specific perceptions and ways of using the body. I believe I have provided some indications in this direction and, above all, made it clear that the choice of any medicine will involve a user's perception of health and sickness and, furthermore, that this perception by and large reflects this user's class positio — that is, his place within the social structure. This holds true both for clients as well as for doctors and specialists in different forms of healing.

References

BOLTANSKI, L.
    1968   *La découverte de la maladie*. Paris: Centre de Sociologie Européenne (mimeo). Translated to Portuguese and published in BOLTANSKI, L., 1984. *As classes sociais e o corpo*. Rio de Janeiro: Graal.
BOURDIEU, P.
    1979   *La distinction. Critique social du jugement*. Paris: Editions de Minuit.
DURKHEIM, E.
    1960   *Les formes élémentaires de la vie religieuse: le système totémique en Australie*. Paris: PUF.
LOYOLA, M.A.
    1982   Cure des corps et cure des âmes. Les rapports entre les médecins et les religions dans la banlieue de Rio. *Actes de la Recherche en Sciences Sociales* 43: 2-43.
    1983   *L'Esprit et le Corps*. Paris: Editions de la Maison des Sciences de L'Homme.
    1984   *Médicos e Curandeiros, Conflito Social e Saúde*. São Paulo: Difel.

1987a Medicina Popular: Rezas e Curas de Corpo e Alma. *Ciência Hoje* 6(35): 34-43.
1987b Uma medicina de classe média: idéias preliminares sobre a clientela da homeopatia. *Cadernos do IMS* 1(1): 45-72.

MAUSS, M.
1967 *Oeuvres*. Paris: Editions de Minuit, vol. I. (Col. Le Sens Commun).

Biomedical Discourses and Health Care Experiences:
The Goiânia Radiological Disaster

Telma Camargo Da Silva

Abstract

In 1987, in Goiânia, the capital of Goiás state, in Central Brazil, a cesium-137 radiotherapy unit was abandoned by a private medical institute. Informal sector workers collected the unit, took it home, and opened it. The result was severe environmental and populational contamination. The medical responses given by state agencies raise a number of questions about ideological processes that shaped medical knowledge and about the construction of victim identity. This paper focuses on the human body as a representation of contradictions raised between institutional medical discourses and patient experiences in the context of a radiation disaster. I suggest that an understanding of those tensions and contradictions is important for an agenda that advocates human rights and health care monitoring programs for affected populations.

Zusammenfassung

1987 wurde eine Caesium-137 Strahlentherapiekapsel in Goiânia, Hauptstadt des Bundesstaates Goiás, weggeworfen, die einem privaten medizinischen Institut gehörte. Abfallsammler des informellen Arbeitsmarktes hoben die Kapsel auf und nahmen sie mit nach Hause, wo sie sie öffneten. Das Ergebnis war eine schwere Verseuchung der Umwelt und der Bevölkerung. Die Antworten der staatlichen Medizinbehörde werfen eine Reihe von Fragen auf über die ideologischen Prozesse, die das medizinische Wissen formen sowie über die Konstruktion von Identität der Opfer. Dieser Artikel konzentriert sich auf den menschlichen Körper als die Repräsentation von Widersprüchen, die, im Kontext eines Strahlenunglücks, zwischen institutionellen medizinischen Diskursen und den Erfahrungen der Patienten entstehen. Die Ergebnisse lassen darauf schließen, daß ein besseres Verständnis dieser Spannungen und Widersprüche für die Planung von Strategien für Menschenrechte und die Gesundheitsversorgung der betroffenen Bevölkerungen von großer Bedeutung ist.

Keywords: disaster, anthropology of illness and health, body, Brazil

An increasing number of works in the field of the Anthropology of Illness and Health have been using the representation of the body (visual and/or discursive) to analyze people's experience with sickness, healing, suffering and death. For some scholars the body as a metaphor is specially meaningful in the emotional encounter between the anthropologist(s) and the 'natives.' For others, the discourse(s) on the body unveil particular experiences of power and are historically contextualized. The first approach claims for a deconstruction of what its practitioners call the false dichotomy between cultural sentiments and natural passions (Scheper-Hughes & Lock 1987: 28) and give privilege to particular individual experiences (Scheper-Hughes 1993). The second framework conceives the body as a cultural expression of peoples in historical and economical areas (Lock 1993; Comaroff 1993; Haraway 1993). This approach opens the way to observe contradictions of peoples' everyday experiences. While the first approach focuses on privileged individuals' experiences, the second framework considers the social relations involved in the constructions of the body and its representations. Indeed from this perspective different actors and discourses emerged from the same experience. (Burdick 1992; 1993)

In this paper I intend to pursue the theoretical formulations considered under the second approach. I examine the manufacturing of the victim identity through the consideration of different discourses produced about the human body in the aftermath of the Goiânia radiological disaster. I base my study on official documents published by state agencies, the International Atomic Energy Agency (IAEA), Scientific Conferences, grassroots organization, on data collected during preliminary fieldwork done from late 1987 to mid 1990 and on present research for my doctoral dissertation. The focus of my analysis is on the discourses articulated by both medical institutions and people affected by the radiation disseminated by this disaster. I argue that a) the process of categorization is extremely dynamic, involves contradictions and negotiations; b) power relations shape peoples' and institutions' discourses; c) the individuals' experiences intervene in the power relationships.

My analysis points out to some contributions already incorporated by works developed by the Anthropology of Illness and Health as the case of post-structuralists approaches on the discourse's notion. At the same time my discussion intends to collaborate to the anthropological literature on disaster that is an emergent topic. I depart from the Foucauldian assumption that links discourse, power and institution and bring to this paradigm people's everyday experiences. According to FOUCAULT (1972 [1969]: 49) discourse is not defined as a group of signs (signifying elements referring to contents or representations) but as practices that systematically form the objects of which they speak. Thus, Foucauldian notion of discourse move beyond the structuralist focus on the internal logic of language as a relational system homologous with the social order, to a concern with an encompassing image of discourse as constitutive of that social order (KUIPERS 1989). Nevertheless, based on DE CERTEAU's thought (1988), some American anthropologists argue the need to advance Foucault's idea on discourse in adding to his perspective the notion of agency. They claim the incorporation of circumstantial realities of verbal interactions where the discourses take place. In other words, they argue for bringing negotiations, contradictions and resistance that occur on the everyday experience of discursive interactions to the power/knowledge/discourse bond. RAYNA RAPP's (1988) work on amniocentesis in the context of new reproductive technologies is a good example of this viewpoint. She examines the dialogues and practices undertaken by new professionals called 'genetic counselors' and multicultural patients (1988:143). In RAPPs' study, power and knowledge are linked together to multicultural everyday life of people living in NewYork. Distinct ethnic groups and specific cultures are the sites for establishing boundaries between patients and medical professional and among patients themselves.

Although the anthropological literature on disaster in the United States in the last twenty years has dedicated a number of studies to 'natural' (earthquake, flood, avalanche, hurricane) and 'man-made disasters' (chemical, oil spills, gas) Brazilian anthropologists seem not concerned with this topic. While in the United States some reflexions arise on disaster and hazardous environment, the study of populations affected by radiation is still an incipient topic. Nevertheless some works advance elements for the discussion I present here: multiple subject voices emerging in the aftermath of disaster situation. NASH & KIRSCH (1988) examine the rise of different discourses (agents of a corporation, the medical and scientific professions, and the community) concerning the effects of polychlorinated biphenyls (PCBs) in the General Electric plant in Pittsfield (Massachusetts - U.S.A), in the late seventies. They concluded that the construction of consensus among these different discourses resulted from the ability of the corporation to set the direction of the discourse, subsuming the community's own discourse under its own (Id: 170). SUSSER's research on the impact of pollution generated by a U.S. industrial plant, Union Carbide Grafito, Inc., on the lives of inhabitants of a Puerto Rican town, has generated two interesting essays. In the first (1985), the author describes how health concerns and behavior were related to historical experiences, and to political and economic interests. In the second (1992), SUSSER documents the continuity in gender roles that led women to community concerns and examines the combination of changes that propelled women into leadership by the end of the 1980's. Both NASH & KIRSCH as well as SUSSER focus on the movement of transnational corporations, their environmental impact and the process of community empowerment through organization. They make an important contribution to the study of disaster by showing how issues of urban pollution, occupational and environmental health hazards change in response to ongoing conflicts among workers, management, and the communities affected. Following this path, I argue that discourses, experiences and everyday practices must be analyzed within particular historical, cultural, political and environmental contexts in which they are produced, maintained, or transformed.

The Production of Goiânia Radiological Disaster

To contextualize the discourses, I will present some data about the disaster itself and the site where the events occurred. Goiânia is the capital of the state of Goiás on the Central Brazil plateau, with a population of about one million inhabitants. It is a city planned during the 1930s to be the regional capital. The local economy is based on cereal farms and cattle ranches. Goiânia is at 200 km from Brasília, the capital of Brazil, built during the 1960s.

In this city, about the end of 1985 a private radiotherapy institute—Instituto Goiano de Radioterapia—moved to new premises and left behind a cesium-137 radiotherapy unit. The owners of the institute did not notify the licensing authority, the *Comissão Nacional de Energia Nuclear* (CNEN), Brazil's national nuclear energy about the remains of this unit.

In 1987, complex elements increased the gravity of the situation, and revealed the precariousness of the local institutions to handle radioactive material. The old building where the teletherapy unit had been left, was partly demolished without any kind of surveillance. CNEN, responsible for monitoring all radioactive material in Brazilian territory had no control over the actual condition of teletherapy and radiography sources. Simultaneously, with the Brazilian economic crisis of the 80s, unemployment increased, and individuals depending on the informal sector augmented. One of these was the 'catador de papel,' an individual who used handmade metal and cardboard strollers to collect papers and scrap metals to sell to junkyard owners, finally selling the material to recycling industries. Two of these scrap collectors entered the abandoned clinic, took a part of the teletherapy unit to their homes and opened it at the 57th Street, downtown Goiânia, transformed in one of major focus of radiation. Afterwards, they sold the material to a scrap dealer who became fascinated with the blue glow that emanated from the unit at night. Members of the scrap dealer's family and social network were invited to come to his house, see and touch the powder. Among those individuals, some carried the physical and visible inscription of radiation on their bodies because they had, in different ways, physical contact with the cesium-137 source. The skin burns were the result of various actions: opening the teletherapy unit; holding a radioactive piece or putting it on their bodies. For some it looked like carnival glitter and they rubbed their bodies with it. Other, drew a cross on his chest, because maybe it had a magical power. Many took portions of the cesium-137 to their homes and stored it in their kitchens and bedrooms. Some ate meals with their hands contaminated with cesium. These people continued to go to work, to school, taking collective transportation, having a regular daily life without knowing that they were carrying radioactive material on and inside their bodies. In this way some individuals became irradiated, without knowing that they were in contact with radiation.

According to official reconstruction of the events, the authorities discovered the disaster only 13 days after the beginning of the radiation dissemination. (IAEA 1988; IAEA Bulletin 4.1988; FUNDAÇÃO LEIDE DAS NEVES FERREIRA 1990). The result was severe contamination of the environment and of the population. According to the literature, the particular features of the Goiânia radiological disaster made it "the worst radiation accident in the Western Hemisphere." (ROBERTS 1987: 238). Several elements contributed to that characterization: a) the delay between the event and its perception and recognition; b) the fact that the major focus of the disaster area (Sector Aeroporto) was in a densely populated section of the city; c) the way that people used the cesium in their daily lives; d) the lack of an emergency plan for radiological disasters; e) the physical characteristic of the cesium used in this teletherapy;[1] f) the weather pattern in central Brazil in September with abundant rain, high temperatures and winds, which contributed to the dispersion of radioactivity.[2]

Governmental Perception of Individuals Affected by the Radiation

The treatment and care of the people affected by the disaster have been described and discussed in many scientific and professional meetings[3]. Two International Conferences (1988, 1990) were held at Goiânia. The actions undertaken since the discovery of the disaster have been indexed chronologically, and the affected population labeled and classified. There are different notions used to describe who has been affected, undermining theoretical and political point of views. Simultaneously, there also have been debates about the real number of individuals affected by the disaster. According to the International Atomic Energy Agency (IAEA) report, the medical responses were classified as a) Initial and emergency response (1988: 41-60) and b) Long term control.

Several Brazilian and international specialists[4] worked in the first phase under the direction of CNEN, an institution controlled by the military. Then the radiation patients were defined by their

---

1. Contrary to the current use of cesium-137 vitrified form that inhibits dispersion (IAEA 1988:88) this was an obsolete teletherapy unit that contained cesium chloride, highly soluble.
2. The high temperature dried out the wet ground and the high winds caused the resuspection and dispersion of the cesium, that was deposited on the roofs of the houses. (IAEA 1988:88).
3. For instance, a review meeting was organized jointly by the Brazilian National Energy Commission (CNEN) and the IAEA, at Rio de Janeiro, 1988. Eight papers were presented at the Thirty-Third Annual Meeting of the Health Physics Society, Boston, July 4-8, 1988; member of the FUNDAÇÃO LEIDE DAS NEVES participated in various international conferences as the 'Children and Radiation' Conference, Trondhaim, Norway, June 1993.
4. 700 workers participated in response to the disaster, including professionals from CNEN staff, personnel from the Brazilian army, NUCLEBRAS, FURNAS, the state of Goiás, and from private companies. (IAEA Bulletin 4,1988:10). In October, the Brazilian Government asked the International Atomic Energy Agency (IAEA) in Vienna for help. The international team included two U.S. radiation experts (Robert Ricks and physician Clarence Lushbaugh of the Radiation Emergency Center \ Training Sites (REACTS), a World Health Organization; Juan Jimenez of Buenos Aires; Gunter Trexler of Munich; and George Seliodovkin a hematologist from Moscow, who had treated the victims of Chernobyl. Another international specialist, Dr. Robert Gale, treated the victims during this emergencial phase. His participation and the use of GM-CSF was the subject of one of the medical and political debates raised during this disaster (*Science* No. 4830: 1028-1031; *Science* No. 4838) GM-CSF (Granulocyte Macrophage Colony Stimulating Factor) is a new hormone-like drug. It "was used in the treatment of overexposed persons, with questionable results." (*IAEA Bulletin*.4.1988: 13)
   "GM-CSF is one of a family of hormones that stimulate the bone marrow to produce white or red blood celles. GM-CSF specificaly stimulates neutrophils and monocytes, the white blood cells that kill microbes. GM-CSF is not approved for medical use in the United States or Brazil, but is undergoing clinical trials here to determine its usefulness in boosting white cell production in patients with suppressed bone marrow (Science, May 1: 517)" (Science, November 20: 1029)

relationship with the first identified individuals involved in the break in of the teletherapy unit. Kinship, household, professional and social networks were some of the criteria used. The specialists grouped 249 individuals who were considered 'contaminated,' as contaminated was the environment around them. This group was divided based on the level of contamination: a) some had 'only' shoes and clothes contaminated by the cesium-137; b) 129 persons had internal and external contamination. (LEIDE DAS NEVES FERREIRA FOUNDATION 1990:21) The remedial action focused on finding the contaminated individuals, isolating them and undertaking the procedures involving the physical decontamination of bodies. Physical bodies were isolated, secluded and given what the radiation specialists called 'the decorporation of cesium' by using 'Prussian Blue.' To be rescued for 'social life,' those more contaminated bodies had been measured in different ways. Samples of blood, urine and feces were obtained daily to assess the level of internal contamination. A whole body counter was constructed to find out the total doses of each individual. A detailed process of decontamination was undertaken:

"Contaminated clothing was removed and all (individuals) were decontaminated by taking several baths with soap and water." (IAEA 1988: 42)

"Skin decontamination was performed on all patients using mild soap and water, acetic acid and titanium dioxide. Decontamination was only partially successful since sweating resulted in recontamination of the skin from internally deposited cesium-137." (IAEA 1988: 43)

"Decontamination of the patients' skin and dealing with desquamation from radiation injuries and contaminated excreta posed major problems of care. Daily haematological and medical examinations, good nursing care and bioassay of blood cultures contributed to the early detection and therapy of local systemic infections." (IAEA 1988: 2)

While some members of the CNEN, a federal institution, were involved in treating 'contaminated people and environment,' its board was involved in political struggles with the local Government about: a) the localization and construction of the waste repository to fit the radioactive waste produced by those characterized as 'contaminated' people; b) the responsibility for the disaster; c) the adequacy of procedures taken; d) the definition of 'safe' levels of radiation for the liberation of 'contaminated' areas. Along with those issues, the Government of Goiás also faced the discrimination against local industrial and agricultural products as well the stigmatization of local population. The event had a significant impact on the economic stability and the social/political fabric of the state of Goiás. (PETTERSON 1988)

Many local business organizations held a collective effort to face the stigma. The Goiás Commercial and Industrial Association (Associação Comercial e Industrial de Goiás) gave financial and political support to the Federal University of Goiás on the creation of a research center: Núcleo de Acompanhamento ao Acidente Radiológico de Goiânia—NUAC. Goiás economic sector, that usually was not concerned with scientific matters, held a collective effort that could overcome the unknown, i.e. radiation disease, through the production of knowledge. Then, the association between knowledge and economic regional power is clearly established as attested by the important financial contributions of Encol S/A and União Democrática Ruralista Nacional—UDR. (NUAC Archives). The first, a major name on the local building industry; the second, a right wing organization which national leader originated from Goiás and represented cereal farm and cattle ranch sectors, an influential sphere at the local level. The associated effort's ultimate aim was to assure the maintenance of economic production in controlling the disturbed situation:

"The regrettable radiological accident that occurred in Goiânia, in the second half of September, still is and will represent for many years, a source of great concern for the population, what is already attested by important consequences left on cultural, economic and social activities of the state of Goiás.

Thus, it became crucial for facing the crisis an associated effort of all the community sectors. To accomplish this endeavor, it is decisive the investigation of the disaster's real dimensions, its probable consequences along with the assurance of the best modern science resources for the victims and the release of accurate disaster information to the local population." (NUAC—Proposta de Implementação das Atividades do Núcleo).

The economic regional sector undertook more symbolic centered measures. For instance, the transportation of goods and merchandises at inter regional level was used to respond to discrimatory acts. Thus, trucks coming or leaving the city of Goiânia carried slogans written in black letters over write fabric and tied to the truck's body saying,

"The radioactive accident did not kill Goiânia, but you can kill it with your discrimination"
"Goiânia regains its breath and ELIANE & SOARES follows this move"

It is worth recalling that the State of Goiás held a weak political, intellectual, and economic position among other states of the federation. In the very beginning of the aftermath of the disaster this situation reached a critical condition because of the discrimination. In this context, in February 1988, the local government created the FOUNDATION LEIDE DAS NEVES FERREIRA.

The Foundation was established with two major objectives that mixed assistance and scientific research, which is: a) to give direct and permanent assistance to 107 people, including health care, pension, economic compensation, housing, basic food; b) to promote research on the effects of radioactivity.

"The government of the State of Goiás created the Fundação 'Leide das Neves Ferreira' with the aim of giving support to the people involved in the radioactive accident in Goiânia. At the moment 54 people are receiving medical observation and also laboratory, psychological, odontological and social observation. But the population that should receive this observation will be increased, in the beginning to more or less 550 people, this number consisting of individuals who worked on the critical phase of the accident and were exposed to contamination and/or radiation with the Cesium-137. The neighbouring (sic) population of the focuses of the contamination will be included in a project of evaluation and research of (sic) Micronucleus. The global observation will be of 1.104 people.

The importance of inclusion of these last groups in the observation is connected to the evidence that RBE for the late effects may be greater to low than to high doses of irradiaton (sic)." (LEIDE DAS NEVES FERREIRA FOUNDATION 1988. Medical Nucleus)

The foundation design is a response to two different political contexts: 1) a response to the pressures of the 57th Street inhabitants, where the teletherapy unit was broken; 2) a privileged opportunity for the state of Goiás to produce 'scientific knowledge,' and gain national and international prestige, an aim that is on the front page of the Foundation Bulletin, published in English.

"The decision of the Governor of the State of Goiás, HENRIQUE SANTILLO, a Medical Pediatrician, to create a scientific research institution, unknown in the Center-West Region of Brazil, demonstrates his concern with the development of science in a region traditionally forgotten by Brazilian administrators. More than this, it proves that a Governor should act in this field, as well as acting in questions of a purely political nature.

The main concern of the Foundation is based on the implementation of research in the area of medicine, as well as fostering information exchange with the more advance centers in the world. Brazil has already entered the Nuclear Energy Club and the organized society must now accompany and supervises this development. No doubt the Foundation will contribute, in its own specific and clear way, a great deal in this new technological age. As a consequence of the tragedy in Goiânia, the Governor of Goiás instituted the Foundation, which today forms part of the national and international scientific world and is open to the exchange of ideas, experiences, studies, research and results, which aim to protect human beings and the ecological system from the misuse of nuclear energy and its subsequent consequences. Only a scientist in politics could understand these new circumstances." (FOUNDATION LEIDE DAS NEVES FERREIRA 1989)

To carry out its actions, the Foundation categorized the individuals affected by the disaster. First, the medical protocol was established for health monitoring, and four groups were defined[5]

---

5. see note at the end of this paper.

according to individual's level of radiation, professional contact with affected people and domicile in the neighborhood affected by the disaster. Second, a project was designed to evaluate the composition of each group in order to assure to the most affected individuals a permanent health care and financial compensation. In fact, in defining the level of victimization, the project also specified the compensation to be allowed and this became a crucial point of struggle between affected population and the Leide das Neves Foundation.

Thus, at the Governmental level two major categorizations emerged. While the federal CNEN focuses on 'contaminated' people, the local Foundation centers the discourse on the idea of victimization.[6]

'Victim': A Self-Identification Category

But how did the affected people refer to themselves, in this complex categorization involving notions of contamination and victimization? One way to look at the self-identification of the individuals affected by the disaster is through the documents and speeches of the members of the 'Associação das Vítimas do Césio-137.' On December 13, 1987, the inhabitants of the 57th Street organized an association that resulted from: 1. the astonishment of the local population at the secrecy and methods used to evacuate the inhabitants of affected areas; 2. the call for a broader definition of what characterizes the population affected by the disaster; 3. the confrontation with CNEN and Leide das Neves Ferreira Foundation for a better health care with a broader notion of health (i.e., involving physical and mental health, and attention to the nutritional aspect of the individuals)[7] access to individual information about the results of the tests taken at those institutions; and compensation for the material loses; 4. the articulation with national and international grass-roots organizations and with local universities to obtain support for their demands.[8]

"On the evening of September 29, 1987 the 57th Street inhabitants made their first contact with the disaster when the sanitation and police force came to evacuate the residents of house number 68. At dawn, the persons living nearby were also removed from their houses and isolated on the Olímpico Stadium, while the neighborhood did not receive any information about what was occurring. The next morning the space showed the marks of change: string line separated all the houses evacuated. Some 57th Street inhabitants looked for information at the Olímpico Stadium where they were told about the opening of a Cesium teletherapy unit. At that occasion, they were notified that within two or three days everything will be normalized and everybody will return to their houses.

A group of the 57th Street inhabitants took the initiative of founding an Association in response to the absolute lack of information and assistance to the individuals indirectly affected by the radioactive accident. We asked the governmental institutions responses to our claims with no satisfied answers. When we formalized our re-

---

6. At a certain moment, the entire Goiânia population is classified by a foundation as a psychological victim of the 'accident'. (FERNANDES 1988:21) The Foundation itself is a memorials of the victims. The Government of Goiás, bearing the idea of victimization, gave the institutin the name of the six year old girl who died as a consequence of the disaster.
7. For instance, under the pressure of the Association, the number and composition of the 'Basic Food Basket', provided by the Foundation to the 'direct' victims is altered. On March, 1988 the Foundation furnishes 72 baskets to 32 'families'. On Abril 1988, the number change to 127 baskets to 35 'families'. The members of the Association request the additional item—beef—to the following: 1kg of sugar; 2 kg of bean; 5kg of rice; 2 liters of oil; 2 packages of 'Bom-Bril'; 3 units of soap; 2kg of powder milk (FUNDAÇÃO LEIDE DAS NEVES FERREIRA. Julho 1988. Relatório de Atividades).
8. During the crucial moments of the disaster, the Association asked for the help of a German Green Party member to measure the level of radiation at the Aeroporto Section. Then they used these numbers to confront the radiation numbers proposed by CNEN technicians.

quests, mostly on health issues, the State Government asked us to properly organize into an association with registered bye-law. Otherwise, the authorities said, they could not address our claims.
(…) Thus, the association is constituted by people from various zones afffected by the disaster. People whose lives were modified by the accident in various ways: both in terms of health and in terms of losing their homes and jobs. Lives affected by the dislocation of small businesses; the deterioration of property value; the disruption of kinship, friendship and the neighborhood by the stigma raised from the disaster.
(…) We include as the population affected by the disaster: the people directly contaminated; the neighbors of the sites considered as radiation focus and the Abadia de Goiás community compelled to live with the repository of radioactive waste. Thus, we share the same struggle." (ASSOCIAÇÃO DAS VÍTIMAS DO CÉSIO-137. 1989)

Here the victim identity is constructed in confrontation with institutionalized biomedical power. According to the members of the association, the victimized body is not just the visible physically affected body, as thought by the CNEN notion of contaminated individuals. They demand that 'invisible' marks of the disaster, such as the disintegration of social networks, kinship relations, and social and economic dislocations should be included. To do that, they categorize the victims as 'direct' and 'indirect'. The first corresponds to the CNEN notion of 'contamination'. The second, the groups of peoples who did not have direct contact with the radioactive source. But everyday discourse reveals the internal contradictions of the association, separating different social groups. The first distinction is based on one's place in the local economy (i.e., unemployed, underemployed, low skill workers, autonomous small business and liberal professionals). Second, they attempt to isolate those considered by the majority to be responsible for the disaster. Later, in 1991, the notion of victim acquires another characteristic. It is not just an identity built in struggle, a 'mask of confrontation,' to use JOAN VINCENT's notion (1974). Victim takes on the connotation of people twice victimized: by the disaster itself and by the lack of continuous financial and political support of promised health treatment.

Based on observations done on early post-disaster context it seems that three major forces were in confrontation and negotiation in the aftermath of Goiânia Disaster: local government, federal government, and the population affected by the radiation. Each while negotiating a specific agenda simultaneously contributed to the definition of the affected body: a) CNEN had to domesticate and to control contaminated spaces and bodies in 'clearly' defining doses, geographical boundaries in order to competently act as a 'decontaminator' agent; b) the government of Goiás had to negotiate its fragility and to promote on national level; c) the members of the Victims Association, distinctly called themselves victims for a number of reasons, among them the compensation for material loses, health monitoring programs, and to call attention.

It is also important to recall that the definition of population affected by the disaster depends upon particular social actors' understanding of illness and the definitions change through time. In this way this study comes close to MARGARET LOCK's (1994) comparative study on disputes in both North America and Japan associated with organ transplant technology. She claims that there is a correlation between organs transplant option and individuals' death definition. She pursuits her argument demonstrating that the option for transplant is defined by the cultural construction of the death related to social and political order. In North America there is actually a remaking of the death with an increasing medicalization of the mortality and the individuals shared idea of making death useful. In contemporary Japan, there are contested attitudes toward new technology, brain death and organ transplants. She argues that this debate is intimately linked to a widespread ambivalence about the process of Japanese modernization. She concludes, the debate is not really about human suffering, however, but is a manifestation of the struggle by people from a whole range of political persuasions to create a moral order for Japan. In the United States the talk is about commodification of human parts and it calls attention to the flow of organs from the poor to the rich,

Biomedical Discourses and Health Care Experiences:

from the third world to the first world. In Goiânia, the various and controversial definitions of population affected by the radiological disaster and the claims for knowledge production reveal political struggles between various spheres of government, economic pressures and information control more than an actual concern with the well-being of the population affected by the radiological disaster.

The Domestication of Knowledge and the Production of Silence

In 1991, NUAC, the Federal University of Goiás research center was discontinued due to lack of financial support. Then, the local economy already recovered from the impact of the disaster. Consequently, the ruralist leaders like the city business persons withdrew their financial support to advance knowledge on radiation issues. According to NUAC documents, the common effort carried by the University center and Goiás economic sectors was restricted to the emergent phase, when they encountered the visibility of radiation on the decrease commercialization and consumption of their goods. Also, the research financing foundation called Financiadora de Estudos e Projetos—FINEP, whose headquarters are in Rio de Janeiro, approved eight out of twelve projects submitted to appreciation. Nevertheless, the resources were never delivered. Thus, the compromise of NUAC in understanding the environmental, social and health impact of disaster in order to inform the community and help the population to face the 'unknown' was never totally accomplished.

According to CNEN words "Decontamination was undoubtedly the most resource intensive (sic) element in the response to the disaster." (AIEA1988: 80). By the middle of 1988, CNEN decontamination work ended and other activities were initiated as the monitoring of the storage site and research activities. CNEN professionals produced a large number of works on Goiânia disaster, published articles, participated in various international conferences, accomplished academic research for obtaining master's and PhD degrees along with the orientation of students since some professionals work also as professors in Brazilian universities. According to a CNEN director, who was strongly engaged in Goiânia emergent phase, the institution acquired a great experience and developed an important knowledge about the effects of Cesium-137 on the environment and on human bodies. By 1996, Goiânia post-disaster is no more a major research topic at CNEN. The same professional told me that they have answers for all the issues they were concerned with. The idea of 'everything is under control;' 'disasters happen but the radioactivity can be controlled' persist in the aftermath of the Goiânia disaster. Initially, the institution controlled spaces and bodies contaminated to process the major task of decontamination. Later, the CNEN Goiânia office major task is to assure to the local population that Goiânia is a safe place to live: the nuclear waste dump project turned on Abadia Ecological Park, a site planned to be "a tourist attraction" (The New York Times 1995); the institution develops some children's educational project that aims to present the useful aspects of radioactivity. Nevertheless, during some conferences delivered in Goiânia's elementary schools, the professional answers to the children's concern about the health effects of the Goiânia disaster and the health conditions of the affected population do not fit the level of knowledge acquired through the research already developed. In fact, CNEN domesticated contaminated spaces and bodies as they domesticated the disaster experience, but they do not deal with the affected population's everyday questions on health issues.

Almost ten years after the Goiânia radiological disaster, the medical follow up activities is the Leide das Neves Ferreira Foundation responsibility. The number of individuals classified as the affected population increased since a new category was created, named as F.1 and associated to Group II from the initial medical protocol (see footnote 5). This new class incorporates around 40 children: a) children from pregnant mothers at the disaster occasion (intra-uterus life); b) children already born when the disaster occurred; c) children born after the disaster from radioaccidented parents. However, the number of individuals under the monitoring and health care programs decreases: a) One group was cut down from the initial medical protocol[9] b) the current Group III, formed by professional who worked in the accident and by people who lived near the areas contaminated by the Cesium-137 source is not receiving health care from the Foundation. From one hand, some patients chose a private doctor due to personal reason as the stigmatization of the Leide das Neves Ferreira Foundation as a site of treatment. By the other hand, the institution cut down all the researches under progress and limited the area of activities. The Foundation's structural crisis due to internal conflicts (NETO 1994) is worsened when many professionals resign.[10] Those experts had gotten a great deal of experience with the disaster and could not easily be replaced. But again, the major issue here is the way political and economic factors interfere on the health care of the population affected by the disaster. Since the beginning, the foundation's board of directors was decided by strictly political party criteria. That is, each time the head of state government changes, every four years, the new elected governor replaces the foundation president. Consequently, the foundation never advances on its design project; the board habitually does not have any experience with the disaster itself or related issues; the foundation restrains the activities at the minimum of giving health care to a restricted number of individuals. At the same time, the current state government idea of regional modernization with the enlargement of industrial sector strives against the recollection of a radiation disaster. The dramatic cut down of the foundation revenue is a concrete expression of this thought.

After a successful effort in getting some radiation patients to undertake health treatment in Cuba, it appears as though Victims Association has chosen to remain in silence. The first president of the organization retreated from any disaster related issue; most of the active members do not want to talk about the Goiânia Radiological disaster. In spite of the grassroots organization's silence, individuals' voices claiming for cancer cases growth are heard in areas close to spaces contaminated by the Cesium-137 source. At 57th street, inhabitants have reported eight cancers related deaths. According to the Foundation Medical Protocol those individuals are classified on the Group-III. When the institutional medical authorities were asked about the correlation between the radiological disaster and the cancer cases, they immediately rejected any connection at all. However, the dissent must be built on the knowledge arising from epidemiological studies done on the population belonging to the Group-III. Are the Goiânia biomedical specialists truly concerned with this

---

9. In 1996 the medical protocol for medical follow up is different from the one published in 1988 (see note 5):
"*The victims were divided, for medical follow up, in three groups, as follows:*
Group I—56 patients (35 males and 25 females) 4 deaths.
Patients with cytogenetic dosimetry above or equal 0,2 Gy, with radiodermatitis and internal contamination above or equal to 50Mci.
(...)
Group II—46 patients (26 males and 29 females)
Patients with cytogenetic dosimetry below 0,2 Gy, without radiodermatitis and internal contaminal below 50 Mci.
(...)
Group III—515 patients (263 males and 252 females)
People who live near the areas contaminated by the Cesium-137 source. The professional who worked in the accident. This group of people did not undergo any cytogenetic dosimetry but some of them had a whole body count." (CURADO 1995: 5).
10. Up to nine psychologists at the beginning of the Foundation's activites, there is only one in early 1996.

VWB – Verlag für Wissenschaft und Bildung

group in terms of a research topic or is the answer just a matter of political issue? In the international sphere, the literature shows an increasing concern with late effects of low dose of radiation (BERTELL 1985; Children and Radiation Conference 1993, Norway). Thus Goiânia biomedical investigators seem to have a unique opportunity to contribute to a contemporary international debate as long as they establish a real dialogue with the population affected by the radiological disaster.

In spite of physical immediate and/or late mutation on human bodies due to radioactivity, I argue that everyday claims, narratives, and experiences of radiation disease patients are an important element in characterizing the effects of radiation disaster on peoples health. Finally, I believe that a study that combines the analysis of different discourses with the practices undertaken by different actors is fundamental for the definition of a health monitoring program. In fact, the effectiveness of the politics of health care offered by governmental state agencies depends upon the understanding of various definitions of the population affected and the political economic forces that through historical times produced knowledge and engage voices and silence.

Note

(Footnote 5—continued)
The FUNDAÇÃO LEIDE DAS NEVES classified the patients who needed to receive clinical observation in four groups (REPORT OF ACTIVITIES 1988):

"Three groups receive medical observation, of which thee first will be considered of 54 individuals who were contaminated. The second group will be formed by 50 individuals. According to the suggestion given by Dr. Alexandre de Oliveira, the adopted standards for the inclusion of the individuals in the groups to erceive medical observation, were considered by the Nuclear Regulatory Commission and Energy Research and Development Administration from the USA, for significant doses of radiation.
1. Whole body dose, osseous medula and gonods—0.25 GY (25 rads)
2. Superficial dose (skin) of extremities—6 GY (600 rads)
3. Thyroid dose or other (sic) organs—0.75 GY (7 rads)
4. Corporal ativity-equivalent to $^1/_2$ LIA (annual limit of incorporation) for Cesium-137, respecting the rates.
So, 4 populations are receiving medical observation defined as Group I, II, III, IV.

A) Group I (54 people)
Standards
1. Patients with radiodermites and/r
2. Dosimetry of the whole body—20 rads and/or
3. Corporal activity equivalent to 1/2 LIA = 50 MCI
Protocol
1. Monthly clinical consults, during the 1st year after the accident;
2. Laboratorial exams of routine (platelets, hemogram, and EAS) every 2 months up to the 2nd year;
3. Semestral complete biochemistry;
4. Mielogram every 6 months;
5. Medula biopsy every year;
6. Spermogram twice in the 1st year;
7. Immunological status—annualy after exposition;
8. Cytogenetic dosimetry twice a year until the 3rd year after exposition;
9. Back of yee—twice a year;
10. Other exams; according to medical indication (tomograph, resonnance, cytogenetic, cintilography).
11. Photographs of the radiolesions every fortnight.

B) Group II (50 people)
Standards
Relatives or contactents of the direct victims, whose register of irradiation do not reach the registers of group 1 (20 rads; LIA; 50 MCI) without radiodermites.
Protocol
1. Clinical consults every 4 months;
2. Laboratory exams of routine every 4 months until the 2nd year;
3. Other exams: according to medical indication.

C) Group III (ca. 300 people)
Standards
Professionals that worked and work with material contaminated by the Cesium-137 or with patients irradiated or contaminated by the Cesium-137 (Id)
Protocol
1. Annual clinical consults;
2. Annual laboratory exams of routine; (hemograms, EAS);
3. Other exams: according to medical indications;

D) Group IV (500 people)
Standards
Neighbor (sic) population of the 7 first (sic) contaminated points written below:
1. Roberto's house — Rua 57, no. 68
2. Ovidio's house — Rua 63, no. 19
3. Rua 26-A and Rua 15 — Dump yard I — Devair
4. Rua 6, Qd. Q Lt. 18 — Dump yard II — Ivo
5. Rua P-19, Lt. 04 — Dump yard III — Joaquim
6. Rua 17 Qd. 70-A Lt. 2613 — Ernesto Fabiano
7. Rua 16-A, no. 792 — Sanitary Vigilance"
(LEIDE DAS NEVES FOUNDATION 1988)

Acknowledgements

This research is supported by Wenner-Gren Foundation for Anthropological Research — Grant N1 5969.

References

ASSOCIAÇÃO DAS VÍTIMAS DO CÉSIO-137. *ESTATUTO.*
    1988   *Nota de Esclarecimento.* Goiânia. 03/20/88.
    1989   *Histórico da Luta da Comunidade Atingida pelo Acidente com o Césio-137 em Goiânia.* Junho/89.
    1990   *Manifesto. "Três Anos de Agonia e Dor."* Agosto de 1990.
BERTELL, R.
    1985   *No Immediate Danger.* Toronto: Women's Press.
BURDICK, J.
    1992   Rethinking the Study of Social Movements: The Case of Christian Base Communities in Urban Brazil. In: *The Making of Social Movements in Latin America: Identity, Strategy, and Democracy.* Edited by ARTURO ESCOBAR & SONIA E. ALVAREZ, pp. 171-184. Boulder, San Francisco, Oxford: Westview Press.
    1993   *Looking for God in Brazil: The Progressive Catholic Church in Urban Brazil's Religious Arena.* Berkeley, Los Angeles, London: University of California Press.
COMAROFF, J.
    1993   The Diseased Heart of Africa: Medicine, Colonialism, and the Black Body. In: *Knowledge, Power & Practice: The Anthropology of Medicine and Everyday Life.* Edited by SHIRLEY LINDENBAUM & MARGARET LOCK, pp. 305-329. Berkeley: University of California Press.
CURADO, M.P.
    1995   *Health Care for Cesium-137 Accident Victims in Goiânia-Brazil.* Paper presented at the International Symposium on the Commemoration of the 50th Year of the Atomic Bombing. Hiroshima. October 1995.
DE CERTEAU, M.
    1988 [1984] General Introduction. In: *The Practice of Everyday Life*: XI-XXIV. Berkeley and Los Angeles: University of California Press.
FERNANDES, C.R.D.
    1990   Atendimento Psicossocial às Vítimas. In: *I Simpósio Internacional sobre o Acidente Radioativo com o Césio-137 em Goiânia.* Goiânia, 28 a 30 de Setembro de 1988. Anais.Goiânia. Fundação Leide das Neves Ferreira.
FOUCAULT, M.
    1972 [1969] *The Archeology of Knowledge and The Discourse on Language.* Alan Sheridan Smith, Transl. New York: Pantheon.
GALE, R.P.
    1988   Treatment of Radiation Victims in Brazil. *Science* 239(4838): 335.

HARAWAY, D.
    1993   The Biopolitics of Postmodern Bodies: Determinations of Self in Immune System Discourse. In: *Knowledge, Power & Practice: The Anthropology of Medicine and Everyday Life.* Edited by SHIRLEY LINDENBAUM & MARGARET LOCK, pp. 364-410. Berkeley: University of California Press.
HEALTH PHYSICS
    1988   Abstracts of Papers presented at the *Thirty-Third Annual Meeting of the Health Physics Society.* July 4-8, 1988, Boston, Massachusetts, USA. Vol. 54. Supplement: S61-S-64.
INTERNATIONAL ATOMIC ENERGY AGENCY
    1988a *The Radiological Accident in Goìânia.* Vienna: International Atomic Energy Agency.
    1988b Radiation Sources: Lessons from Goiânia. *IAEA Bulletin* 30(4):10-17.
KUIPERS, J.C.
    1989   "Medical Discourse" in Anthropological Context: Views of Language and Power. *Medical Anthropological Quarterly* 3(2): 99-123.
LEIDE DAS NEVES FERREIRA FOUNDATION
    1988a *Projeto de Cadastramento das Pessoas Envolvidas Direta ou Indiretamente no Acidente Radioativo de Goiânia.* Fundação Leide das Neves Ferreira. Goiânia, maio/88. (Mimeo.)
    1988b *Relatório de Atividades* (July).
    1988c *Report of Activities* (Dossier), (September)
    1989   Information Bulletin. Year 1, No. 1. April/89. Goiânia. Brazil.
    1990   *Histórico do Acidente Radioativo com o Césio-137.*
    1990   *Lições do Acidente com o Césio-137 em Goiânia.*
LOCK, M.
    1993   The Politics of Mid-Life and Menopause: Ideologies for the Second Sex in North America and Japan. In: *Knowledge, Power & Practice: The Anthropology of Medicine and Everyday Life.* Edited by SHIRLEY LINDENBAUM & MARGARET LOCK, pp. 330-363. Berkeley: University of California Press.
    1994   *Displacing Suffering: the Reconstruction of Death in North America and Japan.* Paper prepared for a conference on Social Suffering, Bellagio. July 1994.
NASH, J. & M. KIRSCH.
    1988   The Discourse of Medical Science in the Construction of Consensus Between Corporation and Community. *Medical Anthropology Quarterly* 2(2): 158-171.
NETO, S.B. DA C.
    1994   *Fatores do Processo de Tomada de Decisão da Equipe de Sadde numa Instituição de Tratamento a Irradiados por Fonte Ionizante: Um Estudo de Caso.*Thesis for Master's degree. Brasília. D.F.: Instituto de Psicologia da Universidade de Brasília.
The New York Times
    1995   *Tourist Site Springs From a Nuclear Horror Story.* Wednesday. May 3: 4.
NUAC
    n.d.   *Proposta de Implementação das atividades do Núcleo.* (Particular Archive)
PETTERSON, J.S.
    1988   Perception vs. Reality of Radiological Impact: The Goiânia Model. *Nuclear News.* November: 84-90.
RAPP, R.
    1988   Chromosomes and Communication: The Discourse of Genetic Counseling. *Medical Anthropology Quarterly* New Series 2(2): 143-157.
ROBERTS, L.
    1987   Radiation Accident Grips Goiânia. *Science* 238(4830): 1028-1031.
SCHEPER-HUGHES, N.
    1993 [1992]. *Death Without Weeping: The Violence of Everyday Life in Brazil.* Berkeley, Los Angeles, Oxford: University of California Press.
SCHEPER-HUGHES, N. & M. LOCK
    1987   The Mindful Body: A Prolegomenon to the Future Work in Medical Anthropology. *Medical Anthropological Quarterly.* New Series 1(1): 6-41.
SUSSER, I.
    1985   Union Carbide and the Community Surrounding It: The Case of a Community in Puerto Rico. *International Journal of Health Services* 15(4): 561-583.
VINCENT, J.
    1974   The Structuring of Ethnicity. *Human Organization* 33: 375-80.

The Symbolic Geopolitics of Syphilis:
An Essay in Historical Anthropology
SÉRGIO CARRARA

> *All of us have inherited through our Portuguese blood
> a large dose of lyricism. And of syphilis, of course.*
> Chico Buarque and Ruy Guerra

Abstract

This article analyzes some scientific conceptions that Brazilian physicians, particularly syphilographers, developed in relation to syphilis. Particularly in the 1920's, they constructed a uniquely Brazilian version of the disease, as they debated with foreign specialists the origin, symptoms, and incidence of the disease in Brazil. With their formulations they transformed syphilis into a sort of natural symbol, through which they expressed both their claims to a prominent position in the international scientific community and their effort to place the country in the hierarchy of nations, denying that it was forever doomed to backwardness and barbarism because of its hot climate and racially mixed population.

Zusammenfassung

Dieser Artikel analysiert einige wissenschaftliche Konzepte, die brasilianische Ärzte in Bezug auf Syphilis entwikkelt haben. Speziell in den 20er Jahren haben sie eine einzigartige brasilianische Version dieser Krankheit konstruiert, während sie mit ausländischen Spezialisten die Herkunft, Symptome und das Vorkommen in Brasilien diskutierten. Mit ihren Formulierungen haben sie die Syphilis in eine Art natürliches Symbol verwandelt, das sowohl ihren Anspruch auf eine besondere Position innerhalb der internationalen wissenschaftlichen Gemeinschaft ausdrückt, als auch das Bestreben, Brasilien seinen Platz unter den Nationen zu sichern.

Keywords: syphilis, history of medicine, Brazil

Introduction

In the context of Western history, few diseases pose as many interesting issues for historical and socio-anthropological reflection as syphilis. Problems of all kinds arise when we consider the huge scholarly production focusing on the disease ever since it appeared in Europe in late fifteenth century. In its nearly totemic reality, syphilis has always been 'good to think' about the way 'scientific discoveries' are produced,[1] the relations between diagnostic or therapeutic techniques and nosology, the possible compromises between scientific thought and certain moral imperatives and social categorizations, the ethical implications of scientifically-oriented action, the international division of scientific labor, and so on.[2]

Indeed, the universe of syphilis is immense, but I have no intention of perpetuating the notion that specialists in syphilis—syphilographers—have successfully defended since the late nineteenth century: the idea that syphilis is a kind of 'total disease,' attacking every organ in individuals of

---

1. It should be observed that the forerunner of modern socio-anthropological analyses of scientific discourse and practices was precisely a study of syphilis. I refer to a book by LUDWKI FLECK (FLECK 1986 [1935]), who developed his ideas on the basis of an analysis of the German bacteriologist AUGUST VON WASSERMANN's 1906 'discovery' of a serologic test that detected the presence of *Treponema palidum*—considered the agent causing syphilis—in the blood of contaminated persons.
2. Some of these issues have been explored by such historians and social scientists as ALLAN BRANDT (1985), CLAUDE QUÉTEL (1986), and ALAIN CORBIN (1977, 1981, 1982, 1988), among others.

both sexes, every race and every age bracket. On the contrary, my intention is to study a quite specific topic, which I have analyzed at greater length elsewhere (CARRARA 1996). My theme is the way Brazilian syphilographers established the peculiarities of the disease in Brazil from the late nineteenth century through the mid-1940's, and used it as a means for considering the position of Brazil in the concert of nations and—particularly from the 1920's on—attempting to place their country in the context of the so-called "civilized" world. For this purpose, I shall briefly review the dialogue—not always explicit—between Brazilian physicians, particularly syphilographers, and their colleagues abroad.

Throughout the entire historical period examined here, this dialogue focused on three major themes. The first is the idea that syphilis originated in the New World and should therefore be seen as an autochthonous disease in Brazil. The second is the notion that syphilis was hugely disseminated in this country, in comparison with others, due to certain biological, social, and moral features that were peculiar to Brazil. And the third is the idea that these features were partly responsible for the uniquely terrible symptoms that supposedly characterized the disease in the country. Thus, as the Brazilian documentation I have examined makes clear, from the viewpoint of the international syphilography of the period, syphilis in Brazil was to be seen as not just an age-old heritage but also, with its wide dissemination, a sort of attribute of Brazilians, in whom its effects were singularly terrible and crippling.

My object is then the way Brazilian physicians responded to this generic characterization. I shall give particular emphasis to the decisive role played by syphilis since the 1920's in a shift that took place in the endless debates on the causes of the degeneration of the Brazilian people. Whereas at first the culprit was commonly held to be racial miscegenation and the eugenically pernicious effects of interbreeding between Latin races (such as the Portuguese colonizers) and peoples of even 'inferior' stock, sexual pathology came to be increasingly identified as the actual cause, so that a speedier and surer 'redemption' for Brazil seemed to be possible.

A Foreign Disease

At present, most authorities believe that syphilis was unknown in the Old World before the late fifteenth century, but its geographical origin is still a matter of controversy (MACNEILL 1976). No disease has inspired as much heated dispute over its source as syphilis. Because it was one of the most stigmatizing of all maladies, no people or nation was willing to accept the dubious distinction of being considered its birthplace; this 'privilege' was always conferred on the enemy.[3] Wrote a Brazilian syphilographer in the 1920's:

> "No one wants syphilis, as a guest or as a neighbor, let alone as a historical legacy or family patrimony. Its very condition as an undesirable, rejected everywhere, is an obstacle to the establishment of the facts of its history throughout the centuries" (ALMEIDA 1925: iii).

Before it became more or less firmly entrenched during the first half of the twentieth century, belief in the notion that syphilis originated in America and made its insidious way to Europe on Columbus' ships seems to have depended on acceptance of a specific view of the disease. For those—

---

3. Syphilis was always considered a disease of the 'other', the 'foreigner'. Here are direct translations of some of the names it has gone under in Portuguese: American disease, Canadian disease, Celtic disease, Naples disease, Bay of Naples disease, Christian disease, Scottish disease, French disease, German disease, Illyrian disease, Gallic disease, Polish disease, Turkish disease, Portuguese disease. Apparently the most common terms in Brazil until the nineteenth century were *mal-venéreo* (venereal disease) and *mal-gálico* (Gallic disease), often shortened to *gálico*.

and they were many—who believed that syphilis arose by a sort of spontaneous generation in the context of sinful or inordinate sexual behavior, it was difficult to accept that its roots were in America. Sin, after all, was as old as the world itself, and sexual excesses were not a prerogative of Amerindians; thus there seemed to be no plausible reason to think that the ancients were unacquainted with this scourge. As a Brazilian physician wrote in the mid-nineteenth century,

> "If nature intended to punish those who violated its laws by inflicting them with syphilis, for certain it would not have awaited the Discovery of America to cast its fatal blow on offenders, for centuries before the Discovery there lived the Caesars, and Neros, and Heliogabaluses, and Messalinas, and such others prodigies of debauchery" (LIMA 1849: 2).

Up to the turn of the century, even after the relation between syphilis and immorality had come to be seen as indirect, mediated by contagion, the moral significance of the disease was still used as an argument against the so-called American hypothesis. Thus, another Brazilian doctor wrote that many still doubted the American origin of the disease because

> "the Americas have never provided the most obscene instances of corruption, such as those presented by the Old World" (PIRES DE ALMEIDA 1902:77).

The American hypothesis was also to be ruled out if syphilis was a modified form of an older disease, such as leprosy, or the product of astrological or climatic conjunctions, or a mere inflammatory phenomenon.[4] Thus, although not all contagionists believed in the American hypothesis, all who held that syphilis originated in the New World necessarily saw it as a contagious disease. It may well be that, after the 'Pasteurian revolution,' which ensured the victory of the contagionists, confirmation of the American hypothesis was inevitable.

Nineteenth-century Brazilian doctors apparently held widely varying views. Whereas eminent figures believed syphilis was native to the continent,[5] others were already clearly pointing to the discriminatory and stigmatizing nature of the American hypothesis. Some of these authors stated that Europeans, the Spanish in particular, in order to excuse their "treatment of the unfortunate Americans," convinced

> "... the people and even a considerable number of illustrious physicians that pure, innocent America, a land that knew no baseness, where customs were austere, had brought syphilis to corrupt, lustful Europe" (LIMA 1849: 2).

As the American hypothesis came to be increasingly accepted over the first half of the twentieth century, Brazilian syphilographers, a community that grew ever larger and more powerful, undertook an important task in symbolic geopolitics. They set out to demonstrate that syphilis, though of American origin—as was held by such great European specialists as the French physicians ALFRED FOURNIER and E. JEANSELME—was unknown in Brazil before the Discovery. For, as the most important Brazilian syphilographer of the period, EDUARDO RABELO, put it in 1918, syphilis had been "grated onto our virgin soil and transmitted to our wholesome race, in spite of our will" (RABELO 1921: 325). RABELO had no doubt that syphilis had been brought from the Greater Antilles to Europe by Columbus, as the French masters believed. He wrote in a 1925 article:

---

4. The physiological theories of BROUSSAIS and his disciples won many followers in Brazil in the first half of the nineteenth century. As they accepted these theories, they came to believe that syphilis was not contagious, but was caused instead by an irritation of the sex organs, which subsequently spread to the rest of the system. The cause of this irritation was repeated sexual intercourse or sex in supposedly unsanitary circumstances, particularly with menstruating women.
5. One of these, the French physician JOSÉ FRANCISCO XAVIER SIGAUD, who settled in Rio de Janeiro, defended the American hypothesis in his *Du climat e des maladies du Brésil*. According to the most important historian of Brazilian medicine, this work is "the best and most substantial nineteenth-century treatise on the state of medicine in the country" (SANTOS FILHO 1991: 15).

"This is the view expressed by virtually all writers of the time—chroniclers, historians, friends and foes of the Indians, in particular the physicians who, since the return of Columbus' fleet, began to describe, with astounding unanimity, the 'morbus novus,' 'inauditus,' 'ignotus' that, passing from America to Spain, devastated France and Italy as a clear-cut epidemic, just as in these days we still witness the propagation of syphilis in certain European overseas possessions, previously untainted. Proof that it was unknown is given by the fact that it had no name, and for this reason was successively called the Spanish disease, the French disease, the Neapolitan disease, until Fracastoro's poem gave it the name that has stuck to the present day" (RABELO 1921: 325).

But RABELO could not accept that the disease was native to Brazil. To prove his point, he quoted sixteenth-century chronicles and the first systematic observations, then being made, of Brazilian Native peoples, who at the time were still isolated. According to RABELO, all the early chroniclers "were unanimous in their praise of the Indians' skin." It was only in the writings of authors of the latter half of the sixteenth-century (ANDRÉ THÉVET, JEAN DE LERY, GABRIEL SOARES DE SOUZA) and later observers that references were to be found of diseases that might possibly be manifestations syphilis or yaws[6] among Native populations, which by then were in regular contact with Europeans and Africans. In addition, according to contemporary observers who were penetrating the hinterland, such as CÂNDIDO RONDON, MURILO DE CAMPOS, OLÍMPIO DA FONSECA FILHO, and ROQUETTE PINTO, syphilis was unknown among Indian populations that were still isolated.

Also in the 1920's, the thesis that syphilis did not exist in Brazil before the Discovery found a vehement defender in another major Brazilian syphilographer, OSCAR DA SILVA ARAÚJO. In a long, well-grounded discussion of the issue, Araújo questioned the sources used by those who believed otherwise (ARAÚJO 1928). The eminent Professor SIGAUD, writing in the mid-nineteenth century, had defended the American hypothesis on the strength of a text by an eighteenth-century Portuguese traveler, RIBEIRO DE SAMPAIO.[7] This work was clearly of fundamental importance, for it dealt with the Rio Negro area in northern Brazil, the region nearest to the Caribbean. Quoting SAMPAIO, ARAÚJO shows that the symptoms he describes were wrongly identified as syphilitic by SIGAUD because at the time—the mid-nineteenth century—syphilis had not yet been clearly differentiated from other skin disorders and venereal diseases. Thus it seemed most likely that syphilis had been introduced only after the arrival of the Portuguese, either through contacts with other American peoples or, more probably, by European colonists who were already infected.

However, other syphilographers of the period, such as TEÓFILO DE ALMEIDA, still defended the thesis that the disease had not originated in America. In this, ALMEIDA wrote ironically in 1925, he agreed with those North American researchers who "renounce the claim that America was the birthplace of syphilis, even if the exact spot is in the Caribbean" (ALMEIDA 1925: 3). In any case, Brazilian physicians quickly adopted the idea that syphilis had been brought to the country by Europeans (especially the French, and also Portuguese convicts)—in other words, as ARAÚJO observed, that in Brazil, more than in any other country in the world, it was true that "civilization is syphilization."

---

6. The identification between yaws and syphilis provoked sharp disputes in Brazilian medical circles towards the end of the nineteenth century. Apparently the controversy was settled only after 1905, when CASTELANI 'identified' the agent supposedly responsible for yaws, also known as frambesia. This agent was said to be another treponema, *T. pertenue*, morphologically identical to the spirochete that caused syphilis, which, though it could also be treated with mercury, was not sexually transmissible. Yaws occurred particularly in tropical zones in America, Africa, Southeast Asia, and Oceania (BECHELLI 1976: 809).
7. According to the anthropologist NÁDIA FARAGE, RIBEIRO DE SAMPAIO, justice-general of the Rio Negro Captaincy, wrote about two travels in the extreme North of Brazil, one on the Negro River in 1775 and one on the Branco River in 1777 (FARAGE 1991).

This notion spread fast through the dense net formed by Brazilian and foreign specialists at this time, so that soon it was echoed abroad. In the mid-1920's, for instance, it was espoused by the director of the German Society for the Struggle Against Venereal Diseases, H. ROESCHMANN, in his comparative study of the fight against VD in various countries. About Brazil he wrote:

> "As to the genesis of syphilis, the most widely held view is that it was brought to Europe from North America in Columbus' fleet; to South America it was taken by the Portuguese, and it was disseminated among the inhabitants who came into contact with settlers, particularly the coastal populations. As to the people in the hinterland, they remained completely unblemished for a long time" (ROESCHMANN 1929: 37).

As we can see, in the 1920's Brazilian syphilographers managed to pull off an amazing feat: to hold that syphilis was both an American disease, as was believed by European authorities, and a European scourge, as Americans would have it. This curious situation seems to express, on the symbolic plane, the position that Brazilian syphilographers (and, more generally, Brazilian doctors) held in the international hierarchy of specialists: though dependent in relation to European centers, they already had enough power to produce original scientific thought. It also seems to symbolize the place claimed for Brazil in the hierarchy of nations. Surely there were countries even poorer and politically weaker—in the Caribbean, for instance—that could uncomplainingly shoulder the blame for being the source of the disease. Thus the speculations of Brazilian syphilographers concerning the origin of syphilis helped to set Brazil apart from these other nations, and thus to bring it closer to the 'civilized world.'

As we shall see, a similar development took place in relation to another point over which there was disagreement between Brazilian doctors and their European colleagues: whether or not manifestations of syphilis were exceptionally malignant in the tropics.

A More Benign Syphilis

In the late nineteenth century, it was believed that syphilis was a much more serious affliction in hot climates, to the point that it constituted a specific variety in such places, known as exotic or tropical syphilis. As a Brazilian author wrote in the early 1920's, on the basis of the climatic hypothesis

> "Lacapère, among others, found major differences between the symptoms of syphilis in European and Moroccan patients. In the latter, skin and bone lesions of extreme severity predominated over visual and nervous lesions" (GURJÃO 1922: 299).

In the early decades of the twentieth century, as the number of Brazilian syphilographers increased, belief in the malignity of tropical syphilis was progressively eroded. This process seems to have taken place particularly through the differentiation of various diseases whose symptoms were similar to those of syphilis. First yaws was distinguished from syphilis. Then, largely on the basis of medical research done in Brazil, other differentiations were established, so that doctors began to discriminate between syphilis and other tropical diseases affecting the skin. EDUARDO RABELO wrote in 1925:

> "At the time when syphilis, leishmaniosis, granuloma inguinale and phagedenic ulcer were still confused, it was believed that syphilis was a more serious illness in our climate than in other regions" (RABELO 1925: iii).

In 1928, ARAÚJO reaffirmed the idea that the 'myth' of the malignity of Brazilian syphilis could largely be put down to 'misdiagnosis':

> "Patients in our country suffering from crippling diseases were classified as syphilitic. Now we know that these were not serious cases of atypical syphilis, but rather of leishmaniosis, blastomycosis, granuloma inguinale, and so on" (ARAÚJO 1928:69).

Referring specifically to Rio de Janeiro, ARAÚJO wrote that, although the incidence of syphilis was indeed of 'striking proportions,' its symptoms did not fundamentally differ from those of European syphilis, and "its evolution was not more severe than what is usually the case in other countries where the climate is cold or temperate" (p. 28). If syphilis occasionally had crippling effects in the country (particularly in some areas of the Northeast), Araújo argued, this was because the populations involved had undergone less miscegenation and therefore had until then been less exposed to infection. Among these populations, syphilis had the same devastating effects it had had when it appeared in Europe in the late fifteenth century.

Eventually, in the 20s and 30s, using more reliable figures, syphilographers were led to the conclusion that syphilis in Brazil not only presented features that distinguished it from the tropical or malign model, constructed on the basis of observation of African cases, but was on the whole much more benign than European syphilis. In 1938, relying on extensive statistics, the syphilographer HENRIQUE DE MOURA COSTA could confidently write:

> "There are striking differences between the situation in our country and the descriptions by European scholars. Nor can the cases observed in our country be compared to what authors describe as so-called tropical or exotic syphilis" (COSTA 1938: 129).

It seems, then, that as regards syphilis—as indeed in so many other respects—Brazil slowly carved out for itself a niche midway between Africa and Europe. What perhaps is most important here is the fact that Brazil could not possibly have had its very own brand of syphilis, both foreign and benign, if it had not had a number of good syphilis researchers interested in reaching such a conclusion. Similarly, there could not have been good syphilographers in the country if there were not a more or less solid background in syphilography and science in general, which in turn required minimal material and institutional conditions. In the 20s, such conditions seemed to exist in Brazil, at least in the major urban centers.

"Is There a Brazilian Who Is Not Syphilitic?"

As ARAÚJO observed in 1928, the high incidence of syphilis in Brazil, particularly in Rio de Janeiro, had been underscored by reliable authors since the eighteenth century (ARAÚJO 1928:11). In addition to quoting chroniclers who talked of the 'dissolution of mores' and of the widespread occurrence of venereal disease, ARAÚJO observed that in 1798 the Senate of the Rio de Janeiro City Council had made an inquiry in order to determine which endemic and epidemic diseases were most common in the city. Three doctors working in Rio were questioned, and two of them stressed the incidence of venereal diseases. The passages quoted by ARAÚJO show clearly how the perception of the prevalence of these diseases was directly associated with judgments concerning the low morals of the population. Said one of the physicians questioned:

> "Moral and dietary causes have a great influence on the illnesses of the country. Of old it was said that consumption, now so common in Rio de Janeiro, was extremely rare here, as were diseases of the skin. Now, if this matter is investigated more fully, it will be seen that all of these diseases are complicated by the presence of venereal vice. The wealth of this respectable city has led to the introduction of luxury and moral depravity. So it is that there are brothels in the city, where youths spoil their health, corrupt the morals they acquired in a sound upbringing, and contract and spread new diseases" (quoted in ARAÚJO 1928: 12).

The other physician who mentioned venereal disease relied on a line of argument that, in different forms, was to survive well into the twentieth century. This was the notion that slavery was the cause of debauchery, because prostitution was the

"... inevitable consequence of idleness and wealth that is not the fruit of labor, and also of the familiar example of slaves, who know scarcely any other laws than those of nature" (p. 12).

In the mid-nineteenth century, in his treatise on the climate and diseases of Brazil, SIGAUD wrote that "syphilis has existed in the country in every period, *and is now a major disease*" (quoted in ARAÚJO 1928:17; emphasis added). At the same time, certain authors began to point to syphilis as the cause of the 'premature old age' which, according to some, was characteristic of Brazilian youth (AZAMBUJA 1847:3). The concern with syphilis increased in the 1860's, and the illness is often mentioned in annual reports of provincial health inspectors as the one that, together with tuberculosis, intestinal affections, and agues, "does the most harm to the less prosperous populations" of the Empire, to quote the Bahia health inspector of the time (p. 3). Also, the proportion of hospital beds occupied by syphilitic patients began to be computed. According to an article published in a provincial medical journal, the *Gazeta Médica da Bahia*, in 1871, "in order to realize the proportions that syphilis has unfortunately reached among us" all that need be done was to examine hospital statistics: in the 1861-1866 period more than one third of patients in the surgery wards of the Santa Casa de Misericórdia, a hospital for paupers in Rio de Janeiro, suffered from venereal disease (ANONYMOUS 1871: 26). The article went on to say that these figures

"... clearly point to the growth of venereal diseases among us, and suggest that, as this growth continues, since no measures have been taken to neutralize its dire consequences, it will soon reach immense proportions" (p. 26).

Under the impact of the Paraguayan War (1865-1870), the same warnings began to be heard in military circles, and by the 1870's the high incidence of syphilis and other venereal diseases among the troops was raising concern.[8] In 1873, JOÃO JOSÉ DE OLIVEIRA JUNQUEIRA, War Minister of the Empire, said that venereal disease was the most common complaint among soldiers, immediately followed by diseases "of the respiratory and the digestive systems" (quoted in ARAÚJO 1928: 24). The physician JOSÉ DE GÓES SIQUEIRA FILHO estimated that, in 1872-1873 period, one-third of the troops quartered in Rio de Janeiro were contaminated (p. 24). Ten years later, in 1883, in a paper presented at the Imperial Academy of Medicine, the military physician JOSÉ DE OLIVEIRA wrote in an even more alarmed tone:

"While tuberculosis causes the largest number of deaths in the Brazilian Army, and while the victims of gastric disturbances are equally numerous, venereal and syphilitic diseases are even more common. *One may confidently say that there is not a single soldier who has not been treated for venereal disease at a hospital at least once.* In peacetime, Army surgeons are constantly treating cases of gonorrhea, chancre, and bubo. Secondary and tertiary syphilis, exostosis, and rheumatism run rampant" (p. 23; emphasis added).

By the latter half of the nineteenth century, physicians' concern was no longer restricted to Rio de Janeiro. In 1866, Professor CLAUDEMIRO CALDAS wrote in the *Gazeta Médica da Bahia* that "the overwhelming majority of patients in the surgical clinic of the Bahia Medical School are victims of syphilis" (CALDAS 1866: 89). And at the turn of the century, the renowned psychiatrist JULIANO MOREIRA observed that they had said a number of times that "syphilis is strikingly common in Bahia," adding that in Brazil as a whole the disease was "widening its terrible sway every day" (MOREIRA 1899: 113). Apparently the disease was also widespread in São Paulo, where, according to the puzzling estimates of a doctor in the early years of the twentieth century, about 30,000 new cases of syphilis occurred each year, a number equivalent to 10 percent of that population (SOUZA 1909: 7).[9]

---

8. This may have been partly due to the fact that the war disseminated the disease widely among soldiers, or the fact that military doctors began to give it more serious thought.
9. SOUZA arrived at this horrendous figure on the basis of the estimated number of prostitutes living in the city and the number of potentially contaminating sexual encounters they probably had per year.

Thus, since what few statistics existed were quite unreliable, turn-of-the-century doctors grounded their warnings mostly on their own clinical experience and on hospital figures. It is true that, in their estimates of the expansion of the disease in the country, some of them also relied on common sense, which saw Brazil, as MOREIRA observed in 1899, as the ideal home of syphilis. According to him, in Brazilian families it was common for any complaint to be diagnosed as 'the Gallic disease.' Both lay persons and doctors, he wrote, had a tendency to 'widen the circle excessively,' identifying as syphilis "the most insignificant parasitic dermatoses, the most trivial cases of acne, the most obvious instances of blepharitis, the simplest conjunctivitis." It was quite common to hear people say: "Is there a Brazilian who does not have a bit of syphilis?" (MOREIRA 1899: 113).

To MOREIRA, this popular formula, though of course it was 'an exaggeration,' was 'a clear sign of the dissemination of the disease' (p. 113).

Though they had a dissenting position as to the American hypothesis and the notion that syphilis was particularly malignant in the tropics, and though they played an important role in the task of distinguishing syphilis from certain tropical diseases existing in Brazil, the Brazilian syphilographers of the first half of the twentieth century helped to perpetuate the belief—which was already received wisdom at the time—that the disease was extraordinarily widespread in Brazil. Since it was only in the 1940's that cases of syphilis began to be reported by law and that unanimously accepted standardized criteria for diagnosis were developed, all kinds of statistical speculations were possible—and every one of them tended to reinforce this belief. In addition, the disease's Protean nature—its multiple symptomatic manifestations—fueled heated controversies as to what the ideal criteria were for defining a given symptom as syphilis. Some used a clinical criterion that took in an enormous diversity of diseases and congenital or hereditary abnormalities. Others relied exclusively on blood tests that not only were (by our present standards) quite fallible but also allowed different interpretations. In particular, the results of the traditional Wassermann test fell in a continuum ranging from 'strongly positive' to 'strongly negative.'[10]

Obviously, it is not our purpose here to arrive at a true account of the prevalence of syphilis in Brazil. However widely these figures might vary, they always pointed to the generalized perception that Brazil was the ideal place for syphilis. And the notion that all Brazilians were syphilitic sometimes justified the attitude that statistics were really unnecessary when it came to determining the actual incidence of the disease in Brazil. So it was that a physician in the early twentieth century could write:

"As to syphilis and venereal diseases, in Brazil there is hardly any use for statistics, for one might say that the approximate number of patients is the population of the country. An exaggeration? Not at all" (SOUZA 1909: 6).

In the First South American Congress of Dermatology and Syphilography, held in Rio de Janeiro in 1918, the clinician OSCAR CLARK stated, in the beginning of his paper, that

"... the high incidence of lues in Brazil is a historical fact, and even foreigners who travel around our country are led to the conclusion that every Brazilian is syphilitic" (CLARK 1921: 188).

---

10. In her recent history of the WASSERMANN test, ILANA LÖWY writes that "a positive test was viewed—in particular in the first period of enthusiasm for the new method—not as a diagnostic aid, but as an infallible proof of treponemal infection" (LÖWY 1993: 19-20). When, after World War II, new tests were devised that made it possible to detect the presence of the treponema itself in the bloodstream, it was found that the WASSERMANN test gave positive results for countless other diseases, and that for certain populations the number of false positive results might be immense. Thus, LÖWY concludes, "thousands of persons which today would be false positive were diagnosed with syphilis. They suffered not only from the psychological and social consequences of syphilis diagnosis—fear, guilt, shame and social opprobrium—but also from the severe toxic effects of the standard antisyphilitic treatments" (p. 20).

It was this supposedly terrible situation that, up to the 1920's, motivated physician's demands for measures against the disease and criticisms of the inaction of the successive republican governments. When the first nationwide anti-syphilis campaign was started in 1921, the alarm over statistics subsided significantly. But though some measures were taken, mandatory reporting of cases of syphilis was not one of them, so that doctors and syphilographers still had no access to reliable figures. During the 1920's, it became accepted that about one-fifth of the Brazilian population was contaminated. This percentage, considered extraordinarily high, was to remain unchanged up to the early 1940's. The figure was used as early as 1921 by the eugenicist RENATO KEHL in the first educational lecture promoted by the recently created Inspectorship for the Prevention of Leprosy and Venereal Disease. After observing that without mandatory reporting it was impossible to have reliable figures on syphilis, KEHL, drawing on the work of authoritative syphilographers, most notably EDUARDO RABELO, estimated that there were approximately six million syphilitics in Brazil, or about 20 percent of the national population. The number of victims of gonorrhea was, he believed, "without exaggeration," a bit smaller, about 4.8 million, or 16 percent of the population. In contrast, KEHL noted, in "civilized countries" the rates were much lower, and syphilis affected no more than 10 percent of the population.[11] And he added:

"Those who hear me may well think this is an unduly pessimistic view of Brazil's health situation. But I must assure you, on the basis of the conclusions of eminent and indisputable scientists, that unfortunately such is indeed the case" (KEHL 1921: 38-39).

In 1934, when the anti-VD campaign started in the previous decade was discontinued, the alarm over statistics once again stepped up, and Brazil's "syphilized" condition was reaffirmed. One indication of this is an article by EMÍLIO FARO, a physician in the Portuguese Navy, published in the medical journal *Jornal de Sífilis e Urologia*. Faro states that a large part of the population of Portugal is contaminated and that Europeans tend to think that every Portuguese is syphilitic. Then he comments:

"We Portuguese have been deeply affected—formerly because of the great voyages to the East and South America, more recently because of mass emigration to Brazil. There syphilis is so prevalent that one may well say that whoever has lived in the country for some time is undoubtedly syphilitic" (FARO 1934: 184).

In 1940, during the First National Conference for Defense Against Syphilis, held under the dictatorial regime of GETÚLIO VARGAS, specialists made a new effort to estimate the number of affected persons. They concluded that the malady still had a solid foothold in the country, resisting all attempts to contain it, and that it should be seen as a continuing decisive factor responsible for the degeneration of the Brazilian race.

---

11. In order to justify his statement about "civilized countries," KEHL mentioned figures that were in fact quite higher. Quoting FOURIER, he said that in France 13 to 16 percent of the adult population had syphilis; for Germany, BLASCHKO (1906) had estimated that 18 percent "of the bourgeois class" was infected; and for the U.S., DAY & MCNITT had arrived at the following figures: 6 to 13 percent of the "bourgeois classes," 20 percent of "poor whites" and 30 percent of "poor blacks" (KEHL 1921: 33). As to gonorrhea, KEHL wrote that, in the U.S. and Germany, 80 percent of adult men were believed to have contracted the disease before turning 30, and 70 to 95 percent of the prostitutes either had once had gonorrhea or were still infected. In Brazil, he added, since there were no campaigns against prostitution and for the use of prophylactic methods, gonorrhea probably affected 70 to 90 percent of the adult male population and 100 percent of the prostitutes. In Rio, he said, 90 percent of adult men had contracted the illness at least once (pp. 46-47).

Lust, Race, and Pathology

It seems to me quite clear that the perception of Brazil as a country of syphilitics was a corollary of the more general idea that Brazilians were particularly given to sexual excesses.[12] Up to the 1930's, a unique conjunction of climatic and racial factors was used as a strong argument to support the myth of Brazilian lustfulness. Since the beginning of the nineteenth century, at the latest, it was believed that warm climates favored debauchery, by bringing on early puberty. Race also had an influence on sexual appetite. This point is emphasized by the French physician JULIEN JOSEPH VIREY in a study of sexual incontinence and its dangers, where he states that "all Africans from the torrid zone seem to have the fire of concupiscence in their very blood" (VIREY 1836: 54). The same idea is implicit in a Brazilian doctor's 'discovery' that, in Haiti,

> "... concupiscence has to such a degree enfeebled the species that many settlements in the region have been either depopulated or degenerated by the scourge of syphilis" (PIRES DE ALMEIDA 1902: 20).

Though to a lesser degree, Latin peoples, such as the Portuguese, were also noted for their sexual ardor. The Brazilian hygienist AFRÂNIO PEIXOTO wrote in 1913 that sexual abstinence was "a hygienic and moral practice that, among Latin peoples, is transgressed so often that its observance is almost the object of ridicule" (PEIXOTO 1913: 99). So it was that, until the 1920's, many physicians resorted to such climatic and racial hypotheses in order to explain the sexual excess that supposedly characterized Brazilians and was responsible for the enormous dissemination of syphilis in the country.

But whereas the notion of Brazilians as oversexed was to survive more or less intact to the present, by the 1920's its underlying assumptions began to be questioned, particularly racial ones. For instance, in this decade ARAÚJO wrote that several North American authors still believed that syphilis was much more frequent among blacks, since their were sexually more precocious, and another Brazilian syphilographer EGAS MONIZ DE ARAGÃO, in Bahia, had pointed to the "simian, boundless concupiscence" of Brazilian blacks as the reason why extragenital chancres were so common among them.[13] ARAÚJO forcefully rejects MONIZ DE ARAGÃO's 'exaggerated' views, arguing that since the late nineteenth century statistics showed that, in Rio de Janeiro, extragenital chancres were most common among whites, particularly the Portuguese. Hence, if there were 'sexually hyperesthetic' persons, they belonged to the white or near-white part of the population that had come from the Northern Hemisphere and that, as we have seen, around this time was being seen as responsible for the introduction of syphilis in Brazil.

Though it surfaced sporadically until the 1940's, the climatic hypothesis also began to come under attack in the 1920's. In 1922, for instance, an editorial of the medical journal *Folha Médica*, discussing sex education, discarded the hypothesis, arguing that "if the sun's rays bring more heat, on the other hand the basal metabolic rate is lower" (*Folha Médica*, Year III, No. 24, Dec. 5, 1922, p. 279). Thus the greater nervous excitability which allegedly characterized Brazilians began to be

---

12. Well into the twentieth century, such disparate authors as PAULO PRADO, NINA RODRIGUES, GILBERTO FREYRE, and AFONSO ARINOS DE MELO FRANCO still mentioned sensuality or concupiscence as a distinctive trait of the Brazilian national character, or at least one of the nation's major characteristics (LEITE 1983; PARKER 1991). If, as the historian LAURA DE MELO E SOUZA notes (SOUZA 1993), Brazil was born under the sign of the devil, as a land of sin, it could not help but be the land of syphilis as well.
13. Extragenital chancres (for instance, around the mouth or anus or on the hands) were usually seen as signs of unorthodox sexual practices, since the ulcer indicated the place where the *Treponema* had invaded the organism. Because it was commonly believed that the search for 'perverse pleasures' — that is, the transgression of sexual norms — was caused by excessive normal intercourse and the consequent exhaustion of the pleasure extracted from it, the conclusion was that the incidence of extragenital chancres was a good indicator of the sexual excesses of an individual or social group.

attributed mostly to the 'lack of training in self-control' that distinguished them particularly from Anglo-Saxons. It was therefore a problem that might be solved by a sound educational and sanitary policy. The editorialist went on to say:

"We must reject once and for all the demoralizing notion that we are doomed to vegetate forever in inferior forms of civilization" (p. 279).

Indeed, beginning in the 1920's Brazilian syphilographers would tend to give particular emphasis to the influence that social and moral factors—ignorance, poverty, an immoral environment, the legacy of slavery, and so on—supposedly exerted on 'sexual needs,' generating excesses. These factors, which governed the intensity, constancy, and diversification of supply and demand in the sex market, were seen as ultimately responsible for the fast diffusion of syphilis in the country. Most importantly, these causes—unlike such biophysical factors such as race and climate - could be altered more quickly and effectively by means of enlightened action, which would allow the country to develop toward 'higher forms of civilization.' But though they increasingly believed in the possibility of 'redemption,' syphilographers left the myth of Brazilian sexual hyperesthesia fundamentally unchallenged.

Brazilian syphilographers, then, on the whole tended to accept their European mentors' belief in the widespread occurrence of the disease in their tropical country. However, this acceptance led to certain secondary gains for their effort to relocate Brazil in the concert of nations. Together with the notion that syphilis was prevalent in the country, the belief in the disease's hereditary character[14] was a significant factor in the shift away from the traditional emphasis on the racial degeneration of the Brazilian people, so that during the 1920's the issue of miscegenation was gradually replaced by the problem of sexual pathology.[15] If Brazilians were degenerate, this was not due to any constitutional factors, but to disease, mostly syphilis, and this situation could be changed rather quickly.[16]

Perhaps the most radical and influential instance of this shift is *Casa-grande & senzala* [English translation: *The Masters and the Slaves*], published by the famous Brazilian sociologist GILBERTO FREYRE in 1933. This work may be seen as unmistakable proof of the overwhelming impact of 1920's syphilography on subsequent social thought. There are numerous references to syphilis in the book, and FREYRE draws freely on the historical works of OSCAR DA SILVA ARAÚJO. FREYRE paraphrases ARAÚJO when he writes that Brazil became 'syphilized' long before it was 'civ-

---

14. According to CORBIN, it was fundamentally on the authority of two French authors, ALFRED FOURNIER and his son Edmond, that doctors began to ascribe to syphilis "virtually every sort of malformation or monstrosity" (CORBIN 1977: 249), thus making the disease anthropologically relevant. FOURNIER, says CORBIN, heralded "the golden age of syphilis teratology" (p. 249).
15. Although this was the dominant trend, it should be mentioned that in the two major centers of medical thought of the period there were still significant controversies in the 1920's over the importance of miscegenation as the cause of the country's problems. Writes the anthropologist LILIA M. SCHWARCZ: "The physicians at the Rio de Janeiro Medical School affirmed their originality and identity discovering tropical diseases ... Meanwhile, in Bahia doctors did the same by pointing to racial mixture as both our great evil and our supreme difference" (SCHWARCZ 1993: 90).
16. At this time, the call for a struggle for the salvation of the Brazilian race by means of an attack on VD, started by syphilographers at the turn of the century, seems to have been taken up by eugenicists such as RENATO KEHL, forensic-medicine experts and hygienists such as AFRÂNIO PEIXOTO, LEONÍDIO RIBEIRO, and RODRIGUES DÓRIA, and psychiatrists such as ANTÔNIO AUSTREGÉSILO, JULIANO MOREIRA, and HEITOR CARRILHO. Founded by GUSTAVO RIEDEL in Rio de Janeiro in 1923, the Brazilian League of Mental Hygiene saw the fight against syphilis as one of the principal means to reach its ultimate goal: prevention of mental disease in Brazil (COSTA 1981). In 1921, KEHL joined the anti-VD struggle saying that syphilis "destroys not only the individual but also his offspring, and being detrimental to the race poses a major national danger" (KEHL 1921: 7). In 1929, anti-VD campaigns were among the main topics discussed in the First Brazilian Eugenics Congress, held in Rio (STEPAN 1990: 119).

ilized,' and in a discussion of 'social influences' says that 'syphilis may have been, next to malnutrition, the one that had the most deleterious effect on the body and economic energy of the Brazilian hybrid race' (FREYRE 1954 [1933]: 161). He writes:

> "The advantage of miscegenation in Brazil was accompanied by the enormous drawback of syphilization. As the former began to shape the Brazilian—perhaps the ideal type of the modern man for the tropics, a European invigorated by black or Indian blood—the latter began to deform him. Here lies the source of the confusion of attributions that has led many to ascribe to miscegenation what is in fact largely a consequence of syphilization, and to point to the black, the Amerindian, or even the Portuguese race—each of which has produced, in its pure or unmixed state, countless admirable specimens of beauty and physical vigor—as the sources of the 'ugliness' and 'unfitness' of our hybrid populations that are most affected by syphilis or verminosis" (p. 161).

From the 1920's to the early 1940's, the views of syphilographers seemed perfectly compatible with the Neo-Lamarckism that characterized most of Brazilian thought on heredity, in contrast with the situation in such countries as the U.S. and Germany. As the historian NANCY STEPAN pointed out in a recent work, in Brazil and other Latin countries—but not in the Anglo-Saxon world—eugenics meant, above all, sanitation. This, writes STEPAN, is because most Brazilian eugenicists, hygienists, and physicians were 'influenced' by French authors, who were Neo-Lamarckians—that is, they believed that acquired characteristics were heritable. Thus the solution for Brazil's 'racial problem' was centered on the combat against the epidemic and endemic diseases that afflicted the country, the nefarious consequences of which were transmitted to succeeding generations, bastardizing them—a notion that made sense within a Neo-Lamarckian framework.

This intellectual framework made it possible to argue that, if Brazil was a degenerate country, the reason was not climate or miscegenation, as HENRY THOMAS BUCKLE and J.-A. GOBINEAU had affirmed and Brazilian thinkers such as NINA RODRIGUES had believed since the nineteenth century (CORREA 1982). Brazilians were indeed biologically inferior, but this was not an innate condition: it was rather a case of situational inferiority. Within a few generations Brazil could be eugenically redeemed and purified, if only the right sanitary and educational policies were carried out. The races that made up the population would then exhibit their positive attributes, which were only momentarily masked by the harmful effects of certain diseases, such as syphilis, and pernicious habits, such as the sexual excess that caused it.

The growing strength of the hypothesis that the 'Brazilian problem' was largely caused by syphilis rather than by miscegenation contributed to a certain scientific optimism that, according to STEPAN, was typical of the effort undertaken by the Brazilian elite to free the country from the stigmatizing notion that it was doomed to backwardness and barbarism because it was a hot land with a racially-mixed population. In this context, syphilis—which, according to STEPAN, was an important factor in the survival of Neo-Lamarckian ideas around the world[17]—certainly had a strategic value in Brazil. Together with the belief in the extreme diffusion of the disease in Brazil by the sexual excess that characterized the population, the notion that syphilis had hereditary characteristics was largely responsible for the fact that the fight against degeneration in Brazil was carried out mostly in the form of sanitary campaigns that, instead of attempting to eliminate or steril-

---

17. After saying that Neo-Lamarckism prevailed in medical circles in the first half of the twentieth century, STEPAN adds: "The continued reliance on scientifically refined Lamarckian ideas by physicians in these decades reflected not their stupidity or ignorance, but rather the seeming intractability of certain problems in human pathology. Take, for example, the impact of parental venereal diseases on the offspring. Did the child of such parents suffer in 'fitness' and was this unfitness transmitted by heredity? Was there not a 'hereditary-syphilitic' condition? This was the view of the majority of physicians in France, where Lamarckian views had wide currency and the Lamarckian eugenics movement developed" (STEPAN 1990: 120).

ize the biologically 'unfit,' as happened elsewhere in the Western world, tried to cure the diseases that afflicted them.

Examining other sources on the history of medicine and science in Brazil, STEPAN concludes that it was precisely in the 1920's that what she calls 'realistic nationalism' emerged: Brazilians

"... began to reject their traditional dependence on European values and knowledge, and to seek ways to reinterpret their own racial and climatic condition so as to provide themselves with a more optimistic view of Brazil, in keeping with what they believed to be the country's immense natural resources and special racial make-up" (STEPAN 1990: 128-29).

Indeed, Brazilian syphilographers gave a significant contribution to the consolidation of a body of social thought with strong nationalistic appeal, which attempted to value the country's non-European heritage rather than see Amerindian and African roots as the sole sources of all the nation's evils. Just as the essayist PAULO PRADO was stating, in his influential *Retrato do Brasil*, that Brazilians had inherited from the Portuguese the traits of melancholy, greed, and lasciviousness (PRADO 1931), syphilographers were adding syphilis to the list. They also observed, as we have seen, that the forms of the disease found in Brazil were much more similar to the symptoms of European syphilis than to those of the African variety. Finally, as doctors reinforced the notion that Brazil was exceptionally 'syphilized,' they not only consolidated their self-appointed role as saviors of the Brazilian race and nation but also ensured a perception of their sanitary campaigns as adequate and effective means to this end.

References

ALMEIDA, T. DE
  1925   Da origem não americana da syphilis, *Anais Bras. Dermat. Sifil.* 1(7).
ANÔNIMO
  1871   Da freqüência das moléstias syphiliticas no Rio de Janeiro e da necessidade de adoptarem-se medidas que attenuem seus estragos, *Gazeta M* 5(99-101).
ARAÚJO, O.S.
  1928   *Alguns commentários sobre a syphilis no Rio de Janeiro*. Rio de Janeiro: Empreza Gráphica Editora Paulo Pongetti & Cia.
AZAMBUJA, A.C.N. D'
  1847   *Conselhos práticos sobre os meios de prevenir e curar immediatamente as moléstias venéras, precedidos de noções geraes sobr a hisória, propagação, e modo de produção da syphilis em lingugem adaptada à intelligência de todas as classes da sociedade*. Paris: Typ. Fain e Thunot.
BECHELLI, L.M.
  1976   Bouba. In: *Doenças infecciosas e parasitárias*. Edited by R. VERONESI (6th ed.). Rio de Janeiro: Ed. Guanabara Koogan.
BRANDT, A.M
  1985   *No Magic Bullet—Social History of Venereal Disease in the United States since 1880*. New York/Oxford: Oxford University Press.
CALDAS, C.
  1866   Ligeiras considerações a cerca des principaes theorias syphilográphicas. *Gazeta Médica da Bahia* 1(5): 8, 14, and 18.
CARRARA, S.
  1996   *O tributo a Vênos: A luta contra a sífilis no Brasil, da passagem do século aos anos 40*. Rio de Janeiro: Ed. Fiocruz.
CLARK, O.
  1921   Syphilis no Brasil e suas manifestções ciscerais, *2° Boletim do VIII Congresso Brasileiro de Medicina, do 1° Cogresso Sul-Americano de Dermatologia e Sifilografia etc*. Rio de Janeiro: Imp. Nacional.
CORBIN, A.
  1977   Le péril vénérien au debut du siècle: prophylaxie sanitaire et prophylaxie morale. *Recherches*, No. 29, December.

1981 L'hérédosyphilis ou l'impossible rédemption. Contribution à l'histoire de l'hérédité morbide. *Romantisme—Revue du Dix-neuvi*, No. 31.
1982 *Les Filles de noces*. Paris: Flammarion.
1988 La grande peur de la syphilis. In: *Peurs et terreurs face a la contagion—choléra, tuberculose et syphilis— XIXe. et XXe. si.* Edited by BARDET; BOURDELAIS; GUILLAUME; LEBRUN & QUETEL. Paris: Fayard.
CORREA, M.
1982 *As ilusões da liberdade: a escola Nina Rodrigues & a antropologia no Brasil*, tese dout. Dep. Ciências Sociais da Fac. Filosofia, Letras e Ciências Humanas—USP.
COSTA, H.M.
1938 Aspectos e particularidades da sífilis no Brasil—parte especial, *Anais Bras. de Dermat. e Sifilog.* XIII(34).
COSTA, J.F.
1981 *História da psiquiatria no Brasil* (3th ed., revised). Rio de Janeiro: Campus.
FARAGE, N.
1991 *As muralhas dos sertões—Os povos indígenas no rio Branco e a colonização*. Rio de Janeiro: Paz e Terra/ANPOCS.
FARO, E.T.
1934 Profilaxia das doens venéras na marinha de guerra protuguesa. *Jornal de Syphilis e Urologia* 5(54).
FLECK, L.
1986 [1935], *La génesis y el desarrollo de un hecho científico—introducción a la teoría del estilo de pensamiento y del colectivo de pensamiento*. Madrid: Alianza Editorial.
FREYRE, G.
1952 [1933], *Casa grande & senzala—formação da família brasileira sob o regime de economia patriarcal*. Rio de Janeiro: Jos
GURJÃO, H.
1922 A prostituição em Belém: suas causas, localização, fiscalização e assistência médico-sanitária. In: *A prophylaxia rural no estado do Pará*. Edited by H.C. DE S. ARAÚJO. Belém: Typ da Liv. Gillet.
LIMA, J.T. DE
1849 *Breves consideraçãoes acerca da origem da syphilis*. Rio de Janeiro: Typ. Brasiliense de F. M. Ferreira.
KEHL, R.
1921 *O perigo venéro—conferência realizada no dia 25 de julho de 1921, no salão da Associação dos Empregados do Commércio*. Rio de Janeiro: Dep. Nac. de Saúde Publ. e Inspectoria de Prophylaxia da Lepra e das Doenças Venéras.
LEITE, D. M.
1983 *O caráter nacional brasileiro—história de uma ideologia*, (4th ed.). São Paulo: Pioneira.
LOWY, I.
1991 Testing for Sexually Transmissible Diseases. In: *AIDS and Contemporary History*. Edited by V. BERRIDGE & P. STRONG. Cambridge: Cambridge University Press.
MACNEILL, W.H.
1976 *Plagues and Peoples*. New York: Doubleday.
MOREIRA, J.
1899 A syphilis como factor de degenera. *Gazeta M* 31(1).
PARKER, R.G.
1991 *Corpos, prazeres e paixões—a cultura sexual no Brasil contemporâneo*. Rio de Janeiro: Best Seller.
PEIXOTO, A.
1913 *Elementos de Hijiene*. Rio de Janeiro: Francisco Alves.
PIRES DE ALMEIDA, J.R.
1902 A libertinagem no Rio de Janeiro perante a história, os costumes e a moral. *Brazil-Médico* 6(3-47).
PRADO, P.
1931 *Retrato do Brasil—Ensaio sobre a tristeza brasileira*. Rio de Janeiro: F. Briguiet & Cia.
QUÉTEL, C.
1986 *Le Mal de Naples—Histoire de la syphilis*. Paris: Seghers.
RABELO, E.
1921 Orientação acutal da lucta contraa a syphilis, *2° Boletim do VIII Congresso Brasileiro de Medicina, do 1° Congresso Sul-Americano de Dermatologia e Sifilografia etc*. Rio de Janeiro: Imp. Nacional.
1925 Existia a syphilis na época do descobrimento?, *Anais Bras. de Dermat. e Sifilog*. 1(1).
ROESCHMANN, H.
1929 A luta contra as doenças venéreas na Allemanha em coparação com as medidas adoptadas em outros países. *Anais Bras. de Dermat. e Sifilog*. 5(12).

SANTOS FILHO, A.
 1991 *História geral da medicina brasileira. 2.* São Paulo: Hucitec/EDUSP.
SCHWARCZ, L.M.
 1993 *O espetáculo das raças: Cientistas, instituições e questão racial no Brasil, 1870-1930.* São Paulo: Companhia das Letras.
SOUZA, C. DE
 1909 *Da responsabilidade civil e criminal do syphilítico,* Publicade Prophylaxia Moral e Sanitária. São Paulo: Typ. Hennies Irmãos.
SOUZA, L. DE M. E
 1993 *O diabo e a Terra de Santa Cruz.* São Paulo: Companhia das Letras.
STEPAN, N.
 1990 Eugenics in Brazil, 1917-1940. In: *The Wellborn Science—Eugenics in Germany, France, Brazil and Russia.* Edited by M.B. ADAMS. New York: Oxford University Press.
VIREY, J.J.
 1836 *Dissertação acerca da incontinência e seus perigos em relação às faculdades intellectuais e physicas.* Rio de Janeiro: Typ. Nacional.

Personal Improvement, National Development:
Theories of AIDS Prevention in Rio de Janeiro, Brazil[1]

Sean Patrick Larvie

Abstract

This paper analyses and compares models for AIDS prevention in Rio de Janeiro, Brazil. Based on neo-behaviorist learning theory and behavioral epidemiology, Brazil's National Program on Sexually Transmissible Diseases and AIDS proposes a model which conceptualizes the problem of 'risk behaviors' in terms which emphasize individuals' knowledge and behavior. The second model, native to the hybrid environment of professional psychology in Rio de Janeiro, locates the risk of transmission in a complex psycho-social matrix and proposes personal and political transformations as keys to risk reduction. This paper focuses on the tension between these two theoretical models for the management of risk for HIV infection and sexually transmissible diseases. This paper will also explore the ways in which these models theorize the projects of modernization and development, issues which have concerned public health interventions in Brazil since the beginning of the twentieth century.

Zusammenfassung

Dieser Artikel analysiert und vergleicht verschiedene Modelle der AIDS-Prävention in Rio de Janeiro, Brasilien. Das Nationale Programm Brasiliens für sexuell übertragbare Krankheiten und AIDS, basiert auf der neo-behavioristischen Lerntheorie und einer behavioristischen Epidemiologie. Es favorisiert ein Modell, welches ‚Risikoverhalten' als individuell determiniert definiert. Das zweite Modell stammt aus dem hybriden Milieu professioneller Psychologie in Rio de Janeiro. Es sieht das Risiko einer Ansteckung in einer komplexen psychosozialen Matrix und schlägt persönliche und politische Veränderungen als Schlüssel zur Risikominderung vor. Dieser Artikel analysiert die Spannung zwischen diesen beiden theoretischen Modellen, die das Risiko einer HIV-Infektion bzw. ovn sexuell übertragbaren Krankheiten behandeln. Es wird zudem untersucht, wie in beiden Modellen die Projekte der Modernisierung und Entwicklung theoretisiert werden. Diese Themen beschäftigen das brasilianische öffentliche Gesundheitswesen seit Anfang der 20er Jahre.

Keywords: AIDS, psychological models, urban Brazil

Brazil's National Program on Sexually Transmissible Diseases and AIDS was established by government decree in 1986, but its current structure was determined only after the approval of a financing agreement with the World Bank in 1993 (World Bank 1994). In proposing preventive action as its primary strategy for containing epidemics of HIV and other sexually transmissible infections, the Program articulates medical and non-medical knowledge and techniques in an attempt to both improve the health of Brazilians and to modernize the nation's public health system. In this paper, I will compare two approaches to prevention: that proposed by the Brazilian National Program on STD's and AIDS, and that of the psychologists and social workers charged with the task of administering prevention initiatives in the state of Rio de Janeiro. The National Program provides basic frameworks and funding for state and municipal initiatives. A team of professionals working in the state program of Rio de Janeiro, most with backgrounds in psychology and so-

---

1. A preliminary version of this paper was presented in the working group "Pessoa, Corpo e Doença" at the XXth Meeting of the National Association of Post-graduate Social Science (ANPOCS) held in Caxambu, MG, Brazil in October of 1996.

cial work, coordinate and provide technical support for prevention initiatives throughout the state. As gatekeepers to financial and technical resources, and as consultants to and evaluators of prevention programs, these professionals exercise an important role in defining some of the most basic concepts which inform anti-AIDS initiatives in the state. They are called upon to operationalize the model for prevention proposed by the federal government—adapted from the World Health Organisation's Global Programme on AIDS. To do so, they draw on concepts and techniques derived from the hybrid field of professional psychology and from their collective history of activism.

In the past decade anthropologists have focused on the AIDS epidemic in Brazil as paradigmatic of the challenge of creating public health policies which take into account the multiple meanings of sexuality and risk in Brazilian society. PARKER (1988, 1992) has argued that Brazil's sexual culture is organized around the binaries male-active/female-passive, requiring a reformulation of prevention logics developed in the first world, structured according to the medicalized classificatory system of homo-, bi- and heterosexuality. Researchers such as GOLDSTEIN (1994), GUIMARÃES (1994), KNAUTH (1996) and PAIVA (1994) have suggested that the discursive construction of sexuality in Brazil tends to favor male sexual privilege, impeding discussion of the HIV related risks unique to women. Unable to acknowledge publicly or privately the extra-marital sexual activities of their male partners, these authors argue that Brazilian women are unable to admit their risk of HIV infection, largely associated with homosexuality and intravenous drug use. Most of this research was conducted prior to the elaboration of the current National Program, which presents a new context for anthropological research on the concepts of risk and prevention as they are employed in this nation-wide health initiative.

Anthropological research has also focused on the ways in which AIDS has transformed the conceptual and institutional foundations of health care delivery, research and public policy. In a study conducted with both health care professionals and 'lay' patients, MARTIN (1994) documented the multiple and shifting meanings of AIDS as an illness of the immune system. In interviews with physicians specializing in HIV related illness, CAMARGO (1992) has argued that generational and institutional factors strongly influenced the meaning of AIDS as both a sub-discipline within academic medicine and as a specialized form of clinical practice. Here, I propose to analyze the way in which the largely non-medical health care professionals charged with the task of prevention construct and operationalize concepts of risk and risk reduction. The psychologists and social workers who carry out anti-AIDS initiatives in Rio de Janeiro occupy a liminal position within Brazil's National Program. They are hierarchically distant from the positions in which formal theories and policies are developed, yet directly involved in the conception and management of the epidemic at very local levels. In this paper, I will examine one of the principal tensions within prevention initiatives, that which arises from the attempt of program administrators to adapt theoretical constructs imported by the National Program to pre-existing models of prevention and behavior change. The latter are not only quite different than the former, but are 'native' to one of the most important centers of psychology in Brazil, Rio de Janeiro.

This paper is based on fieldwork conducted in Rio de Janeiro between November of 1994 and December of 1996. My research included interviews, observations and a review of official documents at the local, state and federal levels. For the purposes of this paper, I identify two distinct approaches to prevention. The first, which I refer to here as 'imported' or 'official,' is described in the documents of the Ministry of Health, where it has undergone revisions as part of the ongoing work of the National Program on AIDS and STD's. The second I refer to as 'local,' and is characteristic of anti-AIDS initiatives in the city and state of Rio de Janeiro. As I will argue below, although similar in many ways, these two approaches are derived from distinct paradigms for understanding health, illness and the nature of positive change. Both approaches are derived from elite academic and professional discourses, and produce implicit and explicit visions of modernity and progress in which health professionals configure prominently.

The Imperative of Prevention

The AIDS epidemic hit Brazil hard. According to the Brazilian Ministry of Health, 82,852 cases of AIDS have been recorded as of June 1996, with the greatest incidence in the states of São Paulo and Rio de Janeiro. Once represented in popular and scientific discourse as an epidemic limited to upper class gay men who traveled from Rio or São Paulo to cities in the US and Europe (GALVÃO 1992; DANIEL 1991), AIDS has become a chronic health problem among virtually all urban populations and, especially, among women and the poor (GUIMARÃES 1994). Parallel to the AIDS epidemic, the public health system in Brazil suffered a series of financial crises followed by a massive restructuring in the late 1980's. In many areas of the country the public health system is often unable to meet the demand for treatment of illnesses related to HIV infection, or even to meet the basic health care needs of the population. In the past decade, health care has not been a priority for the Brazilian federal government. In 1993, per capita expenditures on health care were less than US $100 (WORLD BANK 1994; BRAZILIAN MINISTRY OF HEALTH 1993).

Since the approval of the World Bank Financing agreement, prevention programs for AIDS and sexually transmissible diseases have begun throughout Brazil, many co-administered with non-governmental organizations working within some of the communities most affected by AIDS. The Brazilian Ministry of Health's investment in the prevention of AIDS and other STD's is clearly reflected in the Program's proposed budget. Of the US $250,000,000 budget proposed in the financing agreement, over 40% of all funds are allocated to prevention, a share significantly greater than that given to any other area, including epidemiological surveillance (19%) or clinical treatment (34%) (BMOH 1993). This distribution of funds is consistent with the directives of the World Health Organization's Global Programme on AIDS, cited by the Ministry as the undisputed authority in the area and as the source of the guidelines for Brazil's National Program.

Prevention is the top priority of the National Program for two basic reasons. First, prevention is seen as the only economically feasible alternative for controlling an epidemic which has become increasingly costly to both the public health system and the national economy. Although economic losses are difficult to calculate, estimates of the direct and indirect costs of AIDS suggest that, without intervention, the epidemic would generate a loss of approximately US $3.5 billions per year, presuming a primary impact among economically active persons and a post-diagnosis life expectancy of just six months (WORLD BANK 1993a and b, 1994, 1995; BMOH 1993). Second, prevention has become the chief focus of national programs throughout the world because "... there are no effective clinical treatments or vaccines available for HIV/AIDS" (BMOH 1996a, b and c). Unable to control the epidemic through improved epidemiological surveillance or through the provision of specialized clinical services, the Brazilian Ministry of Health has attempted to develop new logics of health service provision for the prevention of AIDS and sexually transmissible infections. Overall, the National Program's AIDS prevention strategy reflects a relatively greater reliance on the action of community based organizations and volunteers than on the work of paid medical professionals. This shift in method has required a significant restructuring of the relationships between health authorities and the populations they intend to serve.

The National Program's emphasis on what I refer to as *psychological prophylaxis* reflects a new concept of public health, one which attempts to articulate medical knowledge and institutions with non-medical theories and techniques. In outlining an approach to the epidemic which is essentially psychological in nature, targeting knowledge and behavior related to risk and risk reduction, the National Program performs two important tasks. First, this strategy locates the nature of the problem, as well as the possibilities for its solution, within the bodies and minds of individuals. Second, the manner in which prevention is conceptualized within the Program as a whole identifies psychological theories and methods as key elements of a public health intervention. Historically, Brazil's sexual culture has been described as both unique and problematic, linked to the problems of 'underdevelopment' and to the nationalist projects of modernization and progress (BRAITERMAN 1996; LARVIE 1994; CARRARA 1996). The AIDS epidemic revives historical debates on the relationship between national health authorities and the sexual behavior of Brazilians. Programs which attempt to change thoughts and behaviors in order to reduce rates of HIV infection question not only concepts of risk, health and disease but also the parameters of state sponsored development programs which propose significant incursions into the sexual lives of Brazilians.

The 'Official' Model of Intervention

Elaborated by the World Health Organization (WHO 1989, 1992) and adopted by Brazil's National Program on AIDS and STD's (BMOH 1996c, 1994a, 1993), the 'official' model of intervention is rooted in a psychology developed in the United States and Great Britain which theorizes the relationship between individuals, peer groups and health related behaviors. This paradigm mixes neo-behaviorist concepts of learning and cognitive theory, on the one hand, with 'community' based techniques of intervention designed to increase the overall efficacy of the prevention initiative on the other. This model's concept of risk articulates psychological and behavioral variables with traditional epidemiological criteria. The risks deriving from behavioral factors assume two basic forms, both of which emphasize the knowledge and actions of individuals. First, risk may appear as the absence, or non-possession, of information related to the transmission of HIV. A person who is unaware of, or who cannot understand information about HIV transmission is said to be at heightened risk for acquiring the virus. 'Correct' information about how to avoid sexually transmissible infections may be confounded by 'lay' beliefs or variants from scientific concepts of germ theory or viral transmission. Second, risk may appear as a function of the impact of social or cultural factors on individual behavior. Persons who know how HIV is transmitted, who know how to prevent its transmission, but who live in societies or belong to groups in which preventive measures are negatively sanctioned or insufficiently reinforced by peers are said to lack 'an adequate social environment' thus placing them at heightened risk for AIDS and other STD's (WHO 1991; BMOH 1996).

Because prevention programs must aim to manage risk at the individual level, belief systems and social practices associated with increased risk for HIV infection within a given population must be specifically targeted, leading to a prevention strategy which is said to be 'culturally appropriate' (e.g. among 'gay men' or 'intravenous drug users').[2] Notwithstanding this link between individuals and their immediate social environment, behavioral interventions must, by design, theorize risks associated with HIV transmission as intersecting with factors intrinsically tied to the concept of the individual. Although concepts such as 'behavior,' 'knowledge,' 'self-esteem' or 'self-efficacy' do not refer exclusively to individual level theoretical constructs, they are inextricably linked to the modern concept of the individual characteristic of the social and medical sciences.

In August of 1996, the National Program on STD's and AIDS released a set of manuals to explain the concept of a behavioral intervention to those responsible for carrying out targeted prevention initiatives. The manuals propose to teach volunteers in specific 'communities' theories and techniques of behavioral intervention. These volunteers, called 'multipliers' will then train others—called 'monitors'—within their specific social/cultural groups to carry out the intervention, using both one-on-one peer counseling techniques as well as other methods which seek to transmit information to larger audiences. These manuals insist on both the feasibility and necessity of changing behaviors by providing 'correct' and neutral information based on scientific principles:

"As is known, AIDS is transmitted mostly through sexual contact (…). And, as there is still no vaccine against HIV or STD's, the only medicine is the substitution of risky situations by behaviors which present little or no risk. (…) Behavior change is always possible, since we, as human beings, are not controlled by instinct as in the case of irrational animals. We have basic necessities, such as the need to feed ourselves, to seek sexual pleasure, to rest—but all of these necessities are manipulated by culture, by the customs of each family, people or nation. Therefore, all of our behaviors, including those related to sexual and erotic attraction, may be controlled or modified (…). This intervention fundamentally seeks to transmit information and techniques about how to avoid STD's and HIV infection. It is not an attempt to change behaviors because of moral convictions or out of ethical condemnation." (BMOH 1996a: 31)

Here, both the problem—risky sexual behaviors—and the solution—their substitution for lower risk behaviors—are elaborated within a vocabulary loosely derived from behaviorist psychology and social anthropology. The metaphor of prevention as the only 'medicine' available to correct both individual and collective level risk factors is revealing of the overall logic of prevention initiatives suggested by the Ministry. Much as other clinical interventions, prevention programs are expected to provide relatively swift and demonstrable impacts upon health outcomes.

This model of prevention theorizes risk as a property which distinguishes certain subgroups from others with respect to HIV infection, understood as a hazard to the collective health of the nation. On a different level, that at which theories are required to inform methods of intervention, risk is understood as product of the interaction between individuals and their immediate social and cultural environments. This risk of infection is to be managed through changes in the knowledge and behavior of the individuals who comprise the target population. This model presupposes that humans are basically rational beings and that their thoughts and actions are determined through relatively straightforward cognitive processes. Here, risk is a function of the possession/non-possession of 'correct' or 'adequate' information which, then, goes on to inform the adoption of safer sexual practices for both individuals and groups. The social environment is understood as posi-

---

2. Some medical anthropologists have suggested that AIDS prevention programs need not attempt to manage risk at the individual level, and that attempts to do so place the rights of individuals above those of 'society.' SCHEPER-HUGHES (1991, 1994) has suggested that gay men in the United States may be responsible for the epidemic in that country because of their unrelenting pursuit of 'individualistic' civil rights. She endorses the Cuban system of mandatory testing and forced quarantine and suggests that it might be a solution for Brazil as well.

tively or negatively reinforcing the adoption of new knowledge and behaviors but not necessarily capable of determining the risks of any given individual. According to this model, while the incidence of HIV or other STD's may vary from one sub-group to another, only those variables which theorize individual level thought and behavior will be predictive of the overall risk of infection for a given group or person. While the precise content and form of the information transmitted through a prevention program might vary in order to be more 'culturally appropriate,' the proposed relationship between information and behavior remains invariant. This model suggests that health — defined as the absence of illness — is a universal and invariant value as well as a powerful motivator of individual and collective action.

This model also suggests a theory of deviance and pathology. A person who possesses and understands the 'correct' information about how to prevent transmission of STD's and whose social environment positively reinforces the adoption of new knowledge and practices will always present the behavior changes desired by the formulators of the intervention, unless that person is irrational. Because the concept of health which informs this approach is implicitly theorized as a universal and invariant value, those who do not or cannot respond appropriately to this model of intervention are understood as having inadequate control over their conscious thoughts and behavior. Something within these individuals impedes the conversion of information into behavior change and reduced risk. This block might be theorized as affective, as in the case of compulsive sexual behavior or low self-esteem. An incapacity to act on information may involve external factors such as the use of drugs and alcohol, which impair judgment. In both of these cases, the concept of 'deviance' implicit in this model refers to a reduction in an individual's capacity to exercise adequate control over thought and behavior, a characteristic attributed, *a priori*, to healthy persons.

This model also theorizes, explicitly and implicitly, ideas of progress and development. A positive outcome of a targeted behavioral intervention is signaled by changes on at least two levels. First, the groups which are defined as being at increased risk for sexually transmissible diseases and HIV must organize themselves into a functional communities for the purposes of carrying out the intervention. This organization, in itself, represents a significant change from previous logics of health care delivery in Brazil, which have traditionally emphasized the role of the state in providing health services to a given population. In essence, this aspect of a positive outcome requires that individuals who share epidemiologically significant characteristics form communities for the purposes of providing health care services to themselves, with the informal tutelage of health authorities. The community based organizations must also make the appropriate alterations in the sub-cultural environment to reinforce and sustain changes in behavior. In this sense, the idea of progress implicit in this 'official' or 'imported' model suggests the need for significant social and political reorganization of at least some segments of Brazilian society. The basic principles of change are fully consistent with the neo-liberal social policies of the Brazilian government and the World Bank, emphasizing a reduced presence of the state and a larger role for 'community' organizations.

The second type of change which marks a positive outcome for a targeted behavioral intervention occurs simultaneously on individual and collective levels. For individual behavior change to occur, scientific notions of germ theory must replace other competing ideas which may interfere in the adoption of safer sexual practices. As a corollary, behavior change will occur only when the individual in question makes a rational, cognitive evaluation of risk and chooses the sexual practice which will optimize the possibility of a positive health outcome, defined here as the absence of HIV or STD's. In this sense, this intervention paradigm seeks to install an ethos of scientific rationality peculiar to Western medical and social sciences in populations and geographic locations where a pre-existing or competing ethos is thought to exist.

In summary, the 'official' model of AIDS and STD prevention emphasizes the relationship between 'correct' or 'scientific' information and individual behavior change. The social environment can reinforce—both positively and negatively—the acquisition of new knowledge and the adoption of new behaviors and may itself be the target of prevention initiatives. Risk is understood as a product of both epidemiological and psychological paradigms for the management of health. Successful interventions are marked by community organization and changes in individual behavior occurring at a level which is epidemiologically significant. Populations which cannot be reached through this approach may include individuals who are irrational, lack the capacity to control their thoughts or behavior, or are negatively impacted by cultural dynamics which render them unable to perceive their risk or to adopt safer sexual practices.

The Framework of Interventions in Rio de Janeiro

The set of concepts, methods and techniques used by the professionals who carry out the prevention component of the National Program in the city and state of Rio de Janeiro does not constitute, in a formal sense, a theoretical or methodological model. Instead, I describe the set of ideas and practices which characterize the activities of these health care workers as a framework derived from overlapping disciplinary backgrounds, a shared political critique of the public health care system and a professional ethos which assigns political significance to the everyday paid labor of public servants[3]. I refer to this framework as 'local' not because it is unique to Rio de Janeiro or to a particular group of health care professionals working there, although this may also be true. More importantly, this framework appears in the discourse of those I interviewed as a foil to the model proposed by the National Program, represented as 'official' and as 'imported.' Numerous authors have described a culture of psychology unique to Rio de Janeiro (RUSSO 1994), or to the middle and upper middle classes of Brazilian cities (VELHO 1985). Although the professionals I interviewed were not trained in any single discipline, they were clearly influenced by this hybrid psychological culture, itself an important reference for 'alternative' health care professions and professionals in Rio de Janeiro. Because so much of the informal model which informs prevention activities is derived from commonalties among the health care workers at the state and local levels, I begin with a general description of these professionals.

The team of health care workers responsible for carrying out prevention activities in Rio de Janeiro's state program for AIDS and STD's is divided almost evenly between social workers and psychologists, with one physician specializing in community health[4]. Almost all of the psychologists have post-graduate training in some form of psychoanalysis, though none claims to be a practicing psychoanalyst. Without exception, all of those who provide prevention services for the

---

3. The monthly salary for a 'sanitarista', the category of public service employee in question, was approximately US$ 350.00 at the end of 1996. Despite the low salaries, competition for these jobs is quite stiff.
4. There are a total of 13 people working in the area of prevention in Rio de Janeiro's State Secretary of Health. Of these, nine are directly involved in carrying out the training, supervision and evaluation activities associated with the prevention component of the state program. Of these nine, four are social workers, four are psychologists and one is a gynecologist with a residency in a community health program. It is important to note that the five others not considered here are physicians, do not work directly with the state Program's "target population" and are positions hierarchically superior to the prevention team.

state describe their professional orientations as 'alternative,' or as being outside the mainstream of the disciplines in which they hold university degrees. Post-graduate specialization in public health administration, in group analysis, or in related areas of social or collective health policy mark this group as one which has opted for careers which are not only unusual but also, in the cases of the psychologists and the physician, substantially less lucrative than clinical practice. Most are in their mid to late thirties, having completed their studies during the Brazilian Military dictatorship (1964-1985) or shortly thereafter. The group includes a former organizer of a clandestine communist party during the dictatorship, a union leader and activist, former and current women's health activists and a patient's rights advocate. For many, the political significance of their work derives from both their 'alternative' professional backgrounds and a critique of the clinical relationships said to characterize the public health system. This relationship is represented as essentially authoritarian, inextricably linked to the social and political dynamics which place the physician in a hierarchically superior position relative to the patient of the public health system, frequently poor and without much formal education. According to this critique, the politically conscious public health worker must attempt to revert the dynamics of this relationship which, in turn, will help to empower not only the person seeking assistance but the entire target population. Psychological theory is called upon to theorize the way in which individuals internalize culturally or socially scripted patterns of dominance and submission, and to facilitate politically charged personal transformations.

The 'local' framework of theories and methods which inform prevention programs is structured along two basic axes. The first theorizes the individual, and is anchored in psychoanalytic and psychodynamic theories which seek to facilitate a process of personal transformation. The second theorizes the relationship of the individual to social, political and cultural spheres and draws upon diverse theoretical and practical traditions including radical pedagogy, feminist and gay liberation movements and alternative models of psychoanalytic practice. Like the intervention model proposed by the Ministry of Health, this framework seeks to effectuate change on both the individual and collective levels. Unlike the 'imported' or 'official' model, this approach understands health and health related behaviors as being fundamentally political in nature, and proposes that psychological and social processes associated with HIV infection are inherently linked to inequalities in Brazilian society.

The lack of a substantive critique of social inequities is one of the principal points of divergence between this framework and that proposed by the Ministry. Mocking what she identified as the 'simplistic' and 'shallow' concept of behavior change in Anglo-American psychology, one psychologist working for the State Program in Rio told me that: "... unless these [foreign advisors to the National Program] change their concept of citizenship, they will never be able to change behavior." The opposition between 'official' and 'local' does not simply denote the existence of two competing models, both the products of elite academic and professional discourse. For the professionals I interviewed in Rio de Janeiro, the terms 'official' or 'imported,' serve to locate the speaker within an activist political sphere, relegating the 'imported' model to a competing and opposing ideological position which evokes the specter of imperialism and first world domination of the third.

As in the previous model, the first step for formulating an intervention is to identify its target. According to this framework, interventions must target the set of historical, political, and social relations which lead to the *alienation* which is said to be the cause of practices which endanger health. It is this alienation which complicates both the perception of risk and the adoption of health promoting practices. In the context of AIDS prevention programs, alienation is frequently described as a distancing between body and mind, or as a disparity between the personal experience of intimate relationships and a politicized understanding of the nature of sexuality. Because alienation is theorized as a set of problems imperceptible to most people, AIDS prevention initiatives must facilitate personal transformations, enabling a reflection on the nature of sexuality, intimate relations and the politics of health. In other words, given that most people do not understand that they have a problem, they must undergo a process of change which will facilitate a greater personal freedom or *autonomy* with regard to decisions and practices related to health.

As befits a group of professionals who mix activist and professional logics in the elaboration of interventions, this transformation is both psychological and ideological in nature. A form of consciousness raising (*conscientização*) performs the task of preparing people to reflect on their intimate relations and to consider possible changes in their belief systems as well as in their sexual practices:

> "Prevention work is about offering a space for reflection, for thinking about 'what's my place in the world?', about the collective world of each individual person. The problem here is books, schooling, the idea of culture as a commodity. People without access to this commodity are in less of a position to think about these things ... that's why our workshops are so successful. They attract people with less money who valorize exactly this kind of space and opportunity. [Homosexual men from the lower social classes] like meetings, they break the sense of solitude and offer a safe space. The poorer you are, the more difficult it is to have access to this space." (Maurício, 33, psychologist and coordinator of prevention activities for a Rio based NGO.)

In contrast to the 'official' model's metaphor of prevention as 'medicine,' the concept of intervention appears here as a catalyst, as linked to processes and needs which originate in the social and psychological conditions of the target group. Rather than targeting problematic 'behaviors' and 'beliefs,' in this approach both the professional and the theory involved in the intervention are understood as facilitating a process of change whose outcome cannot be specified *a priori*. Virtually all of the professionals I interviewed locate the underlying problems of the AIDS epidemic in a complex social and political matrix which produces a an environment—with social, political and psychological dimensions—in which self-destructive health related decisions and practices may make sense for a given individual. This concept is termed *vulnerability*, and refers not just to behaviors or practices linked to infection but, fundamentally, to the social and political contexts in which they occur. Lack of access to formal education, poverty and homophobia, in the words of the psychologist quoted above, are the most significant factors which contribute to the vulnerability of the lower and working class homosexual population with which he was working at the time. A mixture of an alternative form of psychoanalysis together with a posture of political activism provide this framework with a theory of risk which is significantly different than that proposed by the documents of the National Program. The primary target of the intervention is not a behavior or practice but, rather, the cultural and social dynamics which constitute the very conditions of that practice of existence:

> "For women, [to reduce vulnerability] means that we'll have to work on the question of inequality and the adversities of heterosexual relationships. Monogamous women who are taking birth control pills are at extremely high risk. You have to understand the social construction of women and femininity."
> [The ideal intervention] "... would inform people about gender differences and the growth of the epidemic. It would discuss the fact that this growth [in the epidemic] is differentiated and what is behind this differentiation. In order to do this, the intervention will have to do some consciousness raising and try to prepare the way for greater autonomy. The professional will have to be able bring up the issue of the body for discussion." (Aparecida, psychologist working for the State Program)

In comparison to the concept of risk in the previous model, the notion of vulnerability offers a relatively greater analytical flexibility. The term refers to a set of political, social and psychological factors which create the conditions for the sexual and drug related practices associated with HIV infection. This concept is key, forming the foundation of not only the problem of AIDS but also the possibilities for a professional intervention.[5] This idea refers, almost invariably, to the socio-psychological matrix which is said to explain the factors which put a person in risk for HIV infection. In this sense, the term marks one of the fundamental axes of difference between the way in which the health professionals I interviewed in the city and state of Rio de Janeiro perceive the concept of prevention and the way in which they understand the 'imported' and 'official' models which come from Brasília. If the 'imported' or 'official' models seek primarily to alter knowledge and behaviors, the framework used by those I interviewed in Rio de Janeiro seeks to alter social and political dynamics. The behaviors which are most closely associated with HIV and other sexually transmissible infections are seen as epiphenomenal to these macro-scale processes.

The personal transformations proposed by this approach—marked by consciousness raising and a reflection on sexuality—are represented as at least a partial solution for the problem of the vulnerability experienced by individuals and groups. Only partial because they are meant to serve as catalysts for a process which will ultimately lead to greater *autonomy*, understood here as a relative freedom from the socio-psychological matrix which provides the conditions for practices and beliefs which might be injurious to individual health. For some, the challenges presented by the task of facilitating 'behavior change' are perhaps most clear in the case of heterosexual women:

> "The reason that many women don't like condoms has to do with the historical construction of heterosexual relationships. And you're not going to turn the tide on a historical process from one day to the next. As I said, behavior change is a question of politics." (Aparecida)

In the same way in which heterosexuality is configured as symbolic of the social and political problems which underlie the epidemic, the process of coming out among gay men appears as an exemplary solution for 'risk factors' which are simultaneously personal and political:

> "I think that people have the capacity to think, they are not dumb. Everyone has already heard of AIDS. But they're afraid, like 'gosh, I'm already homosexual, and now I have to think about this too,' It's a second coming out. For this reason, the process is easier for those who have already assumed an identity as a homosexual." (Maurício).

For the professionals I interviewed, the linking of the personal and political within the model of 'coming out' is homologous to leftist or feminist consciousness raising. Understood as a source of difficulty for prevention programs, the distance between women and their bodies requires a process of personal transformation which takes into consideration the social and historical construction of femininity and gender relations. Low-income populations who are not able to perceive or analyze the mechanisms which permit their oppression must learn to understand health as a value and as a right in order to take action towards avoiding illness. In other words, groups which have historically been denied their constitutional rights—health care being one of them—must undergo significant political and psychological changes in order to understand the value and meaning of health. The concept of personal autonomy, the desired outcome of these interventions, is predicated upon the full enfranchisement of the individual with respect to these constitutional rights. In the words of ÁLVARO MATIDA, director of Rio's state program on STD's and AIDS, without civil rights, there can be no self-esteem.

---

5. This concept is also used by the Ministry, but its use is quite different. See BMOH 1996d.

According to this framework for intervention, the social groups theorized as having increased vulnerability for HIV infection share in common a minority status. For this reason, the concepts of identity and identification are also key to the processes of transformation which are said to promote increased personal autonomy. In the same way that identification as a 'gay' is theorized as facilitating risk reduction for homosexual men, identification with and as a minority would help to mediate risk reduction and the exercise of civil rights for other vulnerable groups. 'Street children,' heterosexual women, prisoners, intravenous drug users, and adolescents all share in common inferior positions within diverse hierarchies of power and dominance. Learning to understand the historical construction of gender would then be considered an aspect of intervention whose importance is on par with that of any actual change in sexual practices.

The techniques most frequently used for prevention initiatives—workshops, experiential workshops, and group dynamics—are meant to create the space and conditions within which this aspect of personal/political transformation can occur. By creating closed environments which foster intimacy among participants, techniques such as role-playing seek to dramatize the negotiation of scripted gender and social relations. These approaches, collectively labeled 'group dynamics,' intend to awaken unconscious feelings physically or verbally within a safe environment. Unlike the 'official' model, this framework assumes that the actions of human beings are governed by both conscious and unconscious thought. And, given that this framework proposes personal autonomy as a marker of a successful program, there is no guarantee that the 'behavior changes' desired by health professionals will result from the intervention. In theory, the analytical capacities acquired in the process of personal transformation would lead to the freedom to negotiate and choose sexual and social practices, including those which might imply risk for HIV infection.

As in the model suggested by the Ministry of Health, the 'local' framework's implicit theory of risk operates on two levels. First, vulnerability derives from historically constructed inequalities, and is a part of the social and political matrix of a society organized hierarchically. Within this society, the property of autonomy—theorized as essential to the processes of thought and action related to health related practices—is distributed unevenly among persons and groups. Machismo, socioeconomic inequalities and homophobia are understood as constituting structural components of Brazilian society and as having a necessary and negative impact on the structure of intimate relations, including those sexual. This macro-level analysis identifies the lack of full citizenship—including sexual citizenship—as epiphenomenal to this social and political backdrop of social inequity. The second level on which this framework's concept of risk operates is essentially psychological in nature. The vulnerabilities which inhere in the social and political structure appear as a reduced capacity for reflection, analysis and autonomy in both thought and action. This framework presupposes that the thoughts and actions of individuals are determined through both conscious and unconscious processes. The techniques used in prevention programs attempt to make these processes conscious and explicit. In contrast to the 'official' model, the possession or non-possession of information related to safer sexual practices is understood here as a matter of secondary importance, subordinate to the individual's capacity for autonomous thought and action.

The concept of deviance is somewhat problematic, in part because this framework tends to theorize the non-adoption of safer sexual practices as essentially normative. Without an intervention into the social and political relations which structure sexuality, it would be unreasonable to expect improved health outcomes. This would be the case of, for example, heterosexual women who claim that they choose not to use condoms as a matter of personal preference. From this point of view, the choice in question—to use or not to use condoms—would most often obey the dominant logic governs heterosexual relations. In the case of men who have sex with men, it makes sense that some might opt for a concept of risk or of safety which prioritizes the need to get along in a homophobic society over the need to assume a homosexual identity and protect oneself from germs. In both cases the need to avoid a conflict of relatively greater magnitude relegates the risks associated with AIDS and STD's to a level of diminished importance. Given these assumptions, the 'local' framework would not mark as 'pathological' those persons who do not adopt a politicized identity and/or do not prioritize changes in their sexual behavior as a strategy for risk reduction.

Even though this framework resists labeling individuals or behaviors as 'pathological,' and is flexible in accounting for variations in understandings of health and risk, the 'local' model nonetheless proposes an implicit theory of deviance. Given that a successful intervention requires substantial personal transformations among members of the target population, the adoption of safer sexual practices is, in itself, an anomaly. In this sense, the 'deviants' would be those who have opted for personal and political change, who have gained autonomy. As might be expected of an 'alternative' psychology, deviance is valued and encouraged. The role of the politically conscious health professional is to facilitate deviance by mediating the processes of consciousness raising and personal transformation. This formulation suggests that society itself is essentially unhealthy and impedes the development of personal autonomy. If this model permits variation in the meanings of health and risk, it is because it understands that some persons, even after an intervention, might opt for practices different from those suggested by the Ministry of Health. As in the case of women who claim to have opted out of condom use as a matter of personal preference, the choice makes sense in its social and historical context and is not necessarily understood as pathological. The historical and social circumstances of the decision making process are. This framework suggests an ideal concept of health which I term 'variant-universal.' Its relativism is limited to an analysis of the imperfections in the social and political spheres. In a perfect world, all people would opt for safe sex of their own free will.

The 'local' framework for prevention also suggests new visions of progress and development, perhaps most evident in two of the signs of a successful intervention: the incorporation of sexuality as a term which organizes diverse realms of experience and the ideal of personal autonomy. In proposing that an understanding of the body as a nexus for social, political and psychological dynamics performs a curative function, *sexuality* imagines profound social transformations. Chief among these is the elimination of sexism, racism, homophobia and the economic inequities characteristic of Brazilian society, part of the concept's implicit critique. As an individual-level marker of a successful intervention, *autonomy* links the psychological constructs of self-efficacy and self-esteem with the juridical concept of citizenship. This concept/ideal suggests that the full attainment of the civil rights guaranteed by the constitution—including health care—requires a significant intervention into the conscious and unconscious thoughts of Brazilians. Although the paradigm employed to identify problems and propose solutions in the 'local' framework is significantly different from that of the 'official' model, they share a faith in the capacity of professionals—duly trained in theory and technique—to bring about positive change.

Self-Improvement, National Development

The National Program on Sexually Transmissible Diseases and AIDS was formulated not just to curb the AIDS epidemic but also as a national development initiative (WORLD BANK 1992; LARVIE 1995). As in previous attempts to control the spread of sexually transmitted disease or to regulate reproduction (STEPAN 1976; CARRARA 1996; HERCHMANN & PEREIRA 1994), the National Program identifies the sexual practices and customs of Brazilians as the target of an initiative meant to modernize public service and improve the health of the nation. Rather than developing an ever more elaborate public health infrastructure, the National Program emphasizes change in individual thought and action. Within this public health strategy, psychological theories and techniques play a key role. On the one hand, psychological theory identifies persons or groups whose sexual practices deviate from ideal models of health. On the other, psychological theories and techniques perform the task of conceptualizing risk and risk reduction in essentially individual terms, permitting interventions which target specific beliefs and behaviors. As elaborated by the Ministry of Health, the National Program asks citizens to organize themselves, acquire new knowledge, change their sexual behaviors and to renounce non-scientific theories of germ transmission. Risk is understood as a product of the interaction between collective level characteristics and individual traits. Those who coordinate prevention initiatives in Rio de Janeiro propose profound psychological and political transformations as the key to halting the epidemic. Risk is seen as deriving from a complex social and psychological matrix characterized by economic inequities, sexism and homophobia.

In addition to divergent theoretical constructions of risk and risk reduction, the two approaches to prevention analyzed here propose distinct visions of progress, modernity and development. The 'official' model theorizes progress as the development of an increasingly rational world in which the determinants of human behavior are both transparent and malleable. The 'lay' beliefs and 'folk' practices believed to be characteristic of some at-risk groups would gradually recede as scientific theories of disease transmission are disseminated and reinforced. Health professionals initiate and supervise this process through precise techniques of diagnosis and intervention, but the target group is responsible for carrying it out. Instead of modernizing the material or professional resources of the nation's health service, this strategy aims to empower groups and individuals so that they can transform themselves through knowledge acquisition and behavior change. In essence, the 'official' model is a proposal for the formation of conscientious citizens who, in theory, would be capable of reproducing rationalized forms of behavior management without the necessity of continuous, state-sponsored interventions.

In the framework of interventions used in Rio de Janeiro, the implicit concept of progress is signaled by increased personal autonomy informed by political awareness. In comparison to the 'official' model, the role of the professional is somewhat more important. Positive change depends upon the presence of someone duly trained in the techniques of linking the sphere of personal experience to the realm of social and political relations. Psychological-pedagogical interventions are proposed as the catalysts of change. Unlike the vision of progress in the 'official' model, the outcome of a successful intervention cannot be specified *a priori*, since individuals would have the autonomy to make choices that do not reduce their risk for HIV or STD's. A successful intervention would, however, assist in reverting social inequities by leading to an increasingly politicized understanding of sexuality and health. If the idea of progress in the 'official' model suggests self-help for the problem of underdevelopment, the 'local' model offers an approach which is relatively more mediated by professional interventions. It might be considered a sort of developmental therapy.

The two models converge on crucial points. First, as is characteristic of development projects in general, both models share a faith in the capacity of technology and professional intervention to identify and solve complex problems. In this case, both the problem and the solution are defined in psychologizing terms, a fact which represents a significant shift in the largely medicalized field of public health administration. Second, both models emphasize investment in the individual and the techniques of psychology as agents of progressive change. Unlike many previous large-scale public health interventions in Brazil (BRAITERMAN 1996; MESSEDER PEREIRA 1994), both models agree that individuals must learn to transform themselves, rather than being transformed by medical specialists. In theorizing an ideal world in which model citizens transform and replicate themselves, the techniques and theories of psychology employed in this model seem to be uniquely suited to the task of both improving health outcomes and redefining the role of the state in the provision of essential social services. Given the corporatist history of public health in Brazil (CASTRO-SANTOS 1991), these models offer the surprising specter of their own obsolescence.

These models of prevention reflect concepts of health and health management peculiar to two very different institutional and professional contexts: that of largely medicalized public health institutions—Brazil's Ministry of Health—and that of the hybrid field of psychology and professional activism—characteristic AIDS initiatives in Rio de Janeiro. Notwithstanding the significant theoretical and methodological differences between them, they share the intent to instill a new ideology in Brazilian society which emphasizes individuality and personal responsibility. As other authors have argued (FIGUEIRA 1985b; VELHO 1985), the uniquely psychologized culture of the middle and upper classes of Brazilian cities is, in itself, both a sign and a mechanism of modernity. In this context, modernity is understood as an ideology which emphasizes the role of the individual as a discrete nexus/agent of thought and action. The 'culture of psychology' is said to work as a mechanism of modernity in that it assists in the transition from a pre-industrial society in which the person is defined relationally to one in which the individual is understood as being the agent-organizer of unique feelings, desires and experiences (JACÓ-VILELLA 1996; SALEM 1992). In the context of the National Program, a psychologized understanding of sexuality, risk and risk reduction also serves as a mechanism of modernization, although one which works somewhat differently. Rather than targeting the middle and upper classes of Brazilian cities, it is aimed primarily at groups whose access to public services of any kind have been problematic at best: low-income women, homosexuals, intravenous drug users, adolescents, sex workers, itinerant prospectors and indigenous populations.

Unlike other moments in the history of Brazilian public health initiatives, the National Program appears to be willing to work with sexual outsiders—including sex workers, transvestites and homosexuals—which were once demonized as inherently insalubrious and even dangerous to the Brazilian nation (PRADO 1931; PIRES DE ALMEIDA 1906; JAIME 1953; BRAITERMAN 1994, 1995; GUY 1991). Rather than proposing their elimination, both models of intervention suggest that these groups could actually be exemplary, forming self-sustaining community-based initiatives to prevent the spread of HIV and sexually transmitted diseases. This strategy also serves as a mechanism for modernization, for implanting the ethos of responsibility and community participation present in both approaches to prevention. The 'fluidity' said to be both characteristic of Brazilian sexual culture and a challenge to prevention programs (PARKER 1988; GOLDSTEIN 1994; SCHEPER-HUGHES 1991) is thus resolved through the formation of new identity-based groups, 'communities' in the language of the Ministry or 'minorities' in the framework characteristic of initiatives in Rio de Janeiro. In this way, AIDS prevention initiatives might be understood as serving to rationalize not only sexual acts but the organization of sexual actors as well. The 'risk groups' which once figured prominently in official Brazilian discourse on AIDS have been replaced by 'communities,' at once the targets and the executors of public health interventions.

The National Program proposes an unusual trade-off. On the one hand, some of the groups historically marginalized for their sexual alterity—most notably gay men and sex workers—are offered support in, of all places, the Ministry of Health. In exchange, this support is predicated on the adoption of new concepts of sexuality, identity and community organization. This shift in the relationship between sexual others and the Brazilian health authorities deserves an analysis more detailed than I can offer here. Nonetheless, it's worth posing the question of whether government sponsored AIDS programs actually have the capacity to place Brazil among what one of the prevention manuals refers to as "the more civilized countries, [where] churches have modernized and accept women as clergy, do not condemn divorce and bless unions between homosexuals" (BMOH 1996a:16).

In this paper I have chosen not to engage important questions about the degree to which either approach to prevention has proven to be effective in achieving its stated goals. Instead, I have focused on the ways in which paradigms for prevention programs articulate conceptual frameworks for the management of AIDS as a problem of collective and individual health. Notwithstanding my reticence to engage the issue of evaluation in this short paper, it seems important to note that, at least discursively, the Brazilian National Program has changed radically from its early days. Rather than warning citizens to 'Watch out or AIDS will get you' or that an AIDS diagnosis is paramount to a death sentence (see HILDEBRAND 1995), current media-based campaigns encourage women to 'love and take care of yourself' by carrying a condom at all times. In essence, the Brazilian Ministry of Health has gone from understanding AIDS as a moral problem with medical sequelae to confronting the epidemic as an issue of public health requiring new and more sophisticated techniques of intervention. To varying degrees, both models for prevention would appear to take into account the largely anthropological critiques of the official response to the epidemic in the late 1980's and early 1990's (see GUIMARÃES 1994; PARKER 1992). While the shift in the Ministry's strategy is largely positive—especially given the early history of AIDS in Brazil—the new approaches to prevention suggest important questions. I would like to close with one: to what extent can largely psychological approaches be effective among populations whose understanding of risk, health and illness may be relatively less psychologized? Given that the theories and techniques used in both models are highly specific to the academic, professional and social circuits in which they were created, their effectiveness among groups who do not share the notion of the modern person/individual on which they are based remains an open question. In this sense, any evaluation of prevention initiatives must begin with a close examination of the interventions' goals—both stated and explicit or implicit in the theory and method upon which they are based.

References

BASTOS, CRISTIANA
    1995 O impacto da AIDS nos estudos de sexualidade: Notas comparadas USA/Brasil. Discussion at the meeting 'Ethnicity and Globalization', sponsored by the Brazilian Anthropological Association; 23-30 June 1995, Rio de Janeiro.

BRAITERMAN, J.
1994 Straight masculinity: Fantastic illusion or glamour acessory? Presentation given at the Center for Feminist Studies, Stanford University.
1996 *Beat it: An anthropology oddity*. Doctoral dissertation in Anthropology, Stanford University.

BMOH (THE BRAZILIAN MINISTRY OF HEALTH), Secretaria de Assistência à Saúde. Programa Nacional de Doenças Sexualmente Transmissíves e AIDS, Bralília
1996a *Manual do Multiplicador: Homossexuais*.
1996b *Manual do Multiplicador: Profissionais do Sexo*.
1996c *Manual do Multplicador: Prevenção às DST/AIDS*.
1994a Projeto de Prevenção des DST/AIDS para populações sob maior risco: Previna.
1994b *Manual do Multiplicador, Para formação de monitores em prevenção de DST/AIDS junto a homossexuais*.

CAMARGO, KENNETH R.
1992 *As ciências da AIDS e a AIDS das ciências: o discurso médico e a construção da AIDS*. Rio de Janeiro: Relume Dumará and the Instituto de Medicina Social—Universidade Estadual do Rio de Janeiro.

CARRARA, S
1996 *Tributo a Venus: A luta contra a sífilis 1900-1945*. Rio de Janeiro: Editora da Fundação Oswaldo Cruz.

CASTRO SANTOS, L.A. DE
1987 *Power, ideology and public health in Brazil, 1889-1930*. Doctoral dissertation, department of Sociology, Harvard University.

DANIEL, HERBERT
1991 We are all people living with AIDS: Myths and realities of AIDS in Brazil. *International Journal of Health Services* 22: 531-551.

ESCOBAR, ARTURO
1995 *Encountering Development: The making and unmaking of the third world*. Princeton, NJ: Princeton University Press.

FIGUEIRA, S.A.
1985a Introdução: Psocologismo, psicanálise e ciências sociais na "cultura psicanalítica.". In: *Cultura da Psicanálise*. Edited by FIGUEIRA. São Paulo: Brasiliense.
1985b Modernização da família e desorientação: Uma das raízes do psycologismo no Brasil. In: *Cultura da Psicanálise*. Edited by FIGUEIRA. São Paulo: Brasiliense.
1981 *O contexto social da psicanálise*. Rio de Janeiro: Francisco Alves.

FRY, PETER
1985 Direito positivo *versus* direito clássico: A psicologização do crime no Brasil no pensamento de Heitor Carrilho. In: *Cultura da Psicanálise*. Edited by FIGUEIRA. São Paulo: Brasiliense.

GALVÃO, JANE
1992 *AIDS e imprensa: Um estudo de antropologia social*. Dissertação de mestrado, Programa de Pos-graduação em Antropologia Social, (Museu Nacional) Universidade Federal do Rio de Janeiro.

GOLDSTEIN, DONNA
1994 AIDS and women in Brazil: An emerging problem. *Social Science and Medicine* 39(7): 919-929.

GUIMARÃES, C.D.
1994 Mulheres, homens e AIDS: O visível e o invisível. In: *A AIDS no Brasil*. Edited by PARKER; BASTOS; GALVÃO & PEDROSA. Rio de Janeiro: Relume Dumará.

GUY, DONNA J.
1992 'White Slavery', Citizenship and Nationality in Argentina. In: *Nationalisms and Sexualities*. Edited by PARKER et. al. New York: Routledge.
1991 *Sex & Danger in Buenos Aires: Prostitution, Family, and Nation in Argentina*. Lincoln: University of Nebraska Press.

HARRAD, D & L. MOTT.
1993 Programa Nacional de Controle das Doenças Sexualmente Transmíssíveis e AIDS: Objetivos, estratégias e ações. (without date) *Programa Nacional de Controle e Prevenção da AIDS*.

HERSCHMANN, M.M. & C.A. MESSEDER PEREIRA.
1994 O imaginário moderno no Brasil. In: *A invenção do Brasil moderno: Medicina, educaçao e engenharia nos anos 20-30*. Edited by M.M. HERSCHMANN & C.A. MESSEDER PEREIRA. Rio de Janeiro: Rocco.

HILDENBRAND, LUCI
1995 *Comunicação oficial brasileira sobre a AIDS: Um percurso pelas linhas e entrelinhas da telinha da tevê*. Doctoral dissertation, Escola de Comunicação da Universidade de São Paulo.

JACÓ-VILELLA, A.M.
1996 *Formar-se psicólogo: Como ser 'livre como um pásaro'*. Doctoral dissertation, Instituto de Psicologia da Universidade de São Paulo.

JAIME, JORGE
  1953 *Homosexualismo masculino*. Rio de Janeiro: Ed Barsoi. 2nd edition.
KNAUTH, DANIELA R.
  1996 AIDS e Mulheres: Um desafio à prevenção. *HIVeraz*, No. 06, December 1996.
LARVIE, PATRICK
  1995 Self-help for bad self-esteem, or the new Brazilian homosexuality. Paper presented for the panel 'Subjects and objects: Toward an anthropology of sexual cultures' at the meeting of the American Anthropological Association, November 1995, Washington D.C.
MARTIN, EMILY
  1995 *FLEXIBLE BODIES*. BOSTON: BEACON.
MESSEDER PEREIRA, C.A.
  1994 "O direito de curar: Homossexualidade e medicina legal no Brasil dos anos 30. In: *A invenção do Brasil moderno: Medicina, educaçao e engenharia nos anos 20-30*. Edited by M.M. HERSCHMANN & C.A. MESSEDER PEREIRA. Rio de Janeiro: Rocco.
MONTGOMERY, S.B.; J.G. JOSEPH, J.G.; M.H. BECKER et. al.
  1989 Critical review: The health belief model in unerstanding compliance with preventive recommendations for AIDS: How useful? *AIDS education and prevention* 1(4): 303-323.
MOREIRA DOS SANTOS, E.
  1995 Comportamentos sexuais, práticas sexuais, *habitus*, trabalho erótico: Uma contribuição ap estudo das sexualidades. In: *AIDS: Ética, medicina e biotecnologia*. Edited by D. DZERESNIA; E. MOREIRA DOS SANTOS; R. SIMÕES BARBOSA & S. MONTEIRO. São Paulo: Hucitec Abrasco.
PAIVA, VERA
  1994 Sexualidade e gênero num trabalho com adolescentes para prevenção do HIV/AIDS. In: *A AIDS no Brasil*. Edited by PARKER; BASTOS; GALVÃO & PEDROSA. Rio de Janeiro: Relume Dumará.
PARKER, RICHARD
  1992 Sexual diversity, cultural analysis, and AIDS education in Brazil. In: *The time of AIDS: Social analysis, theory and method*. Edited by GILBERT HERDT & SHIRLEY LINDENBAUM. Newbury Park, CA: Sage Press.
  1988 Sexual culture and AIDS education in urban Brazil. In: AIDS 1988: AAAS symposia papers. Edited by RUTH KULSTAD. Washington, D.C.: American Association for the Advancement of Science.
PIRES DE ALMEIDA, JOSÉ RICARDO
  1906 *Homosexualismo: A libertenagem no Rio de Janeiro: Estudo sobre as perversões e inversões do instincto genital*. Rio de Janeiro: Laemmert & C.
PRADO, PAULO
  1931 *Retrato do Brasil*. Rio de Janeiro: F Briguiet & Companhia.
RUSSO, JANE
  1994 *O corpo contra a palavra: as terapias corporais no campo psicológico nos anos 80*. Rio de Janeiro: Universidade Federal do Rio de Janeiro.
SALEM, T.
  1992 A 'despossesão subjetiva': Dos paradoxos do individualismo. *Revista Brasileira de Ciências Sociais* 18(7): 62-77.
SCHEPER-HUGHES, NANCY
  1991 AIDS in Brazil or, if you think it's bad here. Presentation at the American Association of Anthropologists, special special session on AIDS, San Francisco.
  1994 An essay: AIDS and the social body. *Social Science and Medicine* 39(7): 991-1003.
STEPAN, NANCY L.
  1985 Biological degeneration: Races and proper places. In: *Degeneration: the Dark Side of Progress*. Edited by Edward J. CHAMBERLAIN & SANDER GILMAN. New York: Columbia University Press.
  1976 *Beginnings of Brazilian science: Oswaldo Cruz, medical research and policy, 1890-1920*. New York: Science History Publications.
VELHO, G.
  1985 A busca de coerência: Coexisência e contradições entre códigos em camadas médias urbanas. In: *Cultura da Psicanálise*. Ediuted by FIGUEIRA. São Paulo: Brasiliense.
THE WORLD BANK: The International Bank for Reconstruction and Development/The World Bank (Banco Mundial), Washington, DC:
  1995 *The World Bank annual report*.
  1995 The International Bank for Reconstruction and Development/The World Bank and the Government of the Federative Republic of Brazil. Acordo de emprestimo (projeto de controle de AIDS e das DST) 16 março 1995. Emprétismo número 3659 BR.
  1994 *The World Bank annual report*.

1993a Documento de Princípios: Brasil. Projeto de Controle da AIDS e DST. 08 outubro 1993. Report n° 11734-BR, Divisão de Recursos Homanos / Human Resources Division, Country Department.
1993b *The World Bank annual report.*
1992 *Tanzania: AIDS assessment and planning study.*
WORLD HEALTH ORGANISATION, Global Programme on AIDS, Geneva:
1985 The global AIDS strategy.
1989 *Guide to planning health promotion for AIDS prevention and control.* WHO AIDS series 5.
1992 *The global AIDS strategy.* WHO AIDS series 11.

"I'm Not Dog, No !":
Cries of Resistance against Cholera Control Campaigns[1]

MARILYN K. NATIONS & CRISTINA M.G. MONTE

Abstract

Popular reactions toward government efforts to control the recent cholera epidemic in Northeast Brazil are evaluated. Intensive ethnographic interviews and participant-observation in two urban slums *(favelas)*, reveal a high level of resistance on the part of impoverished residents towards official cholera control interventions and mass media campaigns. 'Non-compliance' with recommended regimens is described more as a revolt against accusatory attitudes and actions of the elite than as an outright rejection of care by the poor. 'Hidden transcripts' about 'The Dog's Disease,' as cholera is popularly called, voices a history of social and economic inequity and domination in Northeast Brazil. Here, cholera is encumbered by the trappings of metaphor. Two lurid cultural stereotypes, *pessoa imunda* (filthy, dirty person) and *vira lata* (stray mutt dog) are used, it is believed, to equate the poor with cholera. The morally disgracing and disempowering imagery of cholera is used to blame and punish the poor and to collectively taint and separate their communities from wealthy neighborhoods.

The authors argue that metaphoric trappings have tragic consequences: they deform the experience of having cholera and inhibit the sick and dying from seeking treatment early enough. Controlling cholera requires eliminating 'blaming the victim' rhetoric while attacking the social roots of cholera: poverty, low earning power, female illiteracy, sexism, lack of basic sanitation and clean water supplies, medical hegemony, etc. For health interventions to be effective, it is necessary to take into account people's 'hidden transcripts' when designing action programs.

Zusammenfassung

Die Reaktionen der Bevölkerung auf die Anstrengungen der Regierung, die jüngste Choleraepidemie im Nordosten Brasiliens einzudämmen, werden untersucht. Intensive ethnographische Interviews und teilnehmende Beobachtung in zwei urbanen Elendsvierteln *(favelas)* offenbaren einen großen Widerstand seitens der verarmten Bevölkerung gegen die offiziellen Cholerakontrollmaßnahmen sowie die Kampagnen der Massenmedien. Die ‚*Non-compliance*' bezüglich der empfohlenen Lebensweisen wird mehr als eine Revolte gegen die anklagenden Haltungen und Aktionen der Elite beschrieben, denn als gänzliche Ablehnung der Vorsichtsmaßnahmen von seiten der armen Bevölkerung. ‚Versteckte Umschreibungen' [*hidden transcripts*] über die ‚Hundekrankheit', wie Cholera volkstümlich genannt wird, macht die historische soziale und ökonomische Ungleichheit und Herrschaftsrealität im Nordosten Brasiliens deutlich. Cholera ist hier belastet durch die Fallen der Metaphern. Zwei düstere kulturelle Stereotype, *pessoa imunda* (dreckige, schmutzige Person) und *vira lata* (Strassenköter) werden nach unserer Ansicht benutzt, um Armut mit Cholera gleichzusetzen. Das moralisch schmachvolle und entmündigende Bild der Cholera wird benutzt, um die Armen zu beschuldigen und zu bestrafen, sowie um deren Gemeinden von den reicheren Ortschaften zu trennen.

Die Autorinnen vertreten den Standpunkt, daß metaphorische Fallen tragische Konsequenzen haben: Diese beeinflussen die Erfahrung, Cholera zu haben und vehindern, daß sich die Kranken und Sterbenden früh genug einer Behandlung unterziehen. Die Kontrolle der Cholera erfordert es, daß die Opfer nicht länger angeklagt werden, sondern daß stattdessen die sozialen Wurzeln der Cholera angepackt werden: Armut, geringe Einkommensmöglichkeiten, Analphabetentum bei Frauen, Sexismus, das Fehlen sanitärer Einrichtungen und einer sauberen Wasserversorgung, medizinische Hegemonie usw. Damit Gesundheitsstrategien effektiv wirken können, ist es nötig, die ‚versteckten Umschreibungen' der Leute mit einzubeziehen, wenn Aktionsprogramme geplant werden.

Keywords: cholera, health education messages, non-compliance, stigma, Brazil

---

1. This article has been published in *Social Science & Medicine* 43(6): 1007-1024. (Reproduction with permission by Elsevier Science Ltd.)

Cholera's Foothold in Latin America

The global epidemic of cholera—an ancient, acute bacterial enteric disease—continues to spread throughout the world, despite scientists' efforts to control its transmission (AHRTAG 1983). For the first time in this century, cholera is gaining a foothold in the Western hemisphere. In Latin America, the number of endemic cases now rivals those in Asia and Africa. This seventh cholera pandemic, which started in Asia in 1961, spread to Africa, Europe and Oceanic, but had spared the Western hemisphere. That was, however, before January 1991 when toxigenic *Vibrio cholera* O1, biotype El Tor and serotype Inaba, was reported for the first time in some 100 yr in South America (LIMA et al. 1994). Appearing almost simultaneously in several coastal Peruvian cities, the epidemic of *V. cholera* O1 exploded with some 426,000 probable cholera cases and over 3300 deaths reported in Peru alone. It then spread rapidly throughout the continent. Crossing the Andes, the disease swept aggressively eastward to Brazil. By April 1993, 19 (70%) of Brazil's 27 states and territories reported domestically acquired cases of cholera for a total of 27,374 cases, with an incidence of 5.5/100,000 of the population and case fatality rate of 1.6%. But it was in the impoverished Northeast that the epidemic flourished, reporting 87% of Brazil's total cases and an incidence of 16.9/100,000 of the population as compared to 5.5/100,000 for the country as a whole (LIMA 1994: 593). For centuries this drought-stricken region has been scourged by misfortune, disease and death. Both diarrheal diseases attack rates (GUERRANT et al. 1983; VICTORA et al. 1988) and infant mortality rates (UNICEF 1986) in Brazil's Northeast are among the highest reported in the world. Here, endemic poverty, faulty sanitation, contaminated water and food supplies, coupled with high rates of illiteracy and less access to effective health services means that in many northeastern communities, cholera will probably persist for many years to come. Unlike other outbreaks, this latest pandemic will not go away. Instead, cholera is expected to become endemic in the Americas, as it has in Africa.

V. Cholera O1 causes disease by adhering to the mucosa of the upper small bowel, where it produces a potent enterotoxin which stimulates the secretion of isotonic water and electrolytes. While the majority (90%) of cholera cases are mild and many infected persons have no symptoms, they can be carriers and silently infect others. Far fewer (5-8%) experience mild to moderate diarrhea. Cholera's reputation as a killer is restricted to a relatively small proportion of people (2-5%) who develop 'cholera gravis' (LIMA et al. 1994: 2). In such classic cholera cases, infected persons experience severe and profuse watery diarrhea and vomiting resulting in the rapid and profound loss of fluid and electrolytes. So severe may be the losses of essential fluids, that the patient may lose the equivalent of his entire body weight over 2-3 days. These high losses of liquid may, in extreme cases, lead to severe dehydration, with shock in 4-12 hr and death. But today, no one need die from cholera.

As with all diarrheal diseases, the successful treatment of cholera depends on rapid replacement of fluid and electrolyte losses through (preferably) oral or intravenous routes (MAHALNABIS et al. 1974). Before the discovery of rehydration therapy, some 30-50% of severely infected persons died from cholera. These numbers have declined drastically to < 2% with the discovery of rehydration therapy (LIMA 1994: 596). The key is oral rehydration therapy (ORT). ORT was first discovered in Britain in the 1830s, although it was not until the 1960s that the importance of sugar in the solution was discovered (PARKER et al. 1980: 44); glucose significantly increases the body's ability to absorb fluid (MORELLO 1983). In the 1970s and especially in the 1971 cholera epidemic in Bangladesh, the utility of ORT for treatment of diarrheal dehydration was conclusively demonstrated. *The Lancet* has called ORT "potentially the most important medical advance this century" and ranks second only to the discovery of antibiotics in terms of lives saved (MORELLO 1983). The idea is simple; to replace the fluids and electrolytes lost during cholera and other secretary diarrheas; to maintain the patient alive without attempts to cure the diarrhea itself. The treatment is administered in the form of oral rehydration solution (ORS), consisting of water with salts and sugar added. ORS is fed continuously to the patient during the diarrheal episode, obviating the need for intravenous rehydration, which is an effective therapy. The death rate from diarrhea in hospitalized populations has dropped below 1% due to intravenous rehydration (PARKER et al. 1980: 43-44). But it is expensive and necessarily confined to use in hospitals by qualified personnel, whereas ORT can be prepared and administered at home without the need for hospitalization. The exact optimum combination of electrolytes in ORS is a matter of some debate, but the general composition is agreed upon. The World Health Organization (WHO) promotes use of a packaged powder containing sodium chloride, sodium bicarbonate, potassium chloride and glucose in proper proportion, ready to mix with water and use. This oral rehydration solution (ORS) has been found effective, and can be used by laypersons at home.[2] Some planners have argued that it is possible for laypersons to mix an acceptable ORS at home using common table salt and sugar with proper instruction (HARLAND et al. 1981; CLEMENTS 1980; KIELMAN et al. 1977; SHIELDS et al. 1981) and in some cases it is preferable (NATIONS 1982; NATIONS 1983). Although homemade ORS tends to omit sodium bicarbonate and potassium chloride, accurate measures are possible in even the most impoverished households using readily available 1l carbonated beverage bottles (or other containers) to measure the water, and bottle caps to measure the salt (1 level capful) and sugar (7-8 heaping capsful). Homemade ORS has the advantage of being less expensive than WHO ORS and, because of its home preparation, of being more accessible to impoverished mothers. Even locally available crude brown sugar such as lobongur in Bangladesh, has been found effective in such solutions and is, importantly, more accessible to impoverished families (SACK 1980). Cereal-based ORT, in which glucose is replaced by cereal flour (rice, maize, sorghum, millet, wheat or potato), not only may be more available and acceptable to families, but has the added advantage of reducing stool output (MOLLA et al. 1989; MOLLA et al. 1985). Despite the debates about fine points in the composition of the formula, ORT is now unanimously accepted by the international health community and actively promoted by WHO for the treatment of diarrheal dehydration, including that associated with cholera. Its scientific basis is well established (PARKER et al. 1980; HIRSCHHORN et al. 1983) and its ability to save lives has been convincingly demonstrated. It is low cost and low tech, and, theoretically, this should make it accessible to impoverished families, the bulk of those who die from enteric infections, including cholera.

Antibiotics, while helpful, are not essential in the treatment of cholera. Antimicrobial therapy reduces the total volume of fluid loss and shortens the duration of both illness and carriage of vibrios in the feces (GOODENOUGH et al. 1964). However, antimicrobial resistance has been a growing problem in some parts of the world. Family contacts of patients with cholera may be treated prophylactically with tetracycline or doxycycline to prevent illness, however, antibiotic treatment of an entire community, or mass chemoprophylaxis, has not been shown to limit the spread of cholera (LIMA et al. 1994: 5). Other common, but ineffective, prevention measures include vaccination, quarantine or restricting the movement of people and food imports from affected areas. Effective prevention methods are the same as for other forms of diarrhea: drinking un-

---

2. EGEMAN et al. 1980; ELLERBROCK 1979; HARLAND et al. 1981; CLEMENTS 1980; CLEMENTS et al. 1980; KIELMAN et al. 1977; MELAMED et al. 1978; MORAN 1996; NATIONS 1982, 1983; NATIONS et al. 1983; NATIONS et al. 1988; NATIONS & REBHUN 1988; SHIELDS et al. 1981; PIZZARO et al. 1979; THANE-TOE et al. 1984.

contaminated water, handwashing, good home and environmental hygiene and sanitation, and avoidance of potentially contaminated foods (e.g. raw seafood, shellfish, contaminated municipal water, etc.). But the real key to eliminating cholera, as for all diseases linked to underdevelopment, lies in improving the conditions which enable cholera to flourish: poverty, illiteracy, lack of knowledge, economic recession, discrimination against women, lack of safe water and adequate sanitation systems.

Adversity, Accusations and Infectious Agents

Epidemics of particularly dreaded illnesses always provoke a popular outcry. When such adversity as cholera—a virulent, infectious agent which spreads capriciously and kills indiscriminately—strikes, people quickly incriminate: "Shame, shame, who's to blame?" Finger pointing becomes a human passion. It matters not what is pointed but that someone is singled out as responsible for causing the ruthless, mysterious calamity. As SONTAG (1990) says,

"Any disease that is treated as a mystery and acutely enough feared will be felt to be morally, if not literally contagious." (p. 6)

"Demands are made to subject people to 'tests,' to isolate the ill and those suspected of being ill or of transmitting illness, and to erect barriers against the real or imaginary contamination of foreigners." (p. 168)

Punitive notions of disease have a long history, dating back to 1882 and the discovery of tuberculosis, and more recently with cancer and AIDS. In such cases of mysterious malevolence, Sontag points out, accusations of culpability are commonplace. "Who cast the evil eye?" "Who threw the roots?" "Who pointed the bones?" "Who sent the *trabalho* (hex)?" "Who is guilty of transgressing social norms?" There is one burning desire: to identify who caused the suffering. That accusations and folk disease etiologies are interwoven is well documented in the anthropological literature (KLUCKHOHN 1944; RUBEL 1960; TINLING 1967; WINTROB 1973). Only recently, however, has the twisted incriminatory nature of illness accusations been interpreted critically. FARMER (1992) in *AIDS and Accusations: Haiti and The Geography of Blame* makes a perturbing observation. Victims are doubly blamed. They suffer twice: first, debilitating illness followed by image-damaging discrimination.

In Latin America, pinning blame on victims is a pastime (ACHESON 1972; RYAN 1971). The most glaring, recent example is HARRISON's (1985) *Underdevelopment is a State of the Mind* essay. He places blame for lack of progress squarely on poor people's heads, on peasants' supposed fatalistic mentality. Enculturation into a 'culture of poverty' (LEWIS 1966), maintains HARRISON, creates mind sets mired in the muck of helplessness, jealousy and in-fighting. Thus trapped, peasants are seen as unwilling to try to succeed, to take advantage of the many opportunities knocking at their door. Examples of 'Blaming the Victim' as an explanatory principle are plentiful: penniless, peasant mothers are branded 'neglectful' (SCHEPER-HUGHES 1984, 1985); suffering HIV-infected Haitians are labeled AIDS 'originators' (FARMER 1992); malaria-infected, malnourished and massacred Ianomani Indians are said to 'lack initiative,' and the like.

Farmer critiques such accusatory interpretations of illness in rural Haiti by putting poverty first. His objections echo VALENTINE's (1968) and ACHESON's (1972) which took to task LEWIS (1966), FOSTER (1965, 1967, 1972) and others who link poverty to cognitive images of the poor (e.g. Image of Limited Good) and who underemphasize political economy and other structural factors (e.g. discrimination, racism, lack of access to health services and money to pay for care). We agree with FARMER that an interpretive anthropology which fails to consider prevailing political and economic forces is shortsighted especially in impoverished countries where "the hard surfaces of life seem to underpin so much of experience" (p. 529), resulting in a socially unjust interpretation. Taking the calculus of economic and symbolic power seriously, FARMER pushes the "Cult of Blame" analysis to its limits. He argues that faced with accusations, the weaker invent counteraccusations, voicing them in seemingly far-fetched conspiracy theories. Actually they are rhetorical defenses against aggressors' discriminatory and demeaning attitudes. According to FARMER, such conspiracy theories pose explanatory challenges:

> "accusation impute(s) to human agency a significant role in the propagation of a dreaded sickness ... conspiracy theories impute to the powerful evil motives, either the desire to weaken the ranks of outcasts, or to defame black (in reference to Haiti) people. In each case, then, one social group attributes unsavory motives to another" (1992: 234)

Such conspiracy theories are 'weapons of the weak,' according to JAMES SCOTT (1985). They are part of a "hidden transcript" (Scott 1990) expressing popular indignation at political and social domination. Creating convincing conspiracy theories is an art, an art of resistance. This "offstage" discourse is typically produced in response to practices of domination and exploitation, of insults and slights to human dignity, that elites routinely exercise over subordinates (SCOTT 1990: 7). Hidden transcripts are low-profile forms of a shared critique of power and resistance that "dare not speak in their own name."

They are implicit protest, dissent and subversive discourse of underdogs against their worldly fate. Recognizing that elites have privileged access to power, wealth, and health because of their dominate social position, subordinate groups have learned tactical prudence when protesting. Rarely do they blurt out their hidden transcripts in public; elaborate forms of disguise are employed. The public expression of insubordination of subordinate groups is "sufficiently indirect and garbled that it is capable of two readings, one of which is innocuous" (SCOTT 1990: 157).

Cries of "I'm Not Dog, No!" and the creation of far-out cholera conspiracy theories by poor Brazilians pose no direct threat or opposition to the authorized medical position on cholera. But at a deeper level, it is apparent that the euphemisms, folktales, and play-on-words of popular culture encode and conceal double meanings from medical authorities and contest the inequitable social order in northeastern Brazil. This paper explores the hidden transcripts or discourse-gestures, speech, practices-about cholera that is ordinarily excluded from the public transcript of the dominant, medical professional. We describe a rich folk disease taxonomy of cholera. We probe the underlying accusations that provoke poor residents in Gonçalves Dias and *Conjunto* Palmeiras to cry out 'farce!' and resist well-intended medical advice and medications. We describe hurtful, discriminatory accusations which inflict suffering on infected persons and whose originators, in retribution, become the target of popular cholera conspiracy theories. We describe how a positive cholera diagnosis results in social stigmatization, prejudice and discrimination against the infected poor. We argue that conspiracy theories are rhetorical defenses—a kind of symbolic protest—against the crippling accusations of elites. Moreover, we argue that so-called patient 'non-compliance'—mocking cholera prevention messages, lashing out at medical authorities, threatening powerful politicians, shunning doctors' advice, spitting-up medication, and resisting hospital rehydration, etc.—is popular resistance against, not so much cholera care, but the more insidious social diseases of defamation and discrimination.

Cholera and Blame in Brazil

During the recent cholera epidemic in Northeast Brazil, the damaging dynamics of blame were visible. In Ceará state, 16,325 cases were registered in 119 of 184 counties, resulting in 121 deaths in the first 9 months of 1993 alone; 9336 cases have been reported in the capital of Fortaleza (O Povo 1993). These statistics represent only a fraction of all cases. Early in the epidemic, official diagnostic criteria for cholera required a positive laboratory confirmation. As numbers of suspected cases out-paced laboratory facilities, clinical and epidemiological evidence was accepted as sufficient to establish a positive diagnosis. Even so, many cases — Dona Lucimar's and Antonio's below — remained hidden from the 'public transcript' of biomedicine. They suffered cholera's ravening clinical course at home, alone.

With confirmed cholera cases quickly mounting, Brazilian health authorities sounded an all-out alert to contain the spread *of Vibrio cholera*. The disease now threatened not only millions of slum-dwellers in the Northeast, but, perhaps more important to politicians, the economic livelihood of the region (e.g. tourism, seafood export). By the spring of 1993, general panic had set in, particularly in the capital, Fortaleza (population 2 million), which reported the highest cholera attack/mortality rates in the country. Prevention messages were continually broadcast over radio and television airwaves; private school children had daily hand washing drills; five-star hotel restaurants washed vegetables in bleach; and luxury, beach front apartment residents treated private wells with chloride. Overnight, the already dual-class society, sharply divided: cholera-infested and cholera-free. There were those living with cholera and those defending themselves. Imaginary walls quickly rose to seal off the wealthy enclave, Aldeota, from cholera-infected poverty zones of the periphery. Upper-class residents quietly dismissed maids, cooks, laundresses and nannies living in cholera-infested, lower-class neighborhoods. The rich prohibited their children from contacting poorer playmates, using public restrooms and eating in popular restaurants. Northeast bound tourists cancelled trips. Meanwhile, poor residents living in Fortaleza's 300 shantytowns came under intense scrutiny and government-sponsored cholera surveillance. Teams of well-intentioned sanitary workers mapped out high-risk cholera zones, treated community wells and in-home drinking water with chloride, tracked the number and appearance of residents' diarrheal stools and administered prophylactic antibiotics to asymptomatic *Vibrio cholera* carriers. In short, the stated intention of public health teams was to declare war against the rapidly spreading water-borne cholera bacillus *(A Guerra Contra Cólera)*. But according to *favela* residents, the sanitary workers' hidden strategy was to contain cholera in slums and prevent its spread to wealthier neighborhoods.

Two *Favelas*, Too Poor

During the cholera epidemic of 1993 in Fortaleza, Ceará, Brazil, the authors conducted an ethnographic study of cholera-related beliefs and behaviors among residents of two high-risk urban slums — Gonçalves Dias (population 2000) and Conjunto Palmeiras (population 20,000). Gonçalves Dias is a painfully poor favela located only a few blocks from the Federal University of Ceará's (UFC) medical complex and the state's São José's Infectious Diseases Hospital.[3] Some

---

3. State of Ceará's public hospital for infectious diseases is notorious for its large case load of very sick patients, including HIV-infected individuls. Patients receiving treatment at São José Hospital are often stigmatized and feared as carriers of 'dangerous' diseases.

30 yr ago, Gonçalves Dias was an unpaved avenue on Fortaleza's outskirts, until landless peasants invaded one night and staked it out as home. Boring tenacious roots into the packed dirt of Avenida Gonçalves Dias, they built hovels, raised families, and constructed a community along the narrow street. Over the years, residents have been expelled four times from "The Avenida" and their homes, most recently during this project.[4] Pressured by wealthier neighbors, local politicians have ordered families to disassemble their cardboard, tin, adobe and stick homes, pack-up and resettle in government housing projects on the distant outskirts of the sprawling capital city. The resilient residents of The Avenida grudgingly obey the official mandates, only to return when eviction threats subside and the ruling politicians leave office. Today Gonçalves Dias consists of some 440 tightly-packed houses with common walls. No privacy. Life is public. The most common house construction is clay molded over stick frames forming two vãos or rooms, with mostly earthened floors. Pictures and posters of Catholic saints, deceased relatives, soap opera stars, pop musicians and political candidates adorn the otherwise drab walls. During the rainy season, (Dec-March), tropical downpours literally dissolve away the protective clay walls. The larger vão, measuring some 2 x 2 m, doubles as a living room and bedroom, the second, smaller vão at the rear is the kitchen. As many as 10 people sleep in the front vão by stringing up hammocks, crisscross on three levels: low, medium and high. Bed-wetting infants and cholera defecating adults sleep on the low rung. More than 80% of the houses have no sanitary facilities; raw sewage flows throughout the favela in open gutters. Adults defecate in an empty tin can filled with dirt. At night they fling the contents in a vacant space. The children defecate anywhere convenient. Using old newspapers or banana leaves, mothers scoop up the feces and toss (rebola) them outside. Simple coal-burning fires heat the family's two cooking pots: one larger for simmering beans, and another smaller for preparing the baby's porridge (mingau) and boiling water to prepare coffee. Electricity is often tapped illegally from energy lines servicing wealthier neighbors. Women's income as laundresses or maids in wealthier homes is more stable than their often sporadic male partners'. Older children (5-10 yr old) often care for newborns while mothers work. Child-adults they are. Exclusive breastfeeding is rare. The diarrheal attack rate in children 0-5 yr is extremely high: 11.4 illnesses/year (SHORTLING et al. 1987). Sixty-eight percent of children aged 3-5 yr presenting diarrhea have one or more parasitic infections (PENNIE et al. 1996). Of 244 children born to 43 families (5.7 children per family) 60 or 24.6 had died when surveyed in 1983 (GUERRANT et al. 1996); 52% died with diarrhea, 10% with pneumonia, and four (7%) with measles. On weekends Gonçalves Dias bustles with life: red-lipped adolescents, in glove-tight short-shorts and sensual, off-the-shoulder mid-rift blouses, jive to the pounding tropical Lambada, forró and Axé rhythms, which drown-out the blasts of shotguns, screams of battered women, cries of hungry infants, bickering of neighbors, bartering of drug dealers and violent arguments between a group of men downing shots of cachaça[5] at the local bar.

The second slum, Conjunto Palmeiras[6], conjures up a romantic, tropical imagine at first. Palmeiras refers to the clusters of lush, green palm trees that line Ceará's coastline, their trunks

---

4. Recently, the 440 families of Gonçalves Dias were evicted for the fourth time due to government plans to build a road through the *favela*. As appraisers valued homes for expropriation, one resident sobbed: "I've lived here 17 years! This is home. I was raised here. My kids were born here. Even my *anginho* (dead infant) is buried here. What *micheira* (spare change) do you think I'm going to get for my house of dirt and sticks? It will never pay for all what is mine here!"
5. The name of a popular and potent alcoholic beverage brewed from sugar cane.
6. A *conjunto* is a government-subsidized, planned resettlement community built on large tracks of cheap land distant from the city for displaced slum dwellers and migrants. Eviction, abandonment, and overcrowding of the small, identical box-like homes is common due to high fixed rents.

swaying rythmatically and their tattered fonds rustling in the soothing trade winds. But the idealistic image quickly gives way to another sobering reality. Conjunto Palmeiras is a planned resettlement community. It is an endless sea of identical, poorly constructed clay and brick row-houses which are home to some 20,000 people who relocated (often forcibly) from higher-priced city lots or migrated from the drought-stricken interior (sertão) in search of a better life. Conjunto Palmeiras is located on Fortaleza's periphery, just past Jangurursu, the municipal dump, where the garbage of some two million people is deposited, scavenged, saved and sold daily. Like Jangurursu, Conjunto Paimeiras is a dump, only a human one, where it seems society's throw-aways are left to decompose. While potable water was installed in 1988 following requests by community leaders, no sewerage network or public garbage collection service exists. There is only one paved street in town on which old buses run sporadically. A branch of the polluted Coco River borders on the south. Most community activities occur in a small square around which the main school, church, market, community radio, birth center and day-care center are located. Animals roam freely in public places, where rubbish and feces often mix. Socio-economic conditions, while generally poor, vary among residents (MONTE 1993). Classified as 'very poor,' are 25.5% of families who live in mud homes with straw roofs, earthen floors, no sanitation and having a radio as the only appliance, if any. The majority (51.4%) are 'poor' households of unplastered brick with straw roofs and cemented floors, always possessing a radio, sometimes a television but very rarely a refrigerator. Most have access to piped water outside the house and some have pit latrines. 'Less poor' households (23.1%) are brick structures, sometimes plastered with tile roofs and ceramic floors, with access to piped water (sometimes within the house,) pit latrines and having a radio, television and refrigerator. Some 50% of households have six or more members, with 93% having at least 3 children < 5 yr of age. Children suffer frequent diarrhea; 30% of those < 5 yr of age had experienced diarrhea with severe or moderate dehydration in the previous 2 wk (LIMA, personal communication). Male unemployment, burglary, drug abuse, mental stress and violence against women (rape, domestic violence, murder) take their toll. But the demoralizing affliction in Conjunto Palmeiras is political abandonment and disenfranchisement. Families live on the periphery of modern life, shut-out from the opportunities and dreams of Fortaleza's better-off families.

These two *favelas* sadly reflect the conditions of many impoverished and forgotten Brazilian communities. Until very recently, there seemed little hope for change. The first democratically-elected president after some 20 yr of military rule was entangled in scandal and eventually processed for impeachment by the Brazilian National Congress. The distribution of wealth—already the world's third most disparate—is widening, leaving the already privileged few (10%) even wealthier and the other 90% more destitute than ever (WORLD BANK 1990). The number of infants dying from preventable causes persist at disgraceful levels, despite increasing sophistication of modern medicine. Between 1980 and 1986 the infant mortality rate (IMR) was 64.1, 98.8 in the underdeveloped Northeast and 44.6 in the affluent, industrial south; Fortaleza's IMR of 104.6 was far higher than Rio de Janeiro's (O POVO 1993: 2) and São Paulo's (GUERRANT et al. 1996: 1) in the same year (UNICEF 1992). Violence and police brutality are at all time highs. In 1993—during the cholera epidemic—the world was stunned by Brazil's brutal, police violence; the indiscriminate massacre of III prisoners in the Carandiru Prison in São Paulo, assassination of sleeping street children in the Candelária in Rio de Janeiro, and extermination of residents in Vigário Geral *favela* north of Rio de Janeiro. (Here, on 30th August, some 30 hooded Military Police invaded the *favela* at dawn and unmercifully executed 21 innocent residents—20 workers and one student—in streets, bars and homes (VEJA 1993).

VWB – Verlag für Wissenschaft und Bildung

Getting Behind the Official Cholera Story

Thus, the research upon which this chapter is based was 'reality driven.' Medical researchers at the Federal University of Ceará (UFC) sensed 'something was wrong' in Gonçalves Dias, where since 1985 they had surveyed households daily to detect diarrheal illnesses. Residents, normally cooperative, were now incredulous and resistant. They challenged—overtly and cryptically—researchers' authority to intervene and control cholera's spread. Behind the health workers' backs, residents dumped chlorinated water from their clay pots, spit out prophylactic antibiotic pills, falsely reported illness episodes, neglected to collect stool samples, refused hospital transfers, sarcastically mimicked and distorted official cholera prevention slogans, etc. It was apparent that some critical social forces were at play whose identification would be vital if cholera transmission was to be controlled in this community or others. University enteric diseases specialists, thus, summoned a team of social scientists with experience in infectious diseases in northeastern Brazil to gather privileged insights and commentaries on cholera from residents.

To begin we took a broad, holistic look at cholera. Our agenda was (deceptively) simple: to identify how social and cultural forces at myriad levels interact with *Vibrio cholera,* infecting families living in urban poverty. We thought it essential to 'see' cholera through the eyes of poor Brazilians who suffer most its consequences if our results were to be useful for re-writing the educational messages-gone-wrong. What is it like to be poor, hungry, and sick with cholera? What is it like to depend on inaccessible health professionals for your life? How does it feel to know what causes the suffering, yet be powerless against it? Penetrating local moral worlds of families living in poverty was the only way, we were convinced, to gain these insights into and commentaries on cholera as 'lived-experience' (KLEINMAN et al. 1986). Our search began knowing that such second-hand readings of suffering would never be complete. We aimed to probe the meaning-laden interior worlds of cholera-infected persons, while not losing sight of the political and economic forces that put them at risk in the first place. Given the epidemic nature and immediate need for social input in cholera control efforts, we worked quickly drawing heavily on Rapid Ethnographic Assessment (RAP) methodologies (SCRIMSHAW et al. 1987).

During two months (March-April 1993) at the epidemic's height, we conducted 80 in-depth, open-ended interviews with key informants living or working in Gonçalves Dias and *Conjunto Palmeiras*: poor mothers (n = 33); children (n = 11); persons sick with cholera (n = 9); community health agents (n = 7); community members in strategic positions to observe cholera-related behavior (n = 7); caretakers of cholera patients (n = 6); Afro-Brazilian *Umbanda* healers (n = 2); community leaders (n = 2); folk-Catholic healers (n = 2); and a traditional midwife (n = 1). Interview data were enriched and validated by observing in-home and community water use and storage practices, defecation, sewerage disposal, food preparation, animal contact, community organization, medical compliance, self-care, healing rituals and contact with hospitals and visiting health agents. Because both authors had conducted extensive ethnographic research in the two communities and maintained affective ties with many of the women and their families, rapport and immediate entry into the communities was facilitated. The researchers' familiarity with the communities and ties of trust, allowed for immediate access to a far more difficult-to-reach arena; the 'backstage' (GOFFMAN 1959) and 'hidden transcripts' (SCOTT 1990) of cholera.

The authors conducted all 80 interviews in Portuguese in either the homes of persons suffering cholera, at health posts, traditional healing centers (i.e. *terreiros* or Afro-Brazilian *Umbanda* centers), community wells or washing holes. Each interview lasted from 1 to 3 hr. All interviews were tape-recorded and then transcribed completely before translation. A series of techniques were employed to ensure validity and reliability. Questions were checked for adequacy during the pilot study and monitored during data collection. Triangulation (DENZIN 1970) between informants, between investigators, within methods and between methods was used to validate the data collected. We analyzed the content in order to identify themes, which were then compared with accumulated anthropological research and knowledge. Three aspects of the interviews impressed us: 1. the frustration, anger and revolt of adult informants when discussing cholera; 2. the severe physical suffering of cholera patients, many presenting classical, fulminating cases of infection; and 3. the resistance of cholera infected persons to seek official medical care. Reluctant patients were often hauled—severely dehydrated or unconscious—to nearby emergency rooms by relatives and neighbors.

Ritual Resistance of the "Dog's Disease"

Dona Zilnar[7], traditional healer and mother of 22 children[8], eyed suspiciously the printed paper reporting laboratory results of her feces exam collected by University of Ceará field researchers. "So what does it accuse?"[9] she pointedly queried. Unable to read the findings herself, her eldest daughter answered "P-o-s-i-t-i-v-e ... Positive for what devil thing?" Dona Zilnar provoked. "Vibrino cholera" replied the community health worker, surprised with Dona Zilnar's unusual reaction. She continued aggressively:

> "Hear me, this business of cholera doesn't exist. Here in Gonçalves Dias we don't have cholera, no! There doesn't exist anyone with cholera here! ... I'm not even going to speak with Our Lady Aparecida[10] about this thing because for her, there doesn't exist cholera ... Somebody invented it! They are inventing it! And they are going to invent much more to come!" (Dona Zilnar, traditional healer).

"I'm Not Dog, No!"[11] screamed Dona Zilnar uncontrollably as she waded the paper with the printed positive laboratory results into a small ball and flung it at the feet of the now terrified community health worker. "What do you think I am, some low-down vira lata (stray mutt dog)[12]?" Dona Zilnar's anger and frank denial of cholera alerted our attention: Why the upset? What in the cholera diagnosis sets her off? Why a vira lata of all things? The medical team found curious not only her refusal to hear the community health worker's laboratory results, but the deeper, visceral revolt against her admirable intentions. Probing in greater depth the clinical histories of two individuals with cholera, Dona Lucimar and Antonio, we discovered painful stories of suffering. In severe cases of cholera, the intestine is infected with such rapidity and virulence that there is no time to resort to folk remedies, traditional healers and local pharmacy attendants. Even if there was, poor Brazilians know homemade teas are no weapon against such fulminant diarrhea and

---

7. All names of ethnographic informants are pseudonymous. Geographical names are cited.
8. Of *Dona* Zilnar's 22 live births, only 15 of her children are alive today. Seven died during infancy from preventable diarrheal dehydration, measles and malnutrition.
9. That informants use the verb 'to accuse' to refer to findings of the medical examination, is indirect evidence that accusatory pressures are routinely exerted by medical professionals.
10. The term refers to Brazil's patron saint and one of few *negra* (black) virgins recognized by the Roman Catholic church.
11. The phase "I'm Not Dog, No!" is the title of a popular song originally written by EURIPIDES WALDICK SORIANO in Portuguese as *Eu não Sou Cachorro Não!* and aired on country radio during the early 1970s, years of military rule and political repression. Recently the title was translated into English as "I'm Not Dog, No!" and the song re-interpreted by *brega* (funky folk) singers, FALCÃO and TARCISIO MATOS.
12. Portuguese term which literally translates as 'turn can,' vividly describing stray mutts or mongrels who roam streets in poor neighborhoods and *favelas* turning over garbage cans in search of food.

Cries of Resistance against Cholera Control Campaigns

vomiting. Pragmatically, they seek intravenous rehydration at hospitals as the 'only way out' (o jeito) in severe cases of 'The Dog's Disease,' (doença de cachorro) as cholera is popularly called.

Case 1: Dona Lucimar, all sucked out from inside by the dog's disease

> Oh my God! I woke up with that fine pain ... my guts ringing out dry, totally twisted inside ... I prayed to Saint São Sebastino[13] that it wasn't cholera. I ran to the backyard ... it was only water ... squirt, squirt, squirt ... urinating out of my anus ... all over my panties and new pants ... shit, shit, shit and more shit! ... *Oh! Doença de cachorro* (Dog's Disease) ... humiliating, so awful. I was tempted to throw my pants away, but they were new! ... When dawn arrived I was very weak ... a sour taste in my mouth ... looked like I'd been sick for a week ... all sucked out from the inside. I made a tea from orange peel, *goiabeira*[14] and *pitanga*[15]. My boy had four pakkets of oral rehydration solution (ORS) ... 'I don't even like the taste of ORS ... but, I dissolved one quickly and drank it! I drank tea, drank ORS, drank tea, drank ORS, drank tea, drank ORS ... I didn't have anyone to take me to the hospital ... I don't like the hospital ... I only went by force because of the attack ... the taxi driver didn't take me ... afraid I would die. They called an ambulance. My daughter was yelling and crying ... when I woke up, I was in the Intensive Care Unit ... all broken up and done in!

Case 2: Antonio, cut out the death robe

> At about 10 p.m. Antonio threw open the door, ran right for the toilet ... shitting and vomiting all night ... burning with fever. He would sleep, run to the bathroom, cry, then pray, pray at the feet of the *Padre* Cicero[16] to stop it (diarrhea) ... It's a really horrible disease ... does away with one's meat (flesh) ... very strong stomach ache, leg pains so bad you can't stand up, vomiting. I said, Antonio, my son, let's go to the São José Hospital, boy. But he didn't want to go, he wanted a medicine for his headache. I said, 'my son, your medicine is the hospital!' I feed him orange peel tea, but he sickened. There wasn't any way out (*não tem jeito*). By 9 a.m. he couldn't stand up ... white, white, white, and when a *morena*[17] is white ... cut out the death robe. I hadn't a dime for a taxi, so I dragged him, walking and praying to Our Lady of Perpetual Help. São José Hospital is only two blocks away, but he sat down ten times. He couldn't walk anymore. When we arrived, I cut in front of the long line ... He fell into the doctors' arms ... his eyes rolled up ... his pulse jumped up his arm ... I went crazy, out of my mind. I grabbed the doctor and pleaded ... For the love of God, don't let my son die. The next day I hunted for a hospital (to admit him) ... only a mother would do this! There was nothing, no vacancy, nowhere ... 'Give me the medicine,' I said, 'I'm taking him home because its the same God at home as in the hospital!'

The Great Cholera Invention or "Piling-on-the Illness"

Dona Lucimar's, Antonio's, and others' stories of suffering we collected are personal accounts of 'experience-as-lived' and should be taken at face value. Even so, hard data verifying 'real disease' exist: both *Dona* Lucimar and Antonio suffered laboratory-verified infections with *Vibrio cholera*. Curious, then, are reactions of infected patients and families: they deny cholera and label it an imaginary illness, an 'invention.'

---

13. The term refers to the Catholic saint revered in *Umbanda* as protector against epidemics.
14. *Psidium guayava L.* is an oil extract from leaves used popularly to treat diarrhea.
15. *Stenocalyx micheli Berg* is a medical plant whose leaves are used to make tea to treat diarrhea.
16. Miracle-performing Catholic saint of Juazeiro do Norte, Ceará who is a central figure in popular folk healing in Northeast Brazil.
17. The term refers to a Brazilian of mixed African and European descent.

A closer look at our data shows that poor Brazilians in our study employed four strategies to negate the existence of this life-threatening cholera epidemic. First was flat-out denial, as *Dona* Lucimar's comments show and the following reinforce:

"They did an exam ... cholera. But it isn't so! It's really cachaça. The poor guy drinks a lot, you see. They invented that it's cholera!" (daughter of 68-year-old cholera patient)

"The symptoms of cholera? I don't know, I don't even want to know." (mother)

"Half the people here don't believe cholera exists, even seeing my son, Jono, almost under the ground (dead). They think a person is behind it all ... putting things in their head ... they don't believe it!" (mother)

"We've had diarrhea all our lives ... even before there existed this medicine thing ... They invented it (cholera). A mosquito bites and instantly its malaria, yellow fever, dengue, this and that. They invented all this! They just loaded this cholera thing on top of us ... pile on that illness, that's it." (cholera patient)

At times during fieldwork we heard comical-sounding comments about cholera, despite its lethal nature. Health workers interrogated residents for detailed information about cholera, while residents responded by playing a curious hide-and-seek game. "Who was the first person you sought when the diarrhea began?" "I don't know what you're talking about." "When did you decide to go to the hospital for rehydration?" "Cholera is make-believe, an invention!" and so on. Below, a short excerpt from one such truncated and frustrating dialogue between a community health agent and a poor mother in *Conjunto* Palmeiras confirms this:

Q: Mrs Sonia, have you heard any comments from people here about cholera?
R: Here? No.
Q: No one passing by here conversing, "So-and-so is feeling this or that, with cholera?" Nobody talking about cholera, Sonia?
R: No, nobody talking about this, no.
Q: So many people gather here in front and nobody even comments much about this illness? Nobody says anything? Nobody is afraid?
R: No, we don't talk about this.
Q: Nobody feels anything, you know? Nobody comments anything, no?
R: No, here, no. Thanks to God, no. Thanks to God.

A second strategy was to deny outwardly that cholera exists, while fearing inwardly the illness. As with the virulent *Doença de Criança* (The Child's Disease; NATIONS 1992), the mere mention or faintest vision could 'call' the life-threatening illness to healthy bodies. Informants' denial of cholera could be construed as a culturally-constructed protection against the unbearable, against the unspeakable. As seen in the following dialogue between a visiting nurse and a recuperating patient, even dreaming about cholera was forbidden.

Q: Do you talk about cholera with your friends?
R: No, converse, no.
Q: Why not?
R: Because I could dream, no? And then I will have it ... For this reason I don't talk about it.
Q: If you dream, it can happen, ugh?
R: Yeah, the cholera.
Q: You don't talk about cholera, so you won't call it?
R: Yeah, if you say it, it will run after and grab you!

A third strategy was to render cholera trivial, commonplace and insignificant. Selective popular perceptions transformed virulent cholera into 'ordinary diarrhea' or just about anything, so long as the word cholera was not uttered. Below we see how cholera was acknowledged, but assigned an amorphous identity like 'the disease,' or left nameless.

"I thought it was *the illness,* because it gives righ away vomiting, fever, diarrhea, pains in the legs." (cholera patient)

"Exist, it exists. Only people don't have a name for it yet ... lack of interest." (indigenous midwife)

Cries of Resistance against Cholera Control Campaigns

Other informants trivialized cholera's virulence. A death-threatening infection was transformed into "a little annoyance ... a little thing," or "teething diarrhea *(dentinho)*, a normal part of growing up." Said informants:

"My grandmother and my mother already talked about these illnesses. Exist, they exist ... *the common diarrhea* that we've always had ... What are you saying, that we can't have a *little diarrhea*? The person has a little diarrhea and the exam shows cholera. Invention!" (traditional healer)

"When the girl comes with the exam results I'm going to fight with her because I don't believe it exists (cholera) ... in the past they said everyone in the world had *diarrhea, no?* ... now nobody can have it (diarrhea) and it is already this or that ... this business of cholera." (mother)

"We never encountered an adult with cholera, more children, and even so the mothers would say, 'My child had diarrhea because of teething,' they would never say it was cholera. This is teething diarrhea *(dentinho), business of cutting teeth!*" (community health worker)

Informants also downplayed cholera by equating it with clinically similar, yet far less virulent, dehydration, and lethal, intestinal infections. Said one informant:

"There doesn't exist cholera, my daughter, no. There exists the name that they are calling it only. When you have diarrhea you loose a lot of liquid from your body, no? ... you die in 24 hours ... your intestine is eating your entire body ... it's really only a profound intestinal infection, with fever and headache that we feel. It isn't cholera, its only an intestinal infection!" *(Umbanda* healer)

Cholera's demotion by informants to a less virulent intestinal infection status was true even with confirmed laboratory results, as seen in the case of *Dona* Rita:

Q: Tell me about your cholera illness?
R: I didn't have cholera, no!
Q: No? Then did you see this type of illness in adults before?
R: No, with this name, no ... the illness I've seen.
Q: Without the name cholera?
R: Yes, without the name ... just diarrhea, acute diarrhea ... it gives hotness in the intestine, it's an intestinal infection.

Finally, a fourth popular strategy for denying cholera's existence was ridiculing the illness—to *leva na brincadeira* (to take it as a joke), as Brazilians say. Making cholera the brunt of jokes and teasing is what six teenagers, ages 10-15 yr, did when we interviewed the group in Gonçalves Dias. Laughs, smirks, and elbow nudges emerged, and nobody had anything serious to say about cholera-until one of the boys bellowed out: "I don't know anything about cholera. I'm not a favelado[18]. I live in Aldeota (wealthy section of Fortaleza)!" Like dominos, the teens fell contagiously into uncontrollable fits of laughter, playfully back-slapping one other. "Hey, that's a good one!" "You said it, what a joke!" However, laughing off cholera was a strategy employed by all ages. A 34 year-old, severely ill patient from Gonçalves Dias joked:

"I spent three days shitting without stopping. We just took it as a big joke. People in the street would tease, Hey, are you *Colorido?*[19] We would all start to laugh ... until yesterday ... I almost died, so skinny, all sucked-out from inside!"

---

18. Term for an "inhabitant of a *favela* or urban slum," which is also used derogatorily to refer to someone poor and unhygienic. (NOVO DICIONÁRIO AURÉLIO 1986).
19. This phrase is a clever double play on words, "I'm Collorido," the catchy cmpaign slogan used by ex-President of Brazil fernando Collor de Mello, loosely translates into English as "Color me Collor." The accompanying television image showed drab black and white photos coming alive when painted yellow, green and blue (Brazil's national colors). Popular usage here refers to being infected with cholera, a pun on words since the National Congress of Brazil, in a historic and unprecedented action, impeached President Fernando Collor de Mello for corruption and ideological misrepresentation.

Cholera: More than Meets the Eye

The obvious question remains: why go to such culturally-orchestrated lengths to deny a life-threatening disease like cholera? What hidden social forces trigger this (apparently) illogical reaction? Families in Gonçalves Dias and *Conjunto* Paimeiras believed there exists not cholera the disease, but rather cholera the conspiracy. They maintained that an organized plot exists to segregate rich from poor, or worse to 'do in' poor people through massive genocide, thereby preserving the prevailing inequitable social structure. That the conspiracy threat was foremost on informants' minds was evident in the following passages:

"They are going to do away with us, creating illness and hunger." (cholera patient)

"There are many rich nearby that want to do away with this *favela*, for it to vanish. They say only thieves and drug addicts live here ... now they've added cholera! They are even saying this!" (mother)

"When I pass the alley they (better-off neighbor women) harass me, 'Hey women, do you live in Gonçalves Dias? ... it's only cholera ... Hope your (anus) is all plugged up!' They even made a petition to evict us ... They want to do away with us!" (laundress)

"Nobody wants to come close ... when I took my nieces to nursery school, they said, 'Oh, no, for the love of God, leave them at home, they might have cholera and it could spread to the others!'" (aunt)

That cholera was invented as an excuse to 'execute' the poor was reinforced, according to informants, by images used in the 'War Against Cholera' Campaign of the Ceará State Health Department in early 1994. The official mass media campaign, like that described by NICHTER (1990), was built upon an unfortunate metaphor: warfare. Along with soldiers from the Brazilian National Armed Services, the populace was called to 'battle' against cholera *(lutar contra)*, to 'combat cholera' *(combater)*, to form gangs *(arrastões)* (of delinquent youths) to 'raid and loot' against cholera. But residents we interviewed perceived the battle and looting directed not against cholera, the water-borne bacillus, but against 'we the cholera poor.' Drawing upon a 'battle' metaphor was especially inappropriate in 1993 for residents of Brazil's teeming *favelas*. The massacre at Carandiru Prison in São Paulo, the assassination of street kids in the Candelária in Rio de Janeiro, and the extermination of residents of Vigário Geral, were nightmares too recent in memory.

For this reason, drawing upon a 'warfare' metaphor in the official cholera eradication campaign was especially inappropriate. The official anti-cholera campaign poster showed a blindfolded man with a red 'X' over his face. The caption read: "Cholera, Don't Close your Eyes to Life: Help Combat Cholera" (Fig. 1). No more vivid and convincing evidence was needed, residents lamented, that the true 'battle' ahead was against the 'cholera poor;' they were being 'identified during house-to-house searches, rounded-up, tested, blindfolded and done-in.' The blindfolded man depicted on the poster, we were told by informants, was 'marked to die' and ready for execution with his hands bound behind his back, even though authorities had literally 'covered-up the real truth.' Who was behind the sinister plot to spread cholera and exterminate the poor? When interpreting the poster, one 45 yr-old, semi-literate woman let her imagination roam. "The government was announcing that they would pay a ransom for anyone the community captured with cholera and turned-in to authorities!" Why did she believe a ransom would be paid by authorities? To that question, the woman, without hesitation, pointed to the bottom right of the poster. It read: "This material was sponsored by the Northeast Bank of Brazil," accompanied by the bank's familiar logotype.

As GOFFMAN (1963: 46) has noted, "it is possible for signs which mean one thing to one group to mean something else to another group, the same category being designated but differently characterized." The soldiers, battles, raids, looting, blindfolded man, and red "X" meant one thing to State Secretary of Health Cholera Control workers and something quite different to families living in poverty. To authorities they were innocuous terms aimed at energizing the community; to poor families they were symbols of military, police, criminal and drug lords' brutality—omnipresent in Brazil's favelas—which foreshadowed horror and death. Termed 'stigma symbols' by GOFFMAN (1963), such signs are 'especially effective in drawing attention to a debasing identity discrepancy, breaking up what would otherwise be a coherent overall picture, with a consequent reduction in our valuation of the individual" (1963: 43). The poster's 'stigma symbols' are, thus, highly effective in transforming the poor cholera victim into a poor' cholera criminal who deserves justice: to be captured, blindfolded and put before the firing squad.

Fig. 1. Official cholera campaign poster interpreted as war against the infected poor, marked for erradication, that is, 'execution.'

Residents of Gonçalves Dias and *Conjunto* Palmeiras pinpointed as responsible wealthy bankers and financial institutions and implicated an amorphous "them," referring to the power elite in general (FREYRE 1963; LIPSET et al. 1963). They also earmarked the dishonorable ex-President of Brazil, Fernando Collor de Mello, as well as politicians, the pharmaceutical industry, land developers, doctors, foreigners and visiting scientists. Revolted residents explained:

"There isn't research in rich houses, who wants to know if cholera is there? Nobody goes. They only visit poor *favelas* because it's the rich who are paying to know this information." (cholera patient)
"The government invented this cholera because it really isn't to help us. Better to forget, to write us off at once ... like they say, the poor are only worth something buried." (cholera patient)
"Politicians have their reasons ... they just want to win votes." (community leader)
"They say they are going to give the poor food, but they just invent illness like cholera so pharmacies can get rich selling us medicines instead." (community health worker)

Health care professionals were also implicated in the cholera conspiracy, with the exception of community doctors who were largely exonerated. Implicated were distant, alien doctors working in Rio de Janeiro or São Paulo.

"Doctors, not like Dr A. (UFC project physician), no. But you can bet on ones from Rio de Janeiro and São Paulo ... they're only interested in cholera so they can rise" (advance in their careers).

The appearance of asymptomatic carriers of *Vibrio cholera* added more fuel to the conspiracy fire: positive results without symptoms raised immediate suspicions that medical professionals were inventing the disease as part of the cholera conspiracy. That doctors failed to isolate an etiologic agent from diarrheal patients, reinforced an image of medical incompetence and duplicity. Said one women suffering from diarrhea but testing negative for cholera:

"The community health worker did the first exam, a second exam ... nothing! 'What is it now, AIDS?,' I asked. 'Are you crazy woman! It isn't AIDS!,' she said. 'Tell me, no worms, no nothing ... well then, what devil of diarrhea is this anyway?'" (cholera patient)

If such down-home explanations fail to convince, a great global cholera conspiracy is entertained. SONTAG (1990) in *AIDS and Its Metaphors,* suggests that "there is a link between imaging disease and imaging foreignness." It lies perhaps in the very concept of 'wrong,' which is archaically identical with the non-us, the 'alien' (1990: 48). Informants counterattack the highly industrialized and wealthy nations—Japan and the United States of America—as responsible for both inventing and planting cholera in the impoverished Northeast:

"There doesn't even exist cholera in São Paulo, no way. It was invented outside Brazil." (traditional healer)

"It was a band of people over there that invented cholera. The same that invented dengue ... the Japanese. It already came from there to here, cholera. They invented the robot ... they work, do everything, equal to a person ... even weave a hammock. So they invented robots so nobody will work. And invented cholera to do away with us because they can't raise our salaries." (mother)

"We all saw Dr R, the American (doctor), help by putting medicine,in the well water ... but the other Americans with him, they only want women to stop having babies, to exploit us." (cholera patient)

The Menace of Metaphors

Let's assume, for now, that cholera was invented and introduced into Brazilian *favelas* as part of an elitist's conspiracy—a global conspiracy—to exterminate the poor. The next question is: how exactly do the elite link impoverished Brazilians to the morally disgracing and disempowering imagery of cholera? Embedded in informants' narratives we discovered one devastating way: metaphors. In *Metaphors We Live By,* LAKOFF & JOHNSON say "the essence of metaphor is understanding and experiencing one kind of thing in terms of another." (1990: 5) This is possible because the metaphor is built into the conceptual system of the culture in which we live; it is embedded in our values, perceptions and systems of meaning. When making a direct association between two domains is too abstract, unclear, difficult, or even risky-for whatever reason—metaphors are used to define and assign meaning, thus giving us a new understanding of our experience. First, the metaphor highlights certain features while suppressing other aspects of the concept that are inconsistent with metaphor. Second, the metaphor does not merely entail other concepts, but it entails very specific aspects of these concepts. Third, because the metaphor highlights important experiences and makes them coherent while masking other experiences, the metaphor gives a new meaning. By highlighting and hiding, can come to "see" humans living in poor housing conditions without much to eat in terms of non-humans with animal motivations, actions and characteristics. Without these channeling metaphors, but others, we might just as well "see" *favelados* as devoted Catholics, as working mothers, as migrant laborers etc.

As harmless as metaphors—a simple figure of speech—may appear, LAIR RIBEIRO (1992) maintains that metaphors are the most powerful way to communicate because they have "condensed power." In the realm of disease, "nothing is more punitive than to give a disease a meaning." (1992: 17). As SONTAG explains:

"the subjects of deepest dread (corruption, decay, pollution, anomie, weakness) are identified with the disease. The disease itself becomes a metaphor. Then, in the name of the disease (that is, using it as a metaphor), the horror is imposed on other things. The disease becomes adjectival. Something is said to be disease-like, meaning that it is disgusting or ugly ... Feelings about evil are projected onto a disease. And the disease (so enriched with meanings) is projected onto the world" (1990: 58)

From informants' perspectives, the elite in Brazil seem to have a corner on using menacing metaphors. They are accused of subliminally (some may argue unconsciously, or even unwittingly) feeding into pre-existing stereotypes, equating poor people with degrading and humiliating cultural images and then playing on these potent metaphors to link the poor directly to cholera. Two such culturally construed images are the *pessoa imunda* (filthy-dirty person) and *vira latas* (stray mutt dogs). Both are cognitive constructions of the defiling, repulsive and repugnant. Both are common images in the everyday world of *favelados*. Both came to our attention because of the frequency with which they appeared in fieldnotes and transcriptions. We will now explore these two culturally-forged images, showing how the *favelado's* identity, the Dog's Disease and cholera became inexorably bound.

Filthy, Dirty Person *(Pessoa Imunda)*

"We ARE the cholera!" pronounced 18 yr-old Rosa in a matter-of-fact tone of voice, sending shivers through us. For after I month in the field, the force of a metaphor to spoil personal identity was becoming apparent. How had this young woman, recovering from a serious cholera infection, come to internalize that she, herself, her person, was equivalent to contaminated, polluted, dangerous and feared feces?

Being physically dirty or lacking personal hygiene is particularly abhorred in Brazilian culture. Taking innumerable baths per day, using deodorant and dousing oneself with cologne (from sweet smelling herbal water to imported French perfume, depending on class), wearing clean, pressed clothes and spotless shoes in public are valued across socioeconomic groups in Northeast Brazil. The 'cult of cleanliness' is inculcated in young Brazilian children via such animated carton characters as *Sujismundo (Dirty* World) and *Cascão,* two filthy-dirty little boys, who because they never bathe are the brunt of jokes and teasing by playmates. Given this cultural abhorrence of poor personal hygiene, the dirty or the unkept are especially degrading and defiling images, spoiling one's identity.

We learned that prior to the current cholera epidemic, the *favelado's* image, in society's eyes, had already been firmly wedded to that of a *pessoa imunda* (filthy, dirty person).

"They nicknamed us *favelados* because we are poor, we live in a *favela,* we are *imunda* (filthy dirty), we don't have a salary, we don't have good nutrition." (12-year-old girl)

"It makes no difference, if I clean outside because my neighbor is so *imunda*. She raises pigs ... her children walk without shoes ... she throws the sewerage on the street ... and when it rains this dirtiness washes in front of my house." (mother)

Early in 1993, when cholera advanced quickly throughout Ceará, mass media prevention campaigns mentioned that fecal-oral contamination spreads cholera (Fig. 1). What residents 'heard' on radio and television, however, was a different and more damaging message: cholera is caused not by the water-borne bacillus but by miasmic *imundicie, a* popular word meaning 'filthy squalor,' the worst kind of dirtiness or pollution. The *mundo imunda,* the filthy world they were forced to live in 'causes cholera.' Urban squalor—*imundicie*—was everywhere: 'foul atmosphere,' effusions *(catinga)* from decaying pigs' feces and open sewerage, decaying food from the nearby dump, garbage, rot, children playing with mud and walking without shoes, flies landing on feces then on food, proximity to the city's mortuary and bloody run-off water, homemade ice cream with decaying fly remains, and spoiled food scavenged from the dump. The generalizing of a specific infective process into an atmosphere found in urban slums—into *imundicie* and *imundas* (filthy, dirty) persons—was used to moralize cholera and to stigmatize infected persons by associating them with impurity, deviancy and disdain. *Favelados were* stigmatized as *imundas* persons; *imundicie* causes cholera, cholera is, therefore, *favelados. Favelados* are cholera.

It is no wonder, then, that an official national cholera campaign slogan in late *1992—Fora Cólera!* (Get Out Cholera!)—did little to endear our informants to the government's control efforts. The slogan *Fora Cólera!* is a subliminal play on the words *Fora Collor!* (Get Out [President] Collor!) which, just months before in September 1992, had been the rallying cry, chanted by millions of Brazilian citizens who took to the streets to demonstrate and force the impeachment of the then President of Brazil, Fernando Collor de Mello. Instead of 'Get Out Cholera!' families heard, 'Get out, you filthy-dirty crook! Get out, you worthless cholera-infected person.' The official message, rather than mobilizing persons to eradicate *Vibrio cholera* and, thus, protect themselves against infection, galvanized them against the (perceived) unscrupulous motives of the elite.

Doença de Cachorro: The Dog's Disease

"Cholera, rabies, *Doença de Cachorro* (The Dog's Disease)." *Dona* Zilnar rambles the three words off so quickly, that they are hardly distinguishable. She has her reasons. In Portuguese the words are intimately related. *'Cólera'* is a pseudonym for *'raiva,'* or rabies. According to the dictionary *(Novo Dicionário Aurélio da Lingua Portuguesa),* the word *'cólera,'* of Greek and Latin derivation means: 1. a violent impulse against that which offends, wounds or causes us indignity; that angers or provokes *raiva;* 2. a ferocity of animals; 3. agitation; and 4. an infectious, acute, contagious disease, that can manifest as an epidemic, and is characterized in its classical presentation by abundant diarrhea, prostration and cramping. A *colérica* person is first a *raivosa* or angry person, and second a person infected with *V. cólera*. The dictionary defines the word *raiva*, of Latin deviation, as first rabies, a viral disease that attacks mammals, and second as *V. Cólera*. A *raivosas* person is one attached by rabies and second one full of anger, full of *cólera (Novo Dicionário Aurélio da Lingua Portuguesa).*

In northeastern Brazil, people use the word cholera for rabies. Dogs foam at the mouth because of cholera. A *colérico* dog bites and passes *raiva*. People vaccinate their dogs against cholera. Given the linguistic resemblance of cholera and *raiva*, then, the metaphorical play that associates poor persons with *vira lata* dogs is fairly straightforward. *Favelado is* cholera is *raiva* (rabies) is The Dog's Disease (as is cholera) is dog is *vira lata* (an especially scraggly, unkempt kind of dog who scavenges food from garbage cans). Metaphorically speaking, *favelados* are *vira latas*. In the eyes of the poor, how society treats a rabid stray mutt is also how it will symbolically treat a cholera-infected *favelado*.

Stray Mongrels *(Vira Latas)*

Thus, when *Dona* Zilnar screams "I'm not dog, no!," she is not referring to dog as Man's Best Friend—the pedigreed, pampered poodles rich *Madames* parade along Fortaleza's beachfront as *Dona* Zilnar begs money from tourists. The dogs *Dona* Zilnar refers to are another type: *vira latas*. They are the abandoned beasts that roam Fortaleza's *favelas*—hungry, diseased, unkempt, and unloved. Informants' colorful and degrading descriptions of *vira latas* would give anyone reason to revolt, if likened to them:

> *"Vira lata* is a *bruto* (ugly, wild beast) animal, a stray mutt that runs loose in the four corners of the city, wild on the streets. Everybody who sees them wants the right to do something—kick, throw rocks, hit—do all sorts of violence to these *vira latas* because they don't even have an owner." (community health worker)

> *"Vira latas* suffer a lot. They are born at home, but when they grow a little bit they must go to the streets. They scavenge garbage cans-turn them over-looking for any scrap of food. They are common animals like any other type" (without pedigree). (12-year-old girl)

> *"Vira latas* don't have a place to stay ... where they find someone to give a little scrap of food, they stay, but they are always an embarrassment to everyone *(desprezo de todos)."* (cholera patient)

> *"Vira latas* are full of illness. You can almost get sick just looking at one. They are filthy-dirty ... never vaccinated against rabies. If they are crazy and bite someone, this illness is very dangerous (for people) ... They don't have anyone to do anything for them. They are *brutos* (wild, beasts). They don't know anything." (community leader)

Given that being likened to a *vira lata* is bad enough, the term *vira lata* is also used derogatorily in everyday language to refer to female prostitutes (i.e. commercial sex-workers). An English equivalent is 'whore.' The metaphorical implication is that prostitutes, like stray dogs, belong to no one and everyone, that they have no pedigree, no status, and no inherent rights. A *vira lata* girl is at ready disposal of anyone who desires to use and abuse her in exchange for leftovers—as little as U.S. $ 4.00-5.00 per sexual encounter in Fortaleza. The word dog or *cachorro* alone has multiple derogatory meanings in northeastern Brazil. "Cachorro sem vergonha!" loosely translates as "You low-down bastard without scruples!" Dictionary synonyms for the word *cachorro* include scoundrel (a mean, immoral or wicked person or rascal) and wretch (a person who is despised or scorned) and its feminine version, *cachorra* include shew, strumpet (a prostitute), and harlot (rouge, vagabond, prostitute; *Michaelis Dicionário Prático).* A derivative form of *cachorro, cão,* also refer to a masculine dog, but according to the dictionary, the word *cão* alternatively means 'a contemptible person' *(Michaelis Dicionário Prático)* and in popular usage it signifies the 'demon' or 'devil.' The popular sayings, *Que o cão te carregue!,* (May the devil carry you (to hell))! or *Ele tem parte com o cão!* (He has a pact with the devil!) illustrates in common speech the diabolical connotation of the word *cão* or dog in Portuguese. A *banda de cachorros or cachorrada* literally refers to a pack of dogs; according to the dictionary, it also means a mob (a disorderly and lawless crowd or in slang, a gang of criminals) or alternatively, an ill-conceived, wicked and mischievous trick produced by *cachorros (a* low-down, dishonest person; *Michaelis Dicionário Prático). A cachorrice* is defined as a 'wicked action' or 'conduct dirty trick lowness meanness,' 'indignity' *(Michaelis Dicionário Prático).* Furthermore, anyone living in one of Fortaleza's 300 *favelas* can tell the fate of a *colérico vira lata* dog suspected of rabies: dog catchers hunt it down, restrain the feisty animal with a leash and collar, muzzle and isolate it to keep it from biting innocent victims. In cases of bites, the stray is kept under keen observation. If the unfortunate victim develops symptoms of rabies, the dog is killed. Even in less extreme cases when dogs are not infected with rabies, many well-to-do residents prefer to see them eliminated and deliberately avoid all contact (particularly that of their children) with unvaccinated, stray mutts. As one informant emphasized:

> "SUCAM (Government Infectious Disease Control Unit) must kill these *vira latas*. If not the city will be swarming with these mangy mongrels and this can't be permitted!" (community leader)

As with the cholera eradication campaign poster (Fig. 1), the State Secretary of Health's reported actions reinforced, in people's minds, the menacing metaphors. Headlines in the local newspaper of 13 March 1994 read: *"Secretary of Health is Accused of Executing Dogs."* (O POVO 1994) The International Association for the Protection of Animals filed suit against the Secretary of Health in neighboring Maracanã, and two Health Post Veterinarians for indiscriminately capturing and killing dogs. "The workers from the Health Post capture dogs in the street without any respect for laws governing their sacrifice (all animals are entitled to an eight-day period after capture to locate the owner or process an adoption)," the article reported. The Health workers were accused of 'extreme brutality' in sacrificing the animals: the captured dogs were hit over the head with a nail protruding from a two-by-four board and their throats slashed with a large knife.

To *Dona* Zilnar and her neighbor friends, the *vira lata* metaphor rings too close to home. Handing her a positive diagnosis for *V. cholera* was like symbolically screaming in her face: "You no good *vira lata!* You filthy, dirty stray mutt! How dare you bite us, you lowly mongrel! You worthless bitch! You cheap whore!" Through *Dona* Zilnar's eyes, identifying her as a *V. cholera* carrier was equivalent to branding her as an inferior, sub-human type only worthy of eating spoiled, leftover scraps of food (like those she scavenges from the garbage bins behind the São Sebastino Market every Friday). She has no pedigree, no family name worth weight. If she strays into well-to-do-neighborhoods, the dog catcher may catch, harness, muzzle and even 'sacrifice' her. In the same way, when health authorities target endemic cholera enclaves, implement door-to-door disease surveillance, erect highly visible cholera treatment, tents in town centers, and set up barricades to contain the disease's transmission, she feels like a huge dog collar is being tightened around the rabid, *cóleric* community. Slowly it is cinched. Once the muzzle is fitted, the leash secured, the, rabid, mad *vira lata* dog restrained, extermination proceeds.

Metaphor, Stigma and Spoiled Identity

Through metaphors the identity of *favelados* is inexorably bound to morally-repugnant cultural images of filth and stray mutts and, in certain instances, prostitutes. In *Purity and Danger* (1966), MARY DOUGLAS argues that every culture is a means of ordering experience. However, every ordering system gives rise to anomalies and ambiguities, which it must be prepared to control when they violate principles of order by crossing some forbidden line. Labeling anomalies or violators as 'impure polluting,' or otherwise 'dangerous' allows society to get rid of them through destruction, banishment, or execution—either directly or symbolically. Because epidemic cholera florishes in unsanitary *favelas* yet disregards socioeconomic barriers, *favelados* are perceived by wealthy Brazilians as one such 'danger' which threatens the rigid class structure of Brazilian society. Order must be restored and violators controlled. One way, is to label *favelados* as impure, polluting, and dangerous, as we have witnessed in *Conjunto* Palmeiras and Gonçalves Dias. Moral sentiments support the rules of purity, according to DOUGLAS. *Favelados* are not only polluting and dangerous, they are labeled as being morally-inferior to upper-class elites. A *vira lata* mutt is a bastard dog (or prostitute), a morally-disgraceful identity in this largely Catholic country. The very idea of pollution occurring through, say, casual contact between the morally-inferior poor and the upstanding elite, may suffice to preserve the sharply drawn class-distinctions in Northeast Brazil, having one of the world's worst distributions of wealth (WORLD BANK 1990). Moreover, with the aggressive spread of the epidemic, the poor often come to be seen by elites as their *adversaries* that can attack, bite, hurt, steal (scraps of leftover food), and even kill. In keeping with the principle of purity and order, these enemies must be destroyed. Adversarial models of health interventions and education can be employed to 'declare war target attack,' 'exterminate execute,' those who threaten class order, temporarily upset (NICHTER 1990).

Through such degrading and animalistic metaphors, *favelados* suffer contamination not only of their intestinal mucosa, but of their social identity. In his classic work on stigma, ERVING GOFFMAN defines stigma as:

> "an attribute that makes him different from others ... of a less desirable kind ... a person who is quite thoroughly bad, or dangerous, or weak. He is thus reduced in our minds from a whole and usual person to a tainted, discounted one. Such an attribute is a stigma, especially when its discrediting effect is very extensive." (1963: 2-3)

Cholera—like tuberculosis, leprosy, and HIV/AIDS—is a mysterious infectious disease that is not only acutely feared but is felt to be morally, if not literally, contagious. A moralistic judgement about the person accompanies the disease. FREIDSON (1979) notes that when a moralistic judgement of blame is made, the bearer may be held responsible for the illness. Medical problems may be stigmatized to the extent that by *social* taxonomy, the illness becomes a *crime* and the sick person a deviant deserving punishment in society's eyes. Even worse, stigma may spoil normal identity permanently (ABLON 1981; BOUTTÉ 1987).

> "Stigma is so closely connected with identity that even after the cause of the imputation of stigma has been removed and the societal reaction has been ostensibly redirected, identity is formed by the fact of having been in a stigmatized role ... one's identity is permanently spoiled. (GOFFMAN 1963:74)

In this largely Catholic world where filth and sexual immorality are formally abhorred, the social labels of *imunda* or, worse, *vira lata* are weighty, image-destroying stigmas. Besides suffering the wrenching cramps of a *V. cholera* infected intestine, cholera patients are seen by many elites as immoral individuals, who are fully responsible for the epidemic. Their identities as mothers, workers, students are spoiled permanently. Even after the cholera epidemic is controlled, the images of *imundicie* and *vira latas* will remain.

Acquiescence to such social stigmatization, however, is seldom a popular response. Rather, labeling and stigmatization more often provoke acts of subtle resistance by peripheral people against the dominant (SCOTT 1985, 1990; COMAROFF 1985). The highly stigmatized do not always accept the very norms that disqualify them. Explain GUSSOW & TRACY:

> "Surely there are other feasible modes of adaptation. One is the development of stigma theories by the stigmatized-that is, ideologies to counter the ones that discredit them, theories that would explain or legitimize their social condition, that would attempt to disavow their imputed inferiority and danger and expose the real and alleged fallacies involved in the dominant perspective." (1986: 317)

So it is with cholera. If poor people cannot confront the elite or revolt violently and vociferously against their unfair characterization and stigmatization, they dig-in and brandish symbolic fists (SCOTT 1985, 1990). Why comply with medical advice? Why obey instructions? Why become a 'dog'? Why be abused, kicked, muzzled or shot? Better to define cholera as an invention, fantasy, or conspiracy and shout out, 'I'm Not Dog, No!' than to internalize its accusatory message. Better to suffer in silence than to assume 'stray dog status' and be buried in the weight of its prejudice. Non-compliance becomes a silent revolt against the injustices of everyday life. "It's rabies! It's cholera! Careful rich one, don't let us bite you!" bellows out *Dona* Beatriz, as two wealthier women pass by. Defiance serves to reverse estrangement and reconstitute the divided self. Bucking authorities, no matter how discreetly, becomes a survival strategy to keep one's identity and passionate human spirit in tact. The force and furor of the backlash churn beneath the surface largely invisible to the public eye.

In both communities we studied, examples abound of resistance, including non-compliance with recommended treatment and public health prevention efforts. Prophylactic antibiotics age expectorated and chloride for sterilizing water pots dumped out, once health workers leave. As informants explained:

"God help me! I'm not taking those pills. They look like rat poison, my sister, it was rat poison!" (cholera patient)

"My green pills I threw over the wall." (mother)

"They brought me drops (chloride) to put in my water pot ... it was nothing but bleach, common bleach, women! Thanks a lot, I said, because I have a little tiny pile of clothes to wash!" (laundress)

Second, as we learned from *Dona* Zilnar and others the implications of the cholera-as-invention posture is that people "hide" their symptoms from health authorities and, hence, grossly underestimate their risk of infection from *V. cholera*. This is particularly true of asymptomatic carriers, because without symptoms it is easier to dismiss one's role in transmitting the disease, especially if cholera is 'make believe.'

Third, many informants experienced exaggerated confidence in supernatural protection. Only spiritual protection was 100 % effective, informants often said. Sick and suffering cholera patients retreated into their homes, into the comfort of their private saints to whom they pray for forgiveness and salvation while self-treating with herbal remedies.

Fourth, we noticed both a marked resistance and delay in seeking biomedical services. Few informants sought out nearby São José Hospital for electrolyte replacement therapy and, then, only when nearly unconscious. Finally, we identified a strange, morbid sense of pending death experienced by cholera infected persons. With the onset of profuse watery stools, they invariably begin bidding final farewells to horrified and frantic family members.

Lessons for Cholera Control

It is clear from the above that to control cholera in Northeast Brazil, it is necessary to 'remove dog collars'—that is, to listen to people's opinions, to include them in the definition of educational messages, and to design and implement control strategies which are socially and culturally appropriate. Experience shows that poor people do participate in learning experiences when opportunity is present. In such a context, people's innate learning skills are stimulated and instructions make sense (FREIRE 1977; DRUMMOND 1975; RIFKIN 1983).

We see none of the crippling fatalism and myopic 'Limited Good' vision so often ascribed to Latin American peasants in our informants' responses.[20] On the contrary, residents in Gonçalves Dias *and Conjunto* Palmeiras have frustratingly down-to-earth ideas about what needs to be done to control cholera in their communities. What they lack is not the will, but the way to implement changes, as comments below attest:

"The government must come to see the situation here. They have been saying a lot about hygiene and we know by experience that any improvement in hygiene is good for health. Why don't they do something about sanitation?" (mother of five young children).

---

20. ACHESON 1972; RYAN 1971; HARRISON 1985; LEWIS 1966; SCHEPER-HUGHES 1984, 1985; VALENTINE 1968; FOSTER 1965, 1967, 1972.

"We have been trying to do something to improve the environment but we receive no support from any institution." (community leader)

"In my family nobody likes drinking chloride water but I force them to do it anyway. They say that cholera can kill us. I don't want to die." (mother)

Based on the above ethnographic findings, we can recommend to health authorities in Fortaleza, Brazil more generally, and, perhaps, to other developing regions, the following strategies to control cholera:

1. Replace moralistic miasmic theories of the spontaneous generation of cholera with the destigmatizing germ theory of water-borne contagion;
2. Promote healthy hygienic practices (handwashing, feces disposal, in-home water treatment) as an integral part of people's daily life routine rather than an extraordinary cholera-linked measure;
3. Mobilize traditional healers and lay persons in early initiation of in-home rehydration with household fluids, herbal teas and oral rehydration salts as an alternative to hospital-based rehydration (NATIONS et al. 1988; NATIONS & REBHUN 1988);
4. Avoid earmarking specific communities or persons as foci of disease-transmission; control measures should be applied across-the-board to all economic classes and all persons in endemic regions;
5. Avoid 'high visibility' control interventions such as community 'cholera tents' and community-wide testing in public places; private, discrete face-to-face instructions will probably be more effective;
6. Avoid fear-driven educational messages; mass media campaigns should speak to specific methods to prevent infection using popular terminology and cognitive images;
7. Most important, eliminate all menacing, stigmatizing metaphors which insidiously discriminate by linking cholera to the identity of the poor.

Anthropology's Contribution to Cholera Control

Because of the life-threatening nature and urgency of epidemics of infectious diseases such as cholera, medical assistance must be mobilized quickly and efficiently to control their spread. In the haste to deliver emergency medical services, the cultural beliefs, perceptions, attitudes and behaviors of threatened individuals are frequently overlooked. Suffering people are often dehumanized by health workers as 'disease hosts,' 'carriers' or 'sources of contamination,' and their communities as a 'target population' or 'foci of disease transmission.' Their human qualities are transformed, or worse, forgotten. Because anthropology treats humans holistically *in* their natural sociocultural setting and captures people's own representations of their day-to-day world, the discipline can help fill the conceptual gap left by medical teams studying infectious diseases. Grasping an emic perspective (HARRIS 1976; BERREMAN 1966), as we have seen in the case of cholera, is fundamental even in such trying, emergency situations. Control campaigns which ignore the anthropology of its 'target population' at best achieve only stunted program impact, far below its full potential, and, at worse, provoke anger, resistance, revolt and rejection among infected individuals and their families.

The specific contributions of anthropology to the study of infectious diseases we identified based on our experience with cholera in Fortaleza, Brazil are as follows:

1. Key-informants' colorful descriptions of symptoms, onset, manifestations, and suffering associated with infection, which draw on cultural representations and are embedded in local systems of meaning, can speed the diagnostic process and provide invaluable insights for health professionals about the disease as 'lived experience' (KLEINMAN et al. 1986); these often differ from standard textbook accounts. Our rich descriptions of cholera episodes 'lived' at home, for instance, paint a real life picture of suffering, generally not appreciated in de-contexualized, biomedical accounts of enteric infections.

2. Knowledge of people's self-care practices and health-seeking behavior in relation to a specific infection, allows health professionals to identify culturally-specific practices and resources in the community to help patients cope with illness at home. Based on this information, health professionals can prescribe interventions that are both accessible and feasible to practice. For instance, we discovered a strong resistance to the addition of bleach to household drinking water as a cholera control measure. Vinegar was identified during the ethnographic study as a more acceptable alternative. We also learned that cholera is treated at home with medicinal herbal teas and patients seek the advise of *rezadeiras,* or traditional folk catholic healers. Based on this ethnographic data, oral rehydration therapy can be successfully mixed with herbal teas and mild to moderate cases of cholera managed at home by *rezadeiras,* lay experts in diarrheal diseases (NATIONS et al. 1983; NATIONS et al. 1988; NATIONS & REBHUN 1988).
3. In-household participant-observation of family members performing daily chores can lead to the discovery of behavioral modes of disease transmission not previously imaged or identified by epidemiologists (NATIONS 1986). Preparation of homemade popsicies with cholera-infected water or the eating of feces-contaminated dirt (geophagia) by children, for instance, were two such behaviors we observed inside homes in Gonçalves Dias.
4. Anthropological analysis of symbolic behavior and hidden transcripts which gets behind the scenes of official presentations can lead to the important discovery of patients' 'non-complaint' behavior and, more importantly, their rational for rejecting well-intentioned interventions, as we have discussed above.
5. Detailed linguistic and ethnographic data on lay terminology and cognition, and explanatory models of illness can help bridge sometimes fatal gaps in doctor-patient communication. Eliciting the metaphorical meanings of the 'Dog's Disease,' for instance, was essential for improving communication with cholera-infected individuals in Fortaleza. As a result, relationships between health care providers and communities, especially poor communities, can be improved.
6. Ethnographic data can guide the re-writing of educational messages gone wrong. By situating messages in the imaginary world of "target" populations, their meaning is more easily understood and, hence, acted upon. Images and terms that provoke anger, disapproval and rejection can be avoided.
7. Rapid ethnographic assessment (RAP), which gleens essential data about infectious disease beliefs, attitudes and behaviors, can give quick responses on how to control disease transmission. The quick turn-around time from data collection to use by program managers, is a positive feature of RAP in emergency, epidemic settings. In such trying situations, program managers are pressed to design and implement control measures immediately. Using RAP methodology in Fortaleza, we were able to provide university enteric disease specialists with preliminary ethnographic observations and impressions after one week of fieldwork, highly focused on the in-household transmission and control of cholera. Simultaneous with data collection and on-going analysis, program managers were continuously up-dated regarding our ethnographic hypotheses and findings. Our general findings, presented here in greater detail, were incorporated into the emergency cholera control program in Gonçalves Dias long before tape recorded interviews were completely transcribed and the final manuscript written. The quickness of RAP methodology together with numerous short cuts taken by the authors in organizing and processing data, permitted the anthropology of cholera victims and their communities to figure squarely in re-designing control efforts in Gonçalves Dias which were more sensitive to people's reality and proved instrumental in reducing the incidence of cholera in this *favela* (Dr. ALDO LIMA, personal communication).

To conclude, an anthropological interpretation of contagious cholera, requires that researchers first understand the local worlds of people exposed to the water-borne, cholera-causing bacillus. Only with probing insights into this day-to-day reality can researchers and communities work together to identify possible strategies which can effectively control disease transmission within households. Without these key cultural insights, as we have clearly seen with cholera, it is difficult, if not impossible, to design highly effective educational interventions to prevent its spread and forsee the 'collateral effects' such culturally-blind messages may provoke. The morally disgracing, disgusting and disempowering illness imagery associated metaphorically with cholera tainted, rather than cured, individuals and communities we studied. It is not so much the cholera-causing bacillus that is feared but the morally-polluting stigmas that are dreaded. A positive cholera diagnosis debases one's identity. Although physically recovered from painful gastric cramping, explosive diarrhea. and life-threatening dehydration, patients rarely heal completely from the wounds of social stigmatization. This 'collateral effect' of cholera prevention campaigns, we have seen, can spark outrage and revolt on people's part, causing them to resist well-intended control measures.

Even if a new anthropologically-sensitive approach can guard against the 'collateral effects' of conventional educational interventions, we must never lose sight that there is a larger issue with which we must contend with equal urgency: the eradication of the true 'Dog's Disease' in developing countries: that is, economic poverty in which families are forced to live.

Acknowledgements

We thank the *Instituto Conceitos Culturais & Medicina (ICC&M)* and Clinical Research Unit, UFC in Fortaleza, Brazil for supporting this work. To families in Gonçalves Dias and *Conjunto* Paimeiras, we are indebted for their privileged personal accounts of what it is like to be poor, sick, and discriminated against because of suffering 'The Dog's Disease.' Special mention must be made of *Dona* Jandira, spirited laundress, whose piercing social critique of cholera proved to 'hold water.' We are particularly grateful to our COS-SAH colleagues at Harvard University Medical School, Department of Social Medicine, for their comments on an earlier draft of this paper resented at a recent faculty meeting in, Chiapas, Mexico (Dr. Paul Farmer's insights on the dynamics of accusations and AIDS were especially helpful as was Dr Steffan I. Ayora-Diaz's reference to James Scott's work on hidden transcripts), Dr. Aldo Lima, M.D. (UFC) for his solicitation of a social diagnosis of cholera, and Maria Auxiliadora de Souza, M.D., MPH, Ph.D. for easing our entry into the homes and lives of women in Gonçalves Dias. Finally special recognition to Mário Roberto de C. Martin, Carmozita Peixoto da Silva, and Inicio de Noiola Gomes Fernandes who made possible our daily treks into the field, always emotionally and physically exhausting.

Note

Except for several structures, the *Favela* Gonçalves Dias no longer exists. In 1995, subsequent to our work, a major road was built through the community, dispersing the homeless families.

References

ABLON, J.
   1981 Stigmatized health conditions. *Social Science & Medicine* 15: 5-9.
ACHESON, J.M.
   1972 Limited good or limited goods? Response to economic opportunity in a Tarascan Pueblo. *American Anthropology* 74: 1152-1169.
AHRTAG (Appropriate Health Resources and Technologies Action Group Ltd)
   1983 Controlling cholera. *Dialogue on Diarrhoea* 52(Mar-May) 1-8.
BERREMAN, G.D.
   1966 Anemic and emetic analyses in social anthropology. *American Anthropologist* 68: 346-354.
BOUTTÉ, M.I.
   1987 "The Stumbling Disease": A case study of stigma among Azorean-Portuguese. *Social Science & Medicine* 24: 209-217.
CLEMENTS, M.L.
   1980 *Sudan community-based family health project: Trip Report,* 21 Aug.-2 Sept., University of Maryland, Unpublished.
CLEMENTS, M.L. et al.
   1980 *Comparison of simple sugar/salt versus glucose/electrolyte oral rehydration solutions in infant diarrhoea.* University of Maryland, Unpublished.

COMAROFF, J.
　1985　*Body of Power Spirit of Resistance*. University of Chicago Press, Chicago.
DENZIN, N.K.
　1970　*The Research Act in Sociology*. Butterworth, London.
DOUGLAS, M.
　1966　*Purity and Danger*. Routledge & Kegan Paul, London.
DRUMMOND, T.
　1975　Using the method of Paulo Freire in nutrition education: An experimental plan for community action in Northeast Brazil. *Cornell International Nutrition Monograph Series No. 3*. Cornell University Press, Ithaca, NY.
EGEMAN, A. & BERTAN, M.
　1980　A study of oral rehydration therapy by midwives in a rural area near Ankara. *Bulletin of the World Health Organization* 58: 333-338.
ELTERBROCK, T.V.
　1979　*Oral replacement therapy in rural Bangladesh with home ingredients*. Bangladesh Rural Advancement Committee, Dacca, Unpublished.
FARMER, P.
　1992　*AIDS and Accusation: Haiti and the Geography of Blame*. University of California Press, Berkeley.
FREIDSON, E.
　1979　*Profession of Medicine: A Study of the Sociology of Applied Knowledge*. Dodd, Mead, New York.
FREIRE, P.
　1977　*Pedagogy of the Oppressed*. Penguin, London.
FREYRE, G.
　1963　*The Mansions and the Shanties: The Making of Modern Brazil*. Knopf, New York.
FOSTER, G.M.
　1965　Peasant society and the image of limited good. *American Anthropology* 67: 293-315.
　1967　Peasant character and personality, In: *Peasant Society a Reader*. Edited by M. POTTER; M. DIAZ & G. FOSTER, pp. 50-56. Little & Brown, Boston.
　1972　The anatomy of envy: a study in symbolic behavior. *Current Anthropology* 13: 165-202.
GOFFMAN, E.
　1959　*The Presentation of Self in Everyday* Life. Doubleday, Garden City, New York.
　1963　*Stigma: Notes on the Management of Spoiled Identity*. Prentice-Hall, Englewood Cliffs, NJ.
GOODENOUGH, W.B., R.S. GORDON JR & I.S. ROSENBERG.
　1964　Tetracycline in the treatment of *cholera*. *The Lancet* 1: 355-357.
GUERRANT, R.L.; L.V. KIRCHHOFF; D.S. SHIELDS, D.S. et al.
　1983　Prospective study of diarrheal illnesses in northeastern Brazil: Patterns of disease, nutritional impact, etiologies and risk factors. *Journal of Infectious Diseases* 148: 986-997.
GUERRANT, R.L.; J.F. MCAULIFFE & M.A. DE SOUZA.
　1996　Mortality among rural and urban families: an indicator of development and implications for the future. In: *At the Edge of Development: Health Problems in a Transitional Society*. Edited by R.L. GUERRANT; M.A. DE SOUZA & M.K. NATIONS, pp. 69-90. Carolina Academic Press. Durham, North Carolina.
GUSSOW, Z. & G.S. TRACY.
　1986　Status, ideology an adaptation to stigmatized illness: a study of leprosy. *Human Organization* 27: 316.
HARLAND, G. ET AL.
　1981　Composition of oral solutions prepared by Jamaican mothers for treatment of diarrhea. *The Lancet* 1: 600-601.
HARRIS, M.
　1976　History and significance of the emic/etic distinction. *Annual Review of Anthropology* 5: 329-350.
HARRISON, L.
　1985　*Underdevelopment is a State of Mind,* University Press of America, Lanham, MD.
HIRSHHORN, N. et al.
　1983　Oral rehydration therapy: the scientific and technological basis. Presented to the International Conference on ORT, 7 June, Washington, DC.
KIELMAN, A.A. et al.
　1977　Home treatment of childhood diarrhea in Punhab village. *J. Trop. Pediat. Env. Child Health* 23: 197-201.
KLEINMAN, A. & J. KLEINMAN.
　1986　Suffering and its professional transformation: toward an ethnography of experience. Paper presented at the First Conference of the Society for Psychological Anthropology, "On Current Thinking and Research in Psychological Anthropology," San Diego, CA, 6-8 Oct.

KLUCKHOHN, C.
1944   *Navaho Witchcraft*. Harvard University Papers of The Peabody Museum, Cambridge, MA, Vol. 22(2).
LAKOFF, G. & JOHNSON, M.
1990   *Metaphors We Live By*. The University of Chicago Press, Chicago.
LEWIS, O.
1966   The culture of poverty. *Scientific American* 215: 19-25.
LIMA, A.A.M.
1994   Cholera: Molecular epidemiology, pathogenesis, immunology, treatment, and prevention. *Current Science* 3: 593-601.
LIMA, A.M. & R.L. GUERRANT.
1994   *Mediguide to Diseases* 5: 1-5.
LIPSET, S.M. & A. SOLARI.
1963   *Elites in Latin America*. Oxford University Press, New York.
MAHALANABIS, D. et al.
1974   Use of an oral glucose-electrolyte solution in the treatment of paediatric cholera: A controlled study. *J. Trop. Pediatr. Environ. Child Health* 20: 82-87.
MELAMED, A. & M. SEGALL.
1978   Spoons for making glucose-salt solution (letter). *The Lancet* 1: 1317-1318.
MOLIA, A.M. et al.
1985   Rice-based oral rehydration solution decreases stool volume in acute diarrhoea. *Bulletin WHO* 63: 751-756.
MOLLA, A.M.; A. MOLLA & S.K. NATH et al.
1989   Food-based oral rehydration salt solution for acute childhood diarrhoea. *The Lancet* 2: 429-431.
MONTE, C.M.G.
1993   Improving weaning food hygiene practices in a slum area of Fortaleza, Northeast Brazil: A new approach. Ph.D. Thesis, 69, London School of Tropical Medicine and Hygiene, University of London, Unpublished.
MORAN, M.
1996   Oral rehydration therapy in home and hospital: experience in rural Nigeria. *Pediatric Nursing* 25: 32-33.
MORELLO, T.
1983   A spoonful of sugar ... *Far East. Econ. Rev.* 119: 32.
NATIONS, M.
1982   Illness of the Child (Doença de Criança): The Cultural Context of Childhood Diarrhea in Northeast Brazil. Dissertation, University of California, Department of Anthropology, Berkeley, CA (unpublished).
1983   Spirit possession to enteric pathogens: The role of traditional healing in diarrheal diseases control. *Proceedings of the International Conference on Oral Rehydration Therapy*, U.S. Agency for International Development, Washington, DC.
1992   The child's disease *(Doença de criança):* Popular paradigm of persistent diarrhea? *Acta Paediatr Suppl* 381: 55-65.
NATIONS, M.K. et al.
1983   Care within reach: appropriate health-care delivery in the developing *world. The New England Journal of Medicine* 310(24):1612.
1986   Epidemiologic research of infectious diseases: quantitative rigor or rigormortis? Insights from ethnomedicine. In: *Anthropology and Epidemiology*. Edited by C.R. JANES; R. STALL & S.M. GIFFORD, pp. 97-123. Reidel, Boston, MA.
1988   Brazilian popular healers as effective promoters of oral rehydration therapy (ORT) and related child survival strategies. *Bulletin PAHO* 22(4): 335-354.
NATIONS, M.K. & L.A. REBHUN.
1988   Mystification of a simple solution: oral rehydration therapy in Northeast Brazil. *Social Science & Medicine* 27, 25 38.
NICHTER, M.
1990   Vaccinations in South Asia: False expectations and commanding metaphors. In: *Anthropology and Primary Health Care*. Edited by J. COREIL & D. MULL. Westwood Press, Springfield, MI.
O POVO
10/9/93 p. 12a.
1994   13 March, p. 25A.
PARKER, R.L. et al.
1980   Oral rehydration therapy (ORT) for childhood diarrhea. *Pop Rep.*, Series L, 2, Nov.-Dec.

PENNIE, R. A.; R.D. PEARSON & I.T. MCAULIFFE.
    1996   The illness burden in poor rural and urban communities: Enteric parastic infections. In: *At the Edge of Development: Health Problems in a Transitional Society.* Edited by R.L. GUERRANT; M.A. DE SOUZA, M.A. & M.K. NATIONS, pp. 149-160. Carolina Academic Press, Durham, North Carolina.

PIZZARO, D. et al.
    1979   Evaluation of oral therapy for infant diarrhea in an emergency room setting: the acute epidsode as an opportunity for instructing mothers in home treatment. *Bulletin of the World Health Organization* 57(6): 983-986.

RIBEIRO, L.
    1992   *Comunicacno Global: A Mágica da Influência.* Editora Objetiva, Rio de Janeiro.

RIFKIN S.B.
    1983   Planners approaches to community participation in health programs: theory and reality. *Contact* 75: 6-13.

RUBEL, A.J.
    1960   Concepts of disease in Mexican-American culture. *American Anthropology* 62: 795-814.

RYAN, W.
    1971   *Blaming the Victim.* Vintage Press, New York.

SACK, D.A.
    1980   Lobon-gur (common salt and brown sugar) oral rehydration solution in the diarrhoea of adults, Dacca, Bangladesh. *Scientific Report* 36, International Centre for Diarrheal Diseases Research, Bangladesh.

SCHEPER-HUGHES, N.
    1984   Infant mortality and infant care: Cultural and economic constraints on nurturing in Northeast Brazil. *Social Science & Medicine* 19: 535-546.
    1985   Culture, scarcity, and maternal thinking: Maternal detachment and infant survival in a Brazilian shantytown. *Ethos* 13: 291-317.

SCOTT, J. C.
    1985   *Weapons of the Weak: Everyday Forms of Peasant Resistance.* Yale University Press, New Haven.
    1990   *Domination and the Arts of Resistance: Hidden Transcripts.* Yale University Press, New Haven.

SHIELDS, D. et al.
    1981   Electrolyte/glucose concentration and bacterial contamination in home-prepared oral rehydration solution: a field experiment in northeastern Brazil. *Journal of Pediatrics* 98(5): 839-841.

SCRIMSHAW, S.C.M. & E. HURTADO.
    1987   *Rapid Assessment Procedures for Nutrition and Primary Health Care: Anthropological Approaches to Improving Programme Effectiveness,* The United Nations University and UCLA Latin American Center Publications, Tokyo, Japan and Los Angeles, UCLA Latin American Center, Reference Series I 1.

SHORLING, J.S.; S. SHORLING & I.T. MCAULIFFE et al.
    1987   Epidemiology of prolonged diarrhea in an urban Brazilian slum. *Clinical Research* 35: 489A.

SONTAG, S.
    1990   *Illness as Metaphor and Aids and its Metaphors.* Anchor Books, Doubleday, New York *(Illness as Metaphor* first published in (1977); *Aids and its Metaphors* first published in (1988).

THANE-TOE et al.
    1984   Oral rehydration therapy in the home by village mothers in Burma. *Transactions, Royal Society of Tropical Medicine and Hygeine* 78: 581-589.

TINLING, D.C.
    1967   Voodoo, rootwork, and medicine. *Psychiatric Medicine* 29: 483-490.

UNICEF
    1986   *Perfil Estatístico de Crianças e Mães nos Aspectos Socio-Econômicos de Mortalidade Infantil em Áreas Urbans.* Instituto Brasileiro de Geografia e Estatística, Rio de Janeiro, pp. 61-70.
    1992   *Crise e Infância no Brasil: O Impacto das Politicas de 1988 Ajustamento Econômico.* UNICEF, Brasilia.

VALENTINE, C.
    1968   *Culture and Poverty: Critique and Counter-proposals.* University of Chicago Press, Chicago.

VEJA
    1993   9 Angust, pp. 18-31.

VICTORA, C.G. & BARROS, F.C.
    1988   *A Saúde das Crianças Cearenses: Um Estudo de 8000 Familias.* UNICEF, Brasil.

WINTROB, R.
    1973   The influence of others: witchcraft and rootwork as explanations of behavior disturbances. *Journal of Nervous and Mental Disease* 156: 318-326.

WORLD BANK (The)
    1990   *Poverty: World Development Report,* pp. 236-237. Oxford University Press, New York.

Signs, Meanings and Actions Associated with Schistosomiasis Mansoni in a Small Village in Brazil

ELIZABETH UCHÔA, HENRIQUE LEONARDO GUERRA,
JOSÉLIA OLIVEIRA ARAÚJO FIRMO, MARIA FERNANDA LIMA E COSTA

Abstract
The present anthropological study was developed to clarify the reasons why a schistosomiasis control programme in operation over a period of 10 years (1984-1994) in a small village in Southeast Brazil proved ineffective in reducing the prevalence of *S. mansoni* infection. Data was collected through in-depth interviews with key informants, and a systematic observation of activities developed by the population in water areas was carried out. Analysis of the content of the reconstructed narratives from informants shows that most of them have good knowledge (biomedical) of the seriousness of disease, of its complications and of the role played by water in the transmission of schistosomiasis. However the information doesn't seem to have affected the informant's habits as a great number of them have not ceased their contact with the contaminated water of rivers, lakes, wells and swamps. The systematic observation of the population's habitual behaviour in relation to water confirms that fact and discloses the information that in houses which are on the water supply, water is frequently interrupted, in that the well pump that provides the village with water is often out-of-order. Other important data concerns the influence that the universe of beliefs and values exert over the attribution of meanings and action in the face of an event. The analysis of the narratives reveals that the information given to informants is frequently re-interpreted as based on their beliefs.

Zusammenfassung
Diese ethnologische Studie entstand, um herauszufinden, warum das über zehn Jahren (1984-1994) durchgeführte Schistosomiasis-Kontroll-Programm in einem kleinen Dorf im Südosten Brasiliens nicht ausreichend war, um das Vorkommen der *S. mansioni* Infektion zu senken. Die Daten wurden durch Tiefeninterviews mit Hauptinformanten gesammelt bzw. stammen aus der systematischen Beobachtung von Aktivitäten der Bevölkerung an den Wasserstellen. Die Analyse der rekonstruierten Erzählungen der Informanten zeigt, daß die meisten ein gutes (biomedizinisches) Wissen über die Schwere der Krankheit besitzen sowie über Komplikationen und die Rolle, die das Wasser in der Übertragung der Schistosomiasis spielt. Jedoch scheinen diese Informationen die Gewohnheiten der Informanten nicht verändert zu haben, da ein großer Teil von ihnen den Kontakt mit dem verseuchten Wasser aus Flüssen, Seen, Brunnen und Sümpfen nicht aufgegeben hat. Systematische Beobachtungen der Gewohnheiten der Bevölkerung in Bezug auf Wasser bestätigen, daß Häuser, die an das Wassernetz angeschlossen sind, häufig ohne Wasser sind, da die Pumpe, die den Brunnen des Dorfes versorgt, oftmals kaputt ist. Ein anderes wichtiges Ergebnis ist, daß das Glaubens- und Wertesystem großen Einfluß auf Bedeutung und Handlungen angesichts eines Ereignisses haben. Die Analyse der Erzählungen ergibt, daß die Informationen, die den Informanten gegeben wurden, in Anhängigkeit vom Glaubenssystem mehrere Male re-interpretiert wurden.

Keywords: schistosomiasis, prevention, local culture, rural Brazil.

Introduction

Recent studies show how social and cultural universes affect practices, behaviours, subscription in health schemes, and the use of available medical services (UCHÔA et al. 1993; AGYEPONG 1992; TAYLOR et al. 1987; HIELSCHER & SOMMERFELD 1985). They also show that the behaviour of some populations, faced up with health problems, is founded on specific social and cultural universes, a fact which emphasises the need for fundamental educational programmes and health planning based on previous knowledge of the outstanding characteristics of the target population's way of thinking and reacting. (HIELSCHER & SOMMERFELD 1985; NYAMWAYA 1987; NICHTER

1989; CORIN et al. 1989; FINCHAM, 1992; GREEN 1992, INECOM 1993) This requirement has become even more evident nowadays, when community commitment and participation are seen as key factors for the success of health programmes (FINCHAM 1992). How effective a program will be depends very much on its acceptance by the community using and participating in it. Thus, for a community scheme to be successful, it is vital that it include a knowledge of the characteristics of the population it is meant for. (INECOM 1993)

Over the last decade, anthropology has developed important theoretical and methodological tools for the systematic study of the ways in which some populations think and act when it comes to health issues. Recent medical anthropological research has given birth to the systematisation of the study of interactions and contradictions between the medical and the cultural models, besides providing parameters that have made it possible to review the issue of social and cultural adaptation of health programmes. The present paper is based on an anthropological study of the way people from a small village in an endemic area in the North of the State of Minas Gerais act and think in the face of *Schistosomiasis mansoni*.

Context

Muquem, where this study was carried out, is a village with 715 inhabitants (1994), located in the Mirabela Municipality of the State of Minas Gerais (Southeast Brazil). In 1995, 91% of the individuals living in the village had a piped water supply in the household (LIMA E COSTA, not published). Muquém was the site of a schistosomiasis control programme that was carried out over a period of ten years (1984-1994), as part of a larger programme sponsored and conducted by the Brazilian Ministry of Health (SUCAM/Fundação Nacional de Saúde).

A detailed description of the study area and control strategies used is described elsewhere (LIMA E COSTA et al. 1995). Briefly, the control strategies included: a) snail surveillance along all streams, and treatment with niclosamide every time snails, infected or non-infected, were found in the streams which were used by the population for different activities; b) stool examination by the Kato-Katz method (KATZ et al. 1992) of everyone living in the village (the population was defined by a complete house-to-house census); c) treatment with oxamniquine of those who eliminated *Schistosoma mansoni* eggs in stools, as well as of those who did not eliminated eggs but were in the 7-14 year age range; d) education activities regarding prevention of *Schistosomiasis mansoni*, based on lectures (for the whole population) and person-to-person information (for those who received treatment). Snail surveillance, treatment with niclosamide, census, stool examination, treatment with oxamniquine and education activities were performed in 1984, 1985, 1988 and 1990. In 1994, all the above mentioned measures were also performed, except for snail surveillance and treatment with niclosamide. During the control programme, stool examination coverage ranged from 93% (1994) to 96% of the total population (1984 and 1990, respectively), and treatment with oxamniquine covered about 80% of those who were eligible.

The prevalence of *S. mansoni* infection decreased from 38% (before control measures in 1984) to 6% (in 1985) and increased progressively thereafter (29, 22 and 34% in 1988, 1990 and 1994, respectively). This was an unexpected result because, in the State of Minas Gerais, a significant fall in the prevalence of infection was observed in most villages covered by the Brazilian schistosomiasis control programme (LIMA E COSTA et al. 1995). The present study was developed to clarify why in this village, where 91% of inhabitants had a piped water supply in the household, the control programme was ineffective in minimising the prevalence of *S. mansoni* infection.

Theoretical and Methodological Frame

This study stems from the interpretative approach where culture is defined as the universe of signs and meanings that enable the members of a group to interpret experience and guide people's actions (GEERTZ 1973). This concept of culture establishes a link between the way members of a community think and act, i.e., between the cognitive and pragmatic aspects of human life, and emphasises the role cultural aspects play in the construction of perceptions, interpretations and actions of the members of a community.

Studies carried out by GOOD (1977), KLEINMAN (1980), GOOD & DELVECCHIO GOOD (1980; 1982) and GOOD & KLEINMAN (1985) introduce the GEERTZian culture concept when approaching different aspects affecting the health area. The authors mentioned above point out that disorders, either physical or psychological, can only be reached by means of cultural mediation, since a disorder is always interpreted by the person suffering from the disease, the doctor and the families (GOOD & KLEINMAN 1985).

KLEINMAN (1980) states that the ways of thinking and acting as concerns health are socially organised responses to diseases. The concept of an 'explanatory model,' coined by this author (1980), systematises the study of models adopted by different kinds of people when facing health problems. KLEINMAN (1980) traces a line separating professional explanatory models from the explanatory models used by the patients and their families.

According to the author (1980), such models are rooted in different sectors of the health care system (popular, folk and professional) and allow for beliefs, patterns of behaviour and specific expectations. This analytical tool makes it possible for researchers to get acquainted with the explanatory models that prevail among members of some specific group, to evaluate the gap between them and the medical models and to plan proper social and cultural interventions; dramatically vital points for the success of any health programme.

GOOD (1977) and GOOD & DELVECCHIO GOOD (1980, 1982) emphasise the diversity of models that sustain the cultural concepts of health problems and the therapeutic efforts to solve them. They also point out that every therapeutic practice is most of all interpretative and demands continuous translation, decoding and negotiation between different semantic systems.

According to GOOD (1977) and GOOD & DELVECCHIO GOOD (1980, 1982), the signification of pathologic cases would be constructed into semantic network illness, through which, cognitive, affective and experiential factors interact in the universe of social relationships and cultural configurations. This network of symbols associated with particular diseases among members of a society would be used by individuals in their interpretation of experience and to articulate it and express it in a socially legitimate way. The importance of this model becomes even more evident when it is disclosed that there is no strict correlation between professional diagnosis, which generally guides health programmes, and the popular diagnosis, which guides the community's behaviour and representations (HIELSCHER & SOMMERFELD 1985). The perception of what is relevant and needs closer attention, of what causes or averts a problem, of what kind of action the problem demands is, for health professionals, determined by a whole range of biomedical knowledge; however, for the members of a community, this perception is determined by a network of symbols that redefine biomedical and cultural concepts besides determining particular ways of thinking and acting in face of a specific health problem.

The analysis model of "systems of signs, meanings and actions" created by CORIN et al. (1989; 1990; 1992; 1992a) seeks to systematise the study of social, cultural end experiential factors that truly affect the identification of a problem area, when it comes to deciding whether to tackle a problem or not and the ensuing choice of the appropriate therapeutic approach.

This analysis model stems from the idea that each community has its own way of building its universe of health problems - by focusing on certain signs, highlighting some explanations and encouraging certain reactions and actions - and aims to identifying the system of signs, meanings and actions that build up perception, interpretations and behaviour in the health area. (CORIN et al. 1990).

CORIN's (1990) methodological proposal is to invert the generally applied procedure in the study of representations by starting all the way back from the pragmatic stage building up again to the semantic stage. Concrete behaviour of individuals serves as the starting point for a study that seeks to identify conceptual logic underlying such patterns of behaviour, as well as the different factors that mediate actualisation of that logic in particular situations (CORIN et al. 1989). Much though the analysis model of the "systems of signs, meanings and actions" was, at first, used in the field of mental health, its contribution to other areas and especially to the study of widespread endemic disease is, no doubt, vital. Very little is known about the signs and symptoms considered relevant by specific populations, or about interpretations culturally associated with each one of them; and even less is known about typical behaviour, into which such perceptions and interpretations are translated. The model analysis of the "systems of signs, meanings and actions" allows for the knowledge of the conceptual logic that organises the field of cultural representations, associated by specific populations with a certain endemic disease and with certain elements of the context (personal experience, cultural habits, environmental factors, etc.) that can affect the translation of those representations into concrete behaviour (of risk, of protection, and in the face of existing health resources).

This model will certainly contribute to the refinement of research into widespread endemic diseases and to the reformation of issues concerning planning and organisation of health schemes, so as to adapt interventions to social and cultural features of the target population. In this study, this model will serve as a guide in the investigation of the different ways people from Muquém think and act in face of schistosomiasis.

Methods and Instruments

According to a proposal from CORIN et al. (1990;1992), the analysis of the "system of signs, meanings and actions" is based on the study of the actor's practices, apprehended from concrete cases. An ethnographic reconstruction of concrete cases must be highlighted.

In order to ensure that the investigation effectively covers the universe of representations and behaviours associated with a specific problem, it is necessary that the limits of the semantic field to be studied are established. With that aim in mind and that of obtaining further information necessary for the ethnographic study itself, a preliminary study was carried out.

In this first part of the study, the team stayed in the village for 7 days and carried out systematic observation of important places in the life of the population (churches, chemist's, health assistance ambulatory, houses of healers, shops, markets, bars, schools, co-operatives, squares, streams, lakes, lagoons, rivers, falls); information circulation (where people get acquainted with what is going on within and outside the boundaries of their village); the existing groups (formal and informal such as youth clubs, congregations, sports clubs, community assistance groups, and people who meet in the bar or square, etc.); local leaders (people who exert formal or informal leadership on the community). The aim of this observation was to identify key informants to be interviewed and water points to be observed in the second part of the study. During this period, 30 locals were interviewed so as to trace the limits of the semantic field, culturally associated with the medical concept of Schistosomiasis and to identify the language locals use to refer to this disease. The analysis of the data collected during this preliminary stage disclosed 36 key informants, the important water points for the life of the community and the elaboration of interview guides which were socially and culturally adequate.

The second part of the study, concerns the ethnographic study and the team had to stay in the village for 50 days. During that period two main activities were developed: a) 36 interviews with key informants and b) systematic observation of the activities developed by the population in the water points identified in the first part of the study.

a) *Interviews with key informants:* The interview guide, which was elaborated in the first part of this study, was used during the interviews with the 36 key informants. Information of different categories was investigated to help in the detailed reconstruction of familiarity, behaviour and symptoms associated with the disease; their ideas about prevention; seriousness and cause; treatment carried out and/or that should ideally have been carried out; possible obstacles to proper treatment; their perception of available resources, more frequent types of contact with water and each informants' source of information.

The interviews were recorded, transcribed and fed into a computer. A first analysis of the content of the information categories (signs, cause, prevention, treatments, contact with water and source of information) was done with the aim to help the team prepare a list of codes, which bears three hierarchical levels (information category, type and content). This list of codes was tested in some of the interviews and was reviewed until it allowed for the coding of all the information into distinct units, with a minimum of ambiguity.

With the help of this list of codes, the interview was broken down into a number of significant units. Afterwards, each interview was fed into a computer with the help of a software *Qualittat* (DEMICHELI & UCHÔA 1995). This software is meant for the identification of the frequency with which information and content categories occur, the correlation between them, and the quick retrieval of the texts related with one or more information category with the subsequent identification of the informant.

After the coding, a first level of analysis was meant to identify 1. the different types of signs associated with Schistosomiasis; 2. the ideas about cause, prevention, seriousness and treatment; 3. the types of contact with water and the type of water supply in the premises of the subjects interviewed and 4. the sources of information mentioned by them. Based on such data, the amount of knowledge the population had about Schistosomiasis was investigated and the impact this knowledge had overt risk behaviour.

On a second level, the analysis examined the contents of several categories of information, by investigating the connotations associated with each one of them, and investigating the articulations and discontinuities crossing the *systems of signs, meanings and actions.*

b) *Systematic observation of the activities developed in water points.* In order to observe in a systematic way the activities performed in the water points identified as significant for the population, a number of regular visits were made to each of these points on different days and at different times. The team stayed in the spot for an average of 1 and a half hours. All of the activities carried out in each place was registered, as well as their characteristics and those of the people who were performing them. A systematic register was made of the people who met in such places, their ages, sex and the part of the body in contact with the water. This data was organised in a table according to distance, degree of frequency and type of activity at each point so as to enable the quick visualisation of the prevailing contacts with water in that locality.

Results

In Muquém, the word *'xistose'* is widely used by the population to refer to the 'vermin/tiny animal/microbe/germen/virus,' to the disease and to the problems caused by it. In general, *'xistose'* is associated with water, and in particular to the water of the rivers. It is believed that *'xistose'* appears/lives/thrives or transforms itself in water.

The association between *'xistose'* and the snail/*'buzinho'* is evident, whereas the kind of relationship established between the microbe and the snail vary. Sometimes *'xistose'* is seen as a vermin/microbe generated from the snail; some other times it is seen as a vermin/microbe/host of the snail. There are other conceptions such as the belief that *'xistose'* is the snail itself.

Although there is no perfect correlation, generally speaking, the semantic field associated with the popular word *'xistose'* corresponds to the limits traced by the medical term schistosomiasis. Thus, we chose to use the word *'xistose'* to retrieve knowledge and reconstruct experiences concerning schistosomiasis.

The *'Xistose'*

Most of the informants stated that they themselves or one of their next of kin have already "spotted a problem of xistose" at some point in their lives. Seldom did any informants declare that they did not know anyone who had *'xistose.'* The great majority had some familiarity with *'xistose.'*

This familiarity with *'xistose'* appears regularly in the narratives. Sometimes reporting their own experiences; other times mentioning cases in the community; still other times reporting information from others sources, each informant, little by little, introduced us to their specific ways of thinking and acting concerning *'xistose.'*

In the set narratives rarely does anyone declare that they have seen a doctor for health problems that were identified as *'xistose.'* This was the case of one of the residents of Muquém who says: "I caught myself feeling pains in the legs, dizziness, stomach ache and headache, so I went to the doctor. He examined me and asked for some tests. I did the examinations. It was sure-fire" (M 30).

In the great majority of cases, people allege they realised they had *'xistose'* through the results of the stools examination, which is periodically performed by the agents of SUCAM/FNS. "I got to know I got it through these people of SUCAM. The people who come examine us, collect the stool, examine it, then they find the vermin," says an informant. (M03) To some extent, this is perceived as a surprising result due to the absence of symptoms: "Everybody here had it. When SUCAM examined us, it turned out we had it, but no one had been feeling anything serious," explains a resident of Muquém (M27). They use very spontaneous language to refer to SUCAM's activities, and, as a whole, SUCAM's job is seen as necessary and beneficial by the population. It is generally believed that *'xistose'* is "very difficult to discover, if you don't do a stool examination. It is only at the second stage of the disease, when it becomes more serious, that it is discovered." (M036). However, precocious diagnosis is immediately associated with treatment and cure. Regular examinations are welcome as they allow for diagnosis and treatment.

In general, *'xistose'* is felt as a serious disease because it can kill, affect the liver, spleen or blood of individuals suffering from it and it can also bring about a number of symptoms. Very few of the informants would refer to *'xistose'* as a minor disease.

Most of the informants believe the contact with the water of rivers, lakes and lagoons is the main source of disease. According to a resident of Muquém, "you are more likely to catch xistose if you have contact with water. For example, bathing yourself, getting into the water sometimes washing your face, putting your legs into the water" (M 21) mainly 'dirty' water that is not treated "where SUCAM does not spray poison" (M02) Some of the informants say that drinking from such water can cause *'xistose,'* "we drink from that dirty water, that is not boiled, this causes *'xistose,'"* says a resident from Muquém. (M 30)

Most of the informants in Muquém believe that *'xistose'* can be averted if contact with contaminated water is avoided; however, their definition of this contact varies a lot; for some, it is confined to bathing oneself: "we cannot bathe ourselves in the water, like this stream here that is *'xistose'* through and through," explains a resident of Muquém. (M 07)

A significant group of informants believe that filtering or boiling the water are two essential procedures in the prevention of *'xistose'*; a resident comments that "they say we have to drink filtered water, many places where people have no filters (...), they have to boil the water." (M 02)

Some of the informants, believe that the best preventive procedure is the treatment of the waters: "if the water is treated, then the disease is truly prevented because it is difficult not to go and bathe there." (M15) Medical treatment is ranked by the great majority of informants as the best solution to the problem. They see this treatment as accessible and effective. A few of the informants mention another treatment approach:

"Take home-made medicine, medicine from the brushwood. Take some 'matruz' and mash it. Take a bulb that grows in the thicket (...) and mash it, too. Put them together and add a leaf of pigeon pea. Then you mash mint leaves and collect the juice. Mix it all and leave outdoors in the dew. Drink some of it everyday. It is good. Helps to kill xistose." (M030)

Personal experience with *'xistose'* and the guidance offered by SUCAM are seen by informants as the main sources of knowledge about the disease. The data presented here shows how familiar the population of Muquém is with the disease and that they have some relevant knowledge about schistosomiasis. Most of the informants are aware that contact with rivers, lakes and lagoons waters can cause *'xistose.'* They also know that avoiding using these waters can avert he disease, whose seriousness they are conscious of. However, for many different reasons, a great many informants are still using the waters somehow.

Another interesting fact is that only few informants lack running water at home. In Muquém, there is an artesian well and a pump that supply water for the houses.

The study of the relation between having running water at home, the informants' knowledge of the disease and other types of contact with water, revealed that about half of the informants have running water at home; that they know that getting into the waters of rivers, lakes and lagoons etc., can cause *'xistose;'* that they know that by avoiding getting into these waters you can prevent it; that they are conscious of how serious the disease is; however, they still keep on having some sort of contact with these waters.

Systems of Signs, Signification and Action towards *'Xistose'*

On a second level, the analysis looked into the context of a number of information categories, investigated connotations associated to each category and articulations and discontinuities between the *systems of signs, signification and actions*. Informants see *'xistose'* as a disease that can bring about many problems for the individuals suffering from it. Although a complete absence of symptoms generally precedes the positive result of the stool examination, some of the symptoms are recurrently associated with the presence or worsening of the disease. People refer to weakness, laziness, tiredness, alterations in the skin, loss of appetite, loss of weight, a bulgy stomach, diarrhoea, vomit, headache, pain in the legs and bad mood.

At first sight, the discourse of the informants on the different ways *'xistose'* manifests itself, seems to outweigh the medical approach to the problem; however, a systematic analysis discloses that signs are organised in a very particular fashion. The connotations associated with each sign and the value attributed to it reveal a specific universe of signification and show that they have very particular ways of thinking and acting towards the disease.

The reports about the manifestations of *'xistose'* set limits to two dominant sign configurations. Each of them combines different elements from the context, values and cultural beliefs that form the population's notions of seriousness and causality, which determine typical behaviour patterns. The first configuration re-ensembles changes in the skin (itches, stains, swellings, rashes, etc.), and the second one includes problems of different sorts such as pain in the legs, loss of weight, a bulgy stomach, vomit with blood and diarrhoea with blood.

Other symptoms such as headache, vomiting, diarrhoea and bad mood are also present in the informants' report; however, such manifestations are not highlighted in their narrative. Moreover, there is no evidence whatever that they are inter-linked or that there are organising systems that allow for an analysis of the groups as a whole. Thus, the analysis of the context will be confined to the two dominant configurations.

a) The First Configuration: alterations in the skin.

Itches are in most cases, associated with the presence of *'xistose'* in the water: "I know when there is plenty of *'xistose'*: we bathe and our body starts itching," says a resident of Muquém. (M02) Some see it as a sign that the *'xistose'* has penetrated into the individual's skin, and a resident explains that the 'itch' starts as soon as you touch contaminated waters and he describes the evolution of the disease: "people who wash in this here river, start itching the moment they come out of the water. A few months later *'xistose'* takes over." (M08)

The changes in the skin (itches, stains, pipocas-Portuguese for popcorn, rashes) are related to the onset of the disease: "You have a bath and then you start itching. You start itching and the skin feels like a piece of sandpaper (...); the spot where you scratch becomes black" explains a resident of Muquém. (M27) Because of these associations described above, some informant believe that changes in the skin have the same value as a diagnosis: "people go fishing there, and start itching, then they have to do examination and it shows they have *'xistose,'*" explains a resident of Muquém (M18) suggesting that the 'itch' confirms the results of the examination beforehand.

In some cases, the ensuing discomfort of such alterations may lead them to seek medical assistance. However, alterations in the skin do not mean that the disease is serious. It is believed that the picture can be reverted with treatment.

b) The Second Sign Configuration

The analysis of the context of the Second Configuration points to 'weakness' as a central sign. Weakness, malaise and tiredness cross the whole set of narratives, following the evolution of the disease.

This evolution is associated with the action of the vermin inside the body of individuals; "it eats us from the inside, damages us inside," explains a resident of Muquém. (M29) Some informant's are more precise and associate the action of *'xistose'* to the onset of some symptoms:

"that diarrhoea with blood can cause it, too (...) sometimes the person loses weight and the stomach swells, too (...) xistose is like a microbe that causes many problems. It makes the spleen swell, and it can thrive in the spleen and liver, too, (...) I've been through it, I know what it is like." (M21)

The idea of the evolution of *'xistose'* leads to the idea of a possibility of total destruction of the individual and a pressing need for intervention:

M 03 – "it's the same problem as that of blood thinning. You lose courage, your legs become tired, the body becomes tired. Then it ruins all your life. If you don't get treated you can even die."

M 18—"like my brother-in-law here who had an operation. So, he says it is harms, I think the "passarinha"(spleen). So you have to be operated on. Then he says that the pit of the stomach started swelling, it started growing ... growing, then he had to be operated on. if you don't, they say you can even die. It gives blood 'provocation.'"

This sign configuration (pain in the legs, weakness, loss of weight, vomiting and diarrhoea with blood and growth of the stomach) is built up from the idea of loss (of strength, appetite, weight and blood) that evokes the progressive destruction of the body (it attacks the liver, spleen, blood or heart) and lends the disease this connotation of seriousness. The following reports depict their perception of the disease's worsening process:

M 03–"It gets into your liver and you start decaying because blood is made by the liver, so it devours the blood of the person, it means that this person only gets worse and worse for the rest of their lives."

For most of the informant's *'xistose'* is seen as a very serious disease that can lead to death, however this seriousness is attributed to the absence of treatment at the onset of the disease:

M 27—"Xistose, if you suffer from it for a long time, do not treat it, it does kill, doesn't it ?"

M 33—"At the beginning it is easy to treat and, if you wait until you get older, it will take over. It goes on until it kills you."

It is believed that evolution and death will only occur if *'xistose'* is not treated, so access to treatment turns out to be essential in the evaluation of the seriousness of the disease. As mentioned before, most of the informants rank medical treatment as the proper indication for the case, besides being the most effective approach. The analysis of the context reveals that medical care is considered easily accessible thanks to the activities of SUCAM in the area:

M 04–"they brought the medicine to our homes. They bring it to our homes."

M 28–"It was free, everything all right, all paid by the State (...). The examinations were free, the drugs were free. I had no problems at all. I did the stools test, waited and the next day there came the medicine."

Such a perception of the treatment as being free, accessible and effective is found in a network data on *'xistose,'* which certainly contributes to their persistence in adopting risk behaviour. That conclusion will be made clearer if we go back to the associations established by the informants from Muquém. They trace a line between serious and minor symptoms; minor symptoms are associated with contact with water and the serious ones with a lack of medical treatment. Thus, wide knowledge of the effectiveness of and easy access to medical care affects perception of the seriousness of *'xistose'* and diminishes the importance of avoiding contact with contaminated waters. ROSEMBERG's (1994) research on the social representation of schistosomiasis in an endemic area in the State of Espírito Santo bears similar associations. According to the author, the perception of risk is derived from having/not having the disease to being/ not being under medical care.

Re-Interpreting Information

In general, Muquém's informants are aware of the risks they are running when in contact with the waters of rivers, streams, wells and swamps. However, the analysis of the context of reports about their perception of causality reveals that this knowledge is, many times, re-interpreted by informants through their own beliefs.

There are some references to water contaminated by stool: "it is because there are no cesspool people do things on the floor ... it goes to the rivers, doesn't it ? And there, people get into the water," explains a resident of Muquém (M 34). Water temperature is also mentioned by the informants from Muquém. A resident in that locality says that "if you bathe in cold water, you'll get it" (M 30); another one explain that "this is because water's allergy sticks to your body." (M 26)

There are also references to the connection between pools of still waters or "muddy waters" and a person's movements in this water "*if you move in it, I think it's easier to get the disease.*" (M 01) The importance given to the water and to the people's movement in it is not very clear; what seems to stand out is that the danger of getting contaminated comes from a conjugation of these two elements.

Another issue crosses the set of narratives bringing about some ambiguity: it is the water treatment carried out by SUCAM/FNS. For many of the people, the spot where you can catch '*xistose*' "is that where people from SUCAM do not pulverise with poison," according to a resident in Muquém (M02); but for some it is not very clear if the water "those where people from SUCAM pulverised poison" (M 23) are free from contamination.

The characteristics of water informants associated with transmission of '*xistose,*' affect their behaviour when trying to protect themselves from the disease. As a certain characteristic (cold, dirty, not treated) is associated with '*xistose,*' only the waters bearing those characteristics, will be avoided. Rivers, lakes, lagoons or wells not bearing such characteristics are freely used.

That re-interpretation of information mediates the impact of their knowledge of the role of waters in the transmission of '*xistose*' over the pattern of behaviour adopted concerning the waters.

Patterns of Behaviour Concerning Water

Every water point considered important for the population of Muquém was systematically observed. Each point was observed on different days, at different times and the team stayed at the spot for about 1 or 2 hours.

The aim was to identify the activities going on at each spot, their characteristics (kind of activity, time spent, part of the body in contact with the water, how long this contact lasted), the people involved in each activity (number of people, sex, age).

The resulting data was set on a table according to the location of each spot observed, degree of frequency and type of activity, so as to obtain a quick visualisation of the more usual types of contact with water (see table 1).

Table 1:

Point observed	Location	Subjects observed	Activities
Bridge 1	Muquém (behind the locality)	over 32	wash clothes, wash face/hands, take animals to drink and bathe, collect water
Fountain 1	Muquém (on the right side of the locality)	16	wash clothes, bathing, wash dishes, wash hair, play, collect water
Brook 1	Muquém (in the direction of the water falls)	11	wash clothes, wash dishes
Source	Muquém (source on the left side of locality)	over 18	wash hair, wash dishes, bathe, wash clothes, collect water, wash legs/arms
Bridge 2	Muquém (on the right of the way in to locality)	14	wash clothes, collect logs, cross, collect water
Stream (valley)	farm	07	water veg. garden, irrigation system, pick up grass, play in the water, wash meat.
Backyard wells	Muquém	01*	wash clothes, drink, water veg garden
Muquém River	Muquém (in the direction of the football pitch)	over 04	cross, play
Dam	farm	*	water used for more chores
Fountain 2	near waterfall	01	wash clothes
Water falls	-----------------------	00	

* Information by residents in the area

Over 95 locals who were involved in some kind of activity related to water were observed. This data confirms the one obtained through the high frequency of the population that has contact with the waters of rivers, lakes, lagoons, brooks or swamps.

In the first place, easy access to water must be noticed; most of the significant water points are located within the limits of Muquém.

In the second place, it must be observed that during field work, the pump from the well that supplies water for Muquém broke down and was not repaired for five days. So, the population had to resort to using the waters of rivers, brooks or inactive old wells. The situation was as follows:

> "On the first day, it was thought that water flow was not strong enough to reach the highest places of Muquém, nothing serious. On the second day, some families informed they had completely run out of water. Some of them were using water reserves, but the number of people looking for outdoor sources was increasing considerably: a good number of residents started washing dishes and clothes only in the fountains. On the third day the situation remained unchanged. On the fourth day even in those houses where water reserves where in good

condition, there was only drinking water left. Some people started carrying and selling water from the brook for the population to fill up barrels. Children and adults—men and women—went to the sources to collect water. There was so much demand for water that the level of water from the springs, wells and fountains went down. People started digging new wells, looking for water. The small source was full of holes. With the shortage, people started worrying only about the cleanliness of drinking water. As a female resident pointed out: "we know people catch *'xistose'* when they bathe, but our main worry is about the water we drink." (She laughed). Drinking water came from the springs; water used for house chores and personal hygiene (cleaning, bathing, for the animals, etc.) was the water being sold, which was collected from the rivers. In the brook, people where competing for space, carriers filling up their recipients, horsemen washing their animals, others bringing their animals to drink, women washing their laundry, children fetching water and others just playing. Old wells were being reactivated to supply the demand for water. The fountains on the right side of the village were crowded: women washing their laundry, cooks and people carrying all sorts of things. Any kind of recipient seemed to be suitable to collect water: pans, buckets, bottles, etc. The shortage of water changed the routine. The kindergarten had to close and the school had to shorten its timetable; everybody was involved in carrying water and washing laundry and dishes. It was all in a big mess, but some were enjoying it. According to a lady, some of them were going to the fountains very early in the morning to spend more time chatting while work was being done. Another lady, a women of about forty, mocked at the situation: "You see girls ?" This is where *'xistose'* is, while she played with the water (splashing it all over). Children who had denied ever using the water of the river were there playing and enjoying themselves. And many of those who had said the water was unsuitable for humans, looked very relaxed using the water to solve the problem brought about by the broken pump. By the way, for the second time in less than 3 months.

The report above made it clear that the information about the presence of running water in the houses in Muquém must be reconsidered.

Conclusion

The analysis of the content of the interviews with the key informants of Muquém shows that most of them have good knowledge (biomedical) of the seriousness of the disease, its complications and the role water in the transmission of schistosomiasis. The informants level of knowledge and the way they refer to SUCAM/ FNS as being an important source of information, leaves no doubt as to the efficiency of SUCAM's information system.

However, all the information about *'xistose'* doesn't seem to have affected the informants' habits, since they still persist in their risk behaviour. Although they are familiar with and have good knowledge of schistosomiasis, and have running water at home, a large number of informants keep on having contact with the contaminated waters of rivers, lakes, wells and swamps.

Systematic observation of the population's habitual behaviour concerning water confirms that fact and allows for an improvement in the identification of the determiners of the situation. Systematic observation reveals that frequency of contact with water relates directly to the kind of access to it. Most of the points of water are located within the boundaries of the village, which makes it easier for the population to have access to the water of rivers, brooks and other sources of water. Moreover, the information that the houses have running water must be reconsidered, in as much as the supply is faulty since the well pump that supplies water for the village is frequently out-of-order.

Another fact of major importance is the influence that the universe of beliefs and values exert over the attribution of signification and action in the face of an event. The analysis of the narratives reveals that the information given to informants is frequently re-interpreted through their own beliefs. Statements about aetiology disclose that some of the water features that are associated with the idea of transmission of *'xistose'* dramatically affect informants' pattern of behaviour when trying to protect themselves from the disease. The statements concerning signs of *'xistose'* reveal that informants from Muquém can tell the difference between serious and minor symptoms; they link the idea of minor symptoms with water, and the serious ones with a lack of medical treatment; medical care is seen as effective and accessible. Thus, such associations affect their perception that *'xistose'* as a serious disease and lessen the importance of avoiding contact with contaminated waters.

Taking such data into account, it is possible to state that re-interpretation of information mediate the impact of the information passed on to informants over the pattern of behaviour that will be adopted by them. They are subject to the articulation that takes place among different items in their context (environmental and symbolic), which allow the system of signs, signification and action to on.

Acknowledgements

This study was supported by grants from Brazilian Ministry of Health (Fundação Nacional de Saúde), UNDP, World Bank and Financiadora de Estudos e Projetos (FINEP). The authors also wish to thank Dr Fabiano Pimenta Junior and the technicians of the Montes Claros District (Fundação Nacional de Saúde) for their support throughout the project.

References

AGYEPONG, I.A.
    1992   Malaria ethnomedical perceptions and practice in an Adangbe farming community and implications for control. *Social Sciences and Medicine* 35: 131-137.
CORIN, E.; E. UCHÔA; G. BIBEAU & G. HARNOIS
    1989   Les attitudes dans le champ de la santé mentale. Repères théoriques et méthodologiques pour une étude ethnographique et comparative. *Rapport technique,* Centre de recherche de l'hôpital Douglas, Centre Collaborateur OMS; Montréal.
CORIN, E.; G. BIBEAU; J.C. MARTIN & R. LAPLANTE.
    1990   *Comprendre pour soigner autrement. Repères pour régionaliser les services de santé mentale.* Montréal: Presses de l'Université de Montréal.
CORIN, E.; E. UCHÔA; G. BIBEAU. et al.
    1992   La place de la culture dans la psychiatrie africaine d'aujourd'hui. Paramètres pour un cadre de références. *Psychopathologie Africaine* 24: 149-181.
CORIN, E.; UCHÔA, E., BIBEAU, G. & B. KOUMARE
    1992a Articulation et variations des systèmes de signes, de sens et d'actions. *Psychopathologie Africaine* 24: 183-204.
CORIN, E.; G. BIBEAU & E. UCHÔA
    1993   Eléments d'une sémiologie anthropologique des troubles psychiques chez les Bambara, Bwa et Soninké du Mali. *Anthropologie et Sociétés* 17: 1-2, 125-156.
DEMICHELI, W.A. & E. UCHÔA
    1995   Qualitat, versão 1: um programa de análise qualitativa em microcomputadores. Laboratório de Epidemiologia e Antropologia Médica, Centro de Pesquisas René Rachou, FIOCRUZ, Belo Horizonte, Minas Gerais, Brasil. (in preparation)
FINCHAM, S.
    1992   Community health promotion programs. *Social Sciences and Medicine* 35: 239-249.
GEERTZ, C.
    1973   *The Interpretation of Cultures,* New York, Basic Books Inc. Publishers.
GOOD, B.
    1977   The Heart of What's the Matter: The Semantics of Illness in Iran. *Culture, Medicine and Psychiatry* 1: 25-58.

GOOD, B. & M.J. DELVECCHIO GOOD.
  1980   The Meaning of Symptoms: A Cultural Hermeneutic Model for Clinical Practice. In: A. *The Relevance of Social Science for Medicine*. Edited by L. EISENBERG & A. KLEINMAN, pp 165-196. Dordrecht: Reidel Publishing Co.
  1982   Toward a Meaning-centered Analysis os Popular Illness Categories: 'Fright-Illness' and 'Heart Distress' in Iran. In: *Cultural Conceptions of Mental Health and Therapy*. Edited by A. J. MARSELLA & G. WHITE, pp 141-166. . Dordrecht: D. Reidel Publishing Co.

GREEN, E.C.
  1992   Sexuallly Trasmited Disease, Ethnomedicine and Health Policy in Africa. *Social Science and Medicine*, 35, 2: 121-130.

HIELSCHER, S. & J. SOMMERFELD.
  1985   Concepts of Illness and the Utilization of Health Care Services in a Rural Malien Village. *Social Science and Medicine* 21: 397-400.

INECOM
  1993   *The International Network for Cultural Epidemiology and Community Mental Health*. Montréal.

KATZ, N.; D. CHAVES & J.P. PELLEGRINO.
  1972   A simple device for quantitative stool thick-smear technique in Schistosomiasis mansoni. *Revista do Instituto de Medicina Tropical* 14: 397-400.

KLEINMAN, A.
  1980   *Patients and Healers in the Context of Cultures. An Exploration of Boderland between Anthropology and Psychiatry*, Berkeley: University of California Press.

KLEINMAN, A. & B. GOOD (eds)
  1985   *Culture and Depression: Studies in Anthropology and Cross-Cultural Psychiatry of Affect and Disorder*.

LIMA E COSTA, M.F.F.; H.L. GUERRA; F.G. PIMENTA JUNIOR; J.O.A. FIRMO & E. UCHÔA.
  1995   Avaliação do programa de controle da esquistossomose (FCE/PCDEN) em municípios situados na Bacia do Rio São Francisco, Minas Gerais, Brasil. *Revista da Sociedade de Medicina Tropical* 29: 117-126.

NICHTER, M.
  1989   *Anthropology and International Health: South Asian Case Studies* Kluwer: Dordrecht.

NYAMWAD, D.
  1987   A Case Study of Interaction Between Indigenous and Western Medicine Among the Pokot of Kenya. *Social Science and Medicine* 25(12): 1277-1287.

ROSEMBERG, B.
  1994   Representação Social de Eventos Somáticos Ligados à Esquistossomose. *Cadernos de Saúde Pública*, 10(1): 30-46

TAYLOR, P.; S.K. CHANDIWANA; J.M. GOVERE & F. CHOMBO.
  1987   Knowledge Attitudes and Practices in Relation to Schistosomiasis in a Rural Community. *Social Science and Medicine* 24(7): 607-611.

UCHÔA, E.; E. CORIN; B. KOUMARE & G. BIBEAU.
  1993   Représentations culturelles et disqualification sociale: l'épilepsie dans trois groupes ethniques au Mali. *Psychpathologie Africaine* 25(1): 33-57.

Blood, Fertility and Contraceptive Practices[1]

ONDINA FACHEL LEAL

Abstract
According to the results of our research, based on ethnographic evidence, working class women in southern Brazil believe that their fertility period either overlaps or coincides with their menstrual period. In the first part of this paper the supporting data will be presented and an attempt will be made to understand the underlying logic behind the social representations of the body, of bodily fluids and of conception. In the second part of the paper the consequences of this logic on the choice and use of contraceptive methods will be investigated. The main hypothesis presented here consists of the fact that ideas about the body which link blood and fertility to each other, and which lead to the idea that blood and sperm are homologous, forms a set of beliefs about the body which are not restricted to southern Brazil and which can therefore be generalized.

Zusammenfassung
Dieser Artikel basiert auf einem ethnographischen Beleg, den wir wiederholt während unserer Forschung im Süden Brasilien fanden. Er besagt, daß Frauen aus der Arbeiterklasse die Vorstellung haben, ihre fruchtbaren Tage überlappten sich mit ihrer Menstruation oder seien direkt mit ihr verbunden. Zunächst werden diese Daten kommentiert und ich versuche die Logik zu verstehen, die hinter dieser sozialen Repräsentation des Körpers, der Körperflüssigkeiten und der Empfängnis steht. Zweitens, werde ich mich mit den Konsequenzen eines solchen Verständnisses für die Wahl und die Anwendung von Verhütungsmethoden beschäftigen. Meine Hypothese ist, daß diese Vorstellungen über den Körper, die Blut und Fruchtbarkeit miteinander verbinden und die darüber hinaus auch Blut und Sperma in Verbindung bringen sich nicht allein auf den Süden Brasiliens beschränken lassen und daher verallgemeinert werden können.

Keywords: contraception, menstruation, women, Brazil

The data used for this research is derived from three sources. The first source consists of ethnographic data I collected in a rural region of the state of Rio Grande do Sul, Brazil, on the border between the latter and Uruguay,[2] and data from VICTORA's ethnography on body representations among working class women in the metropolitan area of the city of Porto Alegre, the capital of Rio Grande do Sul.[3] The second source is Rio Grande do Sul folklore material relating to beliefs and practices on contraception, abortive practices, labor and birth, found in the PPGAS-UFRGS Ethnographic Data Bank.[4] The third source is derived from research I am currently engaged in, on contraceptive and reproductive practices within four *vilas* or *favelas*, mostly shantytowns, inhabited by the working class and served by the Medical Community Services of the city of Porto

---

1. This paper was presented at the *XIII International Congress of Anthropological and Ethnological Sciences*, in the *La Antropologia en la Investigación Sociodemográfica* session, Mexico City, July 29-August 5, 1993.
2. See LEAL 1989. Specific data concerning fertility and menstruation was collected in fieldwork conducted in 1987 and 1988 and are not presented in the 1989 paper, which focuses on male culture and identity.
3. See VICTORA (1991). My paper has taken full advantage not only of the data presented in VICTORA's paper, but also of the rich discussions resulting from her fieldwork.
4. The *Banco de Dados Etnográfico*, a data bank of ethnographic material, belong to the Anthropology Laboratory of the graduate program in Social Anthropology at the Rio Grande do Sul Federal University. It contains specific data on folk medicine. The original material comes from different sources, mostly from the *Instituto Gaúcho de Folclore* (Rio Grande do Sul Folklore Institute). The data pertains to different regions from the state of Rio Grande do Sul, obtained from 1970 to 1980.

Alegre.[5] This research has been made possible through support provided by the World Health Organization.

The data I will be dealing with can therefore be divided into two parts: first there is ethnographic data from rural areas and general folklore material on traditional healing; and secondly, there is ethnographic data on a low-income population, or slum-dwellers, but who also have continuous and easy access to effective community health services and prevention-oriented medical services.

It is important to stress that this paper focuses on the beliefs about reproduction held by individuals who have access to medical services, even though they live in economically precarious conditions. We are dealing with a population which is well integrated in modern society, with access to family planning, contraception (freely distributed) and who also have access to mass media communication. Data originating in rural areas, consisting of beliefs about reproduction, contraception and child birth, will be considered an accessory to the existing representations and practices originating in urban areas.

The main issue of this investigation is the following: we find evidence that there is a collective representation about the female fertility period based on erroneous reproductive and contraceptive practices, in other words, based on practices which are medically ineffectual. Labeling these notions as 'ignorance,' lack of knowledge or as surviving elements from traditional cultures is not useful. These notions are not based on ignorance, or on plain lack of information, given that information about contraception is massively broadcast in the area. Many of my informants had participated in family planning programs, pre-natal care and other such discussion groups organized by local health centers. The challenge to medical anthropology is far more complex: it is not a matter of producing more or better information or publicizing it through other means, and neither is the legitimacy of the medical doctor at stake; and it is also not a matter of making contraceptive methods more easily available, considering that this is already the case. What must be grasped here is the logic underlying the fallacious representations about the body and reproduction.

It is necessary to observe how folk culture refers to modes of 'signification.' The concept of a *cultural matrix*, through which one is able to assign meaning and reorganize cultural elements produced by another group, must be taken into account when seeking to understand the dissonance between medical discourse (including the general media) on the subject of contraception and the actual beliefs and practices of the population. The medical discourse, although ubiquitous, is not recognized as the only possible explanation of the complex processes of pain, symptoms and human reproduction, the latter being our main focus. Elements taken from the medical discourse become coherent only when inserted into a global system of ideas related to the body and the world, thus creating a 'world view' which is taken as a frame of reference for everyday practices. Medical recommendations, specifically on reproduction, an essentially feminine domain, become subordinated to a cultural model of the body specific to the working class.[6]

In earlier fieldwork I observed that women associate their fertility period with menstruation while at the same time making a direct connection between fertility and menstrual blood in magi-

---

5. The investigation started on March 1993 and was sponsored by the Special Program of Research, Development and Research Training in Human Reproduction, World Health Organization. The title of the project is *Body, Sexuality and Reproduction: A Study of Social Representations—Project 91378 BSDA*. The present paper made use of the discussions engendered by this research, not to mention the comments of BERNARDO LEWGOY, DANIELA KNAUTH and DENISE JARDIM, who read the first version of the paper.
6. For a more detailed description of the concept of *cultural matrix*, see MARTIN-BARBERO 1987. Also see BOLTANSKI 1984, who follows the same argument regarding popular class modes of the reinterpretation of the medical discourse. See KNAUTH 1991, for different possibilities on understanding the medical discourse, as related to the same population used in this paper.

cal healing procedures. At the time these associations appeared to be solely evidence of classical conceptions in anthropology which refer to the symbolic equivalence between female blood and semen, for I did not have sufficient data to identify them as part of a more coherent body of social representations. The manner in which this association occurs did not become clear, perhaps because that was not the main target of my investigation.

VICTORA's research presents more consistent data, indicating that women imagine their fertile period to be coincident with their menstrual period. The study's informants believe that conception is possible a few days before and after menstruation. This perception of fertility is analyzed by means of body maps and drawings of the female body the informants were asked to make, and she also observes that women consider their bodies to be unique, with individual fertility periods identified as specific and impervious to medical principles. She then concludes that in this situation menstrual blood symbolizes fertility (VICTORA 1991: 179-9).[7]

VICTORA's work leads me to hypothesize that the equation relating fertility with menstrual blood, which in reality refers to the possibility of conception, is a meaningful inner association amongst the representations of the working classes. In my research the new population under analysis has the same characteristics as his, namely it is urban, low-income and attended by public health services, but is much larger and is not restricted to females. Nevertheless we observe exactly the same equation: although we are dealing with preliminary data, most answers to the question "When is the time women are more likely to get pregnant?" are exactly the same: the answer is preponderantly that the most likely time to get pregnant is during menstruation. Our initial hypothesis assumed that the belief about fertility coinciding with menstruation would be one of the existing popular conceptions about fertility, among others. We verified, however, that a massive homogeneity of belief in the fertility/menstruation equation exists.[8]

When we ask questions about the best timing for conception, approximately 90% of our respondents make a direct association with the menstrual period, modifying only the number of days concerned. Some typical answers are:

" I think there is more of a risk (of getting pregnant) in the three days following menstruation."
"Three days before, and up to three days after, is when one can get pregnant."
"Right after menstruation, when the blood is not entirely dry yet."
"Right after everything (the blood) comes out, immediately after menstruation."

In a generalized representation, the body opens itself to discharge blood and then closes itself. The time period contiguous to this opening, or menstruation, is seen as fertile, 'dangerous' (an expression also used by doctors) and favorable to procreation.

Those individuals who mentioned fertility periods other than during menstruation were then asked if they believed a woman could get pregnant during menstruation as well. The answer was mostly affirmative, although menstruation is also considered a period during which sexual intercourse should be avoided. We therefore have nearly unanimous answers, from both women and men, as to the timing of conception.

---

7. See BOLTANSKI (1979), DUARTE (1988) and LOYOLA (1979), for an analysis on the social representation of the body as a unique and singular entity, in which pain, pleasure and other bodily sensations experienced by an individual becomes the knowledge reference-point for the body.
8. The data refers to approximately 50 cases (40 women and 10 men), aged between 13 and 50. In the ongoing investigation the total number of planned interviews is 100 for each sex. The method utilized consists of an interview and the application of an ethnographically-oriented observation protocol. Each interview takes approximately 10 hours and is conducted in at least three sessions. The investigation includes general ethnographic data from each of the four shantytowns and from their community medical services.

Dates, numbers and calculations presented by the respondents, such as 'the day in the chart' or the 'date taught by the doctor,' are frequently manipulated, possibly because the individual feels tested and wishes to conform to the interviewer's expectations. It is interesting to note that in this number manipulation the numbers *three* and *seven* appear as more or less constantly meaningful to the respondents. Other dates are mentioned as complementary information, such as the days taught by the doctor at the health center or other dates believed to have been the taught dates. *Three* and *seven* are not magical numbers, but indicate a clear connection between the popular and medical discourses. The statement "three days before and three days after, plus one more dangerous day," for instance, add up to seven 'dangerous' days. The individual repeats the recommendation, manipulating the same numbers, the reference is to menstruation, but a displacement of dates occurs. *Seven* is also the number prescribed for 'a rest' after twenty-one days taking oral contraceptives, given that seven and twenty-one add up to the total number of days in a menstrual cycle. As yet another example, *seven* is also identified with medical prescriptions, being the possible number of days for recommended antibiotic use. And information such as "three days before or after the fourteenth day, counting from the first day of the menstrual period" sounds confusing, arbitrary and illogical. In such cases the individual tends to associate the given dates with other dates. Here are some examples:

"The doctor said that a woman is fertile on the eighth day after menstruating, but it's not exactly like that, because it depends on the woman. There are women who get pregnant while menstruating."

"Fourteen days after the period, and three days before and three days after the period, is when a woman can get pregnant."

The use of specific numbers should be investigated, as they may be present in the medical discourse and may be present in the popular discourse for symbolic reasons.

To calculate the length of gestation doctors make use of the date of the last menstrual period, and are therefore able to work out the probable date of conception and the estimated delivery date. In any pre-natal service the date of the last menstrual period will be constantly referred to. In the popular view this logic may be constructed as a strong indicator, not entirely misplaced, of the relationship between menstruation and conception.

Even when the date taught by the health centers is repeated accurately (most of the time it suffers some peculiar modification), the medical information is relativized and other meaningful references recalled which are better equipped to explain reproduction, as in the following example:

"There is the man's erection, then the sperm goes to join the woman's ovule inside the uterus and conception occurs. But this only happens during the fertile period, only 24 hours every month. But this depends on each woman. The books say that the female fertile period is seven days before and seven days after menstruation, but I don't believe that, because my wife got pregnant during her menstruation."

Pregnancy is always considered a *risk*, or a fact that may or may not occur in a universe of random events. In fact, it is not a coincidence that the expression used for becoming pregnant, *pegar filho*, which literally means 'to catch or get a child,' is similar to the expression used for 'catching a disease' or being submitted to an affliction.

Conception is perceived as a contagious state, when bodily fluids come into contact, female menstrual blood being directly analogous to semen, the male fertility fluid. One of our male informants even employed the term 'woman's semen,' or *semen da mulher*, to describe 'the substance produced by the [fallopian] tubes,' or *a substância produzida nas trompas*. Sexual intercourse is represented by a situation involving the exchange of bodily fluids. Blood and semen are vehicles of transmission of pollution as well as of life, emotions and moral elements, and sexual interaction is essentially a social interaction where an interchange occurs. Menstrual blood is the most evident vaginal fluid and is taken to be a token of female essence and 'nature.' The homology of menstrual blood and semen and their roles as vehicles of fertility is a cross-cultural phenomenon.[9]

An entire body of general data, which I consider to be global and inclusive of well-known cultural facts, leads to a direct association between menstrual flow and fertility. This data indicates that both processes are perceived as hot and humid bodily conditions, and that both are necessary for procreation. As an example, among working class women there is a well-known prohibition concerning washing one's hair whilst menstruating:

"If one washes one's hair while menstruating, the blood climbs to one's head and the woman can go crazy."
"If a woman takes a cold shower and washes her hair, the [menstrual] blood goes up instead of down."
"If we get wet, the water can 'cut' (corta) the blood and 'cut' menstruation."

In this symbolic equation, blood is classified as *hot* and water as *cold*. Interestingly, as VICTORA (1991: 121) mentions, these avoidance practices are identical to those defined for the post-partum or post-abortion bleeding periods. It can therefore be conjectured that menstrual blood belongs to the same category as the vital fluids associated with the development of a fetus. An informant says:

"The menstruation which comes right after childbirth smells strongly because it has been at rest for nine months."

We also found representations of the placenta and of pregnancy as a huge clot of condensed blood.[10]

"After nine months the blood that became a huge clot dissolved and flowed."

The logic embedded in the recipes for abortive teas (used 'to let the menstruation come out,' called *chapueradas*) observe the same rationale. It is important to note that within this framework there is no distinction between contraception and abortion, for the very notion of prevention does not exist in the world of reproduction: one can only undo what has been done. In their view, if conception does not occur fetal blood is the same blood as menstrual blood.

Menstrual blood is perceived as different from the blood that runs in a woman's veins, a blood of a different type, of a different consistency and overall nature. While women show repugnance and disgust when referring to their own menstrual blood, they do not manifest the same aversion to blood from a wound. The smell and consistency of menstrual blood is considered strange, and classified as 'strong,' 'disgusting,' 'thick,' and 'gummy' (*forte, nojento, grosso* and *pastoso*).

The non-identification of menstrual blood with the woman's own blood suggests an *alterity*, or 'otherness,' as if the blood belonged to somebody else. After fertilization, this blood stays in the uterus, as if it didn't really belong to the woman's body. In folk terminology, the menstrual state is referred to as 'being with the ox' (*estar de boi*) and as 'receiving guests' (*recebendo visita*).

Abortive teas (*chapueradas*) are based on the magical principles of contiguity, where the 'the similar works upon the similar,' guaranteeing that the tea will have the desired effect (to 'take out,' or *tirar*). The preparation and ingestion of *chapueradas* are subjected to the belief that menstrual blood is a fertile substance, revealing relevant patterns of opposition and association in the social categories of thought. Even though the word *chapuearada* is based on the root *chá* (tea), a

---

9. The ethnographic evidence of the homology between female menstrual blood and male semen is provided by various authors in the anthropological literature, as in BRANDES 1980; DOUGLAS 1986; LÉVI-STRAUSS 1982 and DUARTE 1981.
10. This particular data is derived from ethnographic material, not yet systematized, collected in fieldwork currently underway by JAQUELINE FERREIRA, towards her master's thesis on *Bodily Fluids, Symptoms and Sensations*. The thesis will be presented at the Universidade Federal do Rio Grande do Sul's Social Anthropology Department.

beverage, the boiled mixture is not restricted to oral ingestion, being occasionally introduced intravaginally.

Chapueradas are brews made of herbs such as *erva-de-passarinho*, cinnamon bark, tangerine leaves, boiled wine, bean broth and rum. The recipes regionally, but they must all be ingested when very hot ('boiling') and in combination with 'strong' food and medicine. The most common medications, available at drugstores, consist of large doses of aspirin or other pain-killers, an entire month's dosage of oral contraceptives, Cytotec (ulcer medication of verified abortive side-effects) or heart medication. Medications which require prescription are considered 'strong,' and this characteristic, perhaps in reference to the possibility of side-effects and to the fact that the medicine may be difficult to acquire, leads to the belief that the beverage is effective.

Chapueradas include variations of 'strong food,' such as a specific animal's lard (hard to find), fat, oils and resinous materials boiled along with rusty nails or pieces of iron. With the addition of red wine, bean sauce and fatty substances, the appearance of the brew is not unlike that of menstrual blood, revealing an implicit similarity between the brew and blood, an unconscious correspondence. Also, in order to be able to dissolve the procreation nodule or clot, the brew must be *hot* and *strong*, the same terminology used to describe menstrual blood.[11]

In some cases it is specifically recommended that the *chapuerada* should be *repulsive (repugnante)*, and therefore served only when the deterioration process has already begun. The concept of being *spoiled* is a variation on *strong*, in the sense that a *strong* brew has the power to cause nausea, vomiting, or the power to *throw out*, or expel.

The association between the beverage and menstruation, both categorized as repugnant and 'polluting,' recalls yet again the magical principle of similitude. The *chapueradas* should be ingested in the morning, before the first meal of the day, and the woman must stay in bed, warm and in *resguardo* until the 'menstruation comes out.'

Some kind of magical procedure should be always be present in the making and ingesting of a chapuerada: a healer's spell, specific words spoken in an exact sequence, and often a unique element, almost impossible to acquire, usually consisting of animal waste. The recipe's details involve scarce and unique elements. The magic is necessary to assure the effectiveness of the abortion, but it is always present in combination with a high-dose ingestion of hormones or abortive medication such as Cytotec. The magic can also be seen as an essential element in the 'undoing' of conception, believed to be highly complex and magical itself.[12]

Other abortion practices, such as vaginal douching, *lavagens* and *gotas* (chemical abortion and sterilization) will not be addressed in this paper, but it is nonetheless worth pointing out that they follow the same principles described above, given that they are not identified as abortive procedures but as a means 'to let the menstruation come out.'

Pregnancy or menstrual avoidance rules, as well as abortion practices, are regulated by the principle that blood present inside the body must be allowed to flow out. This belief belongs to a more general conception about natural equilibrium, in which the humoral model of constant fluid circulation, responsible for the body's organization, must also be taken into account. Within this logical scheme, menstrual blood assumes the role of procreator when it comes into contact with semen:

---

11. See KNAUTH 1991, for a description of the classification of food as *strong (forte)* as opposed to *weak (fraca)*, and *hot (quente)* as opposed to *cold (fria)* within this specific ethnographic context.
12. See LEAL 1991, for a description of spells and procedures employed by benzedeiras who perform magic healing in southern Brazil.

"I'm not sure how conception works. The sperm goes there and makes the fetus. The riskiest time [for pregnancy to occur] is during menstruation, for then the blood comes out and the semen stays inside her. Besides that, they must both have orgasms [*gozam*] at the same time."

The statements above are masculine, characterized quite well by the association between blood and semen, both 'generating' substances. A 40-year-old woman states:

"I have a busy life, taking care of the house and the children, but when I wake up in the morning and I am menstruating, I realize I am a woman and so I feel like having sex."

In the above statement menstrual blood is perceived as a sign of femininity, reminding her of her female identity and evoking sexual desire. Narratives containing ideas about desire, *ter vontade*, are recurrent, although contradictory with the ideas about the 'polluting' nature of the menstrual period. In this regard it is important to observe the distinction between the first and last days of the period, between weak and strong flows, and between the corresponding humid and warm state as opposed to the wet and hot one. The beginning and the end of the menstrual period are the times considered pleasurable, but in general the menstrual flow is dirty, 'polluting' and disgusting, a period when sexual intercourse should be avoided.[13]

"If one has sex during menstruation, besides being messy and disgusting, one can get pregnant."
"It's dirty to have intercourse during the menstrual period, and each woman has her own way of getting pregnant."

Here are some examples of male speech:
"A menstruating woman is not clean, she is full of worms (bichada)."
"A man who has intercourse with a menstruating woman can become impotent."

The repulsion, danger and avoidance, shown mostly by males, does not exclude the manifestation of sexual desire present in women's statements. In general women avoid sexual intercourse when the flow is heavy, but at the beginning and at the end of their periods, when 'the body is opening and closing,' respectively, they believe it is the most likely moment for getting pregnant and claim it is the moment of strongest sexual desire. The male fear of impotence resulting from contact with menstrual blood can also be taken as an indicator of the male belief that menstrual blood is powerful and fertile.

Under certain conditions menstrual blood is therefore regarded as pollution, dirt and waste to be eliminated; and under other conditions it is a fluid which cleans the female body, either by leaving the body or as a filter. This can be viewed as another representation of the post-menstrual female body as a favorable setting for gestation. In the game of humoral body meanings, which involve menstruation and conception, the idea of the female body as an entity which opens and closes should be seen as a dominant representation, a key to understanding the logic of reproduction.

The body is continuously envisaged as containing many inner movements, a mechanism of fluid flow responsible for life, in opposition to death, when fluid circulation stops. The female body has the pre-requisites for life: menstrual blood is a female condition indicating fertility, and the uterus, an empty cavity, is where the fetus develops. In a woman's life-cycle, starting to produce menstrual blood indicates the ability to conceive, while the end of production indicates that she is no longer able to reproduce. The blood flow is clean while construed as a generator of life, but it is considered *dirt* (or a filter) when encompassing *things that are not good for the body*, such as an unwanted pregnancy or eliminated blood. In such cases it should be discharged and quarantine practices are necessary.

---

13. In the anthropological literature we find extensive material on how diverse cultures identify menstrual blood with impurity and pollution. See DOUGLAS 1976, and HELMAN 1984. See BRANDES 1980, for more on the perception of menstrual blood as a pollutant and of the menstrual flow as a carrier of the dirt accumulated over the course of the cycle.

The concept of a body that opens and closes itself during menstruation is a main representation, both in feminine and masculine speech. When attempting to conceive, the internal organs of the open body are vulnerable, so vaginal contact should be avoided during heavy flow, even though menstrual blood is fertile. The ideal days for conception are therefore the days immediately before and after the heavy flow. The assumption that conception occurs in *contiguity* with menstruation is widely shared. It reveals a representation of the body as a cultural model, including notions of bodily opening, heat, humidity, as well as a logical need for the existence of a conducting fluid and a sense of boundary (or the absence of it) regarding the female body:

"One should not have sexual intercourse during the menstrual period because the body is open and bleeding."
"Three days before you get your period the uterus stays open and then anything will make you pregnant, even after menstruation when the uterus is not yet closed."
"A woman can get pregnant right after her period, because then she is clean."

Among women there is an avoidance of sexual intercourse during the menstruation's *strong* days, either because it may result in pregnancy or because it is 'dirty,' 'messy,' or 'disgusting.' Among men, an avoidance of menstrual blood is recommended, due to its polluting nature, but note that abstinence is not recommended:

"When the woman is pregnant or when she is menstruating anal sex should be [practiced] so as not to harm the baby."

This statement also contains a reference to the logical equivalence between menstruation and pregnancy.

Firstly, conception is perceived as the 'consubstantiation' of blood and semen, a physically intimate process. Secondly, body conditions such as temperature and humidity play an important role in this model. Thirdly, conception is regulated by the culturally imposed mechanism, similar to a binary operator, of a body that opens and closes itself, allowing fluids to circulate and providing the inner physiological world the possibility of establishing relationships with the external, or social, world. And finally, the entire reproductive process is subject to the influence of what I shall call *a situational logic*, in reference to the haphazardness of life. Following this argument, sexual intercourse must be submitted to different circumstances, as for instance the quality of the relationship, time space and social conditions, in order to result in reproduction.

"People get child [*pegam filho*] if they have orgasms [*gozam*] together."
"May is the most likely month for becoming pregnant because it is the 'month of brides' and 'the month of mothers.'"
"When it's raining, it's humid—I learnt that with the nurses at the hospital."

A very large number of narratives are from women professing to become pregnant during their menstrual period, from women who are 'in between pills,' or who are using an *intrauterine device* (IUD). The examples concerning the pill become clear if we take into account the fact that the use of oral contraceptives is not properly understood and is interrupted precisely during the menstrual discharge. Another issue identified as a problem consists of the fact that hormones diminish the volume of menstrual flow and interrupt the necessary circulation of bodily fluids: "blood that was supposed to come out is kept inside." Given these facts, the administration of oral contraceptives on a daily basis does not make sense. The pills are not taken as recommended, thus compromising their effectiveness and permanently affecting the belief in their effectiveness. The IUD, on the other hand, causes longer and abundant discharges, but is regarded with distrust: how can it avoid pregnancy if it actually produces more fertile blood discharge, deemed fertile? Another negative aspect of the IUD, namely that menstrual blood implies male avoidance of vaginal intercourse, should not be underestimated when considering the reasons for women to avoid the IUD.

These considerations partially explain the contraceptive profile of the population studied. The data considers women in their reproductive period (15 to 49 years) and are the result of two epidemiological researches made six years apart: in 1986, when the Health Service were implanted in the area, and in 1992, when TAKEDA's study was performed (TAKEDA 1993). See the table below for further details.[14]

Table 1: Contraceptive profile of women aged 15 to 49, Valão, Porto Alegre.

Women, aged 15 to 49, Valão, Porto Alegre	1986	1992
Pill	32.7	38.7
Feminine Sterilization	7.8	7.1
IUD	2.9	2.9
Withdrawal	1.6	1.4
Periodic abstinence	2.3	1.6
Vasectomy	–	0.2
Condom	–	2.5
Other methods/ traditional methods	1.3	3.2
Any method	48.0	29.4
Any method, pregnancy wanted	0.7	2.6
Any method, pregnant	2.6	4.1
Other (female or male sterility, menopause, hysterectomy)	–	6.2

Although there is significant use of oral contraceptives (39%), the number of abortions performed constitutes a critical health problem of overwhelming proportions, specially considering that abortions are illegal in Brazil.[15] The IUD is an available alternative for only approximately 2.9% of the women, this data having remained stable during the Health Service's six-year period of existence (the data refers to 1986 and 1993). Both the low rate of IUD use and the irregular use of the pill, with it's resulting ineffectiveness, are probably responsible for the increasing demand for feminine sterilization.

---

14. Statistical data presented here, referring to this specific population, comes from the *Diagnóstico de Saúde da População da Área da Abrangência do Posto de Saúde do Valão*, and was coordinated by CESAR VICTORA & FERNANDO BARROS, *Serviços de Saúde Comunitária, Hospital Conceição, Porto Alegre, 1986*. The second "community health diagnosis" was coordinated by SILVIA TAKEDA. The data presented here, rearranged so as to permit a comparison of the 1986 and 1992 data, is from TAKEDA 1993.
15. Data on abortion is not available, so we consider the data presented at the *44º Congresso Brasileiro de Ginecologia e Obstetrícia, November 1991*: in 1991 there were an estimated 5 million abortions in Brazil (in contrast to 3.5 million births). Also, in the same year 275,000 women were hospitalized with post-abortion complications in INSS (public) hospitals (data from WHO). This data was published in the Correio do Povo, Nov. 1, 1992.

Surgical sterilization (or *ligadura*) has been performed on 7% of the women, a relatively high percentage and the second most common contraceptive method.[16] Even though the Health Service does not offer surgical sterilization as an alternative, their policy of stressing other methods was not sufficient to cause a significant decrease in the observed frequency. The ethnographic data brought into evidence a strong *feminine* demand for sterilization (men behave in the opposite way), accompanied by frequent complaints about how difficult it is to have access to the operation of *ligadura*. Surgical sterilization is considered by woman to be the contraceptive method *par excelence,* in contrast with other reversible alternatives. Also, this female demand for sterilization leads to an increase in the number of cesarean deliveries, given that sterilization can be performed during delivery, exacerbating yet another serious reproductive health problem in Brazil.[17]

The anthropological analysis dealing with the existing structure of thought about the body, and the latter's organizational principles concerning reproduction, helps to explain why 29% of the women studied declare they do not wish to become pregnant but nevertheless do not use any type of contraception. This rate apparently diminished by 20%, a significant improvement relative to the 1986 data. With the necessary approximation to the 1986 data, comparing the tables leads to the conclusion that there was an increase in the use of oral contraceptives. Besides that, the presence of the Health Service has led to incentives towards reproduction, given that effective pre-natal and infant-mother care is provided. The number of pregnant women and women wishing to become pregnant doubled from 3.3% in 1986 to 6.7% in 1992. But since the total population of the area decreased from 7,650 inhabitants in 1986 to 6,565 in 1991 it might be possible to infer that there has been an increase in contraceptive practices different from the ones already mentioned, such as abortion.

The use of traditional methods, such as teas, *chapueradas* and *gotas* increased by 2%, in spite of the presence of the health services, and showed a certain ambiguity in the process. At the same time there is a slight increase in the declared use of the condom, even though an increase in the use of the condom as a contraceptive choice was not detected in the ethnographic investigation. Traditional and less effective methods such as withdrawal and periodic abstinence maintain a constant rate. The new facets of the investigation are the relatively high numbers of sterile women (apart from surgically sterile women), menopausal women (older than 49) and women who underwent hysterectomies. The remaining question is the following: do the numbers reflect an increase in the frequency of abortions performed away from the medical services, either self-induced of performed by midwives and healers (*parteiras* and *benzedeiras*)? It is important to bear in mind that precisely in the last six years the drug Cytotec has been massively diffused. The increase in the use of traditional methods, either by themselves or in combination with 'modern drugs,' leads to a entire new set of issues concerning reproductive health, which should be addressed without delay.[18]

---

16. 7.1%, although apparently a high figure for feminine sterilization, is nonetheless low when compared to the overall figure for Brazil: 27% for women aged 15 to 54, according to 1987 PNAD-IBGE data. Figures presented in the *Relatório da Comissão Parlamentar de Inquérito sobre Esterilização Feminina, Jornal Zero Hora,* Dec. 15, 1992. From the 1987 PNAD data, the rate of feminine sterilization in the state of Rio Grande do Sul is the lowest of all states.
17. Feminine sterilization in Brazil is governed by law, and is only permitted when there are specific clinical recommendations. But C-sections tend to accompany sterilization, thus providing some cover-up for the procedure. See BARROS 1991 and OSIS 1990, for data on the number of sterilizations connected with C-sections.
18. Since abortive practices are drastically disseminated in this population, maybe it is of some relevance to conjecture that there might be a connection between these practices, often performed under extremely precarious conditions, and the impressive rise in AIDS among women in the state of Rio Grande do Sul.

In this paper I have made an attempt to define a coherent logical structure on reproduction based on a cultural model and to show how the representations present in this system relate to existing contraceptive practices among a working-class population sample in southern Brazil. The discernment of this specific symbolic repertoire leads us, on the one hand, to a better understanding of the limited efficacy of some contraceptive methods, and on the other hand, to an explanation concerning the female demand for surgical sterilization, with its associated cesareans, and for extensive abortion practices performed in very precarious health conditions. This analysis also reveals a universe of traditional practices enclosed within urban society's modern medical system.

References

BARROS, F.; C. VAUGHAN; C. VICTORA & Y. HUTTL.
　1991　Epidemic of Caesarean Sections in Brazil. *The Lancet* 338(20): 167-169.
BOLTANSKI, L.
　1979　*As Classes Sociais e o Corpo*. Rio de Janeiro: Graal.
BRANDES, S.
　1980　*Methaphors of Masculinity: Sex and Status in Andalusian Folklore*. Philadelphia, University of Pensylvania Press.
DOUGLAS, M.
　1986　*Pureza e Perigo*. Sao Paulo, Perspectiva.
DUARTE, L.F.
　1986　*Da Vida Nervosa nas Classes Trabalhadoras Urbanas*. Rio de Janeiro, Jorge Zahar.
KNAUTH, D.
　1991　*Os Caminhos da Cura: Sistema de Representacoes e Praticas Sociais sobre a Doença em uma Vila de Classes Populares*. Master thesis in Social Anthropology, Universidade Federal do Rio Grande do Sul (PPGAS-UFRGS), Porto Alegre, Brazil.
HELMAN, C.
　1984　*Culture, Health and Illness*, London, Wright.
LEAL, O.F.
　1989　*The Gaucho: Male Culture and Identity in the Pampas*. PhD Dissertation, Department of Anthropology, University of California, Berkeley, USA.
LEAL, O.F.
　1992　Benzendeiras e Bruxas: Sexo, Genero e Sistem a de Cura Tradicional. *Cadernos de Antropologia Social* 5: 7-22.
LEVI-STRAUSS, C.
　1982　*As Estruturas Elementares do Parentesco*. Petropolis, Vozes.
LOYOLA, M.A.
　1984　*Medicos e Curandeiros: Conflito Social e Saude*. Sao Paulo, DIFEL.
MARTIN-BARBERO, J.
　1987　*Processos de Comunicacion y Matrizes de Cultura: Intinerario para Sair da Razao Dualista*. Mexico, Gili.
OSIS, M.J. et al.
　1990　Laqueadura Tubaria nos Servicos de Saude do Estado de Sao Paulo. *Revista de Ginecologia e Obstetricia* 1(3): 195-204.
RIOS-NETO, E. et al.
　1991　Contraceptive Use and Fertility in Brazil. *Procedings of the Demographic and Health Conference* 1: 113-134.
TAKEDA, S.
　1993　*Avaliacao das Modificacoes nos Indicadores de Saude e Qualidade da Atencao, Seis Anos apos a Implantacao de Unidade*. Master Thesis in Epidemiology, Universidade Federal de Pelotas, Pelotas, Brazil.
VICTORA, C.
　1991　*Mulher, Sexualidade e Reproducao: Representacoes de Corpo em uma Vila Popular de Porto Alegre*. Master Thesis in Social Anthropology. Programa de Pos Graduacao em Antropologia Social (PPGAS-UFRGS), Universidade Federal do Rio Grande do Sul, Porto Alegre, Brazil.

Inside the Mother's Body:
Pregnancy and the 'Emic' Organ 'the Body's Mother'

CERES VICTORA

Abstract

The present paper presents a study about ordinary people's views about the functioning of the reproductive system based on a large anthropological study carried out among low income women living in shantytowns in Porto Alegre, the capital of the southernmost state of Brazil.
Through the analysis of ethnographic material on space, domestic organisation and images of the body this paper discusses 'the body's mother,' an 'emic' organ described by the female informants as 'something' inside the female body that 'looks after the baby before it is born,' and 'looks for the baby after delivery.' Through this example I point out the relationship between embodied cultural experiences of space occupation and knowledge of the body.

Zusammenfassung

Der vorliegende Text zeigt, was gewöhnliche Leute darüber denken, wie der Fortpflanzungsapparat funktioniert, auf einer ethnologischen Studie basierend, die in einem Armenviertel von Porto Alegre, der Hauptstadt des südlichsten Bundesstaates Brasiliens, durchgeführt wurde. Durch die Analyse des ethnographischen Materials über Raum, häusliche Organisation und Körperbilder, diskutiert dieser Text die ‚Mutter des Körpers', ein ‚emisches' Organ, das von den weiblichen Informantinnen als ‚etwas' innerhalb des weiblichen Körpers beschrieben wird, das ‚nach dem Baby guckt, bevor es geboren wird' und ‚guckt nach dem Baby nach der Geburt'. Durch dieses Beispiel zeige ich die Beziehung auf zwischen verinnerlichten kulturellen Erfahrungen von Raumvorstellungen und dem Wissen über den Körper.

Keywords: gender, reproduction, southern Brazil.

Introduction

Within the field of Medical Anthropology, studies of lay and biomedical notions of health and illness have been an important area of research promoting discussions about the health-illness processes in a broader socio-cultural context. In many studies, ethnographic findings highlight that lay people's views of health and illness differ a great deal from their biomedical counterparts, suggesting that an apparent pan-human ever-existing event such as a 'dis-ease' is a highly complex multifaceted process, that may be better treated by healing systems other than biomedicine. (KLEINMAN 1978; GRAHAM & OAKLEY 1981; FARMER 1988; OTS 1990; LANGFORD 1995)

FRANKENBERG's (1986) description of the concept of 'illth' exemplifies what I mean by the multiple meanings of the 'dis-ease' process. Defined in opposition to the idea of wealth, in the sense of well being, 'illth' accounts for the broader social context and implications of what has been described in the medical anthropological literature as the biomedical perspective—the disease—and the person's evaluation of a health problem—the illness. (KLEINMAN 1978; HELMAN 1990). Alternatively to the limiting disease X illness dichotomy, FRANKENBERG (1980, 1986) suggests the concept of sickness "that refers to the way that illth is socially and culturally performed" (1992: 7). That places the 'dis-ease' process in a much broader field of social interactions rather than in the physician's consulting office, by separating the issue regarding lay and biomedical perspectives from the idea of a limiting bi-dimensional interpretation of the same bodily process. In that sense differences in lay and biomedical perspectives do not merely represent problems of the type doctor-patient interaction. Rather they belong in the much wider socio-cultural realm of bodily experience.

It is important to note that the use of words such as 'lay' when referring to ordinary people's views about the body and 'biomedical' when referring to 'western' (also known as 'modern,' 'cosmopolitan,' 'scientific') medicine does not place these perspectives in static opposition to each other, rather both represent a multiplicity of views, and for this reason they are used here in the plural form.

From that follows one of the basic arguments of the present research: people know their bodily facts in different ways. In other words, knowledge of the body is a process that is permanently being re-evaluated by subjects in contact with different life experiences.

This issue has been previously examined by YOUNG (1981) who states:

> "(...) an actor's medical knowledge (beliefs) and his statements are not epistemologically homogeneous, that is he does not know all of his facts in the same way. This is accounted for by the fact that his knowledge is recursive and presocial, in the sense that he continuously evaluates it against his intentions, expectations, and perceptions of events, and sometimes he compares it with other bits of his knowledge of similar events." (YOUNG 1981: 379)

Through traditional participant observation procedures I realised that the same informant could tell me the same fact, for example, a specific medical consultation or a child birth experience in different ways depending on whether we were on our own or if there were other people present as well; whether it was a recent or a past event; whether the informant had had other similar experiences to compare with and, in this case, the experiences would never be told on their own but comparatively. It was also relevant to the narrative their neighbours or relatives experiences or opinions about the event that was recalled or similar events they — neighbours or relatives — had been through. In the case of informants who had had a medical opinion about the event described, the medical discourse would be used as an endorsement of what the person has been through or as proof of medical error. But even if the same story was told differently in different situations each was usually coherent in its own terms.

The informants' discourse was thus analytically explored in different situations: individually, collectively (in group conversations), immediately after an event (such as delivering a baby), some months after important events, in recollections of other people's events, in opinions or gossip about neighbours and relatives.

Research and Methodology

The data presented in this chapter as well as the interpretation of this data refers to my ethnographic research among working class women in Porto Alegre since 1989[1], although a large part of what will be presented here belongs to the most recent section of my research, developed between 1992 and 1994. It includes data about 100 women who have been interviewed for a larger research project developed by the Núcleo de Pesquisa em Antropologia do Corpo e da Saúde — NUPACS.[2] All these women live in four shantytowns in the northern part of Porto Alegre — Vila Dique, Vila Divina Providência, Vila Floresta and Vila Sesc. It also includes data about eleven women who

---

1. For the first part of this ethnographic research see VICTORA 1991.
2. "Body, sexuality and reproduction: a study of social representations," the larger research project which provided part of the data analysed here was funded by the Special Programme of Research, Development and Research Training in Human Reproduction of the World Health Organisation (1993-4).

live in another shantytown in the southern part of the same city—Vila Cruzeiro—as well as seventeen women who were in a Public Hospital (Hospital Conceição) for prenatal or postnatal procedures.

The researched women's embodied cultural experiences can be seen in a range of aspects in various areas of their lives and are discussed here especially in relation to their perceptions of their bodies and their reproductive system. These experiences are clearly related to a working class background and are looked into through their expressed and observed beliefs and practices. The ways their families are organised, the way they relate to other people, the way they raise their children, the way they cook, the way they love, the way they look after the ill—all of these identified primarily as female activities in what is known in the Brazilian anthropological literature as 'popular culture.' The object of analysis are the female views and experiences within this culture.

One of the most relevant aspects of the way of life in the shantytowns is the use of time and space in general and the domestic organisation in particular. These categories—time, space and domestic organisation—have also become an essential analytical tool, basic for the understanding of the images of the body and the reproductive system discussed in this paper. My point is that the particular embodied space organisation experienced by the Brazilian shantytown groups are not isolated facts. Rather, they are consonant with the way they experience their bodily facts, among other aspects of their lives. In relation to that I have discussed elsewhere how the shantytown groups' experience of a more fluid space organisation in the households is coherent with a more fluid notion of body organs and systems. I suggest that this differs from the biomedical images of the body that rely on a much more rigid structure.[3] This is not to say that groups that experience a more rigid space organisation, comply with all biomedical procedures. My claim is that the biomedical principle of a fixed body with organs that are organised in isolated systems is more easily 'assimilated' by such groups than by the Brazilian shantytown ones because their lived experience of space/domestic organisation provides the framework required for such understanding. For the Brazilian groups who live a more fluid space organisation, the body has a more fluid structure, allowing the possibility of organs that move from place to place or are 'awakened' according to the bodily situation, such as the 'emic' organ 'the body's mother' (*mãe do corpo*).

The Pregnant Body and the 'Emic' Organ the 'Body's Mother'

Perhaps the most vivid example of this fluidity in the researched lay models of the body can be found during and immediately after pregnancy, in other words, in the way women perceive their pregnant and post-natal bodies and how they make sense of their sensations.

Pregnancy is a very 'public' state in the shantytowns in the sense that many people get involved, give opinions, advice and cause problems for pregnant women. Pregnant women are seen as suffering significant influence from the immediate social environment and from direct actions performed by them. This is shown in the following statements:

"Everything that happens to you during pregnancy, the baby gets it too. I had problems with my family, and when I went to the doctor, the baby was across the belly. Because of that I needed a Caesarean section." (F., 27 years old)

---

3. See VICTORA 1996.

"I had to do all sorts of heavy work during my pregnancy, carry bricks, cement; the belly was often wet from washing clothes. The baby was born weak, with low birth weight." (C., 25 years old)

In these types of account the women are usually implying that they have not been treated properly according to their distinctive state of pregnancy. The implications of the external/social environment can be seen in the internal/pregnant state. Perhaps the division between an external and internal environment is not so clear cut and the boundaries between the natural body and the social body or the environment are much more complex then this dualistic model allows. In the examples above, problems with the family and a wet belly penetrate the pregnant body and influence the development of the foetus.

The informants, especially those who were in hospital (Hospital Conceição) for anti-natal and post-natal procedures and other informants who were asked to recall previous experiences of pregnancy stated the existence of an organ called the 'body's mother.' This 'emic' organ they describe as an organ that is always inside the body and accompanies the baby during pregnancy. After the baby is born, it looks for the baby, because it misses it. That is why there is movement in the women's belly after birth. Here are some of their accounts about the 'body's mother':

"The 'body's mother' is like a baby, it jumps up and down. But it is always inside the body, it remains inside after the baby is born." (I., 43 years old)

"The 'body's mother' helps the baby to grow; after the baby is born it looks for the baby, you have to massage it to calm it down. [And what do you think about it?, I asked] I don't think, I feel it." (J., 25 years old)

The body's mother as a phenomenological experience, is an organ that moves inside the body — it jumps up and down, it needs to be calmed down. It is alive on its own because 'it looks for the baby.' But at the same time it is a bodily organ like any other that 'is always inside the body.' The reason it is there is to 'help the baby to grow' or just to keep company to the baby while in the belly, as has been told me repeatedly.

It is a friendly organ, like a mother, that gets so attached to the baby that keeps looking for it after it is born, but not for very long. As some informants put it:

"I felt it yesterday, it was bothering me. It looks for the baby. It misses it. It was not painful, it just moved and then stopped." (C., 17 years old)

"The 'body's mother' moves in the body after the baby is born, but not for very long." (T., 36 years old)

I asked a few informants to point or draw the 'body's mother' in a graphic image of the body and they pictured a small circle in one of the sides of the womb and indicated with lines the movements performed by the organ. But the idea of making a drawing of the 'body's mother' in an empty silhouette, a bi-dimensional diagram, was not very adequate because it was clear that the body's mother belonged to distinct type of knowledge, an experiential knowledge. I asked my informants how they first learn about the 'body's mother' and they told me that their mother had told them about it, as follows: "My mum has always told me: it beats like a heart." (C., 26 years old)

"The 'body's mother' is like a little baby inside, it moves. But it is not. I had felt it before and I thought I was pregnant. I told my mum and she said I wasn't, it was just the 'body's mother'." I did a pregnancy test and it was negative." (V., 28 years old)

But, even though women state they have learned about it from an older female relative, several informants said that doctors had confirmed that the movements they felt in the abdomen after giving birth were the 'body's mother.' I suspect that doctors and patients are speaking about movements inside a post-natal body, contractions and rearrangement of internal organs after birth. But although they are actually speaking of the same general phenomena, they imply different meanings. The doctors, so I have been told by some of them, are actually talking about the contracting womb and assume that the womb is the 'mother of the body,' an organ that commands the female being. On the other hand, the women speak of an 'emic' organ. As in the Portuguese language both expressions ('the mother of the body' and the 'body's mother') are the same (*mãe do corpo*) it is hard to confirm.

Two informants also used the term 'womb' to translate what the 'body's mother' is, but kept the meaning they had learned 'at home.'

"The 'body's mother' is the womb, it misses the sac, looks for it after the baby is born." (R., 23 years old)

"If the 'body's mother' is weak, the woman does not get pregnant. It is the womb. I have felt it, it moves side to side, makes noises, has cramps. We feel it after delivering a baby. It is as if you still have a baby inside. Every woman knows that." (M., 44 years old)

The idea that this knowledge is common to all women is also a recurrent one since this type of information is clearly part of the female gender experience among the shantytown groups.

As a distinct organ the body's mother accounts for another bodily event, the psychological pregnancy. As one informant explains:

"I know it moves like a baby in the womb. Sometimes, when a woman cannot get pregnant, she has a psychological pregnancy. It is the 'body's mother' that grows." (F., 27 years old)

In a way similar to the doctors' use of the emic expression *mãe do corpo* to speak about the contracting womb, the women use the 'medical' word, *womb*, implying the 'emic' organ. My understanding is that doctors and patients are not just using different names, they are actually using different models of the body. The same can be said in relation to the 'psychological pregnancy' which in a lay model of the body is seen as growth of the 'body's mother.' Being the 'body's mother' a quite autonomous organ that mirrors the mother's behaviour, it desperately wants a baby, it likes the baby, it looks after the baby and searches for the baby when it is gone.

Embodiment of Cultural Experiences and Knowledge About the Reproductive System

I have argued in the beginning of this paper that there are different ways of knowing our bodies. In many situations the Brazilian shantytown informants reported their bodily experiences as the main source of knowledge, one example of that being the 'emic' organ the 'body's mother' which is experienced primarily through the body. This is not to say that it is not a cultural experience, since its meanings are given within a cultural repertoire, but the body in this case is taken as the grounds of culture, the primary field of perception and practice. (FRANK 1986; CSORDAS 1988, 1993, 1994; OTS 1990; TURNER 1994)

BOURDIEU also stresses the groundedness in the body — a socially informed body — as

"a principle generating and unifying all practices, the system of inseparably cognitive and evaluative structures of a determinate state of the social world." (BOURDIEU 1995: 124)

For BOURDIEU the *habitus* exists because it is incorporated in the body. (JENKINS 1992)

In that sense the idea that women have an organ that changes places, moving from side to side, needs to be seen within an embodied notion of fluid space.

In the shantytowns the houses are usually small, with an average of two rooms, one bedroom and one kitchen/living-room. But in the dynamics of the shantytowns, the division of rooms is not what it seems to be because there are usually more people living in the houses than beds. That is because at night the kitchen and the living-room might 'become' bedrooms where the floor turns into a large bed that will lodge several people.

In such situations, a vast exchange takes place among the houses in the same boundaries. Very often only one toilet is available outside for all. Neighbours frequently watch television together in the evening, even when they have their own television set. They may also use the fridge or just get cold water or ice from neighbours who have a fridge in the hot summer months. This is not exclusive to houses in the same boundaries, but might be extended to other surrounding dwellings. Looking at who-or-what-belongs-where in these boundaries is basic for the understanding of the dynamics of the shantytown, but in these cases concepts such as 'inside' and 'outside' cease to be useful as exclusive categories.

For instance, the idea of boundaries that include and exclude can not be taken literally in a very crowded place. In some situations a fence limits the enclosed dwellings, other times there is no fence at all so inclusion or exclusion depends on knowledge of the place's history.

In relation to separation between houses, it might be difficult to know how many households there are in areas where the dwellings are so close together that they could easily be taken as only one. There is also the case of relatives who, living next door to each other, share so many things that the fact they have separate houses may seem an insignificant circumstance. Besides, there are also 'sleeping' arrangements, where children or teenagers spend the night at neighbour's or relative's houses, either because their parents' house is too crowded or because they are sent to keep a someone else company, or both.

In relation to this last point it is important to note that it is very unusual for people to live on their own. People living alone are pitied by others who will then either incorporate them to their household or send them a child or a teenager to live with them.

This phenomenon has also been observed by SCHEPER-HUGHES in Alto do Cruzeiro, a shantytown in Northeast of Brazil. As she puts it:

> "Actually one is never really alone on the Alto. Should a person suddenly become totally bereft of household members, a neighbour will send someone to live with that 'poor, solitary creature.'" (SCHEPER-HUGHES 1992: 99)

The point I wish to raise is the observed relationship between embodied cultural experiences (such as the experience of space/domestic organisation) and knowledge of the reproductive system. The 'body's mother,' according to the informants is 'something' that 'looks after the baby before it is born,' and 'it looks for the baby after delivery' which reflects cultural notions of space occupation and correlated ideas about how people should dwell.

People in the shantytowns do not think one should be alone. This is even more clear in the case of babies who are seen as tiny and defenceless creatures. The 'body's mother' is there to keep the baby company. The 'body's mother' as a phenomenological experience is a bodily produced knowledge based on embodied (cultural) notions since it is the body that enables the perceptual experience.

References

BOURDIEU, P.
    1995   *The logic of practice*. Cambridge: Polity Press.
CSORDAS, T.J.
    1988   Embodiment as a paradigm for Anthropology. *Ethos* 18: 5-47.
    1994   Introduction: the body as representation and being-in-the-world. In: *Embodiment and experience*. Edited by T.J. CSORDAS. Cambridge: Cambridge University Press.
FARMER, P.
    1988   Bad Blood, Spoiled Milk: Bodily Fluids as Moral Barometers in Rural Haiti. *American Ethnologist* 15(1): 62-83.
FRANK, G.
    1986   On embodiment: a case study on congenital limb deficiency in American culture. *Culture, Medicine and Psychiatry* 10: 189-219.

FRANKENBERG, R.
1980   Medical Anthropology and development: a theoretical perspective. *Social Science and Medicine* 14B: 197-207.
1986   Sickness as cultural performance: drama, trajectory and pilgrimage root metaphors and the making social of disease. *International Journal of Health Services* 16(4): 603-625.
1992   Your time or mine: temporal contradictions of biomedical practice. In: *Time, health and medicine*. Edited by R. FRANKENBERG. London: Sage Publications.

GRAHAM, H. & A. OAKLEY.
1995   Competing ideologies of reproduction: medical and maternal perspectives on pregnancy. In: *Woman, health and reproduction*. Edited by H. JOCOBUS. Routledge & Keagan Paul.

HELMAN, C.
1990   *Culture, health and illness*. Oxford: Butterworth-Heinemann.

JENKINS, R.
1992   *Pierre Bourdieu*. London: Routledge.

KLEINMAN, A.
1978   The failure of western medicine. *Human Nature*: 63-68.

LANGFORD, J.
1995   Ayurvedic interior: person, space, and episteme in three medical practices. *Cultural Anthropology* 10(3): 330-366.

OTS, T.
1990   The angry liver, the anxious heart and the melancholy spleen. The phenomenology of perceptions in Chinese culture. *Culture, Medicine and Psychiatry* 14: 21-58.

SCHEPER-HUGHES, N.
1992   *Death without weeping. The violence of everyday life in Brazil*. Berkeley: University of California Press.

TURNER, T.
1994   Bodies and anti-bodies: flesh and fetish in contemporary theory. In: *Embodiment and experience*. Edited by T.J. CSORDAS. Cambridge: Cambridge University Press.

VICTORA, C.G
1991   *Mulher, sexualidade e reprodução. Representações do corpo em uma vila de classes populares em Porto Alegre*. Porto Alegre: Master Dissertation in Social Anthropology. PPGAS/UFRGS.
1996   *Images of the body: Lay and biomedical views of the reproductive system in Britain and Brazil*. London: Ph.D. Thesis in Anthropology. Department of Human Sciences/Brunel University.

YOUNG, A.
1981   The creation of medical knowledge: some problems in interpretation. *Social Science and Medicine* 15B: 379-386.

Notebook on Migrations[1]
CONTARDO CALLIGARIS

Abstract
The text is a preliminary contribution to the psychopathology of modern migrant populations. It initially proposes and argues for a restricted definition of modern migrations as voyages toward (more) individualism. It then presents some implications of this description as an introduction to the psychology and psychopathology of modern migrations (points 1 through 4). America's specific role as current Mecca of migrations is also explained in this perspective (point 5). Ditto for the quest for affluence — generally evoked as a main reason to migrate, and here understood as a quest for mobility of status (point 6). The case of the recent Brazilian migration to the US is proposed as an example (point 6.1). Finally, the question of potentially negative cultural capital in migrations is raised, specifically concerning Hispanic immigration to the US (point 7).

Zusammenfassung
Dieser Text ist ein vorläufiger Beitrag zur Psychopathologie der modernen Migrationsbevölkerung. Anfänglich schlägt er eine begrenzte Definition von der modernen Migration als eine Reise in Richtung größere Individualität vor. Danach werden einige Zusammenhänge dieser Beschreibung aufgezeigt, die die Einführung in die Psychologie und Psychopathologie moderner Migrationen ausmachen (Punkte 1 bis 4). Amerikas spezielle Rolle als derzeitiges Mekka für Migrationen wird ebenfalls anhand dieser Perspektive erklärt (Punkt 5). Desgleichen die Frage des Überflusses – generell als Hauptgrund für Migration angesehen und hier verstanden als die Frage nach Mobilität von Status (Punkt 6). Der Fall der jüngsten brasilianischen Migration in die USA wird als ein Beispiel dargestellt (Punkt 6.1). Und schließlich, die Frage nach potentiell negativem kulturellen Kapital innerhalb der Migrationen wird aufgeworfen, speziell in Hinsicht auf die hispanische Immigration in die USA (Punkt 7).

Keywords: migration, psychopathology of migration, USA, Brazil, hispanics

1. There is something awkward and irritating in most general surveys of migrations (last in date, THOMAS SOWELL 1996); they seem to subsume just about anything within the same category. Ancient dislocations of entire populations across desert lands, global invasions, creation of encapsulated communities, mass deportations and, finally, every kind of colonizing settlements — they are all 'migrations,' as if GENGIS KHAN were CORTEZ' big brother and Hispanic 'wetbacks' swimming today across the Rio Grande were somehow related to Indians moving to the Fiji Islands.

---

1. This text is composed of edited selected notes from two sources: the draft of the chapter 'Migrations' in a coming book on contemporary individualism, and the preparatory work for a graduate seminar on the psychological effects of migrations, given in the fall 1996 at UC Berkeley, Dpt. of Anthropology. The seminar was considered, in the University's Program, as a Medical Anthropology topic, which it was, since — as the reader who bears with the text to the end will see — it was intended to be a sort of introduction to a discussion about the use (and abuse?) of medical and social benefits by migrant (specifically Latino) populations in the US.
I have chosen the form of notes in order to preserve the diversity of the arguments, without largely exceeding my space. My intention is here to present not conclusions, but the hints that I am following in my current work. Also, many of my remarks are based on extensive but unformal contacts with Brazilian and Hispanic immigrants in the US, and a more traditional academic format would have required a presentation of datas that the stage of my reflections does not yet authorize.
It is worth mentioning that large parts of this text, (particularly its last section) was presented as a lecture to the Hispano-Network in Lawrence, MA in April 1997. To my surprise and relief it produced no indignation. On the contrary.

To introduce one first distinction, I would rather speak properly of migrations only for modern times. Migrations today are a phenomenon remarkably different from any past conquest or exile, since they always, inevitably, suppose to some degree the existence and—ultimately—the success of Western culture, i.e. of a culture that claims the universality of mankind.

The globalized expansion of such cultural background modifies significantly the meaning and the psychological compass of any geographical movement of people or populations.

Changing country and language is a new and different adventure since modern Western culture progressively and surely promoted the idea that humans are to be defined as individuals rather than as members of a community. Beyond the relevance of cultural and social differences, it is therefore presumed that a modern host country will, if not assimilate, at least ideally and legally grant the perspective of full citizenship to the newcomer. The immigrant—different as he/she may be when stepping off the ship or plane—has a reason to believe that he/she may somehow join the culture he/she is moving into, basically just because his/her humanity is, in the end, the only requirement.

Migrations, in this specific modern sense, only happen either from an individualist culture to another individualist culture, or from a traditional culture to an individualist one. In mitigated terms—since individualism and holism are concepts or models, and not perfected entities—we may define modern migrations as voyages toward (more) individualism.

2. There are, of course, exceptions to our restricted definition of modern migrations. In other words, all contemporary movements of people and populations are not migrations in our sense.

On the one hand, people and populations are sometimes led to all sorts of exiles into cultures where the idea of a shared humanity beyond differences is out of the question. People still move from a traditional setting to another one, where they will probably be outcasts, or—at least—inevitably constitute a separate community (Koreans in Japan, for example). Encapsulated communities of 'immigrant' (improper use) populations often preserve jealously the traditions of the original country, and somehow grant a new pride in belonging to the ethnic background of a donor country where, at the time of migration, the emigrant could feel marginal and socially insignificant. For example, if being a Korean immigrant to Japan promises exclusion from the point of view of Japanese society, on the other hand, within the encapsulated Korean immigrant community, being a Korean may represent a value that the migrant had completely lost at home.

More specifically, people often move out of a traditional setting into another one as refugees of expanding Western modernity. The progressive Westernization of traditional communities generally immediately affects the lowest grades of the social hierarchy. The elites keep benefiting—sometimes over decades or even centuries—of a double sanction of their status: they are elites because of their wealth and recognition (in an individualist perspective), and they remain elites (in a holistic perspective), enjoying the privileges of a superior 'caste.' The lowest strata, on the contrary, rapidly lose—in the Westernizing process—the little social significance granted to them by the traditional setting. They thus face the very hard task to play the Western game from way down low, and in a society still regulated by strong traditional hierarchies that hinder their ascension. No wonder that people in this condition may chose to rebuild and consolidate their lost traditional setting, encapsulating it in a foreign holistic context.

In these movements from a traditional community to another, where the movers will be inevitably encapsulated, need may hastily appear as a primary factor. Still, the decision to integrate an encapsulated community within a host country responds to a communitarian longing, and is frequently reactive—to put it briefly, a sort of resistance against the transformation of 'pariahs' (way down, but included and endowed with a specific meaning in their traditional social setting) into underdog of individualism.

On the other hand, the voyage specifically opposed to migrations—from individualism to holism—is generally sporadic. It is often reserved for extended tourism or anthropological curiosity, when it does not constitute a form of conversion (moving to India and Nepal in the 60s), or even—less frequently—a sexual fantasy that eroticizes interpersonal relationships in a strict traditional setting (dreaming of moving into an Arabian harem, or being sold at a slave market).

Another—and more significant—case of movement from individualism to holism occurs when frustrated middle classes leave their individualist setting in quest of a form of power less precarious than the one they may enjoy at home. After the American Civil War, the movement of American Southerners to Brazil (where slavery was still the dominating mode of production) could be a collective inaugural example. More frequently and recently, such movements concern individuals, lacking recognition of status or unsatisfied with the recognition they get, looking for a better established sanction of their affiliation to a superior 'caste.' In many of these cases, the host countries are post-colonial societies: the frustrated migrating middle-classes may therefore (rightly) count on the fact that their 'foreign' Western origins will grant them a sort of automatic advantaged status in the traditional host culture. The spirit of many of Somerset Maugham's short stories is still alive, after the end of colonialism.

All these cases, as movements toward a traditional setting, are exceptions to our restricted definition of modern migrations. Still, in a way, they do not really escape the individualist global background of our times. On the one hand, the choice of encapsulation appears to be often a reaction against expanding individualism. On the other hand, since its very timid origins, individualism has regularly conceived itself as a time of decline and often lamented past and gone golden ages, thus mourning its communitarian past and longing for it. It is hardly astonishing, therefore, that individuals may now and then—whatever the quality of their nostalgia—take, for example, the road to the East, to an ancient colony, or to some tribal setting.

3. If migrations, in our restricted sense, are an individualist phenomenon, they are certainly destined to increase with the expansion of Western individualism. This is pragmatically obvious, since, as we mentioned, individualism makes them somehow easier, or promises to do so.

But there is more: the migrant is, in fact, the prototype of the individualist personality. The choice to migrate is a sort of repetition of the mythical decision of DUMONT's retirant (LOUIS DUMONT 1986)[2], inaugurating Western individualism. The migrant leaves behind the original community—its ties, its order, its (traditional) values—and moves on to a new world with the minimum necessary confidence that his/her singular humanity and actions will alone decide of his or her future in the host community. The migrant also necessarily believes in recognition of one's individual merits as a source of status, rather than in inherited privileges granted by blood and birth.

On the other hand, the 'expansion of Western individualism' is almost a pleonasm. It is amazing that we may sometimes complain or simply wonder at the sight of the ongoing globalization of the world. Or, even worst, consider it as the secret design of hidden speculating forces. A culture that claims that humanity has the species as its only limit needs no special strategy to expand. A

---

2. It is the time to mention the obvious: the concept of individualism and holism used throughout this text are strictly DUMONTian.

society that recognizes any eventual opponent as a fellow human—and therefore as one of its own potential full-size members—is hardly resistible.

The immediate corollary of individualism: universalism ('join the club! different as you may be, you can be accepted as one of ours') exercises an unmatched power of seduction.

3.1. The opposite of the previous note could also be said without contradiction. In fact, if individualism made and makes migrations easier, it is also true that a wider and more intense circulation of people was always a major factor in the development of individualism. The Hellenistic world, Christianity and even more so the canonical moments of modern Western individualism—the 13th, 16th and 18th centuries—were all moments of increased contacts among differences.

There is no need, from our point of view, to establish here a one-way cause-to-effect relationship between migrations and individualism. It is enough and plenty to underline their coalescence.

4. Modern migrations are defined by us as movements from traditional social settings toward individualism.

To some degree, this may even appear as a clear intentionality of the modern migrant: the wish or dream to find access to opportunities limited by his/her capacities and not by his/her birth and blood.

Still, it is obvious that such intentionality does not prevent or exclude an impressive typology of ambivalence, which frequently stands at the root of the pathology (especially the family pathology) of migrations. The term pathology should be understood here according to etymology: as a phenomenology of the complex and painful ways through which the migrants metamorphose themselves and—most of all—their children into individuals.

Obviously, the subjective processes of this transition can hardly be analyzed here. But, in a more social perspective, at least one of its features must be noticed: the passage, so to speak, from holism to individualism is often accomplished between the migrant and his/her first descendants (born or not in the host country). This transition constantly produces a specific difficulty concerning parental authority and authority as such.

The migrating parents owe their authority to a tradition, which—in the long run—they wish to be denied by their own children. It is, they believe (maybe rightly), the best way for the children to submit entirely to the laws of the new society. The trouble, of course, is that they are generally unable to represent in any way authority in the new culture, since—as recent immigrants—they are often granted very little social recognition. The hardly evitable hiatus—between denied traditional parental authority and the laws of the new society that simply do not incarnate in the parents—leaves the children in a vacuum.

This is particularly true at the moment of adolescence, when the immigrant parents naturally want to launch their children as citizens of the new world, and suddenly often discover in their children an explosive mixture made of: a) resentment against the new society for not having fully recognized their parents, b) resentment against their parents for being nobody in the new society, and having, as migrants, somehow abandoned their original community and whatever value their kinship may have (or nostalgically imagine it had) over there, c) despisal of the traditional authority that seems to regulate a kinship they don't really belong to anymore, d) despisal of the rules and laws of the new society, where they may feel that their kinship sacrificed itself and got no recognition in exchange.

The only reference available to these adolescents is then the individualist dream of success that was delegated to them by their (yet) unsuccessful parents.[3] This unique legacy, combined with the inconsistency of both sources of authority (the tradition denied by their parents, and the new society denying recognition to their parents), often produces an urgency to immediately snatch the symbols of status of the new society. Criminal behavior is the way, and it also can be an attempt to finally encounter some manifestation of the new society's law that the parents could not incarnate.[4]

Migrant families invent a number of interesting solutions to this specific difficulty of migration.

We often came upon migrant families where it appears to be necessary for at least one member to steadily maintain his/her ties to the original culture. An ancestor (grandmother, grandfather, for example) may come with the family, or join it later just to fulfill this peculiar function. The ancestor will serve the purpose of insuring a possible recourse to the original traditions (that he/she has not denied) during the laborious process of integration. He or she will thus maintain a parental authority rooted in the original culture, at a time when the migrating project itself may have left the parents symbolically destitute, since, because of it, they are no more what they were in the traditional community and not yet the 'somebodies' they hope to be recognized as. Only inconvenience: for this function to be fulfilled, the ancestor, depository of the original culture, must remain clearly alien to the migrating project and process—carefully kept apart from any possible integration into the new culture.

When an ancestor is not available, the mother is often the one who fulfills this position. In this case, she performs a supplementary (and in most cases temporary) assignment: as a living memory of the family's ties with the original culture, she somehow defends the father's dignity against the corrosive effects of his inevitably stumbling beginnings in the host country. Whatever respect the father still gets by his children, it is due to the memory of a past where a humble, yet consistent place was attributed to the father in the original culture, and the mother is here called upon to testify.

Ancestors and mothers, in these examples, are often destined to be, sooner or later, discarded by their families (their function becoming useless), and by the host country, where they suddenly find themselves completely alien (linguistically and culturally) even after impressive periods of time. They present US immigration authorities with the insoluble puzzle of legal immigrants, with 10, 20 or even more years of residence, totally incapable of naturalizing themselves.

5. Now, it happens that America (the US) is asymptotically becoming today the main, if not the only ultimate destination of modern migrations.

Whatever the mythical opportunity that the US supposedly offer to their immigrants, whatever the multiple historical contingencies that eventually situate America as a dream in many different cultures, there is a sort of fundamental reason for this. America is the incarnation of Western individualism. The most ancient modern democracy, the only known example of a realized social contract (the Cape Cod Compact)—thus confirming alone the individualist myth about the origins of society—, America feeds its own exceptionalism on an almost exhaustive enumeration of the

---

3. In this, by the way—holistic as their background may be—the migrant parents are very often accomplished individuals, since loving one's children narcissically (wanting them to be the happy ones we wished to be and could not) is a distinctive trait of modern individualism).
4. I indulged in these too brief remarks, because I believe they should be kept in mind whenever we stress a specific higher rate of criminal behavior in immigrant populations.

most significant traits of Western individualism. It hardly matters here whether this is conceived as the actual historical destiny of America, or as a consequence of America's narrative identity (of the way it told and tells its own story).

It is not surprising, anyway, that America may thus become (sometimes against all plausible economic reason) the Mecca of modern migrations, if these are defined—as we proposed—as a voyage toward individualism.

This hypotheses should be kept in mind whenever, for example, American culture is accused of shrewd imperialist strategies, and the troubles of America with an impossible demand for immigration are considered as a well deserved nemesis ("You seduced the world, now deal with the hordes agonizing to break through your borders!").

In fact, American so-called cultural imperialism is probably not so much the effect of a 'Hollywood maneuver,' but the cultural consequence of the irresistible expansion of Western individualism, whose deputy America has become.

This amazing historical role tolls several prices, of course.

The first one is inevitably a double paranoia. From the outside, although America is one of the very few countries still open to immigration, paradoxically it is constantly worldwide accused of strictly protecting its borders.[5] From the inside, whatever the immigration policy, America is necessarily and forever split between the universalism it incarnates—that would ultimately lead her to recognize the right to immigrate to America as a sort of universal human right, and—on the other hand—the justified fear of losing herself as a nation.

Decisions in this field may seem consequences of general political orientations. In fact, beyond that, they are negotiated compromises of a major contradiction that is one of America's definitional traits: incarnating universalism as a value may contradict the very idea of nation, but leaving universalism behind would defeat one of the basic ideals of the nation.

The same can be said for multicultural politics. It has been noticed (ironically, cf. PETER BRIMELOW 1995:180)[6], for example, that America protects and cherishes the different ethnic backgrounds of its immigrants and citizens, and that it does not protect or even seems to consider immoral to protect (even more so to enforce) its own chore values. One more contradiction: how can a nation, or a culture praise its own specificity in any way, when this one includes the idea that cultural differences should be praised as such? More exactly: how can it maintain its specificity when this one proclaims that citizenship should not depend on any specificity whatsoever? The contradiction has the taste of logical paradoxes.

In any case, if migrations in America today seem to be a torrid topic (not only for Americans), it is not because of some immediate peculiar urgency, but because they force a sort of showdown between individualism (therefore universalism) as a chore value, and the inevitable communitarian aspirations and necessities of a nation (even of a nation that posts universalism as a chore value).

Following again its prototypical destiny, America thus performs a crucial debate between the main constituents of Western modernity: enlightenment (universalism) and romanticism (national particularism). The laughter so easily produced in the foreign press about the difficulties of Amer-

---

5. It is remarkable, by the way, that, at the end of this century, just about the only countries open to immigration would be English speaking countries (Australia, Canada and the US). A reflection on enlightenment (specifically universalism) and British culture could take some advantage from this observation.
6. BRIMELOW's book—although sometimes frankly xenophobic—should not be despised: it translates a reactive mood whose justification is probably mainly, in my eyes, the current state on Latino immigration in the US (cf. point 7).

ican identity politics, multiculturalism, political correctness etc. is really nervously Freudian: it just reveals in the satirists the repression of a current crucial contradiction throughout Western culture.

5.1. I came to the US as a J-1. I could have chosen an A-1, if I wanted to. But, for some reason, the J-1 seemed more practical at the time.

J-1s and A-1s are not airplanes. A J-1 is the visa granted to international exchange scholars. It was accessible to me since I would be teaching at The New School in New York. The A-1 is the visa that I could have obtained as a journalist for 'Folha de São Paulo.'

In any case, after a few months, I applied for permanent residence as an 'alien of extraordinary ability.' I prepared an extensive documented history of all my major professional achievements, my CV was approved and, after a few months of administrative interlude, together with my family, I drove downtown Manhattan, to the Federal Plaza Building, where we received our permanent resident cards, without any sponsoring by an American employer.

Despite my record—a long-time migrant, native Italian, permanent resident sequentially in Switzerland, France and Brazil—I found the experience unique and amazing.

In Switzerland I had been a student and was authorized to stay on the explicit request of an employer (Geneva's University). In France, I was protected by the European Community's laws.

In Brazil, immigration had been very difficult. A brave try, sponsored by several Universities where I had been lecturing (without holding a tenured position) had been in vain. And, even after my marriage, obtaining rightful legal residence had been a troublesome and uncertain process.

No surprise, in a way, in the case of Switzerland and France. European countries may have been the fruit of successive past invasions by entire populations, but fundamentally they are—so to speak—'natural' countries. Which means that you are born English, French, Italian or Swiss as a sort of natural accident or contingency: that's where the stork dropped you. Memory does not foster a fantasy on the hypothetical human intentions (eventually, of some ancestor) that would stand at the origin of one's national and cultural identity. American countries, on the contrary, are fantasy countries: with the exception of the natives, we are here, in America, because of a dream and a decision to migrate: either our own, or—past as it may be—of an ancestor. How many years may it take before time would turn our presence here into something 'natural,' I really don't know. In fact, I am not sure that time may ever turn being American into a 'natural' attribute: the dreams and desires that brought and bring migrants to this continent are essentially different from whatever animated, for example, the barbarian invasions in Europe. In our own terms—as we established them before—America is the fruit of migrations, Europe is not.

This justifies easily the impervious Swiss and French borders. One can, of course, migrate to France and Switzerland and eventually become French or Swiss, incorporating a sort of national cultural 'essence.' One will never migrate to France and Switzerland to 'make' them, the way migrants came and come to 'make America.' The European message to migrants is clear, although redundant: become one of ours and you will be one.

It is more difficult to understand the Brazilian closure to migrations—a policy that, to my (imperfect) knowledge, is the same throughout Latin America. Here we have an impressive series of nations constituted through migrations, that progressively seem to cherish and defend a sort of national 'essence,' in the European mode. Why is it?

Leaving aside economical rationalizations that simply do not hold, we should try to understand why the tentative constitution of national identities induced South and Central American nations (largely invented through migrations) to resist and oppose migrations.

One common trait of the Latin American national identities may help us understand. Most Central or South Americans will spontaneously talk about the Hispanic or Portuguese colonization in the passive mode: 'We were colonized by ....' This is particularly striking on the Atlantic side, where the remnants of Indian civilizations are scarce. European settlers of the 19th century, hardly ethnically mixed with native Indians, descendants of more ancient Spanish colonizers in Argentina, or of Portuguese colonizers in Brazil—eventually more mixed with Indians but apparently zealous defenders of their 'whiteness'—why would they all identify with the native Indian, when it comes to telling the story of the colonization of their nation?

There is one hypotheses, that—interestingly enough—may also explain why Central and South America closed themselves to migrations.

America is a European dream. But the truth is that, in relation to America, Europe had two different dreams, which indeed produced different colonizers and two different Americas.

A dream of ravenous conquest and greedy exploitation in the South and a dream of liberty in the North. The dream of a perfect Eden found by miracle in the South, and the dream of a hard construction of a new Eden in the wilderness of the North.[7] This basic opposition still is one of the most powerful instruments of ideological explanation of the different destinies of North and South America.

One of its consequences is that North American colonization was the possible support of a proud identification, while Latin American colonization was a shameful and difficult story. If the American nations must find some pole of identification in the vast inaugural myth of colonization, then the best one left for Latin American nations is definitely not the colonizer, but the victim of colonization—the exterminated and conquered Indian. Hence: 'we were colonized ....'

No wonder that many Latin American countries may have closed themselves to migrations in the process of defining their national identities: to whom is identified with the Indian, the new migrant will indeed appear as a caricature of the colonizer, a sheer expression of invasive greed. Even more so, when the identification with the Indian is really a denial of one's actual descent, or at least of one of its significant components.

Apparently, the North American identity allowed a different relationship to the immigrant, who is still supposed and expected to be a 'doer' and a maker of America.

Things, of course, are changing, and we know that, progressively since the 60s, the identification with the victim (the Indian to begin with, then the slave) has become a component of 'being American.' An ideological effort has even been made to somehow deny the different colonizations of North and South America (more exactly, of Anglo and Hispano-Lusitano America). For example, at the time of the fifth centenary of the discovery of America (the continent), the protest against the celebrations of 'greedy, murderous and ethnocentric' Columbus had the amazing effect of suggesting that Columbus would be the common figure of the original colonizer for both Americas, Anglo and Hispano-Lusitano. Which is really quite not the case.

---

7. On the theme of Eden in South American colonization, cf.: SERGIO BUARQUE DE HOLANDA (1985; 4th ed.). For this same theme in North American colonization, cf.: GEORGE WILLIAM (1962). We produced a concise opposition of the two, cf. CONTARDO CALLIGARIS (1992).

This is not obviously the place to propose any understanding of this shift in American sensibility. But we shall see (cf. point 7) that this new identification with the victim in American culture may well have some amazing effects specifically on Latino immigration to the US.

6. Our restriction in the definition of migrations is not just a descriptive criterion. It is most of all a hermeneutic one. It forces, for example, to formulate at least the hypotheses that one of the reasons for modern migrations is not so much need, but the voyage toward individualism.

This statement may be surprising. After all, we are accustomed to believe that migrations simply follow the path of wealth: from a miserable, poor or at least less advantageous setting toward a better opportunity of affluence. In fact, affluence seems to be the explicit reason for migration, recognized by most immigrants when interrogated, focus-grouped or tested.

But, again, affluence is a cultural concept.[8]

On this particular matter at least, HEGEL's 'Phenomenology of Mind' can (and probably should) be read as a remarkable anthropological description of the beginning of modernity; nowhere else, to my knowledge, is the rise of individualist modernity better understood as a passage from the kingdom of need to the one of desire. The specificity of modern desire—as opposed to need—is that no object can satisfy it, since desire is not a quest for a fulfilling object, but mainly a quest for recognition by our fellow humans. Amazingly, HEGEL, at the beginning of modernity, seems to anticipate some of the latest (and still contested) economical theories of our days (cf. FRED HIRSCH 1976), that claim that practically all objects have become 'positional,' meaning that their value is basically calculated through the status they confer (in the eyes of the others, of course).

We may believe or not in the disappearance of the good old bi-univocal correspondence between need and satisfying object. But we at least have to accept that modernity radically transforms our relationship with the objects. They are now inevitably also indexes of a social status that depends on recognition by the others, and no longer on the fatality of our birth.

It is enough, anyway, to imply that affluence in individualist Western modernity is much more than the access door to the satisfaction of needs. Nor is it—like the possession of land through the Middle Ages, till the Physiocrats—the prerogative of a caste. Affluence, in modernity, is never only a dream of fulfillment, but always also a dream of status or of advancement of status.

FREUD (who, by the way, can and should also be read as a descriptive anthropologist of modernity) is here a good companion to HEGEL, claiming that no object satisfies human desire, because all objects become symbolic of some relevant other's love (or not). FREUD proposed a distinction between infantile dreams, where one dreams of the object that may fulfill his/her wish, and adult dreams, where the fulfillment the dreamer seeks consists in having his/her desire recognized and listened to, much more than having it fulfilled by some apparently adequate object.

In this sense, the migrant's dream of wealth is not an infant's dream ("I am hungry, and therefore I dream of a club sandwich"). It is mainly a dream of recognition (as we shall see in the Brazilian example, cf. 6.1).

A modern migrant's dream of affluence cannot be understood as a sheer quantitative preoccupation. Looking for affluence in the modern sense is the same thing as moving on toward an indi-

---

8. Affluence (with its cultural effects) has obviously been the object of the anthropologists' attention. It is surprising, though, how little attention has been given to the fact that the concept itself is cultural. Cf., for example: R. F. SALISBURY, R.F. & E. TOOKER, E. eds. (1982).

vidualistic society, where affluence and not birth may eventually imply status. What is sought is not only—maybe not even fundamentally—material wealth, but a specific social compact.

The dream is about ascending and about a world where mobility is the rule.

6.1. The Brazilian largely illegal recent immigration to the US is here a perfect example.[9] Despite a majority coming from the Brazilian state of Minas Gerais, it includes Brazilians coming from all over the country, but socially rather homogenous: it is basically a middle-class or low middle class immigration.

Obviously, there are a number of sound explanations for this, some material, and others more interestingly ideological. On the one hand, Brazil is not a neighbor of the US. The trip over has to be by air, which implies the existence of a small capital. Few of the illegal immigrants are clandestine border crossers; when they are, their transgression implies a trip to Mexico and the rather costly use of passers. But most illegal immigrants are really over-stayers who entered the country on a tourist visa. Now, obtaining such a visa at an American Consulate in Brazil implies documented (although eventually falsified) economical stable conditions in Brazil. In a way, being middle class is a condition.

On the other hand, one should consider that—in several countries of the so-called third world, and specifically in Brazil—the idealization of America is a trait of the dominating classes, transmitted downward to the middle and lower classes. Brazilian (economical) elites have traditionally embraced the original Portuguese colonizing project, which essentially planned to sponge off the country. They have therefore always considered themselves as coming from elsewhere and belonging elsewhere. They certainly belonged in Europe (Lisbon, Paris and London) for a long time. And they now belong in America. This transition, of course, is the effect of the American cultural success after the war, but also of a sort of democratization of the Brazilian elites: the old refined elites constituted inevitably an aristocracy of taste and established traditions of refinement. Right or wrong, they probably would have never exchanged their shirts custom made Rue de Rennes in Paris, not even against the best Ascott-Changs. But, undeniably, the post-war period and the subsequent Brazilian miracle created and still create (although the miracle seems to be quite over) new waves of economical elites. These ones prefer Orlando and Disney rather than the Louvre, and shopping at Century 21 rather than on Bond Street. No tears need to be shredded, for essentially—for Brazil—nothing changed: its elites still conceive themselves essentially as foreigners and abroad is where they have fun, invest, spend and enjoy life. It happens that this abroad is today—and has been in the last decades—mainly the US.

One can easily imagine, therefore, that the Americanization of the upper classes obviously appears—seen from below—as an indication of the way to go. America becomes the badge of the powerful, therefore the right badge to wear, one of the many—but a relevant one—indexes of status.

The idea of the transmission of the American ideal from the social top down is significantly different from the much more common version that would describe a sort of global Americanization of Brazil through a cultural invasion. There are two good reasons not to believe in this description: the first is that the main global media in Brazil—television and particularly Rede Globo—is not exactly a contractor for American cultural products. The basic instrument of the Brazilian national

---

9. The recent Brazilian immigration to the US is still *Terra* almost *incognita*. For the moment, although several studies are on the way across the US, very few are published. For a specific case (but with some hints on the general configuration, cf.: M. L. MARGOLIS (1994).

cultural unification and also of major cultural progresses—especially in the vast rural areas of the country—have been and are the evening Globo soap-operas. Now, these have always been Brazilian written, filmed and located. Considering Brazilian media and specifically television as an agent of Americanization would be hard to defend.

Our idea, moreover, stresses the social stratification of the country. It gives a chance to understand what specific layer of the population is destined to Americanization and—as a recent consequence—to migration to the US. We shall exclude the very top of the ladder, of course; they either still belong to the ancient elites and would rather be French or English than American, or else they simply don't need to migrate: they already are, in a way, out of the country.[10] We shall also exclude the very lowest layer, which is hardly in contact at all with the modern indexes of status. And we may notice that, between these two extremes, Americanization follows an interesting curve: its highest peak is not in the beginning, nor at the lower end, but somewhere in the middle. In other words—with all due consideration to exceptions—the population most exposed to the American ideal and more prone to migrate is a low middle class that could be defined like this: not rich enough to migrate without leaving the country (no accounts in American Banks, no apartments in Southern Florida, no regular expeditions to the promised land to incorporate Broadway culture and 5th Avenue's fashions); and not poor enough to be out of reach of the multiplication of American traits that compose the icon of the higher social layer to which they are hoping to have access. In other words, it is a specific layer of the middles classes (with, of course, fringes on both sides) which feels all the urge of social ascension and is stiffly hindered by the social and economical archaism of the country.[11]

Now, what is migration for these populations?

Is it a matter of affluence? We could certainly expect them to run after the material indexes of status that they can see in the hands of the upper classes, and to consider that America will give them a better shot.

But the truth is that, for most of them, their American immigration will be apparently a step down on the social ladder, if this one were calculated quantitatively. They will be overqualified and underpaid for most of the jobs available, and—after all—especially for the ones who come from the most advanced urban areas (like São Paulo)—the wages will not be much higher than they were or would be in Brazil. With the difference, of course, that they will be far from their families and the help and solidarity that they could thus be granted, often in the impossibility of obtaining credit of any sort (because of their illegal situation) etc. In other words, from a quantitative point of view, the question rises: why do they stay? Why don't they put an end to their American journey—disappointing from the point of view of affluence?

---

10. In Brazil, non financial services (which includes transportation and turism abroad) will produce in 1997 a deficit of 11 billion dollars, almost equivalent to the commercial deficit. This figure obviously does not include the deficit produced by shopping abroad. In 1996 Brazilians charged their international credit cards for 4.4 billion dollars. And the estimate for 1997 is 5.5. Datas are hard to get, but it seems fair to say that currently about 10% of new condos projects in Miami Florida are sold to Brazilian citizens. Etc. The Brazilian press periodically monitors these facts. We chose our numbers from the news of the day (cf. Folha de São Paulo, 4/27/1997, 4/30/1997).
11. The archaism we are evoking here is well-known. Both the Portuguese colonization and the astonishing relevance and duration of slavery in Brazil have left very strong ideological and social remnants. Underneath a thin neo-capitalist crust, Brazilian social relationships are still very much modeled according to the country's colonial past. Social mobility is therefore at the same time open and, paradoxically, limited by the surviving holistic structures. The (temporary, let's hope) solution of the paradox is a pervasive culture of familiarity and paternalism (particularly in work relationships) which superficially satisfies the individualist mind, and in fact perpetuates a rather stern (holistic) distinction between the elites as a corps and the rest (Indians, slaves, and their kinship ...).

One first answer is easily derived from our previous considerations: for many, the simple fact of staying in America, even if they are locally downgraded, really implies an imaginary upgrade in Brazil. It is a remarkable ideological phenomenon, where the difficulty of ascension at home projects migrants on a journey which, as such, stands as a social promotion. In a way, they are sustained in their otherwise failed project by the envy that supposedly their destiny produces in the ones who were left behind. The percentages of their income that some of them send back to their relatives are not necessarily the sign of their generosity. Ditto for the money they send home to either build a house or accumulate a capital for their return: it does not prove their intention to go back. The transfers are just the evidence of their American 'success,' or even simply a reminder (for the folks back home) that they are in America. Being forgotten would be the supreme disaster, since they often trade a middle class standard in Brazil against an underdog position in the US, and the trade makes sense only if it implies a sort of imagined social upgrade in Brazil, as a direct effect of their permanency on American soil.

Obviously these remarks do not apply only to Brazilian immigration to the US. The case of Portuguese immigration to France, for example, presents a number of analogous traits, particularly concerning the traditional building of a house back home that in many cases will stay abandoned, sort of monument to the imaginary social promotion (in Portugal) of its owners who continue a hard life in France. Now, as we mentioned before, the Brazilian migrants get an extra bonus: not only is their social status enhanced by the envy of the folks back home, but—more fundamentally—through migration, they become foreigners, and thus somehow join the club of the elites.

This first reason to overstay, or simply stay, is generally of short duration. At a certain moment—different for every one, of course, but the two years term seems to be often critical—, the difficulties and the reduction of their social status in America seem to prevail. Whatever the supposed social promotion in Brazil, the hardship of their American new life starts to weigh heavily. Why wouldn't they go back then? The factor frequently at stake does not seem to be necessarily the fear of a humiliating failure. After all, time has passed, and their return can easily be imagined as a somehow happy experience: a lot to tell—some of it invented, and some not—a guaranteed past glory, a capital of exotic seduction.[12]

This is when many immigrants often start talking about a difficulty that concerns Brazilian society as such. Some may declare that they are afraid that their time in America may have changed them to the point where they would find it difficult to readapt to Brazil. Others may vaguely declare that the US will be the best choice for their children's future. Ultimately, they may all agree that—thinking back—this 'difficulty' must have been a silent, but relevant part of the reasons that led them to emigrate in the first place. The difficulty concerns basic aspects of Brazilian society: high criminality rate, lack of security, corruption, lack of a dignified police force, lack of basic services, but also excessive inequality, abusive paternalism, etc. The enumeration slowly composes, piece by piece, the puzzle of Brazilian oppressive political and social heritage.

These Brazilian immigrants thus end up discovering and revealing that their original dream was not, or at least not exactly a dream of affluence, but the dream of a society where affluence

---

12. At this stage, it is probably true that many illegal Brazilian immigrants could decide to go back, if only they had the possibility of eventually returning to the US, since they are already concerned about their capacity to re-adapt to Brazilian society. Now, as over-stayers, they know that getting a new tourist visa after their illegal imigration is going to be impossible for years. The example of quite a few legal residents who, at this stage, decided to go back to Brazil is interesting: they often become pendular immigrants, forever unable to decide between Brazil and the US.

would, of course, decide about status—giving them a chance to rise—but where, for example, difference in status would not be a daily form of oppression and violent dominion.

In a way, they reveal that their dream of affluence was, in fact, in the end, a democratic dream.

Amazingly enough, whatever their decision may be, at this point our illegal immigrants are probably ready for an amnesty and even for naturalization. Useless to say, it is at this point that their migration appears as a real loss for the future of Brazil.

7. Since THOMAS SOWELL's last book (1996), the expression 'cultural capital' has become quite common. It designates apparently the social and professional skills that the immigrants take along with them and that constitute their contribution to the host country.

The advantage of a country constituted through immigration would thus reside in the diversity of the cultural capitals that contribute to its growth and well-being.

Tactfully (and probably tactically), SOWELL seems to neglect the possibility of negative cultural capitals, certainly and justifiably afraid to raise ethnophobic exclusions. But the danger of this otherwise welcome political correctness is to produce a (deliberate or not) denial of contradictions that, if recognized, could be perhaps politically and socially better dealt with.

Obviously, the very idea of negative cultural capitals is problematic in contemporary American ideology. One wonders what extreme difference could appear as negative, if difference as such is rightly proclaimed to be an advantage for the host country. From this point of view, the current political standpoint is the ultimate version of enlightened optimism, and probably of American optimism: a form extreme of confidence in the American exception and its capacities to convert even the cultural capitals that are explicitly opposite to the very idea of diversity as a common patrimony.

But this is not the only case of negative cultural capitals. Let us consider—forgotten by SOWELL—the migrant's dream as a decisive element of the migrant's cultural capital.

As we said before (5.1), cultures originated through migrations are always, explicitly or not, grounded in the original dream of the first colonizers or settlers as a sort of founding myth. The relevance of this historical contingency cannot be underestimated, since cultures produced through migrations are not defined through a set of inherited traditions, they are inevitably defined by the story of the human desires and wishes that brought people over to the land. And the story begins with the wishes and desires of the ones who arrived first.

With the exception we mentioned before (the identification to the victim of colonization rather than to the colonizer or the settler) an American, for example, can hardly define him/herself without a direct mention of the migration of his/her ancestors as a founding moment of his/her identity. And, if there is such thing as an American identity, it must reside in the possibility of declining together the disparate set of human hopes that brought every immigrant to the country. Becoming American is a sort of narrative effort: it mainly means succeeding in integrating our (or our ancestor's) dream of migration into the stream of dreams that originates in the inaugural one.

Migrant dreams are, therefore, inevitable components of the immigrants' luggage. And we should normally think that they are—as such—a positive trait of their cultural capital.

The example of the West Indian immigrants to the US accounts for this. Their integration and documented success in America—comparable to the one of European immigrants—is frequently and rightly mentioned (cf. for example THOMAS SOWELL 1981: 216 ff), mainly to oppose any racial explanation of the difficulties of African Americans. There is more to it: black West Indians came and come to America as migrant dreamers while African Americans are in America as victims of American oppression. The success of the West Indians may be a proof of the relevance of the dream in the migrant's cultural capital, understanding that the capital is what the migrant takes along and offers to the host land, but also his/her own fruitful possession.

During the main successive waves of migrations to America—Irish, Jews, Italians, etc.—doubts were frequently and vehemently raised: Americans often wondered if the cultural capital of the new immigrants would contribute to the nation, or, on the contrary, disrupt it for good. Different religious beliefs (particularly Catholicism) were, as everybody knows, the main arguments, but others were or could have been legitimately raised. Namely, the aspirations of the new immigrants could have been questioned: who could grant that hunger and poverty would ever lead the new immigrants to dream of America in a way that would some day turn them into American citizens?

The fact is that, in the long run, all questions were answered, all doubts silenced and dreams born out of hunger and misery found a way into the stream of the American narrative.

It would be comfortable to bet that the same will happen always, and specifically with the immigration that seems to be the perplexity of the day: Latin American immigration. But there is a difference that should not be denied.

European as well as Asian immigrations both proceed from countries that are not themselves constituted through immigration: they are not expressions of a migrant's dream.

The Latino immigration to the US is a movement from countries constituted through migrations to the same kind of country, from a dream to another dream. Does that make a difference? Maybe so.

Maybe the migrant who is already a disappointed dreamer—the migrant who leaves a land of migration for another—cannot avoid a certain viscosity of his/her original dream. Maybe this migrant cannot avoid taking to the new host land the very same dream that failed in his/her first land of migration.

It is just a hypotheses, justified here by a speculation according to which the migrant who comes from a 'natural' country (in the sense defined before, cf. 5.1) addresses his dream to the new land, which certainly transforms it. While the second-time migrant would keep repeating the question and the quest that the first migration did not satisfy. This migrant would therefore be less disposed to let the new land transform or simply give shape to his/her dream.

Now, this probably minor trait of immigrations from a country constituted through migration (therefore of Latin American immigration) makes, in America, a dangerous encounter.

We said before that history grounded South and Central American national identities on the colonizer's ravenous and greedy dream. We added that this shameful inaugural myth produced a denial and a massive identification with the victims of colonization.

If we had, therefore, to resume the Latin American cultural capital, we may well start with these two elements: a (denied) material greed and a solid identification with the victim.

Again, this characterization would probably not be more relevant than the Irish potato hunger or the feeling of abandonment of the Italian Southerner, if it were not for a peculiar historical contingency on the American side.

The massive recent Latin American immigration coincides with a remarkable change in American national identity, that suddenly praises the victim and invents a new spirit of guilt and reparation. The double heritage of the South American colonization—denied greed and therefore victimization—meets in America today with a new national necessity to expiate.

VWB – Verlag für Wissenschaft und Bildung

The national atonement, begun in the 60s and still going strong, had a very positive function in recent American history. It certainly was at the heart of the civil rights movement's success and greatly contributed to the construction of a somewhat more generous society. For example, in the case of immigration, it produced the privilege granted to family reunion against quotas.

Even so, thirty years after its beginning, African Americans themselves, who were the prime objects of such national atonement, are beginning to realize a fundamental problem: *entitlement to compensation is not and does not produce automatically empowerment.* The million men march was probably the first moment of collective explicit consciousness of this opposition.

Despite this (very recent) awareness, in fact, the Latino immigration of the last decades found, in America, a perfect terrain to maintain without alterations the double heritage of Latin American colonization. Originally identified with the victim of Hispanic colonization, the Latin Americans can claim reparation to the US, that become the direct heirs of Cortez. And the US are caught at a special moment of the story of their identity, when entitling the Latino immigrants to a sort of 'reparation' satisfies its growing taste for atonement and guilt. The arrangement is almost perfect, since even the denied greed finds an interesting satisfaction in the exercise of an unending abusive entitlement.

The conclusion is a situation where—sometimes legitimately—Latino immigrants are largely considered, for example, as using ravenously American opportunities and social benefits, without taking the step of assuming the rights and duties of citizenship.

The story of Portorico could be instructive: the double refusal of any empowerment (both of independence and of the transformation into an American state) seems to eternalize a parody of citizenship substantially made of entitlement.

The coincidence is therefore dangerous.

On the one hand, the American guilt, willing to victimize victims who are not American victims, constitutes a ready-made identity for Latin American immigrants, and imprisons them in a role that leaves them on the margin of American society. A great example is the imposition of bilingual education, where, praising and respecting the specificity of the entitled 'victims,' the school system may well end up segregating Latin American children in a second-class linguistic and cultural zone.

On the other hand, the Latin American heritage may lead even the best intentioned ones within the Latino community to pursue the maintenance of entitlement as the only social and political perspective. The example here can be the recent welfare reform that is depriving long-term legal immigrants of certain benefits, unless they naturalize. The reform did affect some real victims of the pathology of migrations (like the relinquished totemic ancestors we mentioned before—point 4), but to these cases the government agencies are apparently responding. Leaving such cases aside, the reform is pretty coherent with the American feeling about immigration: immigrants are expected to become Americans and thus empower themselves as full-size citizens (remember: the US inaugural myth is not exploitation nor plundering, but composing a social contract).

Now, several activists and commentators (Latino or not) reacted to the reform propagating the necessity to naturalize as a smart trick out. They were thus inventing a monster—becoming American as a way to protect entitlement—and degrading the most serious chance of empowerment offered to an immigrant: the possibility of assuming citizenship.

The scenario that I am sketching is, of course, no destiny at all. The example of part of the Brazilian recent immigration that I offered before may show how things can avoid in the end such a drastic crystallization.

Still, we may consider that the Brazilian immigration had a specific advantage: it started only at the beginning of the 80s, therefore at a time when the atoning mode of the American consciousness was already undergoing criticism, and when the necessity for empowerment in the African American community began to become an explicit ideological theme.

It is also interesting to notice that many of the middle-class Brazilians I have met across the US manifest an identical perplexity when—confronted to a questionnaire—they have to cross out their ethnic background. They declare that they are not Hispanic (since Spanish is not their language) and that they don't feel they are Latinos, since they believe the term is related to Andean South America (the Pacific side, where the Indian heritage is certainly more present). But I suspect that their perplexity is neither linguistic nor ethnic (after all, Brazil invented miscegenation). I suspect that it is a way of separating their path from what they see as a menacing disaster for the Latino immigration.

It is true, in any case, that no previous wave of immigration to the US (Irish, Jew, Italian, etc.) has developed—like the Latino immigration has—a consistent pattern of life-style identification with the African American community. Through this identification, the Latino immigration to the US has elaborated (as any social worker knows) a sort of culture of entitlement.

Now, the African American community, despite a historically well justified reason for grievance, progressively discovers that entitlement for compensation—acknowledged as it may be—does not produce full citizenship: it takes, for that, a decision of empowerment. The Latino immigration holds (way back, from its cultural capital) a grievance against its host country, that would be justified only if Columbus and Cortez had discovered and colonized North America.

Will American taste for atonement keep nursing this imaginary grievance, thus condemning Latinos to a second-class entitled citizenship? Or will America be able to include in her narrative and thus modify the Latino dream of entitlement to favor a dream of empowerment, thus helping the Latino immigrants to make America, like all other immigrants of the past?

The recent aggressive governmental reaction against the culture of entitlement will obviously only solve a minor economical problem for the national budget. The uncertain solution, at the moment, seems to stay mainly in the hands of the people—Latinos or not—directly involved in the entitlement machine: operators of the doubtful American guilt vis-à-vis the victims of Central and South American colonization, and operators of the doubtful Latino grievance. It seems to be up to them to avoid (or not) what would be the first immigration catastrophe in US history: a wave that would produce very little real citizenship.

References

BRIMELOW, P.
  1995   *Alien Nation—Common Sense About America's Immigration Disaster*. New York: Random House.
BUARQUE DE HOLANDA, S.
  1982   *Visão do Paraíso*. (4th ed.) São Paulo: Nacional.
CALLIGARIS, C.
  1992   "Brasil, País do Futuro de Quem?" In: *Vozes Cultura*, São Paulo: Vozes n.6, 86th year, volume 89, December 1992.
DUMONT, L.
  1986   *Essays on Individualism—Modern ideology in Anthropological perspective*, Chicago: University of Chicago Press.
HIRSCH, F.
  1976   *Social Limits to Growth*, Cambridge: Harvard University Press.

MARGOLIS, M.L.
  1994 *Little Brazil—An Ethnography of Brazilian Immigrants in New York City*, Princeton: Princeton University Press.
SALISBURY, R.F. & TOOKER, E. (ed.)
  1982 *Affluence and Cultural Survival*—1981 proceedings of the American Ethnological Society, The American Ethnological Society.
SOWELL, T.
  1981 *Ethnic America,* New York: BasicBooks.
  1996 *Migrations and Culture—A World View*, New York: BasicBooks.
WILLIAMS, G.
  1982 *Wilderness and Paradise in Christian Thought.* New York: Harpers & Brothers.

When Healing Is Prevention:
Afro-Brazilian Religious Practices Related to Mental Disorders and Associated Stigma in Bahia, Brazil

CARLOS CAROSO, NÚBIA RODRIGUES, NAOMAR ALMEIDA-FILHO, ELLEN CORIN & GILLES BIBEAU

Abstract

This article analyses the role of popular religious practices on mental health in the population of traditional communities in north-eastern Brazil. Its objective is to characterize the community health resources and their use by the population, the criteria for their selection, and how health agencies in the popular sector, mainly represented by the Afro-Brazilian 'cult houses,' constitute one of the most important therapeutic agencies for the alleviation of the afflictions of a considerable section of the population. It also attempts to understand whether the use of religious healing to cure mental health problems, via *elevation* or *promotion rituals,* helps to prevent the labeling and stigma associated with such problems.

Zusammenfassung

Dieser Artikel analysiert die Rolle, die populäre religiöse Praktiken in Hinsicht auf die mentale Gesundheit in der Population von traditionellen Gemeinden im Nordosten Brasiliens spielen. Das Ziel ist es, die Gesundheitseinrichtungen der Gemeinde zu charakterisieren und wie diese von der Bevölkerung in Anspruch genommen werden, die Kriterien für die Wahl, sowie, wie Gesundheitseinrichtungen des populären Sektors – hauptsächlich durch die afrobrasilianischen 'Kulthäuser' repräsentiert – eine der wichtigsten therapeutischen Instanzen ausmachen, um das Leiden eines großen Teils der Bevölkerung zu erleichtern. Es wird zudem versucht zu verstehen, ob religiöses Heilen von Geisteskrankheiten – durch *Elevation* oder ‚Promotionsrituale' – das ‚Labeling' und Stigma verhindern, die solchen Problemen anhaften.

Keywords: Afro-Brazilian religion, mental health, Bahia/Brazil.

Introduction

In this paper we focus on the description of the most typical healing activities in the local therapeutic network of three communities in the northern coast of the state of Bahia, in Brazil. We then proceed to relate the sociocultural background of the mentally disturbed individual with the efficacy of the healing practice. We also examine the latter's effect on the labeling, stigmatization, and social reintegration of patients, through the examination of the micro-social construction of labeling-stigmatization in two therapeutic settings, namely the biomedical and the religious.

Labeling theory, also known as societal reaction theory, was very successful during the sixties and early seventies among North American social scientists, but has now become somewhat 'outfashioned' (DAVIS 1980). In the area of mental health, this perspective has adopted a radical social model of disease, where illnesses would be reducible to socially constructed phenomena. In its extreme form, the labeling approach seems to imply that psychiatric disorders do not exist, being produced by a social process of labeling of mentally ill individuals whose behaviors do not conform to local values and beliefs. The reality of mental illness in this theoretical model would be constructed by imposing upon individuals a stereotyped image of mental disorders learned from early childhood (SCHEFF 1966).

Research inspired by this theoretical approach has been almost exclusively concerned with problems and mechanisms of labeling production, whilst neglecting other factors potentially protective for the individual. Indeed, not much research has been performed on the processes of labeling avoidance and stigma prevention, which may be continuously fostered by cultural institutions such as religious traditions, structured around social efforts to rebuild the individual's identity. This paper intends to fill this gap by describing the health practices used by a coastal community in northeastern Bahia to care for their mentally ill. These practices consist of therapeutic resources, social support networks and management strategies for coping with identified cases of mental health problems. In the studied area, as described below, help for mental disorders is searched for in a significant number of religious therapeutic agencies, either from Christian confession (such as Roman Catholic and Protestant) or from other religious traditions, mainly Afro-Brazilian religions.

The point of departure of this study is that

"there exist in most countries lacunae in relevant knowledge, the filling of which could develop bridges between the communities and mental health workers. In particular, mental health services do not take advantage of indigenous knowledge and community resources and often do not consider the potential involvement of both formal and non-formal health resources for the development of mental health interventions. Above all, there is a lack of reliable information as to how communities manage and cope with mental health problems. Such information could be used for innovative interventions that would foster the co-operation between community resources and mental health teams" (INECOM[1] 1993:3).

The main premise of this paper is that in a pluralistic healthcare context, such as the one described here, the illness experience, illness management strategies, formal and informal institutions, community resources and the societal reaction to mental health problems are all interrelated in a highly complex way (CORIN 1993; GOOD 1994). Understanding these relationships and social responses is critical to the development of sustainable, community-based and culturally sensitive mental healthcare systems, involving community groups, institutions, agencies and practitioners, health planners and policy-makers in the design and provision of mental healthcare.

As a methodological point of departure, we have taken KLEINMAN's model of healthcare systems, defined as a "local cultural system of three overlapping parts: the popular, professional, and folk sector" (1980: 50). The professional sector is comprised of organized healing professions, in many societies limited to modern scientific medicine. The folk sector, which is non-professional and non-bureaucratic but is a specialist sector, consists of a mixture of different components, related both to the professional and the popular sector, being closer to the latter. It is relevant to remark that folk medicine is often classified into sacred and secular segments (KLEINMAN 1980: 50-60). In KLEINMAN's view, the popular sphere of healthcare is the largest part in any system, consisting of many levels: individual, family, social network, and community beliefs and activities. For the purposes of this study, the popular subsystem is the main source of interest.

---

1. Since 1990, the International Development Research Center (IDRC) of Canada has promoted the development of an international network called INECOM (International Network for Cultural Epidemiology and Community Mental Health), involving eight core countries: Canada, Brazil, Peru, India, Italy, Ivory Coast, Mali, and Romania. The participating teams in this multi-country collaborative study share the same conceptual and methodological framework. The headquarters of INECOM are located at the Montreal WHO Collaborating Center, a McGill affiliated Douglas Hospital Research Center (INECOM 1993).

Methodology

Research Setting

The scenario of this study is the municipality of Ribeira[2], located in the northern coast of the state of Bahia, which is the site of the Portuguese 'discovery' of Brazil. The capital city of Salvador, founded in 1549, is the oldest Brazilian settlement and was the center of the Portuguese colonial government until 1750 (AZEVÊDO 1969). Between the sixteenth and nineteenth centuries Salvador was a major port of entry for the African slave trade (VERGER 1987). This deeply marked the state's cultural and demographic profile, characterized today by a population which is predominantly of African ancestry (approximately 70%). These distinctive historical and cultural features are manifested in the arts, language, cuisine and particularly in the elaborated rituals of the Afro-Brazilian religions (mainly Candomblé and Umbanda), which synchretize Christian, African, and Amerindian elements (BASTIDE 1978; RÊGO 1980). Currently, the state of Bahia, with a population of over twelve million (according to the 1991 National Census by the IBGE), is the largest and most populous state of northeastern Brazil, the most impoverished region of the country.

The research was conducted in three localities of the Ribeira municipality, which has a total population of 16,149 (IBGE 1991). The first site is a small town divided into two sections, Porto da Ribeira (approximately 3,500 inhabitants), chiefly a commercial entrepôt, and Vila Velha (approximately 2,500 inhabitants), primarily residential, separated by the Velho river. The second site consists of two neighboring fishing villages, Praias (approximately 1,700 permanent inhabitants) and Águas (approximately 700 permanent inhabitants) located by the sea. The third area encompasses various rural scattered segments and/or homesteads around a small village, which are here referred to as Arraial (approximately 1,000 inhabitants).

Porto da Ribeira, a political and administrative municipal seat, is a small urban center where public services such as banking, legal, medical and schools are located, including the only state government-supported high school, which offers limited professional training. The town also manages the economic activities of the urban and rural segments. Commodity products originating in the various villages and other nearby municipalities are exchanged in a Saturday market, where sellers and buyers gather in the central square and around the public market building forming the largest and most important farmers' market in the northern coast of Bahia. The first territorial settlements in the municipality occurred in the eighteenth century (ANTONIL 1955) at Vila Velha, located on the left bank of the Velho river. The lower part of the town is often flooded by the river, which also periodically washes away the wooden bridges connecting the two town segments.

Praias and Águas are two coastal neighboring communities, where the main economic activities are sea and fresh-water fishing, tourism and agriculture (mainly coconut). Praias is a small fishing and agrarian community, located about six kilometers from Porto da Ribeira. Access is possible by car in any weather due to a recently paved road which crosses extensive humid areas dotted by fresh water lagoons. This area is also subject to flooding in the rainy season, which can cause extensive damage to the road. On both sides of this road there are a few traditional cattle ranches, but coconut groves are the predominant scenery in the region. The access from Praias to Águas is made through a coastal all-weather road which cuts across coconut groves, freshwater lagoons, estuaries, mangroves and beaches. The town's economy, formerly based on fishing and the

---

2. Ribeira, as well as the other localities referred in this report, is a pseudonym.

production of coconuts has experienced a marked change in the last twenty years as a result of 'itinerant' and 'residential tourism' (OLIVER-SMITH et al. 1989), the main activity in the summer months. This has resulted in the construction of many new beach houses, belonging to people from inland cities and from the capital, a few hotels, restaurants and bars. Also, a large number of local homes or rooms are rented out during the vacation season, while the family moves to a relative's home, a second home or a smaller house built in the same property.

The social and cultural impact of tourism on community life has caused significant changes in the village and led to social and psychological stress on the inhabitants, who are gradually being displaced by the recent social order brought about by new activities and professional specialties. The replacement of formerly existing structures strikes at various levels, ranging from the spatial redistribution of people who sold their homes to outsiders and moved out of the best areas of the village, to changes in the social and cultural patterns and finally to changes in the political and hierarchical structures resulting from the disappearance of the old elites (KOTTAK 1992).

The most characteristically rural segment of the three sites of the study, Arraial is located about fourteen kilometers north of Porto da Ribeira. The region is marked by the presence of upper dry land areas and estuarine mangroves of the Velho river system. The access to Arraial is made by a narrow, sinuous, unpaved roads which frequently become flooded and blocked by mud and fallen trees during the rainy season or after summer rainstorms. Around the village of Arraial there are small scattered peasant holdings and some larger landed properties where coconut plantations, cattle raising and the cultivation of fruit trees together constitute the region's main economic base. For their basic needs the population relies on agriculture, domestic industry, including the production of manioc flour, freshwater fishing (mostly fish and freshwater shrimp) and catching (various species of crabs and other shellfish) in rivers, lakes and mangroves. The local peasant market meets every Sunday in the central square, becoming the arena for integration and identification with the various neighboring population segments.

The construction of a coastal tourist highway has made a major contribution to the inflow of financial resources into the local economies and has therefore led to recent changes in the productive system and in the patterns of economic relations. Its inauguration in 1993 accelerated development and socio-economic change in the area closer to the coast, increasing the demands on the local health services without delivering any accompanying improvements, but at the same time improving transportation and thus making Salvador's health resources more easily accessible to the local populations.

Fieldwork

The data analyzed in this paper was obtained in a follow-up study of individuals with mental problems. The aim of the study was to identify the therapeutic resources as they are recognized and used by the community. It is crucial at this point to understand mental illness as a socially constructed experience (i.e. as shaped through a series of exchanges between the sick individual and members of his/her social networks). For an adequate understanding of this, the main research strategies were based on qualitative methods: the analysis of secondary sources, focused ethnography, participant observation, interviews and follow-ups of selected cases, consisting of individuals considered mentally ill by members of the community. Particular attention was given to local discourse on mental illness, as well as to the help-seeking process (role changes, decision-making processes, non-professionals and referrals, treatment choices, adherence, etc.). The fieldwork resulted in a detailed description of the various stages of the therapy-seeking process, which lead the individuals to certain therapeutic agencies and agents, procedures and healing events.[3]

From the start, the theoretical and methodological basis of the research supported and emphasized the idea that 'multivocality' is essential for analyzing a community's understanding of mental illness. Consequently, collecting various narratives about one mental illness case proved to be very important for two reasons. Firstly, it helped identify the networks of individuals engaged at varying degrees of responsibility in the decision-making process of treatment and outcome evaluation. Secondly, it represented a step forward towards the understanding of mental illness as constructed through distinct and often conflicting perspectives, which are continually negotiated in interaction contexts and which must be contextualized in order to be properly understood. This resulted in the need for a study of the social networks that play an important role in the management of illness and which might also constitute an important community resource; it also resulted in a study of the therapeutic process itself, regarded as a set of practices that affect the way the illness experience is perceived by the ill and by their network members.

Considering that the domain of medical practices cannot be separated from the domain of religious practice, we were compelled to design research instruments which could take into account their interrelations. The result was the development of three different and complementary data gathering tools. The first protocol was meant to conduct a Key-Informant Interview with a wide range of selected community members, not including therapeutic agents. The purpose here was to analyze the individual's ideas and experiences relative to diseases in general and particularly in relation to mental illness, as well as to analyze the available treatment forms. The second protocol, a Therapeutic Agent Interview, was specifically designed for collecting therapeutic agents' ideas and practices on health, with mental health as a priority. The third, a Guide for Case Follow-Up, consisted of an integrated interview and observation schedule used in the regular visits[4] paid to the mentally ill already identified in cases for the study. In spite of following the same standard interview protocol, questions were adjusted to each specific context in such a way as to accommodate the diversity of religious practices represented in the area, resulting in a better comparative analysis among the multiple voices of the informants. One example of this comparison is the identification of related and unrelated terms, used by informants who belong to different systems, for referring to the same phenomena being analyzed.

Finally, more in-depth qualitative data, which should warrant a better understanding of the research subject-matter was obtained through: 1. systematic observation and focused ethnographic description of the practices of therapeutic agents, especially of the 'clinical encounters,' with the aim of increasing and deepening the information obtained from therapeutic network key-infor-

---

3. The design of the research is consistent with the multi-country research initiative launched by INECOM, comprising two phases: a) analysis of the system of signs, meanings and practices related to mental health; b) identification of the management and coping strategies adopted by people to deal with cases of mental illness. Each INECOM participating country location has followed a similar research design, which does not rely on professional diagnostic categories for identifying mental illness, or behavioral and social problems. It has been guided, instead, by the popular idioms and concepts as expressed by respondents and key informants. The methodological assumption is that actual mental health problems, even considered in different cultural settings, can be placed into one or more of eight categories: 1. Violence towards others; 2. Violence towards self; 3. Delusions (including hallucinations); 4. Withdrawn behavior; 5. Abnormal speech; 6. Abnormal behavior; 7. Anxiety; 8. Depression. For the INECOM (1993) studies, two other categories have been added 9. Mental retardation; 10. Convulsive crisis. For the Bahia research, the sub-categories of 4.1. Neglect, 6.1. Gaze, and 7.1. Impulsivity have been introduced respectively for the categories of 4. Withdrawn Behavior, 6. Abnormal (bizarre) Behavior, and 7. Anxiety; and also a totally new category of 11. Inadequate Social Interaction.
4. The number of visits ranged between a minimum of twelve and a maximum of seventeen.

mants, general key-informants and healing agents; 2. focused observation and follow-ups of individuals under treatment and the reconstruction of previously treated cases, taking the healing agents themselves as key-informants; and 3. self-reported life histories of individuals with mental problems and the history of their families. It is important, however, to emphasize that the present paper covers only preliminary data drawn from this particular section of the fieldwork.

Local Therapeutic Resources

The popular and folk sectors of the healthcare system in Ribeira consist of therapeutic institutions represented by multifaceted religious agencies and agents: Pentecostal and neo-Pentecostal churches, spiritism, one house of Johrei (an Eastern messianic sect), rural and urban prayer healers, and Afro-Brazilian cults (which syncretize popular Catholicism and elements from native American Indian cults, traditional African cults and spiritist cults). Given that the characteristics of these institutions are based on both popular and folk sectors, they will be referred to from now onwards as the 'community health sector,' in our view a broader concept which better reflects the pluralistic healthcare system under analysis.

The diversification and pluralism of therapeutic resources in Ribeira is, in some ways, comparable to that identified by JANZEN (1978) in Lower Congo (ex-Zaire). There, the author brought into evidence the question of the 'therapy managing group' and its pluralistic therapeutic context in a post-colonial society experiencing a process of change. On the one hand, there is the context in Congo, which encompasses the indigenous, pre-colonial medical tradition, the practices of which are centered mostly on the family and on other social networks surrounding the ill individual. On the other hand, there is Western medicine, the practice of which is almost exclusively centered on the diseases and on the individual. Janzen defines his study as 'an ethnographic account of how medical clients of one region in Congo diagnose illness, select therapies, and evaluate treatments,' a process he calls 'therapy management.' He explicitly intends to clarify a phenomenon about which Central African clients have long been aware, namely the dynamics of medical pluralism, in which differently designed and conceived medical systems are used in combination and as a single unit (p. xviii, passim, passim).

Despite the existing cultural differences between Brazil and Central Africa, it is possible to trace some contextual similarities between Lower Congo and the area where we have been conducting our study on community management in mental health. Compared to African ethnography, it is not possible to identify 'native' or pre-colonial medical practices in Ribeira, because the mainly magic-religious community medical practices are heavily influenced both by post-colonial indigenous and by various African traditions, having become consolidated into what is known as the Afro-Brazilian religious tradition. In our view it is exactly this characteristic which makes our study relevant, for it brings into evidence and proves the existence of the therapeutic pluralism of the community sector of the Ribeira healthcare system.

The Professional Sector

The professional sector of the Ribeira municipality healthcare system is limited both in quantity and quality. The primary healthcare available consists of a single twenty-one bed public hospital and one health post located in Porto da Ribeira. However, in the entire municipality there are only two residing general practitioners, who assist patients both in their private offices and in the public health centers, and two non-residing doctors, who take on different shifts in the public hospital during the week and on weekends. Additionally there is one health agent, two dentists, two nurses and ten nurses' aids. In the other research sites there are small health units which offer very irregular medical services when the Porto da Ribeira physicians come to visit. Nevertheless, locally trained lay health agents, who participate in a nationwide community health program, often perform simple health procedures on demand, not including mental healthcare.

When people are stricken by more serious health problems they are forced to seek help in other towns, located in the range of a one to two-hour drive, where there are better equipped hospitals and specialized medicine, such as surgery, psychiatry and other specialties. Alternatively, patients in need of more specialized or intensive care are taken to Salvador, which has the largest concentration of health resources and medical personnel in the state of Bahia. They usually travel in ambulances belonging to the municipality, or on transportation provided by politicians as part of their long term electoral investment. Prescribed medication is frequently supplied by the municipal administration in one of the local pharmacies, and is limited to the availability of public funds. The existing pharmacies also play a very important role in healthcare. Attendants have accumulated experience in dispensing medication over the counter, and often help those who come for counseling.

The local professional sector has no specialized care for the mentally ill. Mental problems are usually treated by general physicians, and those who need specialized care are taken either to other towns or to one of the mental hospitals in Salvador. The latter alternative is the most common, since the construction of the coastal highway made access to the capital city easier.

The Community Sector

Unlike the professional sector, the community sector, consisting of the popular and the folk sectors of the healthcare system, grants various forms of healthcare to the population in the area. Community health resources are represented by forty-two therapeutic agents/healers, including twenty seven rezadeiras/rezadores[5], eleven curadores[6], and four spiritist leaders. Aside form this there are seven evangelical, Pentecostal and neo-Pentecostal ministers who also perform a very important role in local healthcare, and several practicing midwives, whose practices consist mainly of deliveries and care of newborn babies. It is important to notice that some of these midwives also practice 'pray-healing.'

Standing apart from all other local religious agencies, there is also a Johrei temple, an oriental Christian/messianic religion, which practices healing by the transmission of energy through hands. There are few followers of this practice, which is new in the area, brought by a local resident who had been cured of a very serious illness when she lived in Rio de Janeiro and later underwent an initiation to became a religious leader herself.

Among the Christian religions, the God's Kingdom Universal Church, a neo-Pentecostal church founded in Brazil, is expanding at a very fast pace among the poorer segments of the urban populations. It is one of the most active religious institutions in the delivery of healthcare. Besides regular *sacrifícios*[7] required from the followers, healing prayers and exorcism conducted in daily

---

5. Popular prayer healers, who perform healing activities with the use of green leaves and other materials for pray-blessing rituals.
6. Generic name for folk curers, whose healing activity is based on Afro-Brazilian tradition. Actual figures may be higher; this corresponds only to those who conduct rituals and see patients in cult houses.
7. Literally 'sacrifices,' meaning some form of money contributions from the part of the followers, in this case retaining the double-meaning of being indeed a sacrifice for the meager budgets.

rituals and individual consultation and advice given by the ministers, the church offers the so-called *Corrente da Saúde*[8], a specially designed healing ritual regularly held once a week (FRY & HOWE 1975).

The Afro-Brazilian religions are mainly represented by Candomblé, a term used in the area of Ribeira to designate the Afro-Brazilian cults as well as the ritual place and the religious festivities, and by Umbanda, a variant rich in combinations of Afro-Brazilian, Indian and Spiritist (Kardecist) components. Umbanda rituals are based on several forms of religious possession, which makes it distinct from the traditional Candomblé (BASTIDE 1978; DANTAS 1988; NEGRÃO 1996). Since its introduction about twenty years ago, Umbanda is one of the dominant Afro-Brazilian 'cult houses' in the area. These ritual/healing centers will from now onwards be alternatively referred to by the local terms *casas, centros* or *terreiros*. Compared to other religious institutions, there is a high number of *casas* in the area. 'Consultation services,' known as *consultas, demandas* and t*rabalhos*[9], and directed towards the solution of immediate problems and the alleviation of suffering on an individual basis (DANTAS 1988), are available in every casa. However, the community's therapeutic system is permeated by political disputes for power, prestige and clients, which results in great internal competition, limited inter-casa circulation, and a low degree of collaboration among the healers of the different casas, characterizing what VELHO (1975) has called the 'war of orishás.'

As far as mental health is concerned, there is an overwhelming predominance of Afro-Brazilian healing practices in Ribeira. Consequently, we will focus hereafter on this particular religious sector as the main therapeutic network available in the area for three basic reasons: firstly, the *casas* have been recognized as religious healing agencies for longer than the Pentecostals and spiritist agencies, established in the area more recently; secondly, the therapeutic process in the *casas* involves cultural elements represented by magic-religious entities, which make them very distinctive from the therapeutic patterns in the professional sector; and thirdly, the *casas* in Ribeira mobilize a greater number of followers in comparison to Pentecostals and spiritist agencies, specially among the poorer segments of the population.

The Afro-Brazilian Healing Network

Most of the *casas, centros* or *terreiros* of the Afro-Brazilian religions in the area claim to have some degree of specialization in treating mental problems which have supposed magical and spiritual causes. Mental disorders from 'organic' etiology are known to require care in the professional sector. However, treatment is often carried out in the community sector before the professional sector treatment is sought after, or both treatments are conducted in parallel. In the latter case they are expected to support each other: the community sector treatment strengthens the spirit, while the professional sector treatment is limited to the organic aspect of the disease.

The preceding situation may be illustrated by one mental illness case, followed for over one year. The initial treatment for the magic and spiritual aspects of the disease was conducted by an Afro-Brazilian cult. A 26-year-old woman's permanently abnormal behavior was attributed to memory and speech problems caused by witchcraft and spiritual possession, and required medication to 'loosen up her speech,' according to the healer, prescribed by a psychiatrist. The 'paramed-

---

8. It translates literally as *chain for health*. The so called *chains* are daily prayers dedicated to different aspects of life: family, health, money, labor, love.
9. *Consultas, demandas* and *trabalhos*, literally ritual jobs or services, are private divination/healing activities which diagnose and/or prescribe treatments/actions upon the causes of the disease/suffering itself.

ical staff' of the 'cult house' carefully administered the medication, resulting in almost total recovery of the patient. She was kept under continued treatment in the 'cult house,' however, for full recovery, observing the prescribed avoidances until she was allowed to return home (apparently the patient's home was one of the causes of her ailment). In other words, initiation in the cult, serving in the 'cult house' under the guidance of the *zelador*[10], and observation of the ritual obligations, the prescribed behaviors and avoidances, are judged to be the only means to fully regain and maintain health.

The *casas, centros* or *terreiros*, besides their religious importance, are appropriate for fostering social relations and are open to the presence of people of different age groups and social positions. Besides participating in the rituals, followers also watch their friends and kinsfolk go into trance, wear elaborate costumes which symbolize their guiding entities and have sacred identities attributed to them during the ritual. They also chant and perform the rhythmic body motions and idioms of the entities that guide them. The role of the ritual as an arena for socialization is well characterized by the participation of children, who have the opportunity to play around the edges of the ritual territory[11] whilst observing the action and who eventually participate in the *gira de crianças*[12]. As a result of this intensive involvement with various aspects of religious life, very young children can often perform elaborate body motions and display accurate knowledge about the rituals and their various components (for more on socialization in the Afro-Brazilian cults, see SERRA 1968).

The particular form of social interaction present in the Afro-Brazilian cults can be understood by taking into consideration the ritual's organization and the socializing character of its therapeutic activity. This may indeed be one of the reasons individuals become motivated to engage in treatment within this particular religious system. According to GOLDMAN (1985: 50), the two main reasons for the conversion to Afro-Brazilian cults are the illnesses and political manipulation. He recognizes that the cult attracts individuals afflicted with certain diseases because of the powerful means for controlling illness available within the cult, and that in this manner the cult establishes an arena of socio-political manipulation. He does nonetheless claim that the system structure must be held responsible for these trends.

The *incorporação*[13] is an aspect of the therapeutic process. It is a permanently liminal state, present throughout the initiation process, in which the initiated individual becomes acquainted with the dominant entity[14] or entities and learns how to represent and manage them. This initiation process is responsible for the transition from the individual's initial fragmented condition, a result of the disease, to the re-socialized condition, an outcome of the (re)operationalization of one's personal identity in the cult. If on the one hand mental disorders can be understood as a fragmentation experience, on the other hand the 'incorporation' constitutes the transition from a state of illness to a state of health, mediated by a given set of codes negotiated within the Afro-Brazilian

---

10. *Zelador/zeladora* or *pai-de-santo/mãe-de santo* are some of the designations for the leaders of the *casas*.
11. *Caramanchão* is the name given to the ritual space, usually located in the back of the house of the *zelador*.
12. *Gira de crianças* (literally children going round) is the ritual dance, which in some houses may include children, limited to the moment of incorporation of *orishás*, because *caboclos* and *exus* may harm them.
13. The use of the category *incorporação* (incorporation, embodiment), instead of possession, follows the folk use in the area. In this conception incorporation is related to the positive trance, ritually valued and desirable, whereas possession is a trance which is negatively valued, undesirable, and often related to the idea of spiritual or demoniac possession. Authors, such as BASTIDE (1973) and CONCONE (1987), do not make this differentiation and refer only to trance of possession in the Afro-Brazilian religions.
14. Every person is said to "have his or her head" (also in the sense of destiny, fate) dominated by a guide entity, believed to be one's personal saint.

cult system. In this sense, the incorporation is part of a long and complex healing process, achieved through the construction and reconstruction of a sense of self.

By and large, problems that cannot be explained according to any of the recognized disease models, either in the professional or in the community sector, can bring people to seek help in the Afro-Brazilian cults. As an example, individuals who have experienced illnesses with behavioral symptoms recognized to be those of 'craziness' often join *casas* in their quest for therapy. The attributed causes may have been 'possession' or magical actions, such as a *trabalho* or *coisa feita*[15] against the individual.

The therapeutic practices in the *casas* offer models for the construction, socialization and resocialization of the individual who has experienced or is experiencing emotional suffering. In this sense, the *casas* provide the space for this socialization, for this construction and reproduction of identities through re-socialization, and mainly for the operation of culturally based models of the individual. The observation of the social processes, which result in the construction and operation of these models, can only be achieved through the analysis of some of the fundamental aspects recurrent in the identity model developed by the cult.

Again, the choice and combination of treatments is usually determined by the recognized etiology of the affliction. As discussed by YOUNG (1981) in his Mexican study, this may be combined with other variables, represented by the availability of health resources and the economic capability of the individual to bear the costs of a treatment recognized as appropriate, a capability which can be responsible for postponing procedures deemed necessary. The process of disease identification and the decision about which treatment to choose are mediated by various factors, including the social networks to which the sick individual belongs, such as family and kin, neighbors and other members in the community's social networks. In the last instance, through the interpretation of the symptoms and causes attributed to the illness, these networks may be responsible for leading the individual to treatments judged appropriate (YOUNG 1981; POOL 1994).

Models of Therapeutic Rituals

The present analysis takes into consideration the therapeutic character of the various rituals conducted in *casas*, *centros* or *terreiros* in Ribeira, amongst them the so-called *celebration rituals* and *obligation rituals*, which have different meanings for the followers of Afro-Brazilian cults. The variations between the different 'cult houses,' discussed below, are also taken into account.

Celebration rituals are represented by the *festas*, festivities or commemorations in honor of an *orishá*, *caboclo* or *exu*, entities of the Afro-Brazilian religious pantheon. They are public rituals held in every 'cult house' in observance of calendrical obligations based on the celebration dates for catholic saints. In preparation for these special occasions there is often significant work and monetary investment on ritual costumes and foods to be made, and the entertainment aspect is as important as the religious one. The *celebrations* also have their component of *obligation*, despite their public and open character, and the responsibility for their organization belongs to the entire community of followers, even though the *zelador* and his immediate aids have the most important organizational roles.

Obligation rituals are observances of both a calendrical and non-calendrical nature, intended to propitiate the entities to which the individual or the *casa* is ritually bound, perform initiation and

---

15. *Trabalho* or *coisa feita* roughly corresponds to a spell. It consists of both the action and the object upon which the magical action is performed and 'dispatched' to the desired target.

confirmation rituals, or simply fulfill the duties towards one's dominant entities. These observances may be of different kinds, such as the *ingorossi*; *trabalho de chão* and *confirmação*; *batismo*, *zelo* and *cuidado*.

The *ingorossi* is an ordinary ritual prayer which congregates the participants in some 'cult houses' once or twice a week, with the aim of obtaining spiritual protection and advice, and also reaffirming the *filhos-de-fé's*[16] submission to the *zelador*. After the chants and prayers, the *zelador* often goes into a trance and dispenses *consultas* and/or *caridades*.[17] The *ingorossi* encompasses both appeasing and therapeutic aspects, allowing contact between participants and the sacred entities. It operates as a pre-socializing arena, where people are informed and oriented about the need for other propitiation procedures, such as *trabalhos*. These consist of more specialized ritual procedures centered on the ill individual, which may represent the transition of "ritual death and ritual rebirth," such as discussed in DOUGLAS (1976: 120). For those who have already undergone all the initiation/therapeutic procedures, the *ingorossi* is the arena for the ritual re-enactment and reconfirmation of the cure.

When an individual seeks help in a 'cult house' through the *ingorossi* or through an individual consultation, the *guia da casa*[18] identifies the problem, its causes, and either prescribes some common treatment that can be conducted individually by the individual himself or herself (including the fulfilment of neglected obligations towards the entities) or, if necessary, establishes a date for the *trabalho de chão* (the initial cleansing procedure in a ritual initiation) or for the *confirmação* (the next step in the initiation process).

The need for conducting a cleansing service, either the *trabalho de chão* or the *confirmação*[19], is determined by the characteristics of the problem and individual's previous experience with these initiation procedures. The guiding entities of the *zelador* interpret the case based on the observation of the individual's behavioral signs. The *zelador* first examines the causes for disturbance. If the *sofrimento*[20], according to members of one's social/therapeutic network, has not been caused mainly by magical action or supernatural interference, the disturbed individual will not be encouraged to proceed with the magic-religious treatment. In this sense, it is possible to affirm that the adherence to treatments in the 'cult houses' depends on the previous socialization of the individual and/or the family in this system, and that this seems to be a necessary condition for success in this type of treatment.

The *trabalho de chão* requires the ill individual to remain in seclusion in the *quarto*, which is a special withdrawal room (usually located nearby), or in the *terreiro* (reserved for ritual/therapeutic procedures), for periods that may vary from three to seven days, lying down on a bed of green leaves covered by a straw mat, with the objective of *cleansing* the body. During the withdrawal period the individual is daily bathed with *banho de abô*[21], and his or her diet is restricted to prescribed foods, which are served by the *zelador* and his aids (*mãe-pequena/pai-pequeno* or

---

16. *Filhos-de-fé* may be translated as the children of the faith, the ritually initiated followers of a *casa/zelador*. They are often called *afilhado/afilhada* (godson/goddaughter) and the *zelador/zeladora* are called *padrinho/madrinha* (godfather/godmother).
17. *Consultas* and *caridades* are both religious medical encounters. The first is a private healing act which is paid for while the second is a free public act, performed for charity.
18. The dominant entity of the main spiritual leader of the cult house.
19. *Trabalho de chão* and *confirmação* are different stages of the cleansing processes meant to purify the person.
20. It corresponds to suffering, which is pervasive referring both to health problems and to the various experiences of the person (KLEINMAN 1996). It is the folk equivalent of the theoretical category of *affliction* (see TURNER 1968).
21. *Banho de abô* is a ritual cleansing liquid mixture, made of an aged infusion of sacred herbs and the blood of a sacrificed animal.

ekede)[22]. At certain times of the day the individual is engaged in prayer and teachings by the *zelador*. On the eve of the last day the individual is taken out of the *quarto*, given a bath in a stream or lake, and is incorporated to the *candomblé*[23] or *gira* in honor of the novice. This is followed by an animal sacrifice and the *océ*[24] on the following day.

Adopting the model of purity and impurity discussed by DOUGLAS (1976) for comparison, it is possible to explain how the Afro-Brazilian cults manipulate the representations of 'purity' and 'impurity': the former is regarded as a state acquired after the process of initiation or confirmation, creating 'unity in experience' among the participants, while the latter designates illness. This procedure demarcates the liminal state between the illness and the experience following the disease. The various acts designed for cleansing the body represent the beginning of the process of re-socialization of the individual. During seclusion and the associated rites, the ill individual has no role in society. All communication between the individual placed in this ritual liminal state and society is conducted through the *zelador* and his or her aids, or through someone in the 'cult house' responsible for cleaning of the *quarto* and feeding the novice/patient. These individuals help to promote the transition between 'impurity' (illness) and 'purity' (health).

After the *cleansing of the body* the novice/patient can leave the *quarto*, walk within the limits of the 'cult house'/family home, but he or she cannot go out onto the streets, considered uncontrolled territory[25]. In the next few days (the exact number of days is defined by the *zelador*), the individual is taught the secrets of the cult. This is also the time at which the categories defining the individual's future role are submitted to preliminary testing. From this moment onwards the initiated individual must follow some *behavioral avoidances* and *ritual obligations,* and will have formally joined the *casa*. Future obligations include *zelar*[26], or caring for the symbols of her dominant entity, and preparing the yearly *océ* in commemoration of the anniversary of the initiation.

When the *confirmação* is considered fundamental for the success of the treatment and reintegration of the individual, the novice will return to the *quarto* for seven more days, and will undergo similar procedures. This can be done either immediately, or at a later date, when the individual can afford to bear the cost of the procedures, mainly the payment to the *zelador*, and also the heavy physical and psychological burden that is placed upon a individual in seclusion. In spite of the higher status and prestige associated with being a confirmed *filho* or *filha de santo*[27], *confirmação* is usually not voluntary, often happening as a result of a new crisis.

Despite the great importance attributed to the *batismo de santo*[28], a further and very elaborate procedure in the initiation/healing process, none of the followers of the local *casas* in the area of Ribeira had experienced it as part of their initiation process because of the high costs involved in conducting such a ritual.

Obligations represented by the *zelo* performed on the entities of the right side are seen differently from the *cuidado* with the entities of the left, where right and left correspond respectively to

---

22. *Mãe-pequena* or *pai-pequeno* are the ritual assistants, second to the *zelador* in the hierarchy of a *casa*. *Ekede* is the post given to the person in charge of keeping the *casa*.
23. *Candomblé* refers to the ritual dance and chants.
24. *Océ* is a ritual meal made from sacrificed animals, eaten only by the initiated participants.
25. The streets are controlled by the *exus*, trickster entities who act as mediators (or emissaries) between people and the deities, and are often depicted as demoniac entities.
26. *Zelar* means to zeal for the entities of the right side. Different from *cuidar*, literally to take care of, which is the fulfillment of ritual obligations to the entities of the left side.
27. *Filho de santo* or *filha de santo* is the name for those who are initiated and fulfill rituals obligations in Afro-Brazilian cults.
28. Baptism of the dominant entity consists of the ritual reaffirmation of the relations existing between the person, the dominant entity and the *casa*.

good and evil. The entities of the right, represented by the *orishás* (at the celestial level) and the *caboclos* (Indian entities whose actions represent the mediation between nature and culture) are appeased by symbolic food offerings related to each entity, light (candles), and by caring for their symbols. Care for the malignant entities of the left side consists of appeasing the slaves *(exus, pombas giras*[29]) with appropriate food offerings on a regular basis, usually including palm oil (symbolically related to these entities), alcoholic drinks and tobacco. If these procedures are not followed these entities may be used as intermediaries in harming the individual.

It is clear that the re-socializing rituals described above present frequent positive outcomes. Among the aspects taken into consideration in trying to understand this phenomenon, it is important to note that the religious setting contributes to the formation of a model of the individual. The cultural background on which the cult flourishes, however, does so more explicitly and makes use of complementary elements, resulting in a more substantial model. An attempt is also made by the religious leaders to adapt the implementation of the cult's core structural features to the individual, given that beliefs, knowledge of core symbols and ethnic considerations may vary significantly.

Healing and Preventing Labeling-Stigma

Two Healing Experiences

In this section we discuss and compare two cases of mental illness among young women, having accompanied their illness experiences and treatment in the same healing center for approximately two years. Their common features include rural birth, immigration to large cities (Salvador and São Paulo, respectively) and jobs held as domestic servants. But while the first woman was raised within the cultural experience of Ribeira, the second one had predominantly urban values due to her earlier migration and her family's somewhat higher social position. As shall be shown, the differences in their treatment process and outcome are a direct consequence of their different socialization processes.

The first case involves a 23 year-old woman born in a poor rural working family in Vila Velha, who worked in local homes since a very young age. She was living with her family in Ribeira when she first developed symptoms of mental illness, in the form of violence towards others and bizarre behavior. Her mother, a *rezadeira*, took her to the local hospital, where she was seen and medicated by one of the doctors. Following this occurrence, the mother asked a friend to make a *consulta* for the daughter with a *curador*, the Beato do Mato[30], who recommended the use of some herbal baths, a procedure immediately followed by her. The young woman was then taken by a family friend to one of the local neo-pentecostal churches. During the healing session she had a crisis and ran out of the church, ripped off her clothes, entered the nearby cemetery and decorated herself with mortuary ornaments. Her mother then made an unsuccessful attempt to have her seen by a healer in a local *casa*. Next, she took her daughter back to the local hospital, where the doctor medicated her again and warned that she should be sent to a psychiatric hospital in Salvador. The mother, however, fearing that her daughter would become permanently ill, did not allow

---

29. Pomba-gira is the female equivalent of the exu.
30. The *Beato do Mato* is the most prestigious folk healer in the whole area. His home/healing Center is located in the rural area, and may be compared to a folk psychiatric hospital. His *celebrações* and *obrigações* rituals attract hundreds of people residing in the vicinities, in other neighboring municipalities, and migrants living as far as São Paulo, who pay annual visits to keep the obligations to their entities.

her to be taken to the hospital. The young woman was then tied up and taken to the *Beato*. Upon her arrival he removed the ropes and prayed until she calmed down. The full treatment lasted sixty days. During the first two weeks she was placed in the *quarto* a *trabalho de chão*. The remaining time after the treatment was dedicated to her reintegration into normal life. She was gradually introduced to housework until she was finally allowed to return to her family in Salvador, where she found work as a domestic servant. She is expected to return to the healing center at least once a year in fulfillment of her ritual obligations, besides having a number of prescribed avoidances to be followed.

The second young woman was a 30-year-old belonging to a landed rural of some social distinction. She immigrated to São Paulo when she was 13 years old, where she lived with a married sister. She worked as a domestic servant in private homes, including her sister's home, where she engaged in housework and took care of the children, and gave birth to a child of her own fathered by her brother-in-law. She experienced her first emotional crisis approximately ten years after the migration and was taken to a psychiatric hospital where she remained for a certain period of time. Another critical episode was followed by unsuccessful psychiatric and religious treatment in São Paulo, at which point her family brought her back to Ribeira, where she had another crisis, identified by violent and bizarre behavior. The family took her to the local hospital and then finally to the *Beato* for treatment. She remained in the healing center for approximately eight months. The healer admitted that this had been the most difficult case he had ever encountered. One of the main difficulties was the patient's delusive discourse on modern urban themes, often totally incomprehensible for the healer and his aids/family[31]. Other sources of difficulty were the following: her rejection of the rural traditional environment; the local culture, specially the mystic discourse used by the healer and his aids/family; the social conditions; the racial characteristics of the healer and his aids/family (who were black, while the patient was of mixed blood); and, above all, her unfamiliarity with the therapeutic idiom, derived from the Afro-Brazilian ritual tradition.

In the first case, the woman's family took her back to the healing center after she experienced a mild crisis in Salvador. She was under the belief that the crisis had been caused by a failure to observe a prescribed avoidance, namely a prohibition related to cutting one's hair, and fully accepted that she must not cut her hair and must live near her family, a requirement prescribed by her entity[32]. She followed the treatment very closely, regarding the healer and his aids/family very highly and would easily have accepted the idea of spending the rest of her life in the ritual center, if this had been judged necessary for her health by the *Beato*.

In the second case, the patient left the healing center recognizably better. However, she was not considered totally cured by the healer.

Let us now compare the two cases. In the first case the patient had been exposed to the Afro-Brazilian cult tradition from an early age. Her mother had undergone initiation and was a *filha-de-santo* in a *casa* in Ribeira, besides being a *rezadeira*. These two factors certainly contributed towards her compliance to the treatment and towards its positive results, including her reintegration into society in a short period of time. The second woman, on the other hand, had never been directly exposed to this tradition and neither had her family members participated directly in this ritual system. She has spent most of her adult life in São Paulo, participating in an urban modern seg-

---

31. The themes of her delusive speech were the TV stars and the roles played by them, cellular phones, different models of cars, hotels she had been in, and so forth. The healing center is located out in the rural area, where there is neither electricity nor television. Some of the resident members have not even been to the weekly market in Porto da Ribeira, located 18 kilometers away, for about a decade.
32. The individual's characteristics are related to those of their entities, said to 'dominate their heads.'

ment of culture and internalizing its idioms and values, which contrasted quite strongly with those of the healing center and with local beliefs and practices.

As demonstrated above, in these two cases ritual socialization includes, among other things, the belief in the magic-religious causation of diseases, the rigorous fulfillment of ritual obligations, and the observance of prescribed avoidances[33], such as avoiding certain foods and specific situations judged dangerous and behaving in specific ways towards others and towards oneself. Neglecting ritually prescribed observances can result in serious personal harm to the individual and to kinfolk. The observance of prescribed behaviors is an assurance of the state of health, whereas non-observance can revive the experience of a fragmented individual, also referred to as 'out of himself/herself,' or *'fora de si.'*[34]

Labeling and Stigma

In Ribeira the form of treatment offered individuals with mental/emotional problems plays an important role in the labeling of these individuals. When an individual is given formal psychiatric treatment at the onset of a crisis, regardless of the seriousness of the illness, being labeled mentally ill is often a negative experience and may result in the individual carrying the stigma for the rest of his or her life.

Informants in the Ribeira area use labeling categories both for describing and classifying behaviors which may be judged abnormal, but in this case they are based on a different cultural context. Folk terminology such as *doido* (crazy) or *maluco* (loony) are related to psychiatric problems, whereas categories such as *possuído, tomado* and *embruxado* are related to the Afro-Brazilian ritual system.[35] Although these categories may be used to describe the same observed behaviors, the main difference resides in the social meaning attached to them in the various therapeutic contexts, a fact which is very relevant for the future of the individual recognized as having behavioral problems.

Considering two symptoms which are frequently found in descriptions of abnormal behavior will help us understand the importance of the symptoms' social significance, and in particular the latter's effect on labeling and stigmatization of the patient. Symptoms of bizarre behavior are often associated with acts such as taking off one's clothes in public, or chanting and dancing out of context, among others. Symptoms of violent behavior considered abnormal include uncontrollable, apparently illogical, acts of aggression towards others or oneself or towards material possessions and the accompanying verbal manifestations of anger.

These behaviors are primarily seen as the consequence of being in a condition of *juízo fraco* or *mente fraca*[36], a condition of either temporary or permanent mental disturbance. We have observed, however, that when these abnormal behaviors are controlled or reduced in the Afro-Brazilian therapeutic context, the insanity category is reduced to a comparative parameter. In this case, the deviance is minimized by the use of appropriate language when making comments about the behavior of the affected individual. Comments such as "I was crazy myself," or "Everyone

---

33. Commonly called *resguardos* and *cautelas*.
34. It may be translated as 'out of oneself,' in opposition of being aware or in control of oneself.
35. *Tomado, possuído,* and *embruxado* represent different situations of possession. However, the first (translated as "taken") is related to the onset of the domination of good entities, those of the *right side* (orishás and *caboclos*, i.e., Indian entities); the second to domination of bad entities, those of the *left side* (resulting from spiritual of demoniac possession); and the third translates as bewitched (the result of sorcery and witchcraft).
36. These expressions mean 'weak mind' and 'dimwitted.'

thought he was crazy, but he was really bewitched" by individuals of the patient's social network allows abnormal behavior to be left on hold, stripped of the negative connotation responsible for the labeling and stigmatization. An individual who acts strangely or violently in the described manner avoids being labeled insane or mentally ill and is placed under the condition of *tomado, possuído* or *embruxado*, a result of punishment by the dominant entity for breaching of ritual obligations.

Shifting the interpretation of abnormal behavior from insanity to possession, witchcraft or punishment by magic-religious entities reflects positively in the individual's reintegration into society, making it easier for him or her to reconquer his or her previous social roles, which have often been seriously affected or even completely lost. Once the entity is appeased, the evil spirit exorcised or the spell broken, the reasons for discrimination (labeling and stigmatization) also disappear. The individual is now immediately associated with matters of *candomblé,* or initiated in the cult, and is not considered insane, a very different condition from the stigmatized individual who is expected to cause disturbance in his social milieu without warning. Stigmatization generates difficulties in the social re-integration of individuals with psychiatric problems, including serious effects such as social avoidance and even total exclusion from normal social life.

Further Remarks

Our central finding consists of the fact that treatment developed in a specific religious context for emotional-mental problems and performed in the *casas* are mainly based upon the redefinition of the illness and re-socialization of the sick individual and lead to positive outcomes as far as labeling and stigma are concerned. In the popular therapeutic context of Ribeira, disease is commonly defined as suffering and is experienced as the individual's fragmentation. The redefinition of the suffering and the renewal of the individual's identity is attained through ritual initiation and re-socialization acts. This presupposes that the patient has been previously involved in Afro-Brazilian ritual traditions, and has had access to the idioms of treatment and behavior appropriate to the cured/re-socialized individual, providing the ultimate warranty for the treatment's efficacy.

With the objective of discussing and explaining these findings, we shall first dwell upon the anthropological theory on causality of disease (SINDZINGRE & ZEMPLÉNI 1992) and revisit the arguments about the socializing character of the various rites conducted in Afro-Brazilian 'cult houses' as well as those about their role in the construction and reconstruction of the individual (GOLDMAN 1985; DUARTE 1983). Then we will proceed to discuss the implications of interpreting particular agents of these findings from the point of view of labeling.

First of all, it is important to understand the means by which people come to seek treatment in the Afro-Brazilian cult, as well as the role played by certain rituals meant to create/re-create 'unity in the experience' of one who *suffers* or is in 'danger,' as put by DOUGLAS (1976: 13). In other words, the experience of socialization of the ill individual or *sufferer* previous to the treatment is a necessary condition for the understanding of the 'principle' and the 'efficacy of the magic,' such as discussed by LÉVI-STRAUSS (1974). Following GOLDMAN (1985:50), "if we admit that the disease can be experienced as the fragmentation of the individual, we can then understand how possession, which is the symbolic technique for construction of this unit and for maintaining a certain stability, may be structurally linked to it." In this sense, he recognizes that the initiation, through the appropriation of the 'symbolic technique' of *incorporação,* represents (in the synchronic plan) the experiences of *suffering* and *cure*, which are re-enacted in every ritual occasion, bringing about new myths, ritual obligations and re-socialization of the individual.

We believe it is important to analyze the concept of the individual in the Afro-Brazilian cult so as to understand the prevalent help-seeking behavior and treatments used for emotional-mental problems, specially considering the importance of the *casas* as health agencies and the importance of their use of healing techniques based on the context of initiation rituals. If we adopt MAUSS's conceptualization (1974: 226), the concept of individual would also correspond to a level of performing identities, to the extent that the social actors make use of various forms of discourse and actions for building their social life, not only when they talk about themselves but also when they are observed in different situations. In this perspective, treatments in the Afro-Brazilian tradition are individual-centered ritual actions, performed with the objective of 'resignifying' the suffering and reintegrating the individual back into normal life. The concept of the individual in the *casas* of Ribeira refers to the domain of the conscious being, different from the *aparelho* (meaning device or instrument) or *cavalo de santo* (saint's horse), when he or she receives or incorporates the entities, temporarily abandoning their identity, and gaining an institutional identity in the Afro-Brazilian cult. In this context the performance of the afflicted individual, with minimal ritual differences, might be similar to that of other members performing in the same ritual arena, where participants simultaneously incorporate variants of the same entity.

An important inference resulting from this study is that treatments in the Afro-Brazilian tradition subscribe to the model of *rites de passage*[37], operated through what we refer to as *elevation* or *promotion rituals*. This concept is intended to be in symmetrical opposition to GOFFMAN's idea of *degradation rituals*, which was proposed as an important step for the destruction of personal identity in the stigmatization process (GOFFMAN 1963). Elevation or promotion rituals are designed to help develop self-confidence as a consequence of the general attention directed towards the individual, who is placed in the center of the ritual activity designed to alleviate physical, mental, social or psychological suffering and promote well-being. The beneficial results of this set of rituals lead us to hypothesize that such elevation rituals may be responsible for the stabilization and re-ordering of the suffering, for the 're-signification' of the individual's frame of mind, for their gradual reintegration into the local social networks, and for re-socialization under a new identity. Summarizing, this implies the founding of a new individual, one which has been initiated in the ritual, a convert to the Afro-Brazilian religion, different from the fragmented individual at the start of the initiation/treatment.

One of our major findings in this regard consists of the idea that the reconstruction and re-socialization of the mentally ill in the Afro-Brazilian 'cult houses' may result in the denial of an exclusive biomedical interpretation of the problem, thus enhancing the acceptance of the non-stigmatized individual in the community. This hypothesis is in some way related to the ethics of the research. During the preparation for the fieldwork we discussed at length if our interest, centered around mental health problems, would not contribute to the further labeling and stigmatization of the identified cases, and as a result took all the necessary precautions for avoiding this outcome.

However, before naively adopting a labeling perspective, we shall consider a few issues which are critical to this theory. It is true that, following the classical anthropological tradition of siding with the native, labeling theory often avoided presenting the deviant as essentially different from the standard western and modern individual. In this theoretical framework, however, in spite of

---

37. These transition rituals were analyzed by VAN GENNEP (1978) as *rites de passage*, consisting of: *separation, transition* and *incorporation*.

SCHEFF's distinction between primary and secondary deviation (SCHEFF 1966), the potential integration of the deviance and labeling categories into some systemic theory of society is neglected. In fact, to deny the roots of deviance implies to also rule out the analysis of political and symbolic systems which could be precisely taken as sources of the labeling process. In other words, as pointed out by several critics (for example, DAVIS 1980), labeling theory seems to have paid little attention to the issues of power and its implications. The basic argument that labeling theory is limited in scope does not hold fast under pressure from this criticism, appearing incomplete and ahistorical. But to say that it is unconcerned with the global sociological questions is at least equivocal, because various labeling theorists have explored social structural constructions and have made it clear that these were not taken into account because they were to be part of a different scientific question (see BECKER 1963; AKERS 1968; INGLEBY 1980).

On the other hand, labeling theory proposed an in-depth, detailed analysis of personal cases and small-group dynamics, defining the deviant individual or the deviant group as isolated from the larger social context. The adoption of such a socio-psychological orientation has implications at both the theoretical and methodological levels. At a conceptual level, the analysis of the institutional apparatuses of social control (or social protection, as seems to be the case in this research) is achieved by a micro-social study. At a methodological level, the basic claim of labeling theorists that the study of deviance must focus on those who label and on the process of labeling rather than on the deviant themselves sounds very appealing. Heavily committed to the ethnomethodological approach, societal reaction research has overemphasized the psychological sphere of perception and cognition of isolated individuals or subcultures, which is in some way updated by the semiological approach taken in our research.

Rather than focusing on the social determinants of mental illness, the current study may help to understand some of the empowerment mechanisms related to the social construction of the community's mental health. In this way, the information produced will hopefully be useful for creating innovative models of mental healthcare based on self-respect and mutual cooperation between community resources and health teams in areas such as the one explored in this research.

Acknowledgements

This research is the result of a collaboration between the University Federal da Bahia, the University of Montréal, and the Douglas Hospital Research Center at McGill University, funded by IDRC (Canada), through the grant contract # 93-0218. The research team was formed by Adenilson da Silva Fonseca, Cláudia Santos Oliveira, Adriana Bastos Silva and Roselene Cassia de Alencar Silva. Cláudio L. Pereira temporarily joined the research team for a specific study about Pentecostal religious agencies in 1995.

References

AKERS, R.
   1968   Problems in the Sociology of Deviance: Social Definitions and Behavior. *Social Forces* 46: 455-465.
AZEVÊDO, THALES
   1969   *O Povoamento da Cidade do Salvador*. Salvador, Ed. Itapuã.
BASTIDE, ROGER
   1973   *Cavalos de Santo (Esboço de uma sociologia do transe místico)*. In: *Estudos Afro-Brasileiros*. Edited by R. BASTIDE. São Paulo: Editora Perspectiva
   1978   *O Candomblé da Bahia: Rito Nagô*. São Paulo: Cia. Ed. Nacional.
BECKER, H.
   1963   *Outsiders*. New York, Free Press.

BODDY, J.
1994 Spirit Possession Revisited: Beyond Instrumentality. In: *Annual Review of Anthropology. No. 23.* Edited by W.H. DURHAN. Palo Alto: Annual Reviews Inc.
CONCONE, M.H.V.B.
1987 *Umbanda: Uma Religião Brasileira.* São Paulo: FFLCH/USP, CER.
CORIN, E.; E. UCHÔA; G. BIBEAU; B. KOUMARE; M. COULIBALY; P. MOUNKORO & M. SISSOKO.
1992 La place de la culture dans la psychiatrie africaine d'aujourd'hui. Paramètres pour un cadre de référence. *Psychopathologie africaine* 24(2): 149-181.
CORIN, E.; G. BIBEAU & E. UCHÔA. 1993. Éléments d'une sémiologie anthropologique des troubles psychiques chez les Bambara, Soninké et Bwa du Mali. *Anthropologie et sociétés* 17(1-2): 125-156.
DANTAS, B.G.
1988 *Vovó Nagô e Papai Branco: Usos e Abusos da África no Brasil.* Rio de Janeiro: Graal.
DAVIS, N.
1980 *Sociological Constructions of Deviance.* Dubuque, Iowa, W.C. Brown Publications.
DOUGLAS, M.
1976 *Pureza e Perigo.* São Paulo: Perspectiva.
1970 Thirty Years after Witchcraft, Oracles and Magic. In: *Witchcraft, Confessions and Accusations.* Edited by M. DOUGLAS. London: Tavistock Publications,
DUARTE, L.F.D.
1983 *Da Vida Nervosa nas Classes Trabalhadoras Urbanas.* Rio de Janeiro: Zahar/CNPq.
FRY, P. & G. HOWE
1975 Duas respostas à Aflição: Umbanda e Pentecostalismo. In: *Debate e Crítica.* São Paulo. n° 6.
GOFFMAN, E.
1963 *Stigma.* New Jersey, Prentice-Hall.
GOLDMAN, M.A.
1985 Construção Ritual da Pessoa: A Possessão no Candomblé. In: *Religião e Sociedade.* Rio de Janeiro: Campus.
GOOD, B.J.
1994 *Medicine, Rationality, and Experience: An Anthropological Perspective.* Cambridge: Cambridge University Press.
INECOM.
1993 *The International Network for Cultural Epidemiology and Community Mental Health.* Montreal: WHO Collaborating Center for Research and Training in Mental Health.
INGLEBY, D.
1980 Understanding Mental Illness. In: *Critical Psychiatry—The Politics of Mental Health.* Edited by D. INGLEBY, pp 23-71. New York, Pantheon.
JANZEN, J.M.
1978 *The Quest for Therapy: Medical Pluralism in Lower Zaire.* Berkeley and Los Angeles: University of California Press.
KLEINMAN, A.
1980 *Patients and Healers in the Context of Culture: An Exploration of the Borderland between Anthropology, Medicine and Psychiatry.* Berkeley: UC Press.
1996 The Appeal of Experience; The Dismay of Images: Cultural Appropriations of Suffering in Our Times. *Daedalus* 125(1): 1-24.
KOTTAK, CONRAD P.
1992 *Assault on Paradise: Social Change in a Brazilian Village.* 2nd. Ed. New York: Mc Graw.
LEVI-STRAUSS, C.
1974 A Eficácia Simbólica. *In Antropologia Estrutural.* Rio de Janeiro: Tempo Brasileiro.
NEGRÃO, L.N.
1996 *Entre a Cruz e a Encruzilhada: Formação do Campo Umbandista em São Paulo.* São Paulo: EDUSP
OLIVER-SMITH, A.; ARRONES, F.J. & J.L. ARCAL
1989 Tourist Development and the Struggle for Local Resource Control. *Human Organization* 48: 345-351.
POOL, R.
1994 *Dialogue and the Interpretation of Illness.* Oxford: Berg Publishers.
RÊGO, V.
1980 Mitos e Ritos Africanos da Bahia. In: *Iconografia dos Deuses Africanos no Candomblé da Bahia.* Edited by H. CARYBÉ. Salvador: Fundação Cultural do Estado da Bahia e UFBA/São Paulo: Instituto Nacional do Livro.
SCHEFF, T.
1966 *Being Mentally Ill: A Sociological Theory.* Chicago, Aldine.

SERRA, O.
    1968   Na trilha das Crianças: Os Êres num Terreiro Angola. Unpublished Masters Dissertation. Brasília: Universidade Nacional de Brasília-UNB.
SINDZINGRE, N. & A. ZEMPLÉNI
    1992   Causality of Disease Among the Senufo. In: *The Social Basis of Health and Healing in Africa*. Edited by S. FEIRMAN & J. JANZEN. Berkeley: UC Press.
TURNER, V.W.
    1968   *The Drums of Affliction: A Study of Religious Process among the Ndembu of Zambia*. Oxford: Clarendon Press and The International African Institute.
VAN GENEPP, A.
    1978   *Os Ritos de Passagem*. Petropólis: Editora Vozes.
VELHO, Y.M.
    1975   *Guerra de Orixá: um estudo de ritual e conflito*. Rio de Janeiro: Zahar.
VERGER, P.
    1987   *Fluxo e refluxo do tráfico de escravos entre o Golfo de Benin e a Bahia de Todos os Santos dos séculos XVII a XIX*. Salvador: Corrupio.
YOUNG, J.C.
    1981   *Medical Choice in a Mexican Village*. New Jersey: Rutgers.

Is Religious Membership and Intensity a Protective Factor in the Course of Functional Psychosis? A Clinical Study from Brazil

PAULO DALGALARRONDO

Abstract

Longitudinal studies have demonstrated a better outcome of schizophrenia in developing countries. Factors such as family size, industrialization and expressed emotions were suggested in order to explain this. In the modern Brazilian socio-cultural reality religion plays a central role. In the present study a comparison of the length of psychiatric hospital stay of Catholic and Pentecostal patients was conducted. Pentecostal patients had a significantly shorter length of stay. The role of religious affiliation, commitment and social network is discussed, as possible factors associated with the outcome of severe psychiatric disorders in Brazil.

Zusammenfassung

Längsschnitt-Untersuchungen haben gezeigt, daß Schizophrenie in Entwicklungsländern ein besseres *outcome* hat. Faktoren wie Familiengröße, Industrialisierung und ‚ausgedrückte Emotionen' wurden als Erklärungen herangezogen. In der modernen brasilianischen soziokulturellen Realität, spielt Religion eine zentrale Rolle. In der vorliegenden Studie wird ein Vergleich der Länge des psychiatrischen Krankenhausaufenthalts zwischen Katholiken und Pfingstlern herangezogen. Patienten, die den Pfingstlern angehören, blieben für einen signifikant kürzeren Zeiraum im Krankenhaus. Die Rolle der religiösen Zugehörigkeit, die Stärke der Bindung und des sozialen Netzwerks werden als mögliche Faktoren diskutiert, die in Brasilien das *outcome* schwerer psychiatrischer Krankheiten beeinflussen.

Keywords: psychosis, pentecostal churches, length of stay, Brazil

Introduction

In the first half of this century, an increasing number of psychiatrists working in Africa and Asia reported that the majority of schizophrenic patients they treated tended to have short and favorable clinical course and frequently complete remission (LIN & KLEINMAN 1988). Since the fifties, in developing countries, longitudinal follow-up studies have been conducted and demonstrated that the course of schizophrenia is not as malignant as that observed in industrialized societies (MURPHY & RAMAN 1971; LO & LO 1977; WAXLER 1979). More recently, the World Health Organization (WHO) conducted two large multicentric studies on the outcome of schizophrenia (with structured interviewing techniques and specific diagnostic criteria), which confirmed the better outcome in pre-industrial societies (SARTORIUS et al. 1977; SARTORIUS et al. 1986). Indeed, in the last decades the better prognosis of schizophrenia in developing countries has become the single most important cross-cultural finding (LIN & KLEINMAN 1988).

COOPER & SARTORIUS (1977) have suggested that this difference could be explained by some possible factors: differential survival effects upon vulnerable individuals, social isolation, family size and structure (extended kinship networks), specialization of work roles, size of community and concepts of mental illness. According to these authors, explaining religious and magical concepts and systems might reduce the rejection and stigmatization of the mental ill.

Religiosity is a complex phenomenon, often neglected as a covariable in clinical and epidemiological surveys (LARSON et al. 1986). Its possible positive or negative influence on the etiology, treatment and outcome of mental illness remains controversial (ERICHSEN 1974; BERGIN 1983).

Brazil is a predominantly Catholic country. From the 1950s until now, new Evangelic churches, especially the Pentecostal ones, have shown a tremendous increase, from 1-2% to more than 10% of the whole population. These sects, originating in the USA, expanded dramatically in Latin America (ROLIM 1985). Until now, the mental health implications of this process have not been systematically studied.

Sociologically a sect is defined by: voluntary association, exclusiveness, frequent proselytism, self-concept of the member as an elect, high level of lay participation, opposition to the dominant religion and hostility or indifference to the secular society (WILSON 1959; BOURGEOIS et al. 1975).

The present study is based on the description of socio-demographic and clinical profile of the first 300 consecutive patients admitted from December 1986 to November 1988, in a 12-bed general hospital psychiatric inpatient unit, in Southeast Brazil.

Patients and Methodology

The patients (166 female, 134 male) had a mean age (±SD) of 34.0±14.6 years. Sixty-eight percent (N=204) came from the projected catchment area, 21.3% (N=64) from outside this area but still from São Paulo State and 5% (N=17) came from other states. Forty-five percent (N=134) were never married, 41.3% (N=124) were married, 7.7% (N=23) were separated and 4.0% (N=12) were widowed. Seventy-five percent (N=113) were Catholics, 22% (N=32) were from Protestant Pentecostal churches and 2.8% (N=4) were atheists.

The distribution of diagnostic categories is presented in Table I. Patient's length of stay was related to the following sixteen socio-demographic and clinical variables: age, gender, birth place, marital status, education, occupation, distance from residence to hospital, religious affiliation, insurance coverage, referral source on admission, clinical indication for admission, clinical diagnosis, number of previous admissions, duration of mental illness, type of discharge and clinical state at discharge. The statistical comparisons of length of stay among different groups were done by t-tests, tests of regression and correlation.

Table1: Diagnosis Distribution

Diagnosis (ICD-9)	N	%
Functional Psychosis (295-298)	178	58.7
Neurosis, Personality, Disorders and Parasuicide (300-302)	52	17.3
Alcohol / Drug Abuse / Dependence (300-302, 291-292)	29	9.7
Organic Brain Syndrome, Mental Retardation and Other (290, 293-294, 317-319, other)	43	17.3
Total	300	100

Results

The mean length of stay (±SD) for the whole patient group was 19.4±18.7 days. Distance from domicile to hospital (p<0.10), clinical diagnosis (major disorders Staying longer (p<0.05) and religious affiliation (Pentecostals staying less than Catholics) (p<0.05) correlated significantly with length of stay.

Pentecostal patients (N=32) were younger (72.5% of them were less than 30 years old in comparison to 49.0% of the Catholics), with more women in the group (68.8% in the Pentecostal group and 53.7% in the Catholic group), and presented a diagnosis of functional psychosis much more (86.0% in the Pentecostal group and 61.3% in the Catholic).

Discussion

Although distance from domicile to hospital and clinical diagnosis were found to predict length of stay, this discussion will focus on religious affiliation [as the former two variables were discussed elsewhere (DALGALARRONDO 1990)].

In our sample diagnosis distribution was clearly different between Pentecostals and Catholics (p<0.05). SPENCER (1975) found in the psychiatric hospitals of West Australia (7,546 new admitted patients) that members of the sect 'Jehovah's Witness' were three—fold over—represented in the schizophrenic group (p < 0.001). More recently, in a community mental health center in Israel, WITZTUM et al. (1990) described (561 new admitted patients) a predominance of schizophrenia (28.5%) among the ultra-orthodox group 'Baalei Teshuva,' in comparison to the general patient group (15.2% of schizophrenia) (p<0.001).

These data might suggest that a sect membership is either a risk factor predisposing to a schizophrenic illness, or that pre-psychotic or even psychotic persons are more likely to join a sect. However, LIN et al. (1978) have demonstrated that groups that do not ascribe to the norms and dominant values of a society will only refer their most severe cases to the official medicine. Furthermore, affiliation with a sect usually means the rejection of secular society and psychological explanation of mental disorders (WITZTUM 1990). Thus, these disproportions in diagnosis distribution appear to rely on different health care seeking behaviour, filters and service utilization.

Field studies should be conducted in order to clarify this issue. A comparison of the data for converted persons with those who have derived their faith from their parents would be a strategic line of research (SPENCER 1975).

Especially surprising in this study was that Pentecostal patients had a shorter length of stay. They were predominantly schizophrenics, bipolar and major depression patients, diagnostic groups which rather predicted a longer length of stay for the whole sample.

Why did Pentecostal affiliation predict a shorter length of stay? Studies on sociology of religion have shown that in Brazil, Pentecostal churches are most Fundamentalist, with strict moral rules and emotionally intense rituals. Exorcism and faith healing are frequent practices. In comparison to Catholics, they have a more intense religious practice, with a world view and symbolic universe much more based on magical beliefs, stronger social control and probably closer social support over members. It is not unlikely that these groups may function as a stronger social network and thus contribute to less rejection and stigmatization of psychotic patients (SPILKA et al. 1985).

Unfortunately, religious affiliation was not included in the multicentric studies of the WHO. VERGHESE et al. (1989) in a controlled study in India, using the same instruments as the WHO studies but including religious intensity, have found increased religious activities as a protective factor for the outcome of schizophrenia.

Albeit descriptive, our data strengthen the importance of including religious affiliation and intensity as a covariable in mental health studies. In order to test the hypothesis that Pentecostal affiliation in Brazil may represent a protective factor in the course of schizophrenia, a controlled prospective study is needed. This study should be sensitive to the cultural dimension (as proposed by ROGLER 1989). As FABREGA (1989) has stated "... selfhood cannot be viewed as similar cross-culturally, and insofar as schizophrenic illness disturbs the integrity of the self, its manifestations and course can be expected to bear the impact of distinctive cultural influences on the self."

References

BERGIN, AE
 1983 Religiosity and Mental Health: A critical reevaluation and meta-analysis. *Professional Psychology: Research and Practice* 14: 170-834.

BOURGEOIS, M.; M. KHALEFF & D. LOBROUSSE
 1975 Une secte religieuse, ses malades mentaux, son médicin et ses psychiatres. *Annales Medico-Psychologiques* 1: 160-167.

COOPER, J. & N. SARTORIUS
 1977 Cultural and Temporal Variations in Schizophrenia: A speculation on the importance of industrialization. *British Journal of Psychiatry* 130: 50-55.

DALGALARRONDO, P.
 1990 *Repensando a Internação Psiquiátrica: A proposta das unidades de internação psiquiátrica de hospitais gerais.* Master thesis. State University of Campinas (UNICAMP), Campinas, SP, Brazil.

ERICHSEN, F.
 1974 Bemerkungen über das sogenannte „religiöse" Erleben des Schizophrenen. *Nervenarzt* 45: 191-199.

FABREGA, H.
 1989 The Self and Schizophrenia: A cultural perspective. *Schizophrenia Bulletin* 15: 277-290.

LARSON, DB; EM PATTISON; DG BLAZER; AR OMRAN & BH KAPLAN
 1986 Systematic Analysis of Research on Religious Variables in Four Major Psychiatric Journals, 1978-1982. *American Journal of Psychiatry* 43: 329-334.

LIN, KM & AM KLEINMAN
 1988 Psychopathology and Clinical Course of Schizophrenia: A cross-cultural perspective. *Schizophrenia Bulletin* 14: 555-567.

LIN, T.; K. TARDIFF; G. DONETZ & W. GORESKY
 1978 Ethnicity and Patterns of Health-Seeking. *Culture, Medicine and Psychiatry* 2: 2-13.

LO, WH & T. LO
 1977 A Ten-Year Follow-Up Study of Chinese Schizophrenics in Hong-Kong. *British Journal of Psychiatry* 131: 63-66.

MURPHY, HBM & AC RAMAN
 1971 The Chronicity of Scizophrenia in Indigenous Tropical Peoples. *British Journal of Psychiatry* 188: 489-97.

ROGLER, LH
 1989 The Meaning of Culturally Sensitive Research in Mental Health. *American Journal of Psychiatry* 146: 296-303.

ROLIM, FC
 1985 *Pentecostais no Brasil: Uma interpretação sócio-religiosa.* Ed. Vozes, Petrópolis.

SARTORIUS, N.; A. JABLENSKY; A. KORTEN; G. ERNBERG; M. ANKER & JE COOPER
 1986 Early Manifestations and First-Contact Incidence of Schizopherenia in Different Cultures. *Psychological Medicine* 16: 909-928.

SARTORIUS, N., JABLENSKY, A. & R. SHAPIRO
  1977 Two-Year Follow-Up of the Patients Included in the WHO International Pilot Study of Schizophrenia. In: *Psychological Medicine* 7: 529-541.
SPENCER, J.
  1975 The Mental Health of "Jehovah's Witnesses." *British Journal of Psychiatry* 126: 556-559.
SPILKA, B., SHAVER, P. & LA KIRKPATRICK
  1985 A General Attribution Theory for the Psychology of Religion. *The Journal for the Scientific Study of Religion* 24: 1-20.
VERGHESE, A.; J.K. JOHN; S. RAJKUMAR; J. RICHARD; BB SETHI & JK TRIVEDI.
  1989 Factors Associated with the Course and Outcome of Schizophrenia in India. *British Journal of Psychiatry* 154: 499-503.
WAXLER, NE
  1979 Is Outcome for Schizophrenia Better in Nonindustrial Societies? *The Journal of Nervous and Mental Disease* 167: 144-158.
WILSON, BR
  1959 An Analysis of Sect Development. *American Sociological Review* 24: 3-15.
WITZTUM, E.; D. GREENBERG, D. & H. DASBERG
  1990 Mental Illness and Religious Change. *British Journal of Medical Psychology* 63: 33-41.

Narrowing Worlds: On Alzheimer's Disease and Biography in Brazil
ANNETTE LEIBING

Abstract
This paper introduces the current 'lived metaphors' relating to Alzheimer's disease in Rio de Janeiro's middle class. They consist of biographically explained 'stress' and typical personality traits. This 'person-centred' approach (as opposed to regarding illness as a 'thing' affecting a passive person) founds present suffering in the person's past, humanises this syndrome which often called 'death before death' — the latter view here perceived to be anchored in a post-modern world. Further shall we see that SELYE's 'stress model' has influenced the way Alzheimer's is explained by the Brazilian middle-class, as well as in current 'alternative' academic approaches.

Zusammenfassung
Dieser Text beschreibt die aktuellen ‚gelebten Metaphern' der Mittelklasse Rio de Janeiros in Bezug auf die Alzheimersche Krankheit. Sie bestehen aus biographisch erklärtem ‚Streß' und typischen Persönlichkeitsmerkmalen. Diese ‚personenzentrierte' Herangehensweise (im Gegensatz zu einer Sicht, die Krankheit als ein ‚Ding' beschreibt, das eine passive Person befällt) gründet gegenwärtiges Leiden in der Vergangenheit der Person und humanisiert auf diese Weise das Syndrom, welches häufig ‚Tod vor dem Tod' genannt wird – letzterer Begriff wird als in einer postmodernen Welt verankert verstanden. Zudem werden wir sehen, daß das SELYEsche Streßmodell einen Einfluß auf die Art hatte, wie die brasilianische Mittelklasse Alzheimer heute erklärt und ebenfalls anzutreffen in ‚alternativen' akademischen Modellen.

Keywords: Alzheimer, cultural context, history, urban Brazil.

> *Our sense of being a person is shaped not simply by our active memories, however; it is also a product of our conceptions of 'memory.'*
> (Allan Young, *The Harmony of Illusions*)

"Animals are lucky," wrote NIETZSCHE (1984), "for they have no history." But if diseases[1] like Alzheimer's restrict normal access to past experiences (e.g. KERTESZ & MOHS 1996), or return somebody to bygone times (cf. SHOMAKER 1989; HAMILTON 1994) or erase verbalized memory completely (e.g. ABRAMS et al. 1995: 1151), the importance of biography—a central feature of humanity, it seems—is cast in doubt.

Tracing the roots of the disease in a person's history one is bound to notice a decisive difference between the non-professional discourse on Alzheimer's in urban Brazil and the dominant biomedical concept (although we shall see that exceptions do exist). Including biography in the aetiology leads to regarding the disease as lived experience and not as a 'thing' or a neurochemical process

---

1. Because of the name's inclusion of the term 'disease' we will continue to use it instead of 'syndrome' which would be more adequate (SHUA-HAIM & GROSS 1996). The differentiation between 'illness' and 'disease' is not made because all forms of suffering consist of biological and socio-cultural elements. It is further important to mention that in this text we will part from a category that is constructed by a certain number of symptoms which the majority of Western doctors today would call 'Alzheimer's disease.' It is not focus on but implicit in this article that 'Alzheimer's disease' like most diseases is not a natural category (cf. COHEN 1995; GUBRIUM 1986; HERSKOVITS 1995; KITWOOD 1988; LEIBING 1996, 1997; LYMAN 1988).

taking place in the brains of passive people. This difference and its socio-cultural background will be the main topic of this paper.

Nowadays Alzheimer's disease ranks among the most feared diseases of an ever ageing humanity. The 'dementia epidemic' (HENDERSON 1987) can affect 4% of those of over 65 and up to 32% of 90 year old North Americans (GAUTHIER et al. 1996); other studies talk of 50%[2] of the oldest old. While RORSMAN et al. (1985, 1986, in JORM 1990) were not able to find any changes in the rate of incidence or survival in a longitudinal study of Alzheimer's disease in Southern Sweden over the last 25 years, and KOKMEN et al. (1988, in JORM 1990) did not observe any changes in a US community over a stretch of 15 years either (cf. also ROCCA et al. 1991), it still seems as though the above-mentioned 'apocalyptic demography' (ROBERTSON 1991) has only entered people's awareness in the last 20 years — and in Brazil only since the beginning of the 90's.

Can it be that Alzheimer's disease always existed, and has only moved into the foreground in step with a growing proportion of the old and oldest old in a multitude of cultures, or are we dealing with a post-modern construction of a 'disease of time' (YOUNG) in which "... people classified in a certain way tend to conform to or grow into the ways that they are described; but they also evolve in their own ways, so that the classifications and descriptions have to be constantly revised?" (HACKING 1995:21)

In my eyes both theories appear to be correct. Historically, as I have shown elsewhere (cf. LEIBING 1997b), there seems to be a 'period of invisibility' concerning Alzheimer's disease which began shortly after ALOIS ALZHEIMER's death in 1915 and ended only in the 1970s. BARRY REISBERG wrote in one of the first books about the disease:

"It is difficult to discuss a condition for which no name exists. Indeed, it is very easy for people to completely ignore or deny a condition which they do not even have a word for." (1981: 3)

And further on:

"Although physicians have not been as negligent as laymen in that at least physicians have always had a word for this disorder, they have until very recently done very little more than name it. Once the diagnosis of senile dementia was made, neither clinicians nor researchers devoted much more time, effort, or thought to the condition." (1981: 5)

The 'period of invisibility' did not exist when looking back within today's dominant paradigm of biomedical research, but as we will see futher on, there *where* scientists working on dementia — like ROTHSCHILD — but the discussion took place in a different scientific sphere — one which we will partly encounter again in popular Brazilian "lived metaphors" (JACKSON 1996: 9) concerning dementia.

The only undisputed risk factor — beside genetics in the very rare 'familiar' form — today is age (e.g. JORM 1990) and the growing number of older persons worldwide (e.g. KALACHE 1996; ALBERT & CATTELL 1994) would therefore also mean more people with Alzheimer's disease. On top of this OPIT (1988) writes that according to his opinion senile dementia went hand-in-hand with modern community-care and the closure of hospitals and institutions linked to it, whereupon the previously hospitalised ('de-ranged') elderly were moved back into the range of vision. When looking back, however, we still cannot be sure which values and kinds of 'Weltanschauungen' were and are connected with terms like 'senile dementia,' 'presenile dementia,' 'Alzheimer's disease' (as used in 1907 as opposed to terms used today)[3], 'senile psychosis,' 'Presbyphrenia,' etc. And when SHAKESPEARE has Henry the Fourth say: "How ill white hairs become a fool and jester" (SHAKESPEARE 1977), or King Lear describes himself as: "a very foolish old man, Fourscore

---

2. For a survey of the epidemiology of Alzheimer's disease see among others JORM (1990); HENDERSON (1994).

and upward, not an hour more or less; And, to deal plainly, I fear *I am not in my perfect mind*" (cf. MINOIS 1989: 281-287; italics mine, A.L.), then it's not quite clear whether an old person's return to (a second) childhood was regarded as an integral part of ageing or as a pathological process—a debatable point on which scientists have not been able to agree up to the present (A.S. HENDERSON 1997; MORRIS et al. 1996; POLLEN 1996; FÖRSTL et al. 1995; GUBRIUM 1986; ALZHEIMER 1911 u.a.).

If we look for comparisons in other cultures we will find that BRAUN et al. (1996) report that Vietnamese immigrants into the US knew of typical symptoms shown by elder family members, even though "[f]or the most part, respondents felt these symptoms were a natural part of aging" (1996: 222) and generally a doctor is only consulted if extremely strong symptoms appear. BARKER (1990), however, reports that the Niue people in Polynesia make a clear distinction between healthy (and respected) and decrepit (and neglected) elderly people. The latter show a great deal of "memory problems and confusion" (1990: 304) and are not worth any care or respect. As a result, they are not granted the status of 'elders' but are regarded as ghosts. To mention a last example for different categorisation and illness strategies resulting from it, as well as possible different effects on epidemiology with regard to senile dementia—COHEN (1995) describes a predominantly audible senility ('the mad voice') in India, the main symptom of which is annoyance rather than loss of memory and the related culture-specific concepts of 'hot brain,' 'sixtyishness,' and 'weakness' which the label 'Alzheimer's disease' renders meaningless.

Therefore, I regard the second hypothesis (of postmodern construction) as complementary to the first one, even though in need of further analysis:

This article intends to give a short view of the current biomedical discourse on Alzheimer's disease, which I regard as closely related to North American values in a post-modern world. Then I shall turn to the Brazilian popular discourse (interlinked with the professional one) in order to juxtapose it with the former. Both of them deal with the factor time/memory/biography ["Each of us becomes a new person as we redescribe the past" (HACKING 1995: 68)], but mirror different kinds of 'Weltanschauung.' The 'post-modern' discourse is characterised by its look ahead in a world continually renewing itself in which the demented person fades away ('degenerates'); the 'Brazilian' one by a *look back*, in which old age as well a person suffering from Alzheimer's is regarded as a result of the past, a '*desgaste*' (being worn out). Even though the discourses cannot both be simplified in such a way and at the same time remain fully distinguishable from one another, it is still possible to demonstrate the 'look back' with the help of illness narratives (KLEINMAN 1988) quite clearly in the Brazilian context. This is due to the fact that the biomedical discussion of old age and dementia is relatively new in this country. Terms like "Alzheimer's disease" or "dementia" are known to a relatively small elite, but they are being circulated by specialists in geriatrics, neurologists and general practitioners, and on a small scale, by the mass media.

---

3. It was KRAEPELIN who had coined the term 'Alzheimer's disease' in the 8th edition of his Handbook of Psychiatry (1910) for the presenile form of dementia which ALZHEIMER had described in 1907—although doubts were often voiced whether this 'new' disease could be distinguished from the normal process of ageing. Following a suggestion of KATZMAN in 1976, both the presenile and senile form of dementia were from then on called 'Alzheimer's disease.' Neurologist DAVID POLLEN, who as a directly involved scientist witnessed the birth of the new category, describes in his book "Hannah's Heirs," that the National Institute of Aging was being founded at that time. This lead to hostilities from colleagues worried about the new competition and their funding. The erstwhile director, Robert Butler, was trying to secure more funds and as POLLEN writes, "Katzman's more inclusive definition of Alzheimer's disease would serve as that wedge. (POLLEN 1996: 80)

Memory Disorders and Postmodernism

> *Nowadays the old are the least experienced, for experience is only useful and therefore respected in an unchanging world or one assumed to be unchanging.*
> [GÜNTHER ANDERS, *Antiquiertheit der Erfahrung und des Alters; (The Outdatedness of Experience and Old Age)*]

HACKING (1995) has pointed out in his brilliant analysis that "the multiple personality epidemic ... broke out" in the USA around 1982 and ran parallel to the growing interest in Post-Traumatic Stress Disorder (YOUNG 1995)[4] and the current concept of Alzheimer's disease (e.g. POLLEN 1996: 85) reflecting at the same time the rise of neopragmatism (GOODMAN 1995). Since all those categories deal with 'diseases of the memory' they lead to the question in which socio-cultural context 'memory' once made and still continues to make sense and takes part of the actual construction of the 'epidemics.'

The Multiple Personality Disorder analysed by Hacking predominantly bases on sexual abuse during childhood. Its—conscious or subconscious (i.e. deeply buried)—memory is supposed to lead to the parallel existence of differnt personalities in one person. In contrast to mainly buried memories in Post Traumatic Stress Disorder or Multiple Personality Disorder, which can be brought to the surface by 'experts,' the slow but irreversible loss of memory due to Alzheimer's disease changes the perception of the afflicted person radically: The philosopher H. TRISTRAM ENGELHARDT, JR. (1986) for example restricts the term 'person' to those who are 'self-conscious, rational, and in possession of a minimal moral sense,' although he adds that a secondary, conferred or social status of being a person exists: It is granted to people who enjoy particular esteem, even though they are not persons 'in the strict sense' (SMITH 1992; see also LEIBING 1996, 1997; HERSKOVITS 1995). Consciousness and rationality, on the other hand, are closely related to memory and an undisturbed time perception (MARKOWITSCH 1995: 1189). "You have to begin to lose your memory, if only in bits and pieces, to realise that memory is what makes our lives ... Without it, we are nothing," writes LUIS BUÑUEL in his memoirs (see SACKS 1990).

In Greek and Roman times citizens were trained in *memoria* and, as HESIO (ca. 800 B.C.) emphasised, memory was the 'spiritual source of the arts, the mother of the Muses.' But more than that: "The virtue of prudence; it built character, good judgement, citizenship and piety. Good memory was a sign of moral perfection" (CARUTHERS 1990, in FINGER 1994: 332). Today 'simple rememberance' is regarded as less positive than analytical thinking, just as the nostalgia of most old people and their 'looking back' are looked down upon, as G. ANDERS observed above. With regard to this HARVEY (1995:303) writes about identity in a post-modern world:

> "The assertion of any place-bound identity has to rest at some point on the motivational power of tradition. It is difficult, however, to maintain any sense of historical continuity in the face of all the flux and ephemerality of flexible accumulation. The irony is that tradition is now often preserved by being commodified and marketed as such. The search for roots ends up at worst being produced and marketed as an image, as a simulacrum or pastiche (...) The photograph, the document, the view, and the reproduction *become history precisely because they are so overwhelmingly present*. At best, historical tradition is reorganized as a museum culture ... (one from which all trace of oppressive social relations may be expunged; italics mine, A.L.).

---

4. "The diagnosis [of PTSD, note A.L.] achieved general acceptance only in 1980 ..." (YOUNG 1995: 5)

At the end of the 70's and beginning of the 80's which we have determined as the approximate start of the 'epidemics' of 'memory disorders,' HUYSSEN (1984, in HARVEY 1995: 39) writes:

"[I]n an important sector of our culture there is a noticeable shift in sensibility, practices and discourse formations which distinguishes a post-modern set of assumptions, experiences and propositions from that of a preceding period."

This (more or less) new fragmented, post-modern world is characterised by "the ephemeral and the fleeting" (HARVEY). The growing trend towards a society ruled by disposability, according to Harvey's analysis, does not only give rise to the problems connected with quick disposal goods, but also with values, traditions and lifestyles; furthermore with the attachment to stable things, human relationships and places of residence (homes). ALVIN TOFFLER (1970, in HARVEY op.cit.) points out the resulting fundamental changes in human psychology and the reactions to "the bombardment of stimuli": "the blocking out of sensory stimuli, denial, and cultivation of the blasé attitude, myopic specialisation, reversion to images of a lost past ..., and excessive simplification" (p. 286).

All these strategies can also be found in descriptions of Alzheimer patients—as 'egocentrism' (cf. HAMILTON 1994) or summed up as 'troublesome behaviour' (EASTWOOD & REISBERG 1996)—deprecatory descriptions of a pathological process that can also be regarded in quite a different way[5]—and ultimately leads to the extinction of humanity: "The body is yours, a shell ... But the light has gone from your eyes, Windows of a vacant house," as it says in the poem of a North American caregiver (in GUBRIUM 1986: 131). Another example of the "funeral that never ends"[6] is quoted by KLEINMAN (1988: 83) from the illness narrative of an Alzheimer patient's husband:

"I couldn't let Anna go to the nursing home ... She told me that when this darn disease started; she said, 'Dalton, please don't put me in an institution if it gets bad.' I promised her I wouldn't. It has broken my heart to see her mind go. It's as if, I can barely say it, *she were gone already*. ... I've learned to feed her, bathe her, even take her to the bathroom ... I think people think I'm batty for doing this. But we were so close. She and I were everything to each other ... But this is the worst. *To see the mind go, so that there are no memories*, it, well, sir, it is a living hell. (italics mine, A.L.)

The process of 'continually growing less' is part of the Western concept that ageing means losing, "... so that the problem of senile dementia is an account of a particularly feared loss in our culture" (OPIT 1988: 194).

The process of becoming 'non-person' can be regarded from a different perspective, that of a concept of ageing contrary to the pragmatic motto "[t]here is no virtue which is final; all are initial" (EMERSON). The following quotation from EMERSON, representative of classical pragmatism en vogue again today, concerning old age and the 'look ahead' is given to illustrate my argument:

"Nature abhors the old, and old age seems the only disease; all others run into this one. We call it by many names—fever, intemperance, insanity, stupidity and crime; they are all forms of old age; they are rest, conservatism, appropriation, inertia; *not newness, not the way onward* ...[T]he man and woman of seventy assume to

---

5. Newer studies show (e.g. KITWOOD 1988; SMITH 1992; HAMILTON 1995; STAFFORD 1992; VASZ 1996) that the person can be discovered even in an advanced stage of Alzheimer's disease, if the context in which this happens can be transcended. STAFFORD (1992: 403) in the frame of *Biosemiotics* writes:
"An alternative biosemiotic might see the signs of dementia in their 'Thirdness'—as the organism's attempt to mediate underlying decline in the face of its ongoing environmental press. Wandering, paranoia, hoarding, 'egoism,' and even moaning itself would move from being clinical indices of disease (Seconds) to symbols of adaptation–the self's attempt to sustain itself by bringing order to a chaos; by projecting fears to a hostile world; by reverting to the earliest sources of security and meaning; by convincing oneself that one is still alive in an elemental and primordial yawp of existence."
6. One of the first descriptions of a caregiver whose husband suffered from Alzheimer's, at the end of the 70's, which was published in a popular US newspaper.

know all, they have outlived their hope, they renounce aspiration, accept the actual for the necessary and talk down to the young ... Nothing is secure but life, transition, the energising spirit." (EMERSON 1995 [1841]; italics mine, A.L.)

Alzheimer's disease was detected in the brain by ALOIS ALZHEIMER at the beginning of the century and is predominantly described to the present day as a mechanism of pathological (untimely) ageing under a genetic influence (cf. POLLEN 1996); "Alzheimer's disease appears to result from a degenerative process characterised by *loss of cells* from the cerebral cortex, hippocampus, and subcortical structures, including selective cell loss in the nucleus basalis of Meynert ... [with] an autosomal dominant genetic pattern ..." (ABRAMS et al. 1995), a mechanistic model, described by KITWOOD (1988) as 'the technical frame' (however cf. EISENBERG 1995; BAUER 1994). Uncertain secondary factors like aluminium in the drinking water, school education, thyroid dysfunction or head trauma (cf. ABRAMS et al. 1995; JORM 1990; A.S. HENDERSON 1988 a.o.) can contribute to an outbreak of the disease, without the mechanistic metaphor of brain failure being discarded and only secondary to the continuing view of a "progressive neurodegenerative disorder" (CUMMINGS & KHACHATURIAN 1996). Even though there are first tentative attempts to incorporate social and psychological factors in the aetiology of Alzheimer's disease as well, they seem to carry little weight in view of dominant neuropathological thinking.

The 'biography' factor in conjunction with certain personality traits, which characterises the Brazilian illness narratives of Alzheimer's disease, can upon close observation also be identified in the professional discourse. It is not my intention to legitimise the lay discourse with the help of the professional one, and neither to present one as the truth and the other as exotic, but to demonstrate how interwoven both of them are. Nor should the 'Brazilian' view be romanticised, something which occasionally happens in anthropologic analyses and, regarding biomedicine as hostile instead, the implicit question of true and false that comes up if two discourses are placed side by side makes sense only in as far as it points to a puzzle whose many parts form what FOUCAULT (1994) calls *genealogy*. This form of critical historical analysis in the first line turns to that *subjugated knowledge*, which "... have been disqualified as inadequate to their task or insufficiently elaborated; naive knowledge, located low down on their hierarchy, beneath the required level of cognition or scientificity." (p. 41) These *savoir des gens* are not seen as "opposed primarily to the contents, methods or concepts of a science" but "to the effects of the centralising powers which are linked to the institution and functioning of an organised scientific discourse within a society such as ours." (p. 43)

A further aspect that moves the 'biography' factor into the foreground, lies in the important role that biography plays in chronic diseases, in the reconstruction of the new context (cf. KLEINMAN 1988; FRANK 1996; WILLIAMS 1996). For a person with Alzheimer's disease this is practically impossible because of the direct or indirect transmittance of anticipated death. However, the inclusion of biographical factors could be seen as having therapeutical potential, which has gained little attention until now (cf. GOLDSMITH 1996; VASZ 1996).

On Biography and Alzheimer's disease

> *Factors that narrow the individual's life also influence the occurrence of senility.*
> (DAVID C. WILSON 1955)

Most scientists, including ALOIS ALZHEIMER, did and still do agree that the typical neurodegenerative process in the brain[7] is secondary to still not known factors. Even genetic predisposition which time and again has been called upon, does not suffice to explain the disease, at least in its predominant 'sporadic' form. Furthermore it seems that a whole number of factors have to come together to trigger the disease. Looking back, there is a possible correlation between suffering/depression during the life and Alzheimer's disease later on, although without conclusive results (cf. JORM 1990). Other risk factors have been studied but none of them regarded as decisive for all cases. This insecurity leads to a view of the actual process of the disease which is passed on to the caregiver who, in a simplified way, receives the message, 'we don't know and there is nothing we can do about it except relieve symptomatically part of the suffering.'[8] An interviewed specialist on Alzheimer's in Rio de Janeiro about possible risk factors and cure:

"We don't know [the risk factors], but because of the existence of the sporadic form of the disease, which is the form most often found, we don't even know whether it is not an error of the ageing process. The fact is that this depositions [of beta amyloids] are being studied, we know already the precursor of the protein. In 10 years we will have a way to avoid this disease ... It is from the genetics that we will gain the cure. You can have environmental influence, whatever it might be, but you can't change the environment. You will only be able to change the deposition of the protein, which is markedly genetical and organical. You won't change the environment, but will have changed the chain."

In the years after World War II the perception of illness changed from the immediacy of a lesion to a process of becoming ill (ARMSTRONG 1988), already anticipated by some authors: The first pointer to biographic factors in the development of 'senile psychosis,' the term used for the late onset form of dementia, was given by DAVID ROTHSCHILD, who was both neuropathologist and clinical psychiatrist at the Harvard Medical School. In his 1937 article "Pathologic Changes in Senile Psychoses and their Psychobiologic Significance" he calls attention to the incongruence of the severity of brain pathology and the amount of symptoms in mental processes. In addition he also found comparable alterations in the brains of non-demented persons, a fact which before him GELLERSTEDT (1933) had already shown. ROTHSCHILD assumes that these differences are due to different abilities to compensate in the people concerned. The inability to deal with personal problems (see also WILSON 1955), particularly where old age is concerned, could be one of the factors allowing a person to lose his ability to compensate: "I agree that the difference between senile dementia and normal senility probably lies in the life history of the individuals." (p. 787) "One should consider the whole person with his life history and his everyday experiences and his reactions to these experiences, especially in later life." (p. 788)

He further develops this reactive view of pathological processes in an article in which he points out premorbid personality, intelligence and psychological stress—additional factors in a process of senile dementia (ROTHSCHILD & SHARP 1941):

---

7. The typical plaques and tangles can also be found in the brains of persons who do not show any symptoms like impaired memory, a.o.
8. This seems to be somehow different in the US where some optimism is transmitted regarding certain drugs and a possible avoidance of quick decline (cf. GUBRIUM 1986).

"... the person's capacity to compensate for the damage [of senile lesions, A.L.] seems to be the factor which determines whether or not a psychosis will occur. Here one must reckon with unfavorable traits of personality, innate or acquired, which may be associated with a weak capacity, ..., but psychologic stress and strain may also play a role by lowering the patient's resistance ..." (p. 53)

In 1952 (SANDS & ROTHSCHILD 1952) he further enlarges on the personality profiles that can be found in the prehistory of senile dementia with significant frequency, particularly dependency and rigidity, from which he concludes that "... there is reason to believe that the organic process itself may be influenced by rather remote factors in the life history of the individual, including his personality." (p. 239)

A modern version of this could be summed up by the term 'psychoneuroimmunology,' a branch of medicine which analyses environmental influences and their complex interaction with the central nervous system, the endocrinium and the immune system in a sometimes linear or non-linear form (e.g. KROPIUNIGG 1990; LYON 1993; KAPLAN 1991). These analyses focus on acute as well as long-term stress and its resulting consequences for a person's health. Whether a certain factor is perceived as stressful depends undoubtedly on the cultural background (YOUNG 1980), but the wider cultural context and a critical analyses, e.g. why a woman in a certain society feels powerless, in this kind of thinking rarely is included—although it opens the possibility of doing so.[9] A possible line of argument is "The social construction of the human brain" (EISENBERG), e.g. influenced by neonatal handling (MEANEY et al. 1988) or stressful life events and their effect on neurochemical processes like, for example, the role glucocorticoids play in ageing (SAPOLSKY 1992). Without discussing this and neighbouring fields (for a discussion see MILLER 1996), I would like to outline an example of the abovementioned relationship between biography and Alzheimer's disease.

BAUER (1994) and BAUER et al. (1992) point out the innate immune mediator interleukin-6 which can be found only in the brains of demented persons, whereas amyloid plaques and neurofibril degenerated tangles, the 'typical marker' of Alzheimer's disease, can also be found in the brains of the non-demented. It has been proved with the help of animal experiments that apart from viral and bacterial stimuli psychic stress can also lead to the rise in the interleukin-6 level: "Interleukin-6 therefore seems to be a central 'psychic-near' agent in processes concerning the immune system and may well be a mediator in psychoimmunological processes."[10] (1994: 29) A complex model of stressful life events and unfavourable personality traits, which he found as a pattern in his patients—like the avoidance of conflicts, an inclination to dependency and the tendency to be social can in BAUER's opinion—in connection with a predisposition—lead to neuropathological changes such as Alzheimer's (also cf. SAPOLSKY 1994, 1992; LANDFIELD 1994; ZHOU et al. 1993; CYNADER 1994; EISENBERG 1995 a.o.).

In a second example KITWOOD (1988) proposes a psychoanalytically oriented approach to the experience of a 'lost self' in the process of dementia:

---

9. One example would be SAPOLSKY's observation (1992) that subordinated individuals hypersecrete cortisol when exposed to frequent psychological stress, but that the physiological correlates depend on the *sort of society* in which the dominance/subordination occurs and on whether it is a stable or an unstable dominance. But also personality, social control, the possibility of letting out aggression are variables in defining whether social status can be a risk factor for disease or not. Writes SAPOLSKY: "As a physiologist, it is clear to me that physiology per se accounts only a very small piece of these complex systems." (p. 281)
10. Estrogens, which lately have been proposed as a possible protection from Alzheimer's, because the number of female Alzheimer patients who took estrogens in relation to a control group which did not, was 2.5 times less, impede as well the synthesis of interleukin-6 (BAUER 1994).

"For some persons the experiencing self is mainly a locus of pain, sealed off from consciousness by psychic defences. Many, living without awareness in the world they take for granted, are scarcely aware of its existence. So they live on the ground of their adapted selves, mistaking this for the true psychic reality. In terms of Marcuse's radical version of psychoanalytic theory (1956), they follow the 'performance principle' of a particular social order." (p. 177)

It continues:

"The key topic to be investigated would be the history of the self in those who do, and those who do not, become demented. On the one hand it would be necessary to look at the adapted self, lived out through social roles and in conformity to others' expectations. How far, and by what means, is the adapted self of middle life maintained as the person moves into old age and undergo its many deprivations? On the other hand it would be necessary to chart the vicissitudes of the experiential self... Has it been developing and expanding as the life course has progressed, or has it been yet further protected by psychic defences as the person faces the difficulties of later life ...?" (p. 177)

Evidently, it has been impossible to provide a full presentation of the wide range of differing views which only occupy rather outsider positions in the field of university research. But they are based on old ideas (the 'stress model') which will be taken up again when they will be related to the current Brazilian urban discourse on Alzheimer's disease.

Alzheimer's Disease and Brazilian Context

The following study was carried out in Rio de Janeiro, the country's city with the greatest number of old people. Their share of 10% of the population is comparable to urban centres in most Western countries (VERAS 1994). It is not possible to give a general description of this group due to its heterogenity. Extreme class differences and vast differences in access to the markets of a fast developing country with an ever changing set of values (cf. LEIBING 1995) — further render a uniform description virtually impossible, even if we talk only about the middle class (cf. BOSI 1994; LINS DE BARROS 1987). But over the last years an improvement in the standing and visibility of old people from the middle class could be observed, they were 'discovered' as consumers and an important group of voters. Another reason why there is a relatively strong body of middle class older people in Rio de Janeiro is the fact that this city was the Brazilian capital until 1960 and when Brasília became the new one, many people from administrative posts stayed behind.

VERAS (1994), VERAS & MURPHY (1994), ALMEIDA FILHO et al. (1984) and BLAY (1989) note a high prevalence of psychiatric disorders among the older population in the urban centres of Rio de Janeiro, Salvador/Bahia and São Paulo. Though the reasons for this are not clear, poverty, exclusion from active life and disregard for the old in a society which worships youth are possible factors.

So far no statistical data on Alzheimer's disease are available, but based on some first studies VERAS (1994) and VERAS & MURPHY (1994) estimate that the figures for dementia — without differentiating between Alzheimer's disease and other forms — are generally a little higher than in developed countries: "It may well prove to be the case that there really is significantly more dementia in the elderly population of this rapidly developing population, many of whom have lived their lives in circumstances of exceptional hardship." (VERAS & MURPHY 1994: 291)

In the present study caregivers of Alzheimer patients were interviewed. One group was contacted by a local Alzheimer organisation (n = 52) who filled in a questionnaire with predominantly open questions about the illness of their relative, concerning the ill person as well as his/her treatment. Parts of the interviews were and are still being backed up by a personal interview. Additional data were gained by persons diagnosed as suffering from Alzheimer's disease in an outpatient unit at the Institute of Psychiatry, Federal University of Rio de Janeiro, but we will focus mainly on the first group which consists of persons from the middle class.[11]

In both groups female patients as well as the interviewed caregivers outnumbered males by a ratio of 2:1. In the first group the women tend to have relatively little school education, while the men completed a higher education in most cases. The women were mostly housewives, which is the norm for their peer group; most frequent among the men were military occupations, followed by retail jobs, though the figures are not statistically significant. 93% of the ill persons were Catholics.

The 'Lived Metaphors' of Alzheimer's Disease in Rio de Janeiro

Generally we could observe that people differentiate between normal and pathological ageing. A person that becomes disoriented in very old age and is possibly weak and fragile as well is often referred to as 'caduco/a,' which describes a condition comparable perhaps to SHAKESPEARE's 'second childhood' and is part of the process of ageing, though not an unavoidable one. But if it is accompanied by aggressive or self-destructive behaviour, excessive sadness or if other family members are greatly disturbed by night-time wanderings a doctor is consulted. *Caducar*, the verb, means to disappear, to lose forces not being used anymore or to annul a contract because of missing the deadline or not fulfilling the established conditions (FERREIRA 1986). The underlying concept of senility is that it results from a relatively long lifespan and represents a possible end of a lived life. But if we look at the connotations of 'caducar' we see a strong negative conception of old age and it is probably the integration in daily activities and sociocultural status, as well as thankfulness, that determine the value and personship of the elderly in Brazil, still considered the country of the youth and where there are still strong family bonds but which are weakening more and more in urban contexts. Premature disorientation can also be called 'caduco/a,' but the term then acquires a negative connotation and is not regarded as normal.

One of the first questions, later repeated in the questionnaire, was how the informant explained the illness. Frequently, two parallel explanations were given. First, there was, for example, 'of genetic origin' or 'an illness with unknown causes' or 'medical science still cannot explain it'—explanations that are often given by the doctors whom we have consulted.

Few people limited themselves to these phrases. Most of them followed them up with explanations relating to the ill person's biography. However, the majority of informants gave such explanations, involving wear from a hard life, in the first place:

> "That's what I'm asking myself. From the medical point of view it was a number of factors, but I believe that it depends—what I know is that my mother had a hard life. My grandparents died early, a godmother took her and soon died as well, she was sent to an orphanage.
>
> 32 years ago she married my father and took care of the household, but she always was a nervous person. She took care of the household, dad and me. My father was always up to something, because he loved hanging around in bars and she turned her attention to me. She always demanded a lot from me, didn't want me to have dates, I was only supposed to study." (Example 1)

A further example (a son talking about his father):

---

11. This is due to the larger number of interviews in this group. The second one of a poorer origin will be described and compared in a further publication.

"Maybe his being overly worried about his work during his lifetime, for my father worked a lot in his shop, but, sure, it wasn't just that. His temperament was very strong (sic!); he was very worried, but one can't say that the cause of Alzheimer's was just life's worries. Its origins don't yet have any concrete causes, but I think it was because he had many worries in life; that's what contributed to the disease." (Example 2)

A second group connected the cause of the disease with a specific event in the past, for instance "a great injustice that was done to him [a long time ago] and gave him such a strong headache that he started to cry" or the disease had already lain 'like a seed' within the person and a traumatic experience that occurred a short while before the first symptoms appeared then set off the pathological process:

"I believe it is a genetic problem but as far as I know these diseases are little investigated ... Maybe her distancing herself started the disease, I'm not sure ... My mother lived far away from her relatives, in one of Rio's suburbs, without telephone, with my father. Her favourite sister died. No activities like work or going to the bank." (Example 3)

Such a narrowing of the world was often described, but much less than (or in combination with) losses [*perdas*]: "The shock of her husband's death caused the illness." So we could observe two main (simplified) models for anchoring the origins of Alzheimer's disease in the past. The first one is closer to the actual biomedical model although there the significance of the time between predisposition etc. and first symptoms is denied (see above). The second one relates to the 'alternative' models in academic studies as has been shown above.

```
(emotionally "closed up"; sometimes)
predisposition/
genetics/- - - - - - - - - - - - - - - - - one or more losses - - - - - - first symptoms
no explanation
```

```
emotionally 'closed up'
- - - - - loss - - - - - loss - - - - - loss - - - - loss - - - - - first symptoms
- - - - - much work
```

Figure 1: Anchoring Alzheimer's disease in the past.

Neither model, the 'genetics' and the 'wear and tear' one, is exclusive and both contain one more decisive element which will be discussed in the next part of the text, the personality.

Biography and Personality

Reading all of the interviews[12] makes it apparent that there is an astonishing number of similarities in the personalities and biographies of the ill persons and the links between them — similarities strongly reminiscent of the abovementioned studies, even if they lack the concomitant neurochemistry. The prototype of these life-and-personality narratives would be someone with a 'strong personality' (as in example 2) on the one hand though emotionally closed up (but many times described as very communicative, at the same time), a diligent worker, often with a need to maintain or better their social status, with a slant towards perfectionism, someone to sacrifice

---

12. A more detailed analysis of the interviews will be given in a future publication.

him- or herself for others, especially in the case of the women, who has often had to struggle. The woman could be a (perfect) housewife, a man might be in the army. Painful losses of beloved persons or treasured things plus an often unhappy childhood complete the picture.[13]

The 'Happy Ones'

We put thirteen of the 52 persons questioned into a sub-group called 'the happy ones.' Because of the mostly negatively connoted lived metaphors used to describe the origin of Alzheimer's disease (but there was a lot of admiration, too), we were wondering whether these persons, described as 'happy' in their adult lives, would differ from the rest. Twelve of the thirteen were women. We do not know whether judgements given by the relatives match the impression the ill persons have of themselves, nor to what degree the current disease overshadows and influences their 'look back,' but it was interesting to note that among this group there was the greatest number of relatives who limited themselves to explaining Alzheimer's with 'Don't know why' or 'genetics' as if Alzheimer's for a happy person would not make sense. Nearly 50% of them (n=6) actually mentioned other cases in their family, although the number itself is too small to draw any valid conclusions from this.

The absence of men in this group is striking and possibly due to different gender specific expectancies.

Apart from this, these illness narratives showed the same pattern of biography/personality plus loss which is to be found in persons not described as happy. The only significant difference was that the relationship to their parents was described to be good or excellent, with the exception of two cases. This would support the hypothesis that neonatal handling or the well established positive influence on development of a warm and caring home can provide a protective influence in later life.[14]

The illness narrative about an 80 year old woman, an ex-secretary and ex-teacher, provided by her daughter, illustrates the interplay of these factors:

"At first she just tended to forget things, but when she learned that her husband had cancer and then died, her condition deteriorated rapidly. Before her husband's disease her life had been simple and happy. All her life she had been cheerful and extroverted, there had been few things that knocked her down, she always bore herself well. And now her mind has gradually been extinguished. Her elder sister became absent-minded [*ausente*] as well, right from the day she stopped working.

The doctors say she is doing great, there is nothing one can do about it. In my mother's case the death of my father was fatal and in some respects her reaction was a certain surprise to us, since she had been very active, strict and very cheerful. Her apartment meant a lot to her. But right after that death all this lost its importance and she doesn't want to live in her beloved apartment any more ... Her father was loving and cheerful, engineer, her mother housewife, tender and protective. She had a happy childhood and she had been cheerful from when she was very little on, her mother and aunt said. Her teen age had also been carefree for her and her four brothers and sisters. As a young adult she then tragically lost her brother and one sister whom she loved dearly. Her marriage and relationship with her husband were happy and he remained her friend and companion until old age. She was crazy about the five of us children and loved to have a full house. Her marriage lasted 53 years.

---

13. A prototype, as opposed to a stereotype, only reflects what the majority of a certain group would consider as 'typical' without necessarily including all elements or idiosyncrasies (cf. HACKING 1995:272).
14. And as SAPOLSKY (1994:103) observed: "Perhaps we can even risk scientific credibility and detachment and mention the word 'love' here, because the most ephemeral of phenomena lurks between the lines of this chapter; something roughly akin to love is needed for proper biological development, ... [Y]oung organisms were able to teach this fact to surprised scientists in a classic set of studies conducted in the 1950s through the 1970s, studies that are, in my opinion, among the most haunting and troubling of all the pag*es of science."*

VWB – Verlag für Wissenschaft und Bildung

All our life we regarded her as strong. She never tired, was never scandalised by anything, was cheerful in a natural way, very temperamental and quick to make friends. She always worked to contribute to financing our education. In this respect she was absolutely serious—duties came first. She always reacted positively to the difficult stretches in her life, and those were numerous." (Example 4)

This is probably the happiest history of all, but some of its details will turn up again in the next section, which deals with the less cheerful Alzheimer patients, i.e. a sense of duty where work is concerned, a 'strong personality,' traumatic losses and keeping a 'stiff upper lip' as part of the character. Before that, another 'happy' example:

"I believe she fell ill because she suffered many losses in a short time. I got married in early 1979 and my sister shortly afterwards. A month later my father died and she found herself alone in the flat. Six months after that she was run over by a car and had to spend two months in bed ...

The doctor told me that Alzheimer's disease cannot be attributed to a single cause and that it is still being investigated ... But let me tell you, her father was a peasant and had a good relationship with his daughter, just like her mother, who was a housewife. Then again her parents used to beat her a lot and her father did not let her go to school. And she grew up in great poverty. Today she speaks of them with great tenderness and does not believe they are already dead ... As a teenager she was a great beauty and had a lot of admirers, who all, as she said, were 'just after one thing.' At night she locked herself into her room so that the men could not get in. Only at the age of 38 she married my father and had us two daughters. My father hardly earned anything and she always worked as well, opened a boarding house. She cooked the food for all those people and looked after the house and us ... I don't know how she managed to do it all. She always was a fighter and we studied thanks to her. Well, what was she like? She had a strong personality, was very communicative, made friends wherever she went and helped whoever needed help. If she wanted something, she would go for it no matter what she had to do to get it." (Example 5)

The 'Unhappy Ones'

This group is characterised by a certain general rigidity and an emotional reclusiveness, usually in connection with a troubled life mastered with the help of hard work. The story of a pensioner who had a middle echelon post in the army and showed the first symptoms when he was 57 years old, as his son reports:

"In the years before his disease he did a lot of sports and it was his big dream to win the big tournaments. When he only came in third he was quite depressed. He argued a lot with his second wife—he had split up with my mother at the end of the eighties. He had never shown a lot of emotion to us children or to other relatives. One relative seems to have shown the same symptoms as he did, so my mother said. A striking feature all his life was his pessimism. He always acted 'tough' and did not show his emotions to other people. It is as if it had accumulated all those years, together with a genetic factor for the disease and then he fell in the bathroom a short while before, and he had to have 18 stitches in the back of his head, which, even though the doctors deny it, accelerated the disease in my opinion.

He never knew his father, and never talked about the subject. My father did everything for his mother and often he said she was the most important person in his life. She died in 1971 when he was 41 years old, and he never got over her death. About his childhood I only know that he played a lot and without restrictions in the suburb, but he had a negative view of his stepfather and avoided him wherever he could. His real father did not acknowledge him. At a young age he joined the navy. He had a lot of fights, often nearly fatal, with other boys in the neighbourhood and one in the navy with a superior when he was 23 or 24 years old, whereupon he was demoted, which greatly frustrated him.

My father was a very reserved person in the family and also did not have any real friends. His marriage with my mother had its ups and downs, but he loved us children very much. It's just a pity that he had such difficulties in expressing it. He used a lot of physical force to solve certain problems outside his home. But he had a great sense of responsibility, and we did not lack anything. He took himself to be superior and was sometimes quite sarcastic. (Example 6)

A last female example is related by the patient's daughter. Her mother, a former teacher (without university education), showed the first symptoms (mistakes in what she wrote and gaps in her memory) at the age of 66. At that time she was looking after her more than 90-year-old and very sick father.

> "Other female members of my mother's family showed similar symptoms. But it is not just that. My mother became a widow at the age of 27. She only lived for her children, her grandchildren, after that for her mother, who became ill and was cared for by my mother until she died. I read a lot about the whole stuff, I know about chromosome 21 and so on. But I think dissatisfaction about life, sadness, stress and the closing up in an ever shrinking world, can lead to self-destruction.
>
> Her father was a truck driver and a distanced person and her mother a housewife. With her she got along well. She was the only one of the kids who never was beaten by her mother.
>
> Her childhood was not very happy, because she went to a boarding school run by nuns, from which she only left to marry.
>
> The death of my father was traumatic, it was a car accident ...
>
> My mother never did anything alone, don't know why, no cinema, visit or shopping. She worked in a school and in a pharmacy to help her sister. In her free hours she did everything for her church and for us, never complained about life. She always showed herself to be a very strong person." (Example 7)

In one third of the narratives the concept of a 'strong personality' was used to describe a character confronting life, controlling, ordering, and a fighter. A certain depressive or sad backdrop can also be felt in the majority of the cases and we could speculate here, whether long lasting depression, resulting from a certain life history and personality in a culture in which these characteristics are lived in a way that there is no 'stage' to transform suffering into a culturally valued play (see PFLEIDERER 1994), might lead to neuropathological changes, as, for example, SAPOLSKY (1992), BAUER (1994:52) or JORM (1990) tentatively consider possible. This interrelation of the cultural and biological is something rarely thought of and even neglected in medical anthropology, due to the typical polarisation of 'biological' and 'social' sciences, although LOCK proposes a dialectic between this as "local biologies" (1994: 39).

Discussion

Whereas the 'look ahead' deals with the further development of the disease, the 'look back' centres on its aetiology. In the majority of cases modern biomedical research endeavours to halt the degenerative process in the brain although this is as well eyed by a 'looking back' in search for possible risk factors, but not like in the Brazilian middle class discourse where the history is part of the present suffering. This does not mean that the afflicted person in Rio de Janeiro does not 'grow less,' but the change goes more in the direction of the SHAKESPEAREan second childhood than towards becoming a non-person. My doubt is, and this requires further research, as to whether the medicalization of dementia diminishes the cultural necessity of the inclusion of, although childish, parents into a traditionally caring Latin family structure as mentioned by an interviewed psychiatrist who works at a (private and well equipped) home for older people. In this home, except for two persons, everybody is perceived as demented:

> "To interview the relatives won't be easy here because many of them nearly never come. They feel guilty about leaving the mother or father behind, although the old people are very well treated with nice rooms, TV, air-conditioning etc. So they prefer not to come and not being reminded all the time of what they have done. They feel that it is against nature to leave the parent to an institution. I think they try to convince themselves that because it is a disease they have to be cared for by doctors."

Even if an article does not suffice to acquaint the reader adequately with the coherence and closedness of the lived metaphors, it should have become apparent that the dementia process makes sense to the persons interviewed and is experienced and interpreted within a rich cultural frame. It is not the question whether this approach is 'truer' than the biomedical one (or rather ones). Instead I want to place subjugated knowledge alongside other research and in closing attempt to explain why they make sense in the Brazilian context.

A striking feature of both the Brazilian middle class discourse as well as in 'alternative' biomedical knowledge of Alzheimer's disease is the interweaving of biomedical models and experienced context. *Perdas* (losses), strain resulting from these losses (or as SELYE would say—"exhaustion") and certain personality traits remind us of HANS SELYE's stress model, which has survived in a modified form in the work of scientists like BAUER and SAPOLSKY, as well as in the non-professional discourse, probably not only in the Rio de Janeiro middle class but in many cultures worldwide. Here we are dealing with common sense or 'tacit knowledge' (YOUNG 1980) and, at a first glance, an appeal for more openness where psychological and sociocultural factors in pathological processes are concerned than the biomedical discourse, which concentrates on the neurodegenerative process. Young, however, rightly warns that since "the stress discourse is a social discourse—it claims to situate pathogenesis within everyday experience—its specificity has important ideological consequences in the sense of legitimising existing social arrangements." (p. 144) Life events gain the status of objectivity and are deprived of the context with the consequence that social contexts are placed within the individual and are thus naturalised. It should be noted that none of the persons interviewed asked about the social context within which the so frequently mentioned hard life endured by a strong and at the same time closed personality takes place; although researchers, like VERAS & MURPHY (s.a.) did ask about the social context.

But it is not only the culturally integrated stress model that gives sense to the process of dementia. The structure of this model is reinforced by traditional Brazilian concepts of being a person. The Brazilian society possesses a diversity of interrelated contexts, in which a person defines her-/himself in different ways (cf. DUARTE in this volume): individualistic and holistic, hierarchic and 'igualitaire' values compete with one another. The individual biography as shown here is regarded as potentially causing the disease. This goes back to the principle of balance in humoral medicine (cf. FOSTER 1994) where certain sickening factors finds entrance into the body while the necessary catharsis to rid the body of these negative influences cannot take place in a closed up personality (the person might be extroverted at the same time, but is described as 'emotionally closed up'). Similarly this can happen to anybody who sacrifices him- or herself for others or works too much felt as being in an unhealthy state of imbalance and wearing himself out with the years.

Although there is an ever growing trend towards psychological knowledge to explain suffering, especially in better educated classes (DUARTE 1986), the humoral principle of balancing opposites is still widely recognised. However, this principle has undergone a radical transition and, as I see it, perverted itself and turned *against* the people as I have shown elsewhere (see LEIBING 1991, 1994). The currently dominant opposing pair of 'strong-weak' has largely displaced the 'hot-cold' dichotomy which LÉVI-STRAUSS [1955] still described as being strongly representing Brazilian life. It was in the 50's that a forced industrialisation took place in Brazil and many established values vanished in favour to a 'savage capitalism' as it is called in Brazil, meaning a capitalism with a hierarchic structure and nearly no guaranteed rights. Theoretically, following the logic of humoral medicine, a 'strong' disease like Alzheimer or mental illness (see LEIBING 1990) ought to be cured with the help of a weak medicine (or, as before, a hot disease with a cold remedy), or a weak person eat strong food to regain her/his strength. But actually a (socially and healthwise) weak person suffering from a 'strong' disease will regard himself as too weak for the required strong (and not weak) medicine prescribed by the doctor explaining part of the 'non-compliance' often observed in Brazilian patients. Here again, the question of the social origins of diseases is topicalised ("I am weak" which can be socially as well as physically), but the origin of the disease is placed within the individual. But not only that, someone who is poor, without power ('weak'), often cannot stand the necessary medicine. It should be noticed however that certain biographical elements (hard work, early losses etc.) and certain personality traits do not determine a disease like Alzheimer's but rather contribute towards it in a certain context. What I refer to here is the 'body in everyday lifel,' as CASSELL (1984) writes, not a particular organ.

In relation to Alzheimer's this means that, as YOUNG pointed out, the *individual* biography is seen as sickening, but not the wider social context ('social biography'). But in contrast to FOUCAULT or ARMSTRONG (1988), however, I see here potential for a contextually justified intervention: The subjective biography should not only be retrospectively considered with regard to a certain disease, nor completely ignored as in the neurobiological paradigm. Instead one could work with the concept of an 'embodied personhood' as LOCK & SCHEPER-HUGHES (1990:70) write, because if we conceive of "… someone living out and reacting to his or her assigned place in the social order, then the social origins of many illnesses and much distress and the 'sickening' social order itself come into sharp focus."

The instances of a 'narrowing world' described by the Brazilian informants and by 'alternative' scientists—whether occuring early in life or only when ageing—could be seen as an individual process or as a wider societal way of coping in a world which does not seem to have space for everybody.

Acknowledgements

This study was financed by the National Council of Scientific and Technological Development (CNPq), grant no. 300664/95-8. Further thanks are due to my colleagues Márcia Dourado and Cristiane de Oliveira Magalhães, the APAZ (the local Alzheimer organisation), specially Dr. Jacov Guterman and Lúcia Lerner, as well as Dr. Jerson Laks for supporting this project. Lorenz and Claudia von Usslar helped with the translation of this text.

References

ABRAMS, W.B.; M.H. BEERS & R. BERKOW (eds.)
   1995 *The Merck Manual of Geriatrics, Second edition*, Whitehouse Station, NJ: Merck & Co.
ALBERT, S.M. & M.G. CATTELL
   1994 Population aging and comparative demography. In: *Old Age in Global Perspective, Cross-cultural and cross-national views*, pp. 35-56. New York: G.K. Hall & Co.
ALZHEIMER, A.
   1907 Über eine eigenartige Erkrankung der Hirnrinde. *Allg. Zeitschrift f. Psychiatrie* 64: 146-148.
   1911 Über eigenartige Krankheitsfälle des späteren Alters. *Zeitschrift f. die ges. Psych. und Neurol.* 4: 355-356.
ARMSTRONG, D.
   1988 Space and time in British general practice. *Biomedicine Examined*. Edited by M. LOCK & D. GORDON, pp. 207-226. Dordrecht: Kluwer Academic Publ.
BARKER, J.C.
   1990 Between humans and ghosts: The decrepit elderly in a Polynesian society. In: *The Cultural Context of Aging, Worldwide perspectives*. Edited by J. SOKOKOVSKY, pp. 295-314. Westport: Bergin & Garvey.

BAUER, J.
1994 *Die Alzheimer-Krankheit, Neurobiologie, Psychosomatik, Diagnostik und Therapie*. Stuttgart: Schattauer.
1992 The participation of interleukin-6 in the pathogenesis of Alzheimer's disease. *Research in Immunol.* 143: 650-657.
BOSI, E.
1994 *Memória e Sociedade, Lembranças de velhos*, São Paulo: Companhia das Letras.[1973]
BRAUN, K.L.; J.C. TAKAMURA & T. MOUGEOT
1996 Perceptions of dementia, caregiving, and help-seeking among recent Vietnamese immigrants. *Journal of Cross-Cultural Gerontology* 11(3): 213-228.
CASSELL, E.J.
1984 *The Place of the Humanities in Medicine, What the humanities have to offer medicine*, Hastings-on-Hudson: The Hastings Center.
COHEN, L.
1995 Toward an anthropology of senility: Anger, weakness, and Alzheimer's in Banaras, India. *Medical Anthropology Quarterly* 9(3): 314-334.
CUMMINGS, J.L. & Z. KHACHATURIAN
1996 Definitions and diagnostic criteria. *Clinical Diagnosis and Management of Alzheimer's Disease*, S. Gauthier (ed.), London: Martin Dunitz.
CYNADER, M.S.
1994 Mechanisms of brain development and their role in health and well-being. *Daedalus* 123(4): 155-166.
DUARTE, L.F.D.
1986 *Da Vida Nervosa nas Classes Trabalhadoras Urbanas*, Rio de Janeiro: Zahar/CNPq.
EASTWOOD, R. & B. REISBERG
1996 Mood and behaviour. In: *Clinical Diagnosis and Management of Alzheimer's Disease*. Edited by S. GAUTHIER, pp.175-190. London: Martin Dunitz.
EISENBERG, L.
1995 The social construction of the human brain. *Am J Psychiatry* 152(11): 1563-1575.
EMERSON, R.W.
1995 Circles, in: Selected Essays [1841]. In: *Pragmatism, A contemporary reader*. Edited by R.B. GOODMAN, pp. 25-33. New York: Routledge.
FERREIRA, A.B.H.
1986 *Novo Dicionário da Língua Portuguêsa*, Rio de Janeiro: Nova Fronteira.
FINGER, S.
1994 *Origins of Neuroscience, A history of explorations into brain functions*. New York: Oxford University Press.
FÖRSTL, H.; R. ZERFASS; C. GEIGER-KABISCH; H. SATTEL; C. BESTHORN & F. HENTSCHEL.
1995 Brain atrophy in normal ageing and Alzheimer's disease. *British J Psych.* 167: 739-746.
FOSTER, G.M.
1994 *Hippocrates' Latin American Legacy, Humoral medicine in the New World*, Langhorne: Gordon & Breach.
FOUCAULT, M.
1994 Genealogy and Social Criticism. In: *The Postmodern Turn, New perspectives on social [1972] theory*. Edited by S. SEIDMAN, pp. 39-45. Cambridge: Cambridge University Press.
FRANK, A.
1996 Reconciliatory alchemy: Bodies, narratives and power. *Body & Society* 2(3): 53-72.
GAUTHIER, S.; L.J. THAL & M. ROSSOR
1996 The future diagnosis and treatment of Alzheimer's disease. In: *Clinical Diagnosis and Management of Alzheimer's Disease*. Edited by S. GAUTHIER, pp. 59-365. London: Martin Dunitz.
GELLERSTEDT, N.
1933 Zur Kenntnis der Hirnveränderungen bei der normalen Altersinvolution. *Upsala Läkareförenings Förhandlingar* 5(6): 193-408.
GOLDSMITH, M.
1996 The value of 'life story'. In: *Hearing the Voice of People with Dementia, Opportunities and obstacles*, London: Jessica Kingsley Publ., pp. 86-96.
GUBRIUM, J.F.
1986 *Oldtimers and Alzheimer's: The descriptive organization of senility*. Greenwich: Jai Press.
HACKING, I.
1995 *Rewriting the Soul, Multiple personality and the sciences of memory*. Princeton: Princeton University Press.

HAMILTON, H.E.
  1994   *Conversations with an Alzheimer's patient, An intersectional sociolinguistic study.* Cambridge: Cambridge University Press.
HARVEY, D.
  1995   *The Condition of Postmodernity, An enquiry into the origins of cultural change.* [1990] Cambridge, MA: Blackwell.
HENDERSON, A.S.
  1997   The spectrum of cognitive decline, in: *Cadernos do IPUB (special issue on aging;* A. LEIBING, ed.). (forthcoming).
  1994   *Dementia.* Geneva: World Health Organization.
  1988   The risk factors for Alzheimer's disease: A review and a hypothesis. *Acta Psychiatr Scand* 78: 257-275.
HENDERSON, J.N.
  1987   Mental disorders among the elderly, Dementia and its sociocultural correlates. In: *The Elderly as Modern Pioneers.* Edited by P. SILVERMAN, pp. 357-374. Bloomington: Indiana University Press.
HERSKOVITS, E.
  1995   Struggling over subjectivity: Debates about the 'self' and Alzheimer's disease. *Medical Anthropology Quarterly* 9(2): 146-164.
JACKSON, M.
  1996   Introduction: Phenomenology, radical empiricism, and anthropological critique. In: *Things as They Are: New directions in phenomenological anthropology.* Edited by M. JACKSON, pp. 1-50. Bloomington: Indiana University Press.
JORM, A.F.
  1990   *The Epidemiology of Alzheimer's Disease and Related Disorders,* London: Chapman and Hall.
KALACHE, A.
  1996   Ageing worldwide. In: *Epidemiology in Old Age.* Edited by S. EBRAHIM & A. KALACHE, pp. 22-31. London: BMJ Publishing Group.
KAPLAN. H.B
  1991   Social psychology of the immune system: A conceptual framework and review of the literature. *Soc. Sci. Med.* 33(8): 909-923.
KERTESZ, A. & R.C. MOHS
  1996   Cognition. In: *Clinical Diagnosis and Management of Alzheimer's Disease.* Edited by S. GAUTHIER, pp. 155-174. London: Martin Dunitz.
KITWOOD, T.
  1988   The technical, the personal, and the framing of dementia. *Social Behaviour* 3: 161-179.
KLEINMAN, A.
  1988   *The Illness Narratives, Suffering, healing and the human condition,* Basic Books.
KROPIUNIGG, U.
  1990   *Psyche und Immunsystem, Psychoneuroimmunologische Untersuchungen.* Wien: Springer-Verlag.
LANDFIELD, P.W.
  1994   The role of glucocorticoids in brain aging and Alzheimer's disease: An integrative physiological hypothesis. *Experimental Gerontology* 29(1): 3-11.
LEIBING, A.
  1997a Doença de Alzheimer e Cultura: A antropologia de uma doença "biológica." In: *Cadernos do IPUB* (special issue on aging; A. LEIBING, ed.), (forthcoming)
  1997b Rita Hayworth também Envelhece—Doença de Alzheimer e Saúde Mental neste Século. In: *Paradigmas da Atenção Psicossocial.* Edited by P.G. DELGADO (ed.), (forthcoming).
  1996   *Reflexões sobre a doença de Alzheimer,* Paper presented at the Ist Congress of Mental Health of the State of Rio de Janeiro, November 20-23, Rio de Janeiro, Brazil.
  1995   "Alles mit der Hüfte": Überlegungen zu Kultur und Psychiatrie in Brasilien. *Jahrbuch für Ethnomedizin* 4: 221-230.
  1994   *Blick auf eine verrückte Welt, Kultur und Psychiatrie in Brasilien.* Münster: LIT-Verlag.
  1991   [Araújo, A.] Herr Doktor, es sind die Nerven, Zur Relevanz "traditioneller" Erklärungsmodelle in der Schulmedizin am Beispiel Brasilien. In: *Traditionelle Heilsysteme und Religionen.* Edited by R. WIEDERSHEIM et al., pp. 157-168. Saarbrücken: Dadder.
LÉVI-STRAUSS, C.
  1988   Traurige Tropen. Frankfurt/Main: Suhrkamp. [1955]
LINS DE BARROS, M.
  1987   *Autoridade e Afeto, Avós, filhos e netos na família brasileira,* Rio de Janeiro: Zahar.

LOCK, M.
  1993 *Encounters with Ageing, Mythologies of menopause in Japan and North America*. Berkeley: University of California Press.
LOCK, M. & N. SCHEPER-HUGHES
  1990 A critical-interpretive approach in medical anthropology: Rituals and routines of discipline and dissent. In: *Medical Anthropology, A handbook of theory and method*. Edited by T.M. JOHNSON & C.F. SARGENT. New York: Greenwood Press.
LYMAN, K.A.
  1989 Bringing the social back in: A critique of the biomedicalization of dementia. *The Gerontologist* 29(5): 597-606.
LYON, M.L.
  1993 Psychoneuroimmunology: The problem of the situatedness of illness and the conceptualization of healing. *Culture, Medicine and Psychiatry* 17: 77-97.
MARKOWITSCH, H.J.
  1995 Cerebral bases of consciousness: A historical view. *Neuropsychologia* 33(9): 1181-1192.
MEANEY, M.J.; D.H. AITKEN; C. VAN BERKEL; S. BHATNAGAR & R.M. SAPOLSKY
  1988 Effect of neonatal handling on age-related impairments associated with the hippocampus. *Science* 239: 766-768.
MILLER, T.W. (ed.)
  1996 *Theory and Assessment of Stressful Life Events*, Madison: International University Press.
Minois, G.
  1989 History of Old Age, From Antiquity to the Renaissance, Chicago: The University of [1987] Chicago Press.
MORRIS, J.C., STORANDT, M., MCKEEL JR., D.W. et al.
  1996 Cerebral amyloid deposition and diffuse plaques in "Normal" aging. *Neurology* 46: 707-719.
NATIONAL INSTITUTE OF AGING/NATIONAL INSTITUTES OF HEALTH
  1995 *Alzheimer's Disease, Unraveling the mystery*, NIH publication no. 95-3782.
NIETZSCHE, F.
  1984 [1873] *Vom Nutzen und Nachteil der Historie für das Leben*. Edited by M. LANDMANN, Zürich, Digogenes.
OPIT, L.J.
  1988 The problem of senile dementia. *Social Behaviour* 3(2): 181-196.
PFLEIDERER, B.
  1994 *Die besessenen Frauen von Mira Datar Dargah, Heilen und Trance in Indien*. Frankfurt: Campus.
POLLEN, D.A.
  1996 Hannah's Heirs, The quest for the genetic origins of Alzheimer's disease (expanded [1993] edition), Oxford: Oxford University Press.
POLLITT, P.A.
  1996 Dementia in old age: An anthropological perspective. *Psychological Medicine* 26: 1061-1074.
REISBERG, B.
  1981 *A Guide to Alzheimer's Disease, For Families, Spouses and Friends*, New York: The Free Press.
ROBERTSON, A.
  1991 The politics of Alzheimer's disease: A case study in apocalyptic demography. In: *Critical Perspectives on Ageing: The political and moral economy of growing old*. New York: Baywood Publ. Co., pp. 135-152.
ROCCA, W.A.; A. HOFMAN; C. BRAYNE, C. et al.
  1991 Frequency and distribution of Alzheimer's disease in Europe: A collaborative study of 1980-1990 prevalence findings. *Ann Neurol* 30: 381-390.
ROTHSCHILD, D.
  1937 Pathological changes in senile psychoses and their psychobiological significance. *Am J Psych* 93: 757-788.
ROTHSCHILD, D. & M.L. SHARP
  1941 The origin of senile psychoses: Neuropathologic factors and factors of a more personal nature. *Diseases of the Nervous System* II(1): 49-54.
SACKS, O.
  1990 The lost mariner. In: *The Man who Mistook his Wife for a Hat and other clinical tales*, [1987] New York: Harper Perennial, pp. 23-42.
SANDS, S.L. & D. ROTHSCHILD
  1952 Sociopsychiatric foundations for a theory of the reactions to aging. *J Nervous and Mental Diseases* 116: 233-241.

SAPOLSKY, R.
   1994   *Why Zebras Don't Get Ulcers, A guide to stress, stress-related diseases, and coping.* New York: W.H. Freeman & Co.
   1992   *Stress, the Aging Brain, and the Mechanisms of Neuron Death.* Cambridge: The MIT Press.
SHAKESPEARE, W.
   1977   *The Portable Shakespeare, Seven Plays, The Songs, The Sonnets, Selections from the other plays.* New York: Penguin Books.
SHOMAKER, D.J.
   1989   Age disorientation, liminality and reality: The case of the Alzheimer's patient. *Medical Anthropology* 12: 91-101.
SHUA-HAIM, J.R. & J.S. GROSS
   1996   Alzheimer's syndrome, not Alzheimer's disease. *JAGS* 44(1): 96-97.
SMITH, D.H.
   1992   Seeing and knowing dementia. In: *Dementia and Aging, Ethics, values, and policy choices.* Baltimore: The Johns Hopkins University Press, pp. 44-54.
STAFFORD, P.B.
   1992   The social construction of Alzheimer's disease. In: *Biosemiotics.* Edited by T.A. SEBEOK, pp. 393-406. Berlin/New York: Gruyter.
VASZ, R.
   1996   *Interview given at the Institute of Psychiatry, Federal University of Rio de Janeiro,* Research program "Alzheimer's disease and Brazilian urban context".
VERAS, R.P.
   1994   *País Jovem com Cabelos Brancos, A saúde do idoso no Brasil,* Rio de Janeiro: Relume Dumará.
VERAS, R.P. & E. MURPHY
   1994   The mental health of older people in Rio de Janeiro. *Intern J Geriatric Psychiatry* 9: 285-295.
WILLIAMS, S.J.
   1996   The vicissitudes of embodiment across the chronic illness trajectory. *Body & Society* 2(2): 23-47.
WILSON, D.C.
   1955   The pathology of senility. *American Journal of Psychiatry* 111: 902-906.
YOUNG, A.
   1995   *The Harmony of Illusions, Inventing Post-Traumatic Stress Disorder,* Princeton: Princeton University Press.
   1980   The discourse on stress and the reproduction of conventional knowledge. *Soc Sci Med.* 14B: 133-146.
ZHOU, D.; A.W. KUSNECOV; M.R. SHURIN; M. DEPAOLI & B.S. RABIN
   1993   Exposure to physical and psychological stressors elevates plasma Interleukin-6: Relationship to the activation of Hypothalamic-Pituitary-Adrenal Axis. *Endocrinology* 133(6): 2523-2530.

Psychiatry: Its Science and Its Ethics

João Ferreira Da Silva Filho

The specific object of psychiatry is the psychically-ill man, the one who suffers from his human condition. Thus, it is impossible for psychiatry to ignore our humanity, the biological, political and philosophical issues implicit in the human condition.

The acknowledgement of differences is the basic act in all mental health actions. This acknowledgement begins with the acceptance of differences in approaches and points of view. It is necessary to affirm the ethics implicit in each formulation and, in this way, make possible the debate. This debate should arise from the will to know so as to better understand, not from the will to prescribe norms of conduct or to create restrictive laws and codes.

It is important to be aware that in the mental health area a limited knowledge will tend to lead us to the murky realm of moral judgements and thence to attempts at restricting the freedom of those whose actions escape understanding.

Another relevant issue in this discussion is related to the scientific nature of psychiatric knowledge. It starts and continues in the clinical experience, which articulates the patient's speech with the doctor's nomination.

Some psychiatrists, two hundred years after the birth of psychiatry itself, still think they owe something to general medicine. Their attempts at paying this debt quite often leads them to disregarding what should be their commitment to the criterion of truth in medicine, *the clinic*, and to their specific object of work, *the mental patients*.

It is important to remember that when skulls were opened, only speechless brains were found. Brains do not speak the language of lesion. In fact, the clinical experience *does not speak the language of lesion*. It simply speaks. It speaks with signs, symbols and senses. It is the clinical experience that articulates medicine and psychiatry, leaving the field open to all forms of approaching and describing madness. This has nothing to do with the truly insane search for efficiency and efectiveness.

Pragmatism advises us to try that which promises us results. But does pragmatism itself bring results? Modernity is basically a process of disenchantment of the world, of dissolution of the cosmos and of the magic. The logics of pragmatism, in search of effectiveness, aims at filling these gaps and, though telling us how to reach what we want, tells us nothing about why we want or how we want that what we want.

The malaise of the modern world was hysteria—the theatralization of the subect—or paranoia—the delirious projection. These days, to the adepts of the pragmatics of efficiency, neither would Anna O. have experiences to be dramatized into symptoms nor would President Schreber have any subjectivity to be projected into the world order. Nowadays, all histories are true since they are invented from beginning to end. The problems of the created therapeutics are produced this way in present times.

Nevertheless, J. Genet is apt to remind us of the true scientific task, "The multiplicity of the name leads us to believe that we are important. We are not. The multiplicity of the name leads us to believe we have power. We do not. It is necessary, thus, to exert constant vigilance upon ourselves and continually work on the issue of the anonymity of the name, a truely exhaustive task." It is this exhaustion, not efficiency, that nurtures science and the clinic.

About the Authors[1]

Naomar Almeida-Filho, M.D. Ph.D. Professor and Dean, Instituto de Saúde Coletiva, Universidade Federal da Bahia, Brazil. Senior Researcher at the Brazilian National Research Council—CNPq. Research Associate, Psychosocial Research Unit, Douglas Hospital Research Center.

Paulo César Alves (B.Soc.Sci., Ph.D.) is a Senior Lecturer at the Federal University of Bahia (Brazil), Departament of Sociology and Postgraduate Programme in Sociology and Anthropology. He is Director of the ECSAS—Health and Social Sciences Centre. He has written numerous articles on the anthropology of medicine and is the co-editor of Saúde e Doença: Um olhar Antropológico (Fiocruz). Among his present interests are research studies on mental health, therapeutic systems, and popular health organizations among urban working class groups.

Gilles Bibeau, Ph.D. Professor at the Department of Anthropology, Université de Montréal. Research Associate, Psychosocial Research Unit, Douglas Hospital Research Center.

Contardo Calligaris is an adoptive Brazilian, and really an Italian. He is a psychoanalyst, and a clinical and social psychologist by Academic training (Ph.D. in Clinical Psychopathology by the Université de Provence). Besides and after several strictly clinical publications, he has written: "Hello Brasil! Notas de um psicanalista europeu viajando ao Brasil" (Escuta: São Paulo 1991), and more recently published a collection of his main contributions to the press (especially Folha de São Paulo, where he has held a column): "Crônicas do Individualismo Cotidiano" (Ática: São Paulo 1996). In 1996, he has been a visiting professor in Medical Anthropology at the University of California in Berkeley, and he currently lives in Boston, MA, where he is finishing a book on bureaucratic personalities, and preparing a long essay on contemporary individualism—both for American publishers.

Kenneth Rochel de Camargo Jr. MD PhD, Associate Professor, Instituto de Medicina Social, Universidade do Estado do Rio de Janeiro, Brazil

Carlos Caroso, Ph.D. Professor, Department of Anthropology, FFCH, and Associate Professor at the Instituto de Saúde Coletiva of Universidade Federal da Bahia, Brazil. Researcher in the Brazilian National Research Council—CNPq.

Sérgio Carrara, DSc, is a Professor at the Institute of Social Medicine (State University of Rio de Janeiro). He is a Social Anthropologist.

Ellen Corin, Ph.D. Professor at the Departments of Psychiatry and Anthropology, McGill University. Senior Researcher, Psychosocial Research Unit, Douglas Hospital Research Center.

---

1. The authors' self-description are unedited, which is why length and content vary greatly. As some, but not all authors included their addresses in their papers, respondents are encouraged to address their comments to: Annette Leibing, Instituto de Psiquiatria, Universidade Federal do Rio de Janeiro, Av. Venceslau Bras, 71 (fundos), 22290-140 Rio de Janeiro, Brazil. E-mail: Leibing@ibm.net. All letters (or e-mails) will be sent on to the respective authors.

Maria Fernanda Lima e Costa, MD, PhD in Tropical Medicine, is Senior Researcher at the Laboratory of Epidemiology and Medical Anthropology, René Rachou Research Institute, Oswaldo Cruz Foundation, Belo Horizonte, and Associate Professor at the Department of Social and Preventive Medicine, Federal University of Minas Gerais.

Paulo Dalgalarrondo, MD, PhD, is Professor at the Department of Psychiatry, State University of Campinas, São Paulo, Brazil.

Luiz-Fernando D. Duarte is a social anthropologist working in the Programa de Pós-Graduação em Antropologia Social, in the Museu Nacional/Universidade Federal do Rio de Janeiro, where he got his Dr Sc. degree in 1985. His academic work has dealt mostly with the culture of the urban working-classes in Brazil, the social construction of the Person and the history of the physical-moral representations of the Self in Western modern culture (including the history of *psychological* ideas.)

Josélia Oliveira Araújo Firmo, MsC in Epidemiology, is Assistant Researcher at the Laboratory of Epidemiology and Medical Anthropology, rené Rachou Research Institute, Oswaldo Cruz Foundation, Belo Horizonte, Brazil.

Henrique Leonardo Guerra, MsC in Epidemiology is Assistant Researcher at the Laboratory of Epidemiology and Medical Anthropology, René Rachou Research Institute, Oswaldo Cruz Foundation, Belo Horizonte, Brazil.

Sean Patrick Larvie is an associated researcher at the Institute for Social Medicine, State University of Rio de Janeiro and a doctoral candidate at the Committee on Human Development, University of Chicago.

Ondina Fachel Leal is Professor at the Institute of Social Anthropology, Rio Grande do Sul Federal University, Brazil. She is the editor of the book "Corpo e Significado, Ensaios de Antropologia Social."

Annette Leibing studied anthropology at the University of Hamburg, where she received her PhD with a doctoral thesis about psychiatry and Brazilian culture. She is currently Professor for mental health at the Institute of Psychiatry, Federal University of Rio de Janeiro and is studying Alzheimer's disease in the Brazilian urban context.

Maria Andréa Loyola is professor of anthropology at the Universidade Estadual do Rio de Janeiro's Institute of Social Medicine.

Madel T. Luz, Social Scientist, PhD, Full Professor, Instituto de Medicina Social, Universidade do Estado do Rio de Janeiro, Brazil

Cristina M.G. Monte, MD, is a Visiting Professor at the Clinical reserach Unit, Federal University of Ceará Medical School, Fortaleza, Brazil.

About the Authors

Marilyn K. Nations, PhD, is Professor at the Department of Social Medicine, Harvard University Medical School, Boston, U.S.A. and Visiting Professor at the Department of Community Medicine Division of Social Medicine, Federal University of Ceará Medical School, Fortaleza, Brazil.

Míriam Cristina Rabelo (B.Soc.Sci., Ph.D.) is a Lecturer at the Federal University of Bahia (Brazil), Department of Sociology and Postgraduate Programme in Sociology and Anthropology. She is Research Coordinator at the ECSAS—Health and Social Sciences Centre and is particularly interested in mental health and religion, an area on which she has written widely.

Núbia Rodrigues, MA. Assistant Professor, Department of Anthropology, FFCH, Research Associate at the Instituto de Saúde Coletiva, Universidade Federal da Bahia, Brazil.

Professor **Jane Russo** is a psychologist with a PhD in Social Anthropology. She studies the social difusion of psychological theories and practices and her PhD thesis, published by the Federal University of Rio de Janeiro Press in 1993, was about the body therapies movement in Rio de Janeiro. She is presently adjunct professor at the Psychiatry, Psychoanalysis and Mental Health Graduation Program of the Federal University of Rio de Janeiro and at the Social Medicine Institute of the State University of Rio de Janeiro, participating in a research program about the institutionalization of the psychological sciences in Brazil.

Telma Camargo da Silva is a professor of anthropology at Goiás Federal University, Goiânia/Brazil. She has done work on popular culture, gender, and health. She has a Master's degree in Sociology of Literature from École des Hautes Etudes en Sciences Sociales, Paris/France. She is a PhD candidate in Cultural Anthropology at The Graduate School and University Center—The City University of New York, U.S.A. Currently, she is completing her doctoral fieldwork research on the representation and experience of radiation illness in the aftermath of the Goiânia radiological disaster.

João Ferreira da Silva-Filho, MD, DSc is psychiatrist and director of the Institute of Psychiatry, Federal University of Rio de Janeiro.

Elizabeth Uchôa, MD, PhD in Anthropology, is Associate Professor at the Department of Psychiatry, Federal University of Minas Gerais and Associate Researcher at the Laboratory of Epidemiology and Medical Anthropology, René Rachou Research Institute, Oswaldo Cruz Foundation, Belo Horizonte, Brazil.

Ceres Victora received her PhD in Anthropology from Brunel University, London, and is currently Lecturer in Anthropology at the Department of Anthropology, Universidade Federal do Rio Grande do Sul, Brazil. She has done research in Anthropology of the Body in Porto Alegre and in London, with particular attention to images of the reproductive system, gender, family and domestic organisation

curare — Zeitschrift für Ethnomedizin
Arbeitsgemeinschaft Ethnomedizin e.V. (Hg.)

ISSN 0344-8622 • dt. u. engl. • 2 Hefte pro Jahr

curare ist ein Forum für Austausch und Diskussion von
- traditionellen medizinischen Systemen
- medizinischer Entwicklungshilfe
- gesundheitspolitischer Planung
- Konzepten verschiedener Kulturen von Gesundheit, Krankheit und Heilung
- dem Verständnis des Leiblich-Seelisch-Geistigen.

Das Paradigma der Medizin als kulturelles System wird kritisch im interdisziplinären und interkulturellen Vergleich hinterfragt und neue Lösungsansätze entwickelt.

1994-1: Psychiatrie im Kulturvergleich
1994-2: Heiler und Heilen im kulturellen Kontext
1995-1: Pilze, Schamanen und die Facetten des Bewußtseins
1995-2: Sucht und veränderte Bewußtseinszustände im Kulturvergleich
1996-1: Kognition – Krankheit – Kultur. Wahrnehmung von Körper und Krankheit in verschiedenen Kulturen
1996-2: Depression
1997-1: Theorie und Praxis
1997-2: Tropengynäkologie

curare – Sonderbände

Gebären – Ethnomedizinische Perspektiven und neue Wege
Hg.: W. Schiefenhövel, D. Sich, C.E. Gottschalk-Batschkus
Bd. 8/1995 • Hardcover • 17 x 24 cm
461 S. • zahlr. Abb. u. Tab., Bibliographie & Filmographie • dt. u. engl.
ISBN 3-86135-560-4

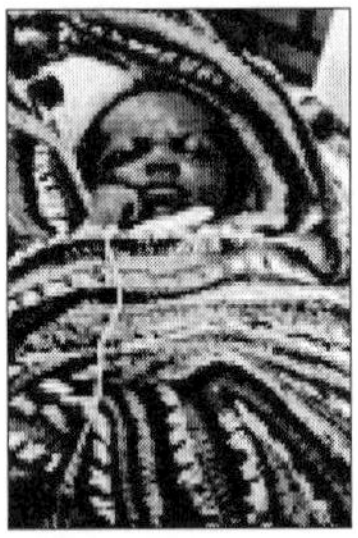

Ethnomedizinische Perspektiven zur frühen Kindheit
Hg.: C.E. Gottschalk-Batschkus, J. Schuler
Bd. 9/1996 • Hardcover • 17 x 24 cm
470 S. • zahlr. Abb., Fotos, Tab. u. Diagr. • dt. u. engl.
ISBN 3-86135-561-2

Transkulturelle Pflege
Hg.: C. Uzarewicz, G. Piechotta
Bd. 10/1997 • Hardcover • 17 x 24 cm
262 S. • dt. u. engl.
ISBN 3-86135-564-7

Frauen und Gesundheit – Ethnomedizinische Perspektiven
Hg.: C.E. Gottschalk-Batschkus, J. Schuler
Bd. 11/1997 • Hardcover • 17 x 24 cm
448 S. • zahlr. Abb. • dt. u. engl.
ISBN 3-86135-563-9

Therapeutische Konzepte im Kulturvergleich
Hg.: C.E. Gottschalk-Batschkus, C. Rätsch
Bd. 12/1997 • Hardcover • 17 x 24 cm
ca. 290 S. • zahlr. Abb. • dt. u. engl.
ISBN 3-86135-567-1
erscheint März 1998

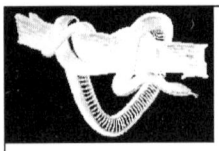

BEITRÄGE ZUR ETHNOMEDIZIN
Hg.: C.E. Gottschalk-Batschkus & Judith Schuler

Anja Manns, Anne Christine Schrader
Ins Leben tragen. Entwicklung und Wirkung des Tragens von Kleinstkindern unter sozialmedizinischen Aspekten • Bd. 1 • 1995 • 125 S. • zahlr. Fotos u. Abb. • 17 x 24 cm • ISBN 3-86135-570-1

Die gesellschaftliche Konstruktion von Befindlichkeit. Ein Sammelband zur Medizinethnologie • Hg.: Michael Stürzer, Angelika Wolf
Bd. 2 • 1996 • 240 S. • 17 x 24 cm • ISBN 3-86135-043-2

MEDIZIN AM ZÜGEL DER EVOLUTION
Hg.: Wulf Schiefenhövel & Judith Schuler

Alexander Braun
Häufigkeit und Verteilung von Erkrankungen bei zwei Naturvölkern Neuguineas
Bd. 1 • 1996 • 141 S. • 89 Abb., Fotos. u. Graphiken • 17 x 24 cm • ISBN 3-86135-571-X

VWB - Verlag für Wissenschaft und Bildung, Amand Aglaster
Markgrafenstr. 67 * 10969 Berlin / Postfach 11 03 68 * 10833 Berlin
Tel. 030-251 04 15 * Fax 030-251 04 12 * 100615.1565@compuserve.com